9/11

AND

TERRORIST TRAVEL

9/11

AND

TERRORIST TRAVEL

A Staff Report of the National Commission on
Terrorist Attacks Upon the United States

Hillsboro Press
PROVIDENCE PUBLISHING CORPORATION
FRANKLIN, TENNESSEE

A Note to the Reader:

This volume represents the complete work of the 9/11 Commission staff report, "9/11 and Terrorist Travel," as published on the 9/11 Commission Web site on August 22, 2004. In an effort to assure the greatest possible accuracy and completeness of this published book, Commission staff reviewed the text prior to publication after consulting Commission management. Small edits were then made where necessary in formatting, grammar, and in a handful of instances, facts. In each case, the factual changes pertained to correcting a wrong number or date, such as "one overstayed" to "two overstayed," or in one case, "September 8, 2001" changed to "July 2001." These changes were necessary to clarify or correct the text. In no case was actual substance altered.

For additional copies of *9/11 and Terrorist Travel*, visit
www.providence-publishing.com
or call 1-800-321-5692.
Providence Publishing Corporation
238 Seaboard Lane
Franklin, Tennessee 37067

Printed in the United States of America

08   07   06   05   04   1   2   3   4   5

ISBN: 1-57736-341-8

HILLSBORO PRESS
an imprint of
Providence Publishing Corporation
238 Seaboard Lane • Franklin, Tennessee 37067
www.providence-publishing.com
800-321-5692

CONTENTS

9/11 AND TERRORIST TRAVEL
STAFF REPORT, AUGUST 21, 2004

Note from the Executive Director   vii

Preface   ix

1. INTRODUCTION: A FACTUAL OVERVIEW
   OF THE SEPTEMBER 11 BORDER STORY   3

2. THE SEPTEMBER 11 TRAVEL OPERATION:
   A CHRONOLOGY   11

3. TERRORIST ENTRY AND EMBEDDING TACTICS: 1993–2001   47
   3.1 The Redbook   47
   3.2 Terrorist Travel Tactics by Plot   48
   3.3 Al Qaeda's Organizational Structure for Travel and Travel Tactics   58

4. IMMIGRATION AND BORDER SECURITY EVOLVE:
   1993 TO 2001   69
   4.1 The Intelligence Community   69
   4.2 The State Department   70
   4.3 The Immigration and Naturalization Service   89

5. PLANNING AND EXECUTING ENTRY FOR THE 9/11 PLOT   111
   5.1 The State Department   111
   5.2 The Immigration and Naturalization Service   130
   5.3 Finding Fair Verdicts   140

6. CRISIS MANAGEMENT AND RESPONSE:
   POST-SEPTEMBER 11   147
   6.1 The Intelligence Community   147
   6.2 The Department of State   148
   6.3 The Department of Justice   150
   6.4 Response at the Borders, September 11–20, 2001   160
   6.5 The Department of Homeland Security   163

Appendix A: *Travel and Identification Documents Digital Images*   169
Appendix B: *The Saudi Flights*   171
Appendix C: *Immigration Histories of Certain Individuals*
             with Terrorist Connections   187

NOTE FROM THE
EXECUTIVE DIRECTOR

THE COMMISSION STAFF ORGANIZED its work around specialized studies, or monographs, prepared by each of the teams. We used some of the evolving draft material for these studies in preparing the seventeen staff statements delivered in conjunction with the Commission's 2004 public hearings. We used more of this material in preparing draft sections of the Commission's final report. Some of the specialized staff work, while not appropriate for inclusion in the report, nonetheless offered substantial information or analysis that was not well represented in the Commission's report. In a few cases this supplemental work could be prepared to a publishable standard, either in an unclassified or classified form, before the Commission expired.

This study is on immigration, border security and terrorist travel issues. It was prepared principally by Thomas Eldridge, Susan Ginsburg, Walter T. Hempel II, Janice Kephart, and Kelly Moore, with assistance from Joanne Accolla, and editing assistance from Alice Falk. As in all staff studies, they often relied on work done by their colleagues.

This is a study by Commission staff. While the Commissioners have been briefed on the work and have had the opportunity to review earlier drafts of some of this work, they have not approved this text and it does not necessarily reflect their views.

Philip Zelikow

PREFACE

IT IS PERHAPS OBVIOUS TO STATE THAT TERRORISTS cannot plan and carry out attacks in the United States if they are unable to enter the country. Yet prior to September 11, while there were efforts to enhance border security, no agency of the U.S. government thought of border security as a tool in the counterterrorism arsenal. Indeed, even after 19 hijackers demonstrated the relative ease of obtaining a U.S. visa and gaining admission into the United States, border security still is not considered a cornerstone of national security policy. We believe, for reasons we discuss in the following pages, that it must be made one.

Congress gave the Commission the mandate to study, evaluate, and report on "immigration, nonimmigrant visas and border security" as these areas relate to the events of 9/11. This staff report represents 14 months of such research. It is based on thousands of pages of documents we reviewed from the State Department, the Immigration and Naturalization Service, the Department of Homeland Security, the Department of Justice, the Federal Bureau of Investigation, the Central Intelligence Agency, the Department of Defense, approximately 25 briefings on various border security topics, and more than 200 interviews. We are grateful to all who assisted and supported us along the way.

The story begins with "A Factual Overview of the September 11 Border Story." This introduction summarizes many of the key facts of the hijackers' entry into the United States. In it, we endeavor to dispel the myth that their entry into the United States was "clean and legal." It was not. Three hijackers carried passports with indicators of Islamic extremism linked to al Qaeda; two others carried passports manipulated in a fraudulent manner. It is likely that several more hijackers carried passports with similar fraudulent manipulation. Two hijackers lied on their visa applications.

Once in the United States, two hijackers violated the terms of their visas. Two overstayed their permitted length of stay. And all but one obtained some form of state identification. We know that six of the hijackers used these state issued identifications to check in for their flights on September 11. Three of them were fraudulently obtained.

The chronology that follows in chapter 2, "The September 11 Travel Operation," is a detailed account of how each hijacker acquired a visa and entered the United States. In all, they had 25 contacts with consular officers and 43 contacts with immigration and customs authorities. They began acquiring their visas in April 1999 and began entering the country in December 2000. They successfully entered the United States 33 times over 21 months, through nine airports of entry, most of which were on the East Coast. Neither the consular officers who adjudicated their visas nor the immigration inspectors who admitted them into the country had any knowledge of fraudulent al Qaeda documents.

The next chapter, "Terrorist Entry and Embedding Tactics, 1993 to 2001," explores the topic of fraudulent documents, which terrorists have long used to support their international travel. Indeed, the CIA studied these documents and published their commonalities as far back as the 1980s. They even made a training video for border inspectors to help them detect such fraud. This effort was abandoned in the early 1990s, just as the United States experienced the first attack on the World Trade Center in 1993. We reviewed information available on terrorist travel practices in the 1990s and identified numerous entry and embedding tactics, unknown at the time of these earlier attacks in the United States owing to the lack of analysis. No government agency systematically would analyze terrorists' travel patterns until after 9/11, thus missing critical opportunities to disrupt their plans.

Chapter 4, "Immigration and Border Security Evolve, 1993 to 2001," provides an overview of counterterrorism activities as they relate to border security in the Intelligence Community, the State Department, and the Immigration and Naturalization Service. Here we explore the evolution of the terrorist watchlist and explain the process of applying for a visa and for gaining entry into the United States. The reader is introduced to the Bureau of Consular Affairs in the State Department and visa policy in general. The various INS units working on counterterrorism are discussed, along with enforcement of immigration law and the immigration benefits system.

Chapter 5, "Planning and Executing Entry for the 9/11 Plot," discusses visa issuance and admission into the United States as it specifically applied to the hijackers. Thus, visa policy in Berlin, the United Arab Emirates, and Saudi Arabia, where the hijackers received their visas, is explored in depth.

Similarly, we review aspects of the admission of the hijackers in detail, noting the immigration violations they committed. On both topics, visas and entry, we include excerpts of interviews with consular, immigration, and customs officials involved in the admission of the hijackers. We conclude with an assessment of how well the State Department and the INS performed in the period prior to 9/11.

"Crisis Management and Response Post–September 11," chapter 6, reports on actions taken by the intelligence community, the departments of State and Justice, and the INS following the attacks, up to the establishment of the Department of Homeland Security. Particular attention is paid to programs implemented by the Justice Department, in some cases as part of the interagency process, including the Interview Project, Visa Condor, the Absconder Apprehension Initiative, and NSEERS, the National Security Exit and Entry Registration System.

Appendix A contains graphics relevant to the 9/11 plot. In Appendix B, "The Saudi Flights," we examine the facts and circumstances surrounding the departure of Saudi nationals from the United States in the days after the 9/11 attack. The procedure followed for each flight, including the inspection of passengers and their belongings, is covered in detail. Finally, in Appendix C, we describe the immigration histories of certain terrorists.

9/11

AND

TERRORIST TRAVEL

1

INTRODUCTION:
A FACTUAL OVERVIEW OF THE SEPTEMBER 11 BORDER STORY

TERRORISTS TRAVEL FOR MANY REASONS, including to train, communicate with other terrorists, collect funds, escape capture and interrogation, engage in surveillance of potential targets, and commit terrorist attacks.[1]

To avoid detection of their activities and objectives while engaging in travel that necessitates using a passport, terrorists devote extensive resources to acquiring and manipulating passports, entry and exit stamps, and visas. The al Qaeda terrorist organization was no exception. High-level members of al Qaeda were expert document forgers who taught other terrorists, including Mohamed Atta, the 9/11 ringleader, their tradecraft.[2]

The entry of the hijackers into the United States therefore represented the culmination of years of practice and experience in penetrating international borders. We introduce our monograph with a retelling of the September 11 events from the perspective of border security as we understand it today.

The conspirators
Twenty-six al Qaeda terrorist conspirators—eighteen Saudis, two Emiratis, one Egyptian, one Lebanese, one Moroccan, one Pakistani, and two Yemenis—sought to enter the United States and carry out a suicide mission.[3] The first of them began to acquire the means to enter two years and five months before the 9/11 attack.

Intelligence about terrorist travel
Three hijackers were known or knowable by intelligence authorities as al Qaeda terrorists in early 2000, but their biographical information was not fully developed and communicated to border authorities for watchlisting at

3

U.S. consulates abroad (by the State Department) and at the border (by immigration and customs border inspectors). The travel plans of all three also were known or knowable in 2000, in part because of cooperation from Arab and Asian country intelligence services and border authorities.

The 19 hijackers used 364 aliases, including different spellings of their names and noms de guerre.[4] As they passed through various countries, their names were recorded by governments and their intelligence and border authorities.

Three were carrying Saudi passports containing a possible extremist indicator present in the passports of many al Qaeda and other terrorists entering the United States as early as the first World Trade Center attack in 1993. This indicator had not been analyzed by the CIA, FBI, or our border authorities for its significance. Indeed, passports seized by the FBI in terrorist investigations were not routinely made available to the CIA for analysis.

Two hijackers were carrying passports that had been manipulated in a fraudulent manner. They contained fraudulent entry-exit stamps (or cachets) probably inserted by al Qaeda travel document forgers to hide travel to Afghanistan for terrorist training. Our analysis of their travel patterns suggests that several more hijackers whose passports did not survive the attacks were likely to have had similar false stamps in their passports. The existence and significance of these stamps was not known to border authorities.

Two Saudis were carrying passports that might have been provided to them by a family member working in the Saudi passport ministry. The Saudi passport authority was rife with patronage and security weaknesses known by then to the State Department and CIA, but they were not the subject of intelligence analysis, diplomatic or security policy, or countermeasures.

Visas

The 19 hijackers applied for 23 visas and obtained 22. Five other conspirators were denied U.S. visas. Two more obtained visas but did not participate in the attack for various reasons.

They began attempting to acquire U.S. visas in April 1999, two years and five months before the attack. Consular officers were unaware of the potential significance of an indicator of potential extremism present in some al Qaeda passports, had no information about fraudulent travel stamps that are associated with al Qaeda, and were not trained in terrorist travel tactics generally.

Two Yemenis were denied visas in Yemen for reasons of U.S. immigration law unrelated to terrorism. At the same time, two Saudi hijackers obtained visas in Saudi Arabia. When these two Saudis later showed up in

Afghanistan, they were selected for the mission in part because they already had U.S. visas. Later, most of the operatives selected were Saudis, who had little difficulty obtaining visas.

In early 2000, four conspirators sought U.S. visas to learn how to become pilots in the plot. An Egyptian and a Lebanese obtained visas easily in Berlin, because they had established ties to Germany and so did not look like intending immigrants. Both presented new passports. A Yemeni who wanted to be a pilot was repeatedly turned down for a visa because he did not have strong ties to Germany, failed to complete the necessary paperwork, and looked like an intending immigrant.

Thirteen of the hijackers presented passports less than three weeks old when they applied for their visas, but the new passports caused no heightened scrutiny of their visa applications.

Two hijackers lied on their visa applications in detectable ways, but were not further questioned about those lies.

Two hijackers were interviewed for reasons unrelated to terrorism. Most simply had their applications approved and their passports stamped with a U.S. visa. Consular officers were not trained to detect terrorists in a visa interview. Terrorism concerns were handled through the watchlist, and all the conspirators' names were checked against the terrorist watchlist without producing a match.

One Saudi, one Moroccan, and one Pakistani were each denied visas for reasons unrelated to terrorism. The last conspirator, the Pakistani, was denied on August 27, 2001, in the United Arab Emirates.

The mastermind of the operation, Khalid Sheikh Mohammed, used a travel facilitator to acquire a visa on July 23, 2001, in Jeddah, Saudi Arabia, using an alias.

Ports of entry

Once the operation was under way, the conspirators attempted to enter the United States 34 times over 21 months, through nine airports. They succeeded all but once. Border inspectors at U.S. airports were unaware of the potential significance of indicators of possible terrorist affiliation in conspirators' passports and had no information about fraudulent travel stamps possibly associated with al Qaeda. No inspectors or agents were trained in terrorist travel intelligence and document practices. The culture at the airports was one of travel facilitation and lax enforcement, with the exception of programs to interdict drug couriers and known criminals.

When they began to arrive at the U.S. airports in January 2000, the pilots traveled alone. With the exception of two of the hijackers, the "muscle" operatives arrived between late April and late June 2001. They came in groups of two or three, and in four cases were screened by the same inspector.

All but one of the hijackers presented visitor visas that immigration inspectors used to decide whether to admit them as tourists or on business. All but two of the nonpilots were admitted as tourists and were granted automatic six-month stays. This allowed them to maintain a legal immigration status through the end of the operation. One of the two nonpilots admitted on business was granted a one-month stay; he, along with another of the nonpilot operatives, was in violation of immigration law for months before the attack.

The one pilot who came in on a student visa never showed up for school, thereby violating the terms of his U.S. visa. Another of the pilots came in on a tourist visa yet began flight school immediately, also violating the terms of his U.S. visa. This pilot came in a total of seven times on a tourist visa while in school. In both cases, the pilots violated the law after their entry into the United States.

Five hijackers attempting entry were referred by primary inspectors for a more intensive review by secondary inspectors. One pilot was referred at two entries, in one case by a customs inspector trained to look for drug couriers, and in the other by an immigration inspector thinking the pilot might be an intending immigrant. One pilot was referred for having the wrong visa and one nonpilot hijacker for failing to have a visa. Two others were referred for failing to complete their arrival and customs forms and for being unable to communicate with the inspectors. No lookouts or visa revocations were posted alerting border authorities to the terrorist association of two of the hijackers until after each has entered the United States for the last time.

Four hijackers were admitted after the secondary inspectors who interviewed them were unable to, or did not, verify information supplied by the operative, misunderstood the law, or failed to follow procedures. One was interviewed at length by a border inspector. The inspector concluded, on the basis of his hostile and arrogant behavior and contradictory statements, that he was unlikely to comply with U.S. immigration law and posed a risk. He was denied entry. The inspector was backed up by his superior, but acted in the face of a general expectation of leniency toward Saudi citizens at that airport.

These entries occurred during a period when approximately 20 million people applied for visas, and more than 10 million people came into the United States through 220 airports of entry.

In the United States
Three hijackers filed applications for change of status to extend their stays in the United States and stayed in compliance with U.S. immigration laws

through September 2001. These were among nearly 600,000 new applications received in September 2000 and were added to a backlog of 3 million others. Two pilots attached the same supporting financial documents to their immigration benefit applications and were adjudicated by the same official in the summer of 2001.

The pending but unadjudicated benefits applications assisted two hijackers in persuading border inspectors to admit them during secondary inspections when they tried to reenter the United States. The adjudications were premised on the validity of their attendance at flight school, but in fact this school should not have been certified to accept foreign nationals. Another hijacker's application allowed him to stay in the United States legally for an extra six months.

While the applications were pending, one hijacker appeared at an Immigration and Naturalization Service (INS) office in Florida and requested a longer length of stay for a companion—possibly another hijacker—that would have enabled the other man to remain through September, when his own visa expired. The inspector refused that request, and realizing that the length of stay granted this hijacker during his secondary inspection was too long, rolled it back to midsummer 2001. The hijacker departed the United States in July and returned again ten days later, thereby acquiring a new length of stay that extended beyond September 11, 2001.

On August 23, 2001, the CIA provided biographical identification information about two of the hijackers to border and law enforcement authorities. The CIA and FBI considered the case important, but there was no way of knowing whether either hijacker was still in the country, because a border exit system Congress authorized in 1996 was never implemented.

One of the two overstayed his visa by less than six months. Without an exit system in place at the border tied to law enforcement databases, there was no way to establish with certainty that he remained in the United States. Thus, there was no risk that his immigration law violations would be visible to law enforcement, and there was no risk of immigration enforcement action of any kind.

Immediate response to the attacks

Immediately after the 9/11 attacks, immigration and customs leadership jointly put in place their agencies' most stringent security precautions, in the process nearly shutting down our borders; the backed-up traffic at the land borders caused a commercial crisis. Because resources were already strained, thousands of other enforcement officials in the National Guard, Border Patrol, and state and local police were needed to help border authorities reduce wait times for those seeking U.S. entry for tourism or business.

Under Justice Department direction, the FBI and the INS initiated a series of counterterrorism-related security programs using immigration law violations as a predicate to interview, detain, and in many cases deport aliens from countries with possible ties to al Qaeda. Also at the urging of the Justice Department, the State Department, together with the FBI, initiated a series of programs to heighten scrutiny of visa applicants from countries with an al Qaeda presence.

In the weeks after September 11, after the national airspace reopened, at least ten flights of Saudi nationals departed the United States. One flight sponsored by the Saudi government carried relatives of Saudi fugitive Usama Bin Ladin. Passengers on the flights were screened by the FBI prior to their departure, but allegations of high-level government involvement spurred theories that passengers received special treatment.

The 9/11 HIJACKERS AND CONSPIRATORS

American Airlines Flight 11—
North Tower of the World Trade Center

Mohamed Atta	Hijacker (Pilot)
Abdul Aziz al Omari	Hijacker
Waleed al Shehri	Hijacker
Satam al Suqami	Hijacker
Wail al Shehri	Hijacker

American Airlines Flight 77—
Pentagon

Hani Hanjour	Hijacker (Pilot)
Khalid al Mihdhar	Hijacker
Majed Moqed	Hijacker
Nawaf al Hazmi	Hijacker
Salem al Hazmi	Hijacker

United Airlines Flight 93—
Pennsylvania

Ziad Samir Jarrah	Hijacker (Pilot)
Saeed al Ghamdi	Hijacker
Ahmed al Nami	Hijacker
Ahmed al Haznawi	Hijacker

United Airlines Flight 175—
South Tower of the World Trade Center

Marwan al Shehhi   Hijacker (Pilot)
Mohand al Shehri   Hijacker
Hamza al Ghamdi   Hijacker
Fayez Banihammad   Hijacker
Ahmed al Ghamdi   Hijacker

Other Conspirators Involved with the Visa Process

Khalid Sheikh Mohammed   Mastermind
Tawfiq bin Attash (Khallad)   Potential Pilot
Ramzi Binalshibh   Potential Pilot
Zakariya Essabar   Potential Pilot/Hijacker
Saeed "Jihad" al Ghamdi   Potential Hijacker
Mushabib al Hamlan   Potential Hijacker
Ali Abdul Aziz Ali   Financial Facilitator and Potential Hijacker

Other Conspirator Involved with the
Visa and Port of Entry Process

Mohamed al Kahtani   Potential Hijacker

2

THE SEPTEMBER 11
TRAVEL OPERATION:
A CHRONOLOGY

THE SUCCESS OF THE SEPTEMBER 11 PLOT depended on the ability of the hijackers to obtain visas and pass an immigration and customs inspection in order to enter the United States. It also depended on their ability to remain here undetected while they worked out the operational details of the attack. If they had failed on either count—entering and becoming embedded—the plot could not have been executed.

Here we present the facts and circumstances of the hijackers' travel operation, including their 25 contacts with consular officers and their 43 contacts with immigration and customs authorities. We also discuss the 12 contacts with border authorities by other September 11 conspirators who applied for a visa. The narrative is chronological, retracing the hijackers' steps from their initial applications for U.S. visas, through their entry into the United States, to their applications for immigration benefits, and up through their acquisition of state identifications that helped them board the planes. Along the way, we note relevant actions by U.S. government authorities to combat terrorism. There were a few lucky breaks for U.S. border authorities in this story. Mostly, though, it is a story of how 19 hijackers easily penetrated U.S. border security.

Overview of the hijacker's visas
The 9/11 hijackers submitted 23 visa applications during the course of the plot, and 22 of these applications were approved. The hijackers applied for visas at five U.S. consulates or embassies overseas; two of them were interviewed. One consular officer issued visas to 11 of the 19 hijackers. Of the eight other conspirators in the plot who sought visas, three succeeded, but only one of the three later sought to use the visa to enter the United States.

Hijackers Nawaf al Hazmi and Khalid al Mihdhar were the first to submit visa applications because they were originally slated to be pilots. The four hijackers who did become pilots applied for visas in 2000. The remaining "muscle" hijackers applied in the fall of 2000 through the spring and summer of 2001, three applying twice.

Most of the hijackers applied with new passports, possibly to hide travel to Afghanistan recorded in their old ones. It is likely that many of the hijackers' passports contained indicators of extremism or showed ties to al Qaeda. However, this intelligence was not developed prior to 9/11, and thus State Department personnel reviewing visa applications were not trained to spot these indicators of a terrorist connection. Visa decisions for the hijackers and conspirators were consistent with a system that focused on excluding intending immigrants and depended on checking a database of names to search for criminals and terrorists.

Overview of the hijackers' entries

The hijackers successfully entered the United States 33 of 34 times, with the first arriving on January 15, 2000, at Los Angeles International Airport. All others entered through airports on the East Coast, including 11 entries through New York area airports and 12 through Florida airports.

The four pilots passed through immigration and customs inspections a total of 17 times from May 29, 2000, to August 5, 2001. Ziad Jarrah was the most frequent border crosser, entering the United States seven times. Mohamed Atta and Marwan al Shehhi came in three times each, entering for the last time on May 2 and July 19, 2001, respectively. Hani Hanjour was the only hijacker to enter on an academic visa, arriving on December 8, 2000. He had already attended both English and flight training schools in the United States during three stays in the 1990s. Hanjour was also the only pilot who already had a commercial pilot's license prior to entry, having acquired it in 1999 in Arizona.[1]

Though Khalid al Mihdhar and Nawaf al Hazmi came to the United States as early as January 2000, the remaining muscle entered between April 23, 2001, and June 29, 2001. They arrived in six pairs and one trio. Four pairs were processed by the same immigration inspector. Only three of the muscle were referred to a secondary inspection for further scrutiny. Of these, only one, Mohamed al Kahtani, was refused entry to the United States.

Entering the United States as tourists was important to the hijackers, since immigration regulations automatically guaranteed tourists six months of stay. Thus the 14 muscle hijackers who entered the United States in the spring and early summer of 2001 were able to remain in the country legally through September 11. The six-month tourist stays also assured the hijackers of sufficient time to make such preparations for their operation as obtaining the identifications some of them used to board the planes on September 11. Fourteen of 15 operatives and all of the pilots acquired one or multiple forms of U.S. state-issued identification. Only Satam al Suqami did not, possibly because he was the only hijacker who knew he was out of immigration status: his length of stay end date of May 20, 2000, was clearly inserted in his passport.

Note: Per an agreement with the Department of State, we have protected the identities of individual consular officers involved with the adjudication of visas to the hijackers. Throughout the chronology, each is referred to as "he," regardless of the person's actual gender. For similar reasons, we have chosen not to include the names of border inspectors in this report.

The Entry of the Hijackers: Acquiring Visas

November 1998
Upon the indictment of Usama Bin Ladin on November 4, a threat advisory was immediately sent by the headquarters of the Immigration and Naturalization Service (INS) to all immigration inspectors at ports of entry. Warning of possible infiltration into the United States by radical Islamic fundamentalists sympathetic to UBL, the advisory called for "hard" inspections of certain visitors from Middle Eastern countries, but only if they were referred to a secondary immigration inspection. This instruction applied to the countries of origin of all of the hijackers.[2]

April 1999
April 3—**Nawaf al Hazmi** applied for a B-1/B-2 (tourist/business) visa in Jeddah, Saudi Arabia, submitting a written visa application, his passport, and a photograph. Hazmi was a Saudi citizen born August 9, 1976.[3] Hazmi's passport was new—issued on March 21, 1999, and it contained an indicator of extremism that has been associated with al Qaeda.[4]

Also on April 3, 1999, the same day that Nawaf al Hazmi was applying for his visa in Jeddah, another of the 9/11 conspirators, **Khallad**, attempted to get a visa in Sanaa, Yemen, using the alias Salah Saeed Mohammed Bin Yousaf. He submitted a written application, a photograph, and a Yemeni passport, issued March 18, 1999, shortly before he applied for this visa. On his application, he listed his date of birth as January 1, 1974, and his nationality as "Yemeni."[5]

Khallad listed his address in the United States as "Bothell W.A.," and gave "Medical Treatment" as the purpose of his visit. Injured while fighting in Afghanistan, he had an artificial right leg. He indicated that he intended to arrive in the United States in April 1999 and stay for a period of "aprox [*sic*] two months."[6]

Khallad was interviewed, apparently by a consular officer, who took notes of their conversation on the visa application. As best as we can tell from the copy we have obtained, the officer wrote "Family in Shobanah and Br (unintelligible)—1 kid—has shops w/family—artificial leg—needs all med info." He denied the application under Immigration and Nationality Act (INA) section 221(g), the provision used to cover denials for incomplete applications or other unspecified reasons, seemingly out of concern that Khallad needed to present more information about his medical condition before he could secure a visa. In general, Yemenis had greater difficulty than wealthier Saudis convincing consular officers they were not intending immigrants.[7]

This is the only visa application we have located for Khallad, though he claims to have applied for one previously.[8]

April 7—**Khalid al Mihdhar** applied for a B-1/B-2 (tourist/business) visa in Jeddah, Saudi Arabia, submitting a written application, his new passport, and a photograph. Mihdhar was a Saudi citizen born May 16, 1975.[9] Mihdhar's passport was issued on April 6, 1999.[10] Mihdhar's passport contained the same indicator of extremism as Nawaf al Hazmi's. But because this indicator of extremism was unknown at the time to U.S. intelligence officials, the consular officer adjudicating their visas had not been warned to watch for it.

Both Hazmi and Mihdhar's visa applications were destroyed before September 11, according to routine State Department document destruction practices in place in Jeddah, so we could not review them. The electronic records of their applications, their photographs, and information about the visas issued to them still exist, however, and are maintained in the State Department's Consular Consolidated Database (CCD), and we have reviewed this material.

It is not possible to state with certainty whether either Hazmi or Mihdhar were interviewed by a consular officer in connection with their visa applications.[11] The consular officer who approved Hazmi's visa stated, "I do not remember these specific applications."[12] State Department computer records did not provide any help in this regard, because they do not indicate whether the applicant has been interviewed.[13]

If either of these two were interviewed, they must have convinced the officer they had good reasons to be going to the United States: both were issued visas after CLASS record checks showed no derogatory information about them. Hazmi's visa was issued on April 3, 1999. Mihdhar's visa was issued on April 7, 1999. Both were one-year, multiple-entry visas.

January 2000
January 15—**Nawaf al Hazmi** and **Khalid al Mihdhar** arrived together at Los Angeles International Airport from Bangkok, Thailand. The two Saudis were admitted as tourists for six-month stays by the same primary immigration inspector, who was unaware of the indicators of extremism likely present in their passports.[14]

Neither Hazmi nor Mihdhar was on the watchlists available to border inspectors. However, Mihdhar was a known al Qaeda operative at the time, and a copy of his passport was available to the intelligence community.[15]

January 18—**Marwan al Shehhi**, an Emirati, was issued a ten-year B-1/B-2 (tourist/business) visa in Dubai, United Arab Emirates.[16] Shehhi submitted a new passport with his visa application. Although his application was destroyed prior to September 11, 2001, pursuant to routine document handling policies, an electronic record was maintained by State.[17] The consular officer who issued the visa said Shehhi probably was not interviewed, explaining that UAE nationals were not interviewed in connection with their visa applications unless—as did not happen in this case—there was a watchlist "hit."[18] UAE nationals were considered good visa risks both on economic and on security grounds.[19]

April 2000
April 2—**Nawaf al Hazmi**'s visa expired,[20] but that expiration had no bearing on his legal status in the United States. Any visitor who enters the country with a valid visa may remain through the length of stay granted by an immigration inspector upon arrival.

April 5—**Mihdhar** and **Nawaf al Hazmi** acquired California driver's licenses.[21]

May 2000
May 17—**Mohammed Atta**, an Egyptian, applied for and on the next day received a five-year B-1/B-2 (tourist/business) visa from the U.S. embassy in Berlin, Germany.[22] The consular officer who adjudicated this visa said Atta "definitely" was not interviewed.

According to the officer, because he was a third-country national who had long been resident in Germany (approximately five years), the visa interview requirement was waived, and Atta was "basically treated like" a German citizen. German citizens do not need visas, as they participate in a "visa waiver" program. Another factor in his favor was Atta's strong record as a student in Germany.[23] Atta's visa application was destroyed prior to 9/11 pursuant to State Department policy then in effect, so we were able to review only the electronic record of his application.

Also on May 17, **Ramzi Binalshibh**, another Yemeni, applied for a B-1/B-2 (tourist/visa) visa in Berlin. He listed Agus Budiman in Washington, D.C., as the person he would be visiting in the United States. Although his application was denied, Binalshibh did not give up on trying to get a visa to the United States, as we will soon see.[24]

May 25—**Ziad Jarrah**, a native of Lebanon, applied for and received a five-year B-1/B-2 (tourist/business) visa in Berlin.[25] The consular officer who issued the visa could not recall whether he interviewed Jarrah. However, our review of Berlin visa policy for third-country nationals suggests that Jarrah was a strong visa candidate, given his long residence in Germany (approximately four years), academic involvement in Germany (at two universities), and Lebanese nationality. Third-country nationals with more than two years of residency in Germany met a threshold for visa approval. The officer who adjudicated his visa has stated that wealthy Lebanese families often sent their children to school in Germany as a way to keep them out of the Middle East's turmoil, and that Jarrah looked like one of those wealthy expatriates.[26]

May 29—**Shehhi** arrived in the United States for the first time from Brussels, Belgium, landing at Newark International Airport in New Jersey. He was admitted by immigration authorities as a tourist for six months. However, he was pulled aside by a "roving" Customs inspector who conducted a secondary inspection. He was admitted after this two-minute examination, during which his bags were x-rayed but he was not personally searched and was admitted. The Customs inspector was trained to look for drug couriers, not terrorists.[27]

June 2000
June 3—**Atta** arrived from Prague, Czech Republic, at Newark Airport as a tourist. He was given a customary six-month stay, valid until December 2, 2000.[28]

June 5—**Binalshibh**'s May application was denied under INA section 221(g).[29] This section was routinely invoked by the U.S. embassy in Berlin, without conducting an interview, to deny a visa application that was incomplete or weak.[30] In such cases, the embassy would send a letter explaining the denial and inviting the submission of further documentation in support of the application.[31] Under the law, such additional information can become part of the original application.[32] The applicant then had six months to have the original denial reversed.[33]

June 10—**Mihdhar** left the United States against the wishes of the operational organizer of the plot, Khalid Sheikh Mohammed. He traveled to Yemen.[34]

June 15—**Binalshibh** attempted a second time to obtain a B-1/B-2 (tourist/business) visa in Berlin.

June 27—**Jarrah** entered the United States for the first time on a tourist visa.[35] He immediately violated his immigration status by going from the airport straight to full-time flight school. He studied at the Florida Flight Training Center in Venice, Florida, until January 31, 2001. [36] Jarrah never filed an application to change his status from tourist to student. This failure to maintain a legal immigration status provided a solid legal basis to deny him entry on each of the six subsequent occasions in which he reentered the United States. But because there was no student tracking system in place and because neither Jarrah nor the school complied with the law's notification requirements, immigration inspectors could not know he was out of status.

June 27—**Binalshibh**'s second visa application was again denied under 221(g), apparently without his being interviewed by a consular officer.

July 2000
July 3—**Shehhi** and **Atta** enrolled at Huffman Aviation to take flight lessons.[37] Neither violated his immigration status: attending flight school was permitted as long as their entrance to the United States was legal and they sought to change their status before the expiration of their length of stay in late November and early December. As required by Huffman, both began training as private pilots.[38]

July 12—**Nawaf al Hazmi** filed to extend his stay in the United States, which was due to expire on July 14, 2000.[39] Yet another opportunity to spot the suspicious indicator of extremism in his passport.

July 1—A consular officer in Berlin interviewed **Binalshibh** in connection with his two visa applications submitted on May 17 and June 15, 2000. This time, a consular officer denied his application under INA Section 214(b), after concluding that Binalshibh had failed to prove that he was not an intending immigrant to the United States.[40] Under this provision, discussed more fully in Chapter 5, the nonimmigrant visa applicant bears the burden of establishing to the satisfaction of the consular officer that they are entitled to nonimmigrant status. The consular officer noted on the application that Binalshibh had a poor academic record at German universities, attending only sporadically. The officer also noted that Binalshibh had no apparent source of income, no apparent job, and was traveling back and forth to the Middle East. All these factors led the officer to consider Binalshibh a bad visa risk. There is no evidence that the officer denied Binalshibh because of concerns about terrorism.

August 2000

August 14—**Atta** and **Shehhi** passed their private pilot airplane test at Huffman Aviation. Atta received a score of 97 (out of 100) in 69 minutes. Shehhi received a score of 83 in 73 minutes.[41]

September 2000

September 3—**Ahmed al Ghamdi**, a Saudi, applied for and received a two-year B-1/B-2 (tourist/business) visa in Jeddah, Saudi Arabia. He presented a new Saudi passport only 13 days old. There is no evidence that he was interviewed.[42]

September 10—**Hani Hanjour** again applied for a B-1/B-2 (tourist/business) visa in Jeddah, Saudi Arabia, submitting a new passport issued on July 24, 2000. His statement on the application that he would like to stay for three years in the United States raised concerns among the consular staff that he was at risk of becoming an immigrant to the United States. A consular employee who screened Hanjour's application forwarded him to a consular officer for an interview. Hanjour told this officer that he was going to attend flight training school in the United States and wanted to change his status to "student" from "tourist" once he arrived in the United States.[43] "Look, you have spent enough time in the States" to know what you want to do there, the officer told Hanjour. His prior travel to the United States, the officer said to him, disqualified Hanjour from receiving a tourist visa in order to go to the United States and find a school "because he had been in the States long enough to decide what he wanted."[44] For these reasons, the officer denied Hanjour's application under INA section 221(g), a general denial that, as noted above, allowed the applicant to return with additional information in support of his application.

September 15—Huffman Aviation's Student Coordinator assisted **Atta** in filling out the student school form I-20M, required by the INS to demonstrate school enrollment.[45] **Shehhi** also received an I-20M signed by this coordinator. Both Atta's and Shehhi's I-539 applications to change their immigration status from tourist (B-1/B-2) to vocational student (M1) were mailed to the INS. Both applications requested that their status be maintained until September 1, 2001. The contents of the applications are substantially the same, including the same financial statement of support, bank statement, and lease.[46] Also in September, the two took flying lessons at Jones Aviation in nearby Sarasota, Florida. They spent a few hours a day flying at Jones, struggling as students because of their poor English. They were aggressive, even trying to take over control of the aircraft from the instructor on occasion. They failed their instrument rating tests there, and returned to Huffman.[47]

September 16—**Binalshibh**'s third visa application was denied in Sanaa, Yemen, under INA section 214(b), the intending immigrant provision.[48] There is no evidence that concerns about terrorism played a role in this denial. The consular officer wrote on the application "no ties" and "previous refusals in Berlin."

September 19—**Atta** and **Shehhi**'s I-539 applications were received by the INS.

September 25—**Hanjour** returned to the Jeddah consulate and, apparently having listened to what the consular officer told him, submitted another application for a student visa. This time, Hanjour stated a desire to attend the ELS Language Center in Oakland, California. A consular official—probably the intake screener—wrote a note on his application indicating that Hanjour had been denied a visa under section 221(g) on September 10. The same consular officer who had interviewed Hanjour in connection with his September 10 application also processed this one. He recalled to us that Hanjour or someone acting on his behalf submitted an INS school enrollment form, or I-20—required to qualify for a student visa—to the consulate late on September 25, 2000.[49] "It came to me, you know, at the end of the day to look at it. I saw he had an I-20, and it [his visa] was issued."[50]

State Department electronic records indicate that this approval allowed Hanjour to "overcome" his September 10 visa denial, another indication that multiple applications can be considered "one case." State Department records erroneously recorded the visa issued to Hanjour as a B-1/B-2 (business/tourist) visa when, in fact, it was an F (student) visa that was printed and put in Hanjour's passport.[51] In addition, Hanjour had already received an approved change of status to attend this same English language school in 1996. But that approval was granted by the INS in the United States, and the State Department had no record of it. The consular officer told us that if he had known this information, he might have refused Hanjour the visa.

October 2000
October 17—**Hamza al Ghamdi**, a Saudi, applied for and received a two-year B-1/B-2 (tourist/business) visa in Riyadh, Saudi Arabia. His application was incomplete.[52] Al Ghamdi listed his occupation as "student" but left blank the question asking the street address of his school. Ghamdi's travel patterns indicated that he may have presented a passport containing fraudulent travel stamps associated with al Qaeda when he applied for this visa.[53] The consular officer who adjudicated his case was not familiar with this kind of manipulation; in addition, he told us that because of the workload in Jeddah, he rarely had time to thumb through passports. Ghamdi was not interviewed, because nothing in his application raised concerns in the mind of the consular officer who adjudicated it and there was no hit in the CLASS system.[54] His visa application was granted.

October 23—**Mohand al Shehri**, a Saudi, applied for and received a two-year B-1/B-2 (tourist/business) visa in Riyadh, Saudi Arabia. His application was incomplete. Al Shehri listed his occupation as "student," but listed the street address of his school as "Riyadh K.S.A." He claimed he was a 21-year-old student who would be supporting himself in the United States.[55] He was not interviewed, according to the officer who issued this visa, because "We only interviewed Saudis if there was a previous denial of a visa application or if there was something wrong with the application."[56] Shehri apparently raised no such concerns. The officer noted that the lack of handwritten notes on the application was a further indication that he had not interviewed Shehri.[57]

October 25—**Binalshibh** applied for a visa again in Berlin, Germany, this time for a student (F) visa to attend aviation school in Florida. He accurately indicated on his application form that he had been denied visas previously in Berlin and Sanaa.

October 28—**Ahmed al Nami**, a Saudi, applied for and received a two-year B-1/B-2 (tourist/business) visa in Jeddah, Saudi Arabia. Nami's application was incomplete.[58] He listed his occupations as "student" but did not provide a complete address for his school. He listed his intending address in the United States as "in Los Angeles." Nami's passport may have contained fraudulent travel stamps associated with al Qaeda.[59] However, his passport did not survive, so we can not be sure. On his application, Nami indicated that "My friend Moshabab" would be traveling with him.

On the same day, **Mushabib al Hamlan**, a Saudi and a friend of 9/11 hijacker Ahmed al Nami, acquired a two-year B1/B2 (tourist/business) visa in Jeddah, Saudi Arabia.[60] Hamlan was selected to participate in the plot but backed out after obtaining his visa, perhaps at the urging of his family.

October 29—**Jarrah** arrived back in the United States, entering in Tampa, Florida, from Frankfurt, Germany, on a tourist visa. He received a six-month length of stay in the United States. He was still in flight school.[61]

November 2000
November 1—**Binalshibh** was denied in Berlin yet again under 221(g) for lack of adequate documentation and failure to show sufficient ties to Germany. His application was incomplete, and his prior denials in Berlin and Sanaa provided powerful grounds for this denial. Consular officials wrote on this application, "Incomplete [application], refused in Sanaa and here, bad case." Once again, there was no evidence that officials were concerned about terrorism. A citizen of a poor, developing country, with tenuous ties to Germany, Binalshibh was considered an intending immigrant and a bad visa risk.

November 6—**Atta** and **Shehhi** took their instrument rating airplane test at Huffman Aviation. Atta received a score of 90 in 122 minutes and Shehhi received a score of 75 in 89 minutes.[62] After passing this test, Atta and Shehhi were able to sign out planes. They did so on a number of occasions, often returning at 2:00 and 3:00 A.M. after logging four or five hours of flying time.[63]

November 12—**Ahmad al Haznawi**, a 20-year-old Saudi national, applied for and received a two-year B-1/B-2 (tourist/business) visa in Jeddah, Saudi Arabia.[64] There is evidence that Haznawi may have presented a passport with fraudulent travel stamps associated with al Qaeda.[65] Haznawi listed his occupation as "student" but left blank the line on which he was asked to supply the street address of his present school. He stated that he would provide financial support for his visit. He was not interviewed.

Also on November 12, **Saeed al Ghamdi**, a Saudi national, sometimes known as "Jihad" al Ghamdi—not to be confused with the 9/11 hijacker of the same name—applied for a B-1/B-2 (tourist/business) visa in Jeddah. Ghamdi's application was denied after he was interviewed by a consular officer who believed he was intending to immigrate to the United States. Ghamdi wrote on his application that he intended to stay in the United States for "12 months," a red flag because the usual period of admission for tourists granted by INS inspectors at ports of entry was six months. Contemporaneous notes by consular staff, probably taken during his interview, state: "To stay one year . . . no job . . . graduated from H.S. last year . . . he has SR [Saudi rials] 10,000 only and staying one year! . . . Not working." Ghamdi was denied under INA section 214(b), the intending immigrant provision. There is no evidence that terrorism concerns played a role in this denial.[66]

November 20—**Majed Moqed**, a Saudi, applied for and received a two-year B-1/B-2 (tourist/business) visa in Riyadh, Saudi Arabia. His application was incomplete. He claimed to be a "student" but left blank the line on which he was asked to supply the street address of his present school.[67] The officer who adjudicated his visa said they did not interview Moqed: "I would have written some notes on the application form if I had."[68] He was not interviewed because, according to the officer who issued the visa, "We only interviewed Saudis if there was a previous denial of a visa application or if there was something wrong with the application."[69] Incompleteness by itself evidently did not trigger an interview.

November 21—**Satam al Suqami**, a Saudi, applied for and received a two-year B-1/B-2 (tourist/business) visa in Riyadh, Saudi Arabia.[70] There is very strong evidence that the passport Suqami submitted with this application had fraudulent travel stamps now associated with al Qaeda.[71] Suqami left blank the line on which he was asked to supply the name and street address of his present employer. The consular officer who issued the visa said he interviewed Suqami because he described his present occupation as "dealer," the word Saudis often put on their applications when they meant "businessman." The officer testified that he asked Suqami a number of questions, including, he believes, who was paying for the trip.[72] Although the officer stated that notes were always taken during interviews,[73] none were written on Suqami's application, raising the possibility that the officer's memory of having conducted an interview was false. In any case, Suqami evidently raised no suspicions and his application was approved.

November 25—**Jarrah** rented a private plane for a one-day trip from Miami to Nassau, Bahamas, with a couple of companions. There is no immigration departure record, but there is a record of his reentry into the country. At the general aviation terminal where Jarrah arrived, he was subjected to both an immigration and customs check, including an inspection of the plane by customs for the presence of drugs, contraband, and currency. Nothing unusual was found and Jarrah was once again admitted as a tourist for six months. Again, he was still in school despite having a B-1/B-2 visa.[74]

December 2000
December 8—**Hanjour** entered the United States for the final time at the Cincinnati/Northern Kentucky International Airport, six months after the entry of the other pilots. He never attended the ELS Language Center in Oakland, California, the stated destination on his second visa application of September 25, 2000. His records do not indicate the length of stay the primary immigration inspector gave him.[75]

December 12—**Zakariya Essabar**, a Moroccan who intended to participate in the plot, submitted the first of two visa applications in Berlin. He indicated that he intended to arrive in the United States on February 15, 2001.[76]

December 19—**Atta** and **Shehhi** took their commercial pilot license tests at Huffman Aviation, completing their schooling. Atta received a score of 93 in 116 minutes and Shehhi received a score of 73 in 99 minutes.[77]

January 2001
January 4—**Atta** departed the United States for the first time, having overstayed his tourist visa by one month. Although his application for a change of his immigration status was still pending, once he departed the country the application was considered abandoned.[78]

January 5—**Jarrah** returned from Dusseldorf, Germany, landing at Newark, New Jersey, and flying onward to Tampa, Florida. He was admitted as a tourist for six months. His flight school education continued.[79]

January 10—**Essabar** was interviewed and was denied a visa under INA section 221(g), on the grounds that he provided no evidence of a job in or other ties to Germany. Essabar applied for a visa again on January 28, 2001, but there is no record of the State Department's ever having acted on this second application. On the same day, **Atta** returned from Madrid to Miami. The primary immigration inspector who screened him told the Commission that he had been working as a primary inspector for less than a year when Atta presented himself. He said he knew that if he took more time than 45 seconds to determine a visitor's admissibility or if he made too many referrals to secondary inspection, he could receive a poor performance appraisal. During an interview with the Department of Justice, Office of the Inspector General (DOJ OIG), in November 2001, the primary inspector recalled some of his encounter with Atta. He told the interviewer that Atta presented an Egyptian passport with a tourist/business visa and an INS student/school form indicating that he was attending school. The inspector determined that Atta needed either an F-1 visa to attend an academic school or an M-1 visa to attend a vocational school, and had neither. The official's "inspection results report" recorded Atta's statement that he had "turned in" a student/school form to the INS in an attempt to change his status, but that he "has not had a response [from the INS], meanwhile he's attending flight training school, already in school for 5/6 months."[80]

The inspector, however, had already begun to process Atta for admission into the United States before noticing the visa problem. The I-94 arrival record, which was stamped and stapled into Atta's passport, indicated that the primary inspector initially approved a one-month stay as a B-1 business visitor.[81]

The second red ink admission stamp (located on the top of Atta's passport in the figure) was that of a B-1 visitor, but the length of stay was left blank. We know this was the work of the primary inspector, as the stamp bears his assigned number. The inspector told us that the blank length of stay on the admission stamp indicated that while he was almost finished processing Atta, he stopped, realizing that Atta needed more scrutiny.[82] He sent him to a secondary immigration inspection for closer examination.

The immigration inspectors the Commission interviewed understood that INS policy permitted a commercial pilot coming to the United States for ongoing training to be admitted as a business visitor for the time necessary to complete his training. However, an alien wishing to pursue such training needed a vocational student visa.[83] The primary inspector initially thought that Atta was already a pilot who was seeking continuing education, and then decided that Atta was studying to become a pilot and had the wrong visa.

The ten-year veteran immigration inspector who conducted Atta's secondary examination admitted him as a tourist for eight months, though Atta had said he was still attending school and though as a tourist his stay should be legally limited to six months. This inspector initially recalled some aspects of this inspection in late 2001, when he was interviewed by the DOJ OIG; he said then that Atta was referred to secondary inspection as a possible overstay on a B1/B2 tourist visa. However, he told the Commission he no longer had any memory of this inspection and could not recall whether he asked Atta for his I-20 student/school form, checked the school/student system to verify Atta's information, or asked Atta whether he was a part-time or full-time student, was attending flight school, or was still in school. He told the Commission that because the student tracking system at that time was "garbage"—full of information that was no longer valid and lacking updates—he would not have checked it to verify Atta's story that he was still in school.[84]

Yet the inspector told the DOJ OIG that he knew Atta had filed for a change of immigration status from tourist to student after conducting a computer check of his records. The inspector seems to have then concluded that this application was still pending and that Atta was admissible. But under INS policy, Atta abandoned his application when he left the country. Thus, Atta's entry into the United States with the wrong visa should have been grounds for his removal.[85]

The Commission sought to understand whether the secondary inspector's understanding of Atta's pending application did, in fact, affect the decision to admit him. In a subsequent 2002 interview with DOJ OIG, the inspector stated that if an alien departed the United States prior to his or her application for change of status being granted, then that application is considered abandoned. If that alien then seeks to reenter the United States as a student, he or she must obtain the correct student visa. Thus, according to the secondary inspector, Atta should not have been admitted. However, in response to a Commission staff question the inspector said that he thought the applicant in such a case "would still be in status; a gray area."[86]

In fact, this was not a gray area. Other inspectors we interviewed, including the primary inspector in this case, said that leaving the United States while an application for change of status was still pending made it necessary for the alien to get a new visa overseas. Indeed, the DOJ OIG concluded that the issue of the pending application was a red herring: all that mattered was whether Atta had the correct visa to enter the United States at the time he applied for entry.[87]

The secondary inspector admitted Atta as a B-2 tourist, which automatically set the length of stay at six months. Only a supervisor could vary this period, allowing a tourist to stay up to one year in the country. Every inspector we interviewed verified this. However, this inspector gave Atta eight months, until September 8, 2001, without supervisory approval. Thus, both Atta's admission as a tourist and his length of stay were improper.[88]

In addition, Atta had overstayed his previous visa by one month when he departed the United States on January 4, 2001.[89] That overstay should have been obvious to a secondary inspector tasked with giving a thorough look at Atta, for his passport would have contained an entry stamp into a foreign country from the week before, and an original U.S. admission stamp dated seven months earlier. Though the overstay did not make Atta automatically inadmissible, it could have been considered. But there is no indication that the secondary inspector who adjudicated Atta's admission took his overstay into account.[90] In contrast, other inspectors have told us that overstays are a typical travel pattern of an intending immigrant, and are normally a red flag for those attempting reentry.[91]

The secondary inspector also could have admitted Atta into the United States for 30 days for a fee of $170, requiring Atta to present paperwork from his school to prove his current student status within 30 days. However, the inspector told us he had not considered the option of a deferred inspection.[92] Such an inspection would have placed Atta in a difficult position: because he was already finished with school, he would have been unable to present paperwork indicating that he was still legally a student.

January 18—**Shehhi** arrived at JFK Airport in New York on Royal Moroccan Air from Casablanca.[93] He was screened by a ten-year veteran of immigration inspections at airports and the New York City seaport.[94] When Shehhi came up to the primary inspection counter, the "room was full, with numerous flights coming in at the same time." The inspector told the Commission that she was suspicious that Shehhi might be an intending immigrant, noting from the stamps in his passport that he had left the United States just a week earlier after a six-month stay. She typed into the computer record: "Sub left one week ago after entry in May. Has extension and now returning for a few more months." She referred Shehhi to a secondary immigration inspection for closer examination.[95]

The secondary inspector told the Commission that Shehhi wore conventional Western clothing, had glasses and facial hair, and "did not look like he had just come from boot camp." Though he had behaved badly in primary inspection, where his refusal to comply with the inspector's instruction to go to the secondary inspection room made an escort necessary, once there Shehhi waited until he was called and was not aggressive. About a dozen other visitors were called into secondary inspection in the ten minutes before Shehhi's referral.[96]

The secondary immigration inspector said that Shehhi had completed the required arrival and customs forms, adding that Shehhi spoke English well during the course of the 10–12 minute interview. "I had the impression Shehhi had money," the inspector said. "I remember looking at his passport, and it showed he had been in and out of the United States and there were other travel stamps. I remember asking how much money he had—he had a substantial amount, three credit cards and more than $2,000."[97]

Shehhi also mentioned applying for an extension of stay in the United States to remain until September 8, 2001; after waiting months for an answer and not getting one, he had finally left. To the inspector, "that seemed reasonable." The inspector told the Commission he was not aware that leaving the country while an immigration benefit application was pending amounted to abandoning that application.[98]

The inspector asked Shehhi the purpose of his trip to the United States, trying to determine if he intended to remain permanently, as the primary inspector suspected. Shehhi told the inspector that he was coming back to the United States for continued flight training, that he had previously attended Huffman Aviation School, and that he was finished with flight school but wanted to log more hours in the sky. The inspector thought Shehhi was seeking private flying lessons, but did not ask Shehhi for supporting documentation.[99]

The inspector did not recall whether Shehhi showed him any papers to verify his previous flight school attendance at Huffman Aviation, nor whether he had asked for such paperwork. "I didn't have any doubt he did go to school, and I didn't think he was trying to use his change of status application to remain here in the United States for illegitimate reasons. My belief was that he was coming back to log flight hours with a private instructor." Under this inspector's understanding of INS guidelines, a pilot here for a form of continuing education, such as private flight lessons, may be admitted as a business visitor. Although the baseline time at JFK International for business visitors was three months, Shehhi asked for four and got it.[100]

The inspection results tell a somewhat different story; they read: "Was in U.S. gaining flight hours to become a pilot. Admitted for four months."

They thus suggest that the inspector actually may have considered Shehhi a student, not already a pilot.

The difference between Shehhi being a student seeking to become a pilot or already was a pilot was not an insignificant nuance. According to immigration law applied at ports of entry, if Shehhi was already a pilot, the B-1 business entry he was granted was arguably legitimate. However, if Shehhi was a full-time student, his admission as a business visitor was erroneous. And because Shehhi, like Atta, had left the country while his application for a change of immigration status was still pending, this application should have been considered "abandoned." In other words, Shehhi needed to obtain the proper student visa overseas in order to reenter the United States. The facts of this adjudication are simply not clear enough to reach a conclusion about the appropriateness of this entry.

January 26—**Jarrah** departed the United States for the fourth time.[101]

February 2001
February 25—**Jarrah** enters for the fifth time at Newark as a business visitor, but still receives a six-month stay. This was unusual, as most inspectors told us that standard operating procedures were to give business visitors a stay of one or three months, depending on the port, and six months only when the visitor could document the purpose of the stay.[102]

March 2001
March 30—**Jarrah** departed for the fifth time.[103]

April 2001
April 12—**Shehhi** obtained a Florida driver's license.[104]

April 13—**Jarrah** entered at Atlanta from Amsterdam and was granted a three and a half month stay on business.[105]

April 21—**Ahmed al Nami** acquired a new Saudi passport, #C505363, replacing the one (#C115007) he had used to acquire a visa on October 28, 2000, in Jeddah, a visa he never used. He may have acquired this new passport because there was evidence of travel to Afghanistan in his previous one.[106]

April 23—**Nami** applied for and received a B-1/B-2 (tourist/business) visa in Jeddah with his new passport. There is evidence from a handwritten note on his application that Nami was interviewed briefly, either by a consular officer or by a consular staff member, to clarify an entry on his application. The words "My friend Mosh" are crossed out under the question asking the "names and relationships of people traveling with you." This is probably a reference to Mushabib al Hamlan, another potential 9/11 hijacker who applied for a visa with Nami on October 28, 2000. Nami also crossed out a box checked "no" under the question asking if he had ever applied for a U.S. visa previously, changing his answer to "yes." It is not clear what prompted this change—possibly his brief interaction with a consular official—but it is accurate. However, he failed to complete his response and state where and when he had previously applied for a U.S. visa. Doing so would have revealed that he was applying for a new visa long before the expiration of the two-year visa he acquired the previous October. Nami's action could have raised questions, had it been coupled with the fact that he was applying with a new passport. But it would not have been noticed by the consular officer who issued the visa, because Saudis were not required to fill in their applications fully, Saudis were rarely interviewed, and State's name check system did not automatically call up prior visa issuances; it called up only prior refusals.[107]

Also on April 23, **Waleed al Shehri** and **Satam al Suqami**, both Saudis, entered together at Orlando from Dubai, United Arab Emirates. Suqami was the only Saudi muscle hijacker admitted on business, and only for one month. Shehri was admitted as a tourist for a six-month stay. Both were admitted by the same primary immigration inspector.[108] Suqami's passport survived the attack: a passerby picked it up from the World Trade Center and handed to a New York Police Department detective shortly before the towers collapsed.[109] Later analysis showed that it contained what are now believed to be fraudulent travel stamps associated with al Qaeda.[110] Upon reviewing color copies of the document, the inspector who admitted Suqami told the Commission he did not note any such fraud.[111] Indeed, he could not have been expected to identify the fraud at the time of Suqami's admission—it was not discovered by the intelligence community until after the attacks.

May 2001

May 2—**Majed Moqed** and **Ahmed al Ghamdi** arrived together at Dulles International Airport in Washington, D.C. Both Saudis were admitted as tourists for six months by different immigration inspectors. Ghamdi's Customs declaration indicated that he had more than $10,000 with him upon entry, but the Customs inspector who processed him did not fill out the required additional electronic forms when money in excess of $10,000 is brought into the United States.[112]

Also on this day, **Shehhi** arrived in Miami and was granted a six-month tourist stay.[113] Meanwhile, **Atta** and, we believe, **Jarrah** were attempting to extend Jarrah's length of stay to September 2001.

ATTA'S WALK-IN INSPECTION AT THE MIAMI IMMIGRATION DISTRICT OFFICE

On May 2, 2001, Atta and two companions stood in a long line at the Miami District Immigration Office. INS district offices adjudicate all types of immigration benefits inspections, including naturalization interviews, applications for permanent residency based on marriage to a U.S. citizen, and deferred inspections for students lacking the proper paperwork upon entry. But Atta had something else in mind. He wanted his companion, who was likely Jarrah, to obtain the same eight-month length of stay that he had (wrongfully) received in January.[114]

By late morning, Atta finally made it to the inspection desk. An inspector from Miami International Airport was getting ready to take a break for lunch at about 11:30 A.M. when three men approached her at the counter. This inspector had worked primary and secondary inspections at airports, as well as of ship crews, since 1988 in Fort Lauderdale and Miami. However, because she had never before worked at this district office, she recalled the encounter with Atta vividly.[115]

One of Atta's companions, proficient in English, spoke first. He told the inspector, "My friends have a question about their I-94 arrival records." When she asked, "Do you need to see immigration?" he said no. The inspector then instructed him to go sit down and that she would help him with his friends, and he complied. She told them that the person needing help should write his name on the sign-in sheet. In large capital letters, he wrote, "ATTA."[116]

Atta told the inspector that he wanted his friend to receive an eight-month length of stay as he had. The inspector recalled taking both passports to see if they had genuine visas. She also looked at the I-94 arrival records in the passports. Atta's companion had received a six-month stay as a tourist, with an end date in July 2001. She also noticed that Atta had been admitted as a tourist for eight months, with a length of stay until September 8, 2001. During this time, Atta was quiet. She told Atta, "Someone gave you the wrong admission and I'm not giving your friend eight months."[117]

The inspector then went to her supervisor, informed him that Atta had been granted an incorrect length of stay, and asked permission to roll it back to six months. The supervisor agreed. The inspector then tore the I-94 record out of Atta's passport, and created a new I-94 for six months, which allowed Atta to remain in the United States until July 9, 2001. On the record she wrote: "I-94 issued in error at MIA [Miami International Airport]. New I-94 issued." The inspector then took a red-inked admission stamp, rolled the date back to January 10, and stamped Atta as a B-2 tourist. She wrote in a length of stay until July 9, 2001, and handed Atta back his passport and new I-94 record. Atta took the documents, said thank you, and left with his companions.[118]

Also on May 2, **Atta** and **Jarrah** acquired Florida driver's licenses.[119]

May 4—**Waleed al Shehri** obtained a Florida driver's license.[120]

May 5—**Waleed al Shehri** acquired a duplicate Florida driver's license, this time with a different address.[121]

May 16—**Waleed al Shehri** and **Suqami** again traveled together, this time out of the country to the Bahamas, where they reserved three nights at the Bahamas Princess Resort.[122] They turned in their arrival record, which was now acting as an exit record, boarded the plane, and arrived in Freeport.[123] The trip was intended to extend Suqami's legal length of stay in the United States.[124] Bahamian immigration refused the two entry, however, because neither had a Bahamian visa.[125] They therefore had to return to their starting point, in this case Fort Lauderdale. Because they never entered the Bahamas, under U.S. immigration law they had never left the United States. After being refused entry by the Bahamian INS at Freeport, they were sent through U.S. "pre-clearance" before boarding the plane back to Miami. By making possible immigration inspections of U.S-bound travelers prior to their arrival, preclearance helped ease the burden of admission at busy U.S. airports. These stations also prevented travelers deemed inadmissible from boarding U.S.-bound planes.[126] In this preclearance process, immigration waived them through but customs stopped Shehri. The inspection lasted one minute; Shehri was not personally searched, nor was his luggage x-rayed. They boarded a plane and returned to Miami.[127]

May 20—**Suqami** joined the millions of overstays in the United States after failing to file for an extension of stay with the INS after he returned from the Bahamas. Had he been allowed into the Bahamas, upon his return to the United States he would have likely been granted an additional length of stay in the country as a tourist. As it was, he remained in illegal status until September 11.

May 24—**Jarrah** obtained a duplicate Florida driver's license.[128]

May 28—**Hamza al Ghamdi**, **Mohand al Shehri**, and **Ahmed al Nami** arrived together at Miami from Dubai, United Arab Emirates.[129] The three Saudis were admitted as tourists for six months by different primary inspectors.[130]

June 2001
June 1—The Visa Express Program was introduced for all Saudi citizens applying for visas in Saudi Arabia in an effort to make the consular work-load more manageable and to reduce the size of the crowds outside of the embassy. The concept was simple. Instead of going to the U.S. consulate to apply for a visa, the applicant filled out the form at one of ten approved travel agencies. After collecting the application, the visa application fee, and the applicant's passport, the travel agency delivered these documents to the embassy in Riyadh or to the consulate in Jeddah, and picked up the package of documents the next day. If the application was approved, then the agency was responsible for returning the passport (now containing the visa) to the applicant. If the consular officials determined that an interview was necessary, then the travel agency was responsible for so notifying the applicant by providing him or her with a letter from the consular section. Applicants were rejected only after an in-person interview.[131] (Visa Express will be discussed in further detail in chapter 5.)

June 8—**Ahmad al Haznawi** and **Wail al Shehri** arrived together at Miami from Dubai, United Arab Emirates. Both Saudis were admitted as tourists for six months by the same primary inspector.[132]

June 10—**Saeed al Ghamdi** acquired a new Saudi passport, #C573895, replacing the one (#B516222) he used to acquire a visa on September 4, 2000, in Jeddah. He may have acquired this new passport because there was evidence of travel to Afghanistan in his previous passport.[133]

June 12—Just like **Nami** (who applied April 23), **Saeed al Ghamdi** acquired a second two-year B-1/B-2 (tourist/business) visa in Jeddah. His application was incomplete and he was not interviewed. Ghamdi's visa application indicated that he had never applied for a U.S. visa before, a curious similarity to Nami's application.[134] This was not true, since he had applied for and acquired a visa on September 4, 2000. However, the State Department computer system was not set up to catch this false statement; as noted above, it called up only prior refusals. Ghamdi's application was submitted by Minhal Travel and processed through the Visa Express program.[135] We considered the possibility that the false answer reflected a mistake by the travel agency personnel, but the same signature appears on both visa applications, and State records indicate that the September application was submitted in person. Thus, it appears that Ghamdi was directly involved in preparing the June visa application containing the false statement. He may have omitted information about his prior visa in order not to raise suspicion about his new visa application in his new passport—without the travel to Pakistan and Afghanistan—when his old visa, which was multiple entry, was still valid.

June 13—**Mihdhar** applied for and received his second B-1/B-2 (tourist/business) visa in Jeddah. Mihdhar's passport had been issued only 13 days earlier and, like up two other hijackers, it contained an indicator of possible terrorist affiliation still unknown at that time to U.S. intelligence officials. His application was incomplete. For example, he listed his occupation as "businessman," but left blank the name and street address of his present employer. Mihdhar's application also indicated that he had not previously applied for a U.S. visa or been to the United States, though he had in fact traveled to the United States on a B-1/B-2 visa issued in April 1999 (also in Jeddah). Thus, his application contained two false statements. However, the State Department's computer system was not set up to catch these false statements by bringing up Mihdhar's prior visa history. Mihdhar's application was processed through the Visa Express program, and his application was submitted by Al Tayyar Travel. It is possible that these questions were answered falsely because of a mistake by the travel agency personnel; and unlike Ghamdi's, Mihdhar's application was signed only on the line for the "preparer" of the application. It is unclear why Mihdhar or the travel agency would wish to hide the fact of his prior travel. Mihdhar may have feared that it could compromise operational security of the 9/11 plot. He also may not have wanted to highlight that he had obtained a new passport since his previous visa.[136]

Consular officials have told us that evidence of the prior visas or travel to the United States actually would have reduced concern that the applicants were intending to immigrate. Thus, if the officers had learned the truth about these issues—and received an adequate explanation for the mistakes on the applications—they likely would have had no good reason to deny visas to these hijackers. On the other hand, if they had interviewed Mihdhar, **Nami**, and **Ghamdi** and received suspicious answers to their questions, the outcome might well have been different.

June 18—The INS belatedly approved **Nawaf al Hazmi**'s extension of stay to January 15, 2001. Technically, the application was late, since the INS received it in July 2000, after his length of stay had expired; they therefore should not have adjudicated it. However, even with this late adjudication Hazmi was still an overstay as of January 16, 2001. Hazmi never knew that his extension had been approved—the notice was returned as "undeliverable" on March 25, 2002.

Also on June 18, **Abdul Aziz al Omari**, a Saudi, applied for and received a two-year B-1/B-2 (tourist/business) visa in Jeddah, Saudi Arabia. There is strong evidence that Omari presented a passport containing the travel stamps now known to be associated with al Qaeda when he applied for this visa since the fraudulent stamps predate this application. Moreover, his application was incomplete, and he listed his home address as a hotel in Jeddah. He was not interviewed. His application was processed through the Visa Express program and was submitted by Attar Travel.[137]

Also on June 18, **Fayez Banihammad**, an Emirati, applied for and received a B-1/B-2 (tourist/business) visa in Abu Dhabi, United Arab Emirates. Banihammad's passport was only five days old. His application was incomplete; a number of sections were left completely blank.[138] The consular officer who adjudicated this visa has stated that interviews were almost never required of UAE nationals in connection with their visa applications, that the UAE was considered a welfare state that took very good care of its citizens, and that the UAE was treated as a de facto visa waiver country.[139] Banihammad, a former immigration officer in the UAE, was not interviewed.[140]

June 19—**Marwan al Shehhi** acquired a duplicate Florida driver's license.[141]

June 20—**Salem al Hazmi**, a Saudi, applied for and received a two-year B-1/B-2 (tourist/business) visa in Jeddah, Saudi Arabia. His application was incomplete, and he listed his occupation as "unemployed." The passport he supplied was four days old and contained an indicator of possible terrorist affiliation.[142] His application, processed through the Visa Express program, was submitted by Ace Travel. According to the consular officer who approved this application, the fact that Hazmi was "unemployed" was not of concern "because they have a terrible unemployment problem in Saudi Arabia, and a lot of people have money but they don't have jobs."[143] Although unemployment would have been a "big deal" in another country, the officer said, Saudis like Hazmi "weren't looking for jobs even though they were unemployed."[144]

June 25—**Nawaf al Hazmi** obtained a Florida driver's license.[145]

June 26—**Hamza al Ghamdi** obtained a Florida identification card.[146]

June 27—**Banihammad** and **Saeed al Ghamdi** arrived at Orlando from Dubai. The two were processed by different primary inspectors. Banihammad was admitted as a tourist for six months.[147] Although he handed in customs and immigration forms using two different names, the anomaly was not noted, because customs and INS inspectors did not review each other's forms. The immigration inspector who admitted Banihammad told the Commission that in the 45 seconds allowed for processing each visitor, it was not possible to fully check the contents of the forms. He said that if he had noticed the two different names forms he would have referred Banihammad to a secondary inspection, suspecting that the Emirati was attempting to hide his true identity.[148]

Saeed al Ghamdi, a Saudi, was admitted as a tourist for six months, but only after a secondary inspection. The Orlando primary inspector who referred him for further examination had worked as an immigration inspector for three years. He said that he insisted that a visitor communicate with him in order to be admitted and that he always asked to see a return ticket. The inspector also told us that he looked closely to see whether the Customs declaration and I-94 arrival form listed a full address of intended destination. Ghamdi met none of these requirements.[149]

The inspector's inspection record reads, "Subject speaks very little English. No return ticket, no address listed; please question."[150] His Customs declaration, listing $500 for a stay of one month, was, according to the primary inspector, "pushing it a little bit, along with the fact that he didn't know where he was going." The inspector confirmed that he did not have the discretion to give Ghamdi the one-month stay he sought—the law required a mandatory six-month stay for tourists traveling on a visa. The inspector referred Ghamdi to secondary inspection so an interpreter could attempt to flesh out his purpose in coming to the United States.[151]

In secondary inspection, Ghamdi convinced a different inspector that he was a tourist and admissible. His secondary inspection report reads: "Tourist. Valid docs. Sufficiently financed. B-2, six months." Although the inspector who admitted Ghamdi does not recall the inspection, which lasted ten minutes, he told the Commission that he did not normally consider money a valid criterion for determining admissibility. He told us that Ghamdi must have had credit cards to supplement the $500 in cash he was carrying. The inspector said he was not concerned that Ghamdi's arrival record failed to list an exact address; central Florida is overflowing with hotel rooms and thus a tourist need not have precise lodging to be admissible. Ghamdi's travel documents looked valid to him as well.[152]

June 29—**Abdul Aziz al Omari** and **Salem al Hazmi** arrived at JFK Airport in New York from Dubai, United Arab Emirates. Both Saudis were admitted as tourists for six months by the same immigration inspector.[153] Omari's passport was doctored, containing what we believe are the same fraudulent travel stamps associated with al Qaeda.[154] The passport survived the attacks on the World Trade Center because Omari's luggage never made it onto the plane when he transferred from his flight from Portland, Maine. Salem al Hazmi's passport contained an indicator of possible terrorist affiliation. We know this because a digital image of Hazmi's passport was found on a hard drive in a safehouse in Pakistan.[155]

Also on June 29, **Ahmed al Nami** obtained a Florida state identification card.[156]

July 2001

July 2—**Hamza al Ghamdi** obtained a Florida driver's license; **Mohand al Shehri**, a Florida identification card. **Moqed** and **Salem al Hazmi** acquired USA identification cards in July.[157] The Hazmi brothers' identifications were found in the rubble at the Pentagon and appeared genuine upon examination.[158]

July 3—**Wail al Shehri** acquired a Florida identification card.[159]

July 4—**Mihdhar** reentered the United States at JFK Airport.[160] He was on no watchlist, though he should have been watchlisted in January 2000.

He was admitted as a business visitor for three months—the standard at JFK for a business entry.[161] His passport contained an indicator or possible terrorist affiliation.[162] Two and a half years later, the inspector who admitted Mihdhar on July 4, 2001, still could not identify the indicator, as the information has yet to be unclassified and disseminated to the field. She did note, however, that Mihdhar's passport, which had been acquired a month earlier, lacked an expiration date; that absence, she told us, could have been a bar to admission had it been noticed.[163]

July 4—**Mohamed al Kahtani**, a Saudi, applied for and received a two-year B-1/B-2 (tourist/business) visa in Riyadh, Saudi Arabia. He was processed through Visa Express. There is no evidence that Kahtani was interviewed.[164]

July 5—In the West Wing, the Counterterrorism Security Group of the NSC, headed by Richard Clarke, hosted an emergency CIA briefing for operational agencies, including INS, Customs, U.S. Secret Service, FBI, FAA, and Coast Guard. The INS and Customs sent two people each to the briefing; none were senior managers. Only one of them had heard any threat reporting on al Qaeda prior to this meeting. The attendees said the briefer told them that there was to be no dissemination of the information discussed at the meeting. The discussion focused on the potential of an overseas target, but a domestic attack was not ruled out.[165] An NSC official recalls a somewhat different emphasis, saying that attendees were asked to take the information back to their home agencies and "do what you can" with it, subject to classification and distribution restrictions.

The midlevel INS intelligence analyst who attended the meeting, who had never been to the White House before, recalled in her interview with us that during the meeting the briefer discussed the possibility of "Mideastern" terrorists attempting entry into the United States using European passports. This same analyst summarized the meeting in a report, briefed her boss, and called the White House after the meeting to request declassification of the information so that she might develop a threat advisory for the ports of entry. She never received a response. Nor did the acting commissioner of the INS at the time, Kevin Rooney, ever hear about the meeting or a potential threat from al Qaeda. However, the Customs attendee at the meeting, somewhat familiar with the atmosphere of threat at this time, decided that the information was important to get to all inspectors in the field through the shared customs and INS computer system, TECS, and prepared a "Terrorism Advisory—Heightened Threat Environment."[166]

July 6—The threat advisory compiled by the Customs officer contained unclassified information that supported the classified information briefed by the CIA the previous day. The message was received by all immigration and customs personnel at ports of entry, but was addressed only to Customs employees. It did not contain any operational information about persons, places, or travel documents. The alert listed five ongoing U.S. trials of radical Islamic terrorists and warned:

> U.S. Customs personnel are requested to be vigilant during the summer months against potential threats from foreign terrorists against U.S. interests domestically and abroad. Recent terrorist trials and convictions (noted below) have created an environment of heightened animosity towards the U.S. from extremists looking for an opportunity to attack. If you encounter suspicious activity suggesting a potential terrorist attack follow your established security procedures, coordinate with the local office of Investigations and advise Headquarters, Anti-Terrorism Intelligence Section.[167]

July 7—**Atta** departed the country, as the abbreviated length of stay he received from the Miami District Office inspector expired on July 9.[168]

July 10—**Haznawi** obtained a Florida driver's license with a learner's permit. **Jarrah** acquired a duplicate Florida driver's license.[169] **Saeed al Ghamdi** and **Banihammad** got Florida state identification cards. **Mihdhar**, **Nawaf al Hazmi**, and **Omari** acquired USA identification cards.[170]

July 17—**Atta's** application to change his immigration status from tourist to student was approved to September 1, 2001. The application was approved by the same person who adjudicated Shehhi's change of status application.[171]

July 19—**Atta** entered the United States for the last time, returning from Madrid on July 19 at Hartsfield Atlanta International Airport. Atta was admitted as a business visitor until November 12, 2001.[172] The primary inspector who screened him did not recall the entry.[173] Because Atta had only been out of the United States for three weeks during the previous 13 months, he should have been flagged as an intending immigrant and was a candidate for a secondary inspection. There was no secondary inspection, however, and Atta was now legally in the United States until the day of the planned attack.

July 23—**Khalid Sheikh Mohamed (KSM)**, a Pakistani and the chief tactical planner and coordinator of the 9/11 attacks, obtained a B-1/B-2 (tourist/business) visa to visit the United States.[174] Although he was not a Saudi citizen and we do not believe he was in Saudi Arabia at the time, he applied for a visa using a Saudi passport under the alias of "Abdulrahman al Ghamdi." On his application, KSM listed his address in the United States as "New York." We believe someone else submitted his application, passport, and a photo to the U.S. embassy in Riyadh through the Visa Express program from the travel agency Minhal Travel,[175] the same agency used by Saeed al Ghamdi for his June 12 application.[176] Because he used an alias, KSM obtained a visa even though he was on the TIPOFF terrorist watch-list since 1996. There is no evidence that KSM ever used this visa under this alias to enter the United States.

ACQUISITION OF VIRGINIA IDENTIFICATION CARDS

Three Salvadoran immigrants living in Virginia, two illegally and one as a lawful permanent resident, were found guilty of helping four September 11 operatives use fraudulent documentation to obtain Virginia identification documents. Two were convicted of helping **Ahmed al Ghamdi** and **Abdul Aziz al Omari** obtain fraudulent residency certificates on August 2, 2001.[177] Another was convicted of providing false residency information on behalf of **Hanjour** and **Mihdhar** after being solicited by the two hijackers at a 7-Eleven in Falls Church, Virginia. For a fee, the Salvadoran falsely certified his old Virginia address as the residence of the hijackers.[178] These residency certificates were then used to support their applications for Virginia identification cards issued by the Department of Motor Vehicles on August 1 and 2, 2001, respectively.[179] The Salvadoran's address was also recycled by **Moqed** and **Salem al Hazmi** to use on their Virginia identification cards issued on August 2, 2001.[180] **Jarrah** followed suit on August 29, using a fictitious residency address and a certification of that address by Hanjour, who again used the address provided to him on August 1, 2001 to acquire his Virginia identification card.[181] One of the men charged in these cases recognized four of these hijackers as having been together at the Arlington, Virginia, DMV on August 2, 2001.[182] In all, the five hijackers based their Virginia identification documents on the residency information of one bribed Salvadoran.

August 2001

August 1—**Mihdhar** and **Hanjour** fraudulently obtained Virginia identification cards in Falls Church. **Ahmed al Ghamdi** and **Moqed** obtained USA identification cards in August as well.[183]

August 2—**Ahmed al Ghamdi**, **Moqed**, **Salem al Hazmi**, and **Omari** acquired Virginia identification cards, with help of Mihdhar and Hanjour. All of these identifications were obtained fraudulently.

August 4—**Mohamed al Kahtani**, a Saudi, the only operative other than Mihdhar who appears to have attempted a solo entry, arrived on August 4, 2001 at Orlando, Florida. He was also the only operative to be refused entry to the United States.[184] Records indicate that Atta was waiting for him at Orlando International while Kahtani was in secondary immigration inspection. Atta did not leave the Orlando airport until after it was clear that Kahtani was going back home.[185]

Both the primary and secondary inspectors remembered Kahtani well. Records indicate that Kahtani presented a Saudi passport with a two-year U.S. tourist visa. The primary inspector said that she recalled Kahtani for two reasons: he was the first Saudi she had ever encountered in her four years at Orlando that claimed to not speak English and his customs and arrival forms were not filled out. More subjectively, he made the inspector feel uneasy. Because she was unable to adequately communicate with Kahtani, she referred him to secondary inspection.[186] The secondary inspector who refused to admit Kahtani into the United States testified before the Commission on January 26, 2004.[187]

The secondary inspector who recommended and gained approval from his supervisor to deny Kahtani entry developed his interviewing skills as a 26-year veteran of the U.S. Army, through limited INS training, and ten years of experience conducting primary and secondary inspections at Miami and Orlando airports. The inspector noted Kahtani's hostility from the moment he called his name through the hour and a half spent interviewing him with the help of a Department of Justice translator. Kahtani was clean-cut with a military build. He had no return ticket and became threatening when asked where he was going, how long he was going to stay, and who was meeting him. Although he had enough cash for a ticket home, he did not have any credit cards.

Kahtani's answers to questions kept changing. Without a return ticket and limited funds, the secondary inspector sought to exclude him as an intending immigrant. The inspector's real concern, however, was that

Kahtani was up to no good. The inspector told the Commission in his written testimony:

> My first question to the subject (through the interpreter) was why he was not in possession of a return airline ticket. The subject became visibly upset and in an arrogant and threatening manner, which included pointing his finger at my face, stated that he did not know where he was going when he departed the United States. What first came to mind at this point was that this subject was a "hit man." When I was in the Recruiting Command, we received extensive training in questioning techniques. A "hit man" doesn't know where he is going because if he is caught, that way he doesn't have any information to bargain with.[188]

This inspector had noted on prior occasions that Saudis coming through Orlando had a reputation for spending a lot of money at Disney World. Denying a Saudi entry was unusual, and inspectors told us they were generally concerned about the repercussions of taking such a step. However, after Kahtani refused to answer any questions under oath, the inspector decided to seek his supervisor's approval to recommend that Kahtani be barred as an "expedited removal," meaning that he could be deported without a hearing. After the inspector was questioned, approval to remove Kahtani was granted. The inspector convinced Kahtani to pay his own way home, saving paperwork and government funds.[189]

Because an "adverse action" was taken against Kahtani, he was required to be digitally photographed and fingerprinted through the INS biometric system. (This action would help to quickly verify Kahtani's identity when he was detained in Afghanistan after 9/11.) His passport was copied, although the inspector noted no fraudulent manipulations. In fact, Kahtani's passport does contain a stamp listed as fraudulent and associated with al Qaeda.[190] The inspector did not check Kahtani's luggage.

August 9—**Shehhi**'s application to change his immigration status from tourist to student was approved through September 1, 2001.

August 23—The CIA sent a classified electronic message to the State Department, FBI, INS and the Customs Service, recommending that **Mihdhar** and **Hazmi** be added to the watchlist database accessible to the INS and Customs. They were suspected terrorists.[191]

August 24—Both **Hazmi** and **Mihdhar** were entered into separate lookouts. These lookouts are automatically checked when passports are scanned at ports of entry. The lookouts were identical, warning of "possible travel to the U.S." Immigration inspectors were instructed to refer them to secondary immigration inspection and to notify investigations and intelligence divisions at headquarters if they attempted to enter the United States. In addition, their passport numbers and travel itinerary were to be recorded.[192] These lookouts were not used by U.S. airlines to screen passengers seeking to fly on domestic flights.

August 27—**Ali Abdul Aziz Ali**, the nephew of Khalid Sheikh Mohammed, applied for a U.S. visa in Dubai, United Arab Emirates. Ali's application stated that he intended to enter the United States on September 4, 2001, for "one week." As a Pakistani visa applicant in a third country, he would have received close scrutiny from U.S. officials. In any event, it was deemed possible that he intended to immigrate, and accordingly he was denied a visa under section 214(b).[193]

August 27—**Hamza al Ghamdi** acquired a duplicate Florida driver's license.[194]

August 29—**Jarrah** obtained a Virginia identification card, with the help of Hanjour and Mihdhar.[195]

August 31—A new listing for **Mihdhar** was placed in an INS and Customs lookout database, describing him as "armed and dangerous" and someone who must be referred to secondary inspection.[196]

September 2001
September 4—The State Department used its visa revocation authority under section 221(i) of the Immigration and Nationality Act to revoke **Mihdhar**'s visa under section 212(A)(3)(b) of the Immigration and Nationality Act for his participation in terrorist activities.[198]

September 5—**Hanjour** obtained a Maryland identification card.[199]

The same day, the INS entered the September 4 notice of revocation of Mihdhar's visa into the INS lookout system. State identified Mihdhar as a potential witness in an FBI investigation, and inspectors were told not to detain him.[200]

September 7—Brothers **Salem** and **Nawaf al Hazmi**, along with **Moqed**, requested that their Virginia identification cards be reissued. **Haznawi** obtained a duplicate Florida driver's license.[201]

September 11—As the hijackers boarded four flights, American Airlines Flights 11 and 77, and United Airlines Flights 93 and 175, at least six used U.S. identification documents acquired in the previous months, three of which were fraudulently obtained in northern Virginia.[202] Suqami, the only hijacker who did not have a state-issued identification, used his Saudi passport as check-in identification for American Airlines Flight 11.[203]

Findings of Fact—Visas

When we examine the outcomes of the 9/11 conspirators' engagement with the visa issuance process, we see they are consistent with a system focused on excluding intending immigrants and dependent on a name check of a database to search for criminals and terrorists. When hijackers or conspirators appeared to be intending immigrants, as happened most often when applicants were from poorer countries, they were denied a visa. If they met that threshold, however, and the name check came up clean, there was little to prevent them from entering the United States. Among our findings:

- Fourteen of the 19 September 11 hijackers obtained new passports shortly before they applied for their U.S. visas.

- Three of the hijackers, Khalid al Mihdhar, Nawaf al Hazmi, and Salem al Hazmi, presented with their visa applications passports that contained an indicator of possible terrorist affiliation. We know now that Mihdhar and Salem al Hazmi each possessed at least two passports, all with this indicator.

- There is strong evidence that two of the hijackers, Satam al Suqami and Abdul Aziz al Omari, when they applied for their visas presented passports that contained fraudulent travel stamps that have been associated with al Qaeda. There is reason to believe that three of the remaining hijackers presented such altered or manipulated passports as well.

- Fifteen of the 19 hijackers were Saudi nationals.

IDENTIFICATION DOCUMENTS
OF THE 9/11 HIJACKERS[197]

Mohamed Atta
FL DL, 05/02/01

Marwan al Shehhi
FL DL, 04/12/01
FL DL duplicate, 6/19/01

Khalid al Mihdhar
CA DL, 04/05/00
USA ID card, 07/10/01
VA ID card, 08/01/01

Nawaf al Hazmi
CA DL, 04/05/00
FL DL, 06/25/01
USA ID card, 07/10/01
VA ID card, 08/02/01
Hani Hanjour

AZ DL, 11/29/91
FL ID card, 04/15/96
VA ID card, 08/01/01
Failed VA DL test, 08/02/01
MD ID card, 09/05/01

Ziad Jarrah
FL DL, 05/02/01
FL DL duplicate 5/24/01
VA ID card, 08/29/01

Satam al Suqami
No DL or ID card

Waleed al Shehri
FL DL, 05/04/01
(duplicate issued with
different address, 05/05/01)

Ahmed al Ghamdi
USA ID card, 07/2001
VA ID card, 08/02/2001

Majed Moqed
USA ID card, 07/2001
VA ID card, 08/02/2001

Hamza al Ghamdi
FL ID card, 06/26/01
FL DL, 07/02/01
(duplicate issued 08/27/01)

Mohand al Shehri
FL ID card, 07/02/01

Ahmed al Nami
FL DL, 06/29/01

Wail al Shehri
FL DL, 07/03/01

Ahmed al Haznawi
FL DL, 07/10/00
(duplicate issued 09/07/01)

Fayez Banihammad
FL ID, 07/10/01

Saeed al Ghamdi
FL ID card, 07/10/01

Salem al Hazmi
USA ID card, 07/01/01
VA ID card, 08/02/01

Abdul Aziz al Omari
USA ID card, 07/10/2001
VA ID card, 08/02/2001

- Two of the Saudi 9/11 hijackers (brothers Waleed and Wail al Shehri) may have obtained their passports legitimately or illegitimately with the help of a family member who worked in the passport office.

- Two of the hijackers were issued visas in Berlin; two were issued visas in the United Arab Emirates. The remaining 15 were issued a total of 18 visas in Saudi Arabia, 14 of which were issued in Jeddah (11 by the same consular officer), and 4 in Riyadh.[204]

- Of the 23 hijacker visa applications, five were destroyed routinely along with other documents before 9/11 and before their significance was known. The visa applications of Nawaf al Hazmi, Khalid al Mihdhar (in 1999), Mohamed Atta, Marwan al Shehhi, and Ziad Jarrah were destroyed.

- All 19 of the still-existing hijacker applications were incomplete in some way, with a data field left blank or not answered fully.

- Twenty-two of the 23 hijacker applications were approved.[205]

- Only two of the hijackers appear to have been interviewed at the visa stage.

- Of the 15 Saudi hijackers, 4 acquired their visas after the creation of the Visa Express Program in June 2001.

- Eight other conspirators in the plot attempted to acquire U.S. visas during the course of the plot; three of them succeeded.

- Of the three who succeeded, one was Khalid Sheikh Mohammed, the mastermind of the 9/11 plot, who obtained a visa in Jeddah, Saudi Arabia, in July 2001 under an alias. The other two who succeeded were Mushabib al Hamlan, who ultimately did not participate, and Mohamed al Kahtani, who was refused entry into the United States.

- Of the five conspirators who failed to obtain visas—Tawfiq bin Attash (Khallad), Ramzi Binalshibh, Saeed al Ghamdi, Zakariya Essabar, and Ali Abdul Aziz Ali—none were denied because consular officials believed they were potential terrorists. They were denied visas either because consular officials believed they might be intending immigrants or because they had failed to submit documents supporting their application.

- Of these conspirators who failed to obtain visas, two were Yemeni, one was Moroccan, one was a Pakistani, and one was a Saudi. Their visa applications were denied in Yemen, Saudi Arabia, the United Arab Emirates, and Germany.

- In summary, a total of 27 individuals—hijackers and other conspirators— attempted to obtain visas during the course of the 9/11 plot. These individuals submitted a total of 35 applications. Of these, 25 were approved.

3

TERRORIST ENTRY AND EMBEDDING TACTICS:
1993 TO 2001

THE RELATIVE EASE WITH WHICH THE HIJACKERS obtained visas and entered the United States underscores the importance of travel to their terrorist operations. In this section we explore the evolution of terrorist travel tactics and organization. We begin with terrorist plots in the 1990s and conclude with the 9/11 attack.

3.1 The Redbook

Since the early 1970s numerous terrorist organizations have provided their operatives with a wide variety of spurious documents. After showing their spurious passports and papers at border control, these terrorist operatives have proceeded to hijack airplanes, plant bombs, and carry out assassinations. These terrorist acts, however, can be stopped. . . .

If we all screen travelers and check their passports, as past experience proves, terrorist will lose their ability to travel undetected, and international terrorism will come one step closer to being stopped!

—The Redbook (1992)

By definition, transnational terrorist groups need to travel to commit terrorist acts. Indeed, without freedom of movement terrorists cannot plan, conduct surveillance, hold meetings, train for their mission, or execute an attack. Terrorists rely on forged passports and fake visas to move around the world unimpeded and undetected. This has been known for more than three decades. It is difficult today to judge with certainty what else was known about terrorist travel methods in the 1970s and 1980s. However, the existence of a CIA training video and manual is evidence of an understanding that terrorists relied on certain tactics when they traveled and that they could be stopped by alert individuals who recognized the use of those tactics.

In the early 1980s, the Central Intelligence Agency produced "The Threat Is Real," a training video to help border officials, customs officers, and consular employees identify terrorists (and other criminals) by analyzing their travel documents. The video drew on an unclassified manual known as the Redbook, also produced by the CIA, which contained information on commonalities among forged passports and travel cachets, or visas, used by terrorists. The 1992 edition of the Redbook claimed that more than "200 people carrying forged passports provided by terrorist groups have been identified **before** they could engage in terrorist acts."[1]

The Redbook focused on five types of travel document fraud committed by terrorists: *forgeries* of some 35 national passports and the travel cachets of at least 45 countries; forged documents terrorists *purchased from commercial vendors; stolen blank passports*, which terrorists could fill in with biographical data of their choosing; information on *genuine altered* passports that had been photo-substituted or given an extended validity date (discussed in greater detail in the Passport Examination Manual, a companion to the Redbook); and *genuine, unaltered passports*, most likely procured with the knowledge of the issuing country or through a corrupt government official.[2]

As the Redbook makes clear, by early 1993, when the first attack on the World Trade Center took place, the intelligence community already had decades of experience with the modes of travel of terrorist groups. But the Redbook ceased publication with the 1992 edition: terrorist travel documents would not be studied in earnest again until after the September 11 attacks owing to a lack of new exemplars.[3] This lack of analysis however, did not reflect a lack of raw data. Law enforcement investigations during the 1990s provided a rich trove of information on the travel tactics of terrorists as they moved around the globe. From the 1993 bombing of the World Trade Center to the disruption of the millennium plot in December 1999, information suggested that al Qaeda continued to employ all five methods of document fraud first noted in the Redbook years earlier, along with some new methods of their own.

3.2 Terrorist Travel Tactics by Plot

During the 1990s, al Qaeda was either directly or indirectly involved in a number of terrorist plots in the United States that partially or totally failed. A study of these plots and how those involved in them moved about clearly indicates that foreign terrorist operatives were being planted in the United States and that foreign terrorist operations were being planned against Americans here at home.

The attempted operations were valuable to those carrying them out despite their lack of success: they gave Islamic terrorists critical operational experience in entering and "embedding" in the United States. Although there is evidence that some land and sea border entries without inspection occurred, these conspirators mainly subverted the legal entry system by entering at airports.[4] In doing so, they relied on a wide variety of fraudulent documents, on aliases, and on government corruption. Because terrorist operations were not suicide missions in the early to mid-1990s, once in the United States terrorists and their supporters tried to get legal immigration status that would permit them to remain here, primarily by committing serial, or repeated, immigration fraud, by claiming political asylum, and by marrying Americans. Many of these tactics would remain largely unchanged and undetected throughout the 1990s and up to the 9/11 attack.

Thus, abuse of the immigration system and a lack of interior immigration enforcement were unwittingly working together to support terrorist activity. It would remain largely unknown, since no agency of the United States government analyzed terrorist travel patterns until after 9/11. This lack of attention meant that critical opportunities to disrupt terrorist travel and, therefore, deadly terrorist operations were missed.

By analyzing information available at the time, we identified numerous entry and embedding tactics associated with these earlier attacks in the United States.

The World Trade Center Bombing, February 1993—Three terrorists who were involved with the first World Trade Center bombing reportedly traveled on Saudi passports containing an indicator of possible terrorist affiliation. Three of the 9/11 hijackers also had passports containing this same possible indicator of terrorist affiliation.[5]

In addition, Ramzi Yousef, the mastermind of the attack, and Ahmad Ajaj, who was able to direct aspects of the attack despite being in prison for using an altered passport, traveled under aliases using fraudulent documents. The two of them were found to possess five passports as well as numerous documents supporting their aliases: a Saudi passport showing signs of alteration, an Iraqi passport bought from a Pakistani official, a photo-substituted Swedish passport, a photo-substituted British passport, a Jordanian passport, identification cards, bank records, education records, and medical records.[6] (See sidebar on Ajaj and Yousef.)

Once terrorists had entered the United States, their next challenge was to find a way to remain here. Their primary method was immigration fraud. For example, Yousef and Ajaj concocted bogus political asylum stories when they arrived in the United States. Mahmoud Abouhalima, involved in both the World Trade Center and landmarks plots, received temporary residence under the Seasonal Agricultural Workers (SAW) program, after falsely claiming that he picked beans in Florida.[7] Mohammed Salameh, who rented the truck used in the bombing, overstayed his tourist visa. He then applied for permanent residency under the agricultural workers program, but was rejected.[8] Eyad Mahmoud Ismail, who drove the van containing the bomb, took English-language classes at Wichita State University in Kansas on a student visa; after he dropped out, he remained in the United States out of status.[9]

AJAJ AND YOUSEF: A CASE STUDY IN FRAUD

This case study illustrates some of the techniques used by two of the 1993 World Trade Center bombing terrorists to enter and remain in the United States. Almost all of these tactics—italicized here for emphasis—would continue to be used by al Qaeda during the 1990s and in preparation for the 9/11 attack.

Using the services of a travel agent in Pakistan and traveling under aliases, on August 31, 1992, Ahmad Ajaj and Ramzi Yousef boarded Pakistan International Airlines Flight 703 in Peshawar and flew to Karachi, Pakistan, and then on to Kennedy Airport in New York City.[10] *They sat in first class* during both legs of the trip, believing they would receive less scrutiny there. Between them, they carried a *variety of documents to support their alias identities,* including identification cards, bank records, education records, and medical records.[11]

Upon Ajaj's arrival at Kennedy, the immigration inspector noted that he was traveling on a photo-substituted Swedish passport. Ajaj was sent to secondary immigration inspection, where he claimed he was a member of the Swedish press.[12] His luggage was searched and officers found *a partially altered Saudi passport and a passport from Jordan,* the documents supporting their alias identities, a plane ticket and a British passport in the name of Mohammed Azan, bomb-making manuals, videos and other material on how to assemble weapons and explosives, letters referencing his attendance at terrorist training camps; anti-American and anti-Israeli material, *instructions on document forgery,* and *two rubber stamp devices to alter the seal on passports* issued from Saudi Arabia.[13] The immigration inspector called an agent on the FBI Terrorist Task Force to tell him about Ajaj, but the agent declined to get involved, instead requesting copies of the file. The inspector also called the Bureau of Alcohol, Tobacco and Firearms, which was "not interested."[14]

Meanwhile, Yousef also was sent to secondary immigration inspection for lacking a passport or a visa that would allow him to enter the United States. He there presented *an Iraqi passport* he allegedly *bought from a Pakistani official for $100.*[15] Upon questioning, Yousef said that the *passport was fraudulent* and that he *bribed a Pakistani official* in order to board the flight. Inspectors also found in his possession an Islamic Center identity card with Yousef's photo and the name Khurram Khan, under which Ajaj had traveled into the United States. They also found a boarding pass in the name of Mohammed Azan.[16] Although their documents were thus oddly intermingled and both men were in secondary inspection, Yousef was not linked to Ajaj. Rather, Yousef was arrested for not having a visa. He made a *claim for political asylum* and was released into the United States pending a hearing.[17]

Ajaj told authorities he had a political asylum claim from a prior entry in February 1992, and was detained pending a hearing. The evidence suggests that Ajaj left the United States in April 1992, thereby abandoning his asylum claim. In fact, it appears that he *traveled under an alias* to attend a terrorist training camp on the Afghan-Pakistani border.[18]

Ajaj later pleaded guilty to a charge of use of an altered passport and served six months in prison. Not surprisingly, Yousef *never appeared for his hearing.* The World Trade Center was bombed on February 26, 1993. Ajaj was released from prison shortly thereafter, although he had no grounds for remaining in the United States. He was arrested in connection with the attack on March 9, 1993. Yousef was indicted on September 1, 1993, but had left the United States on a *fraudulent Pakistani passport.* He was captured in Pakistan and returned to the United States to stand trial on February 8, 1995.

Although Ajaj was arrested for involvement in the bombing, he did not give up on his political asylum claim. He petitioned for a new attorney and an exclusion hearing—held to determine whether someone is admissible into the United States—in Houston, where he had filed his original political asylum claim. Ajaj's request was denied on April 24, 1993, on the grounds that a passport holder from a visa waiver country who uses a fraudulent passport—Ajaj had used a bogus Swedish passport to enter the United States—is not entitled to such a hearing. Not satisfied with that outcome, Ajaj asked to file *a new political asylum claim* and was given ten days by an immigration judge to do so. Thus, Ajaj was able to file a political asylum claim after his arrest for involvement in the bombing of the World Trade Center.

Yousef was sentenced to 240 years in prison; Ajaj was sentenced to 90 years.

The Landmarks Plot, June 1993—*Note: Because most of the conspirators in this plot were married to American citizens they were able to obtain legal permanent residency status or citizenship. As a result, the Department of Homeland Security declined to provide us with copies of their immigration files, citing the Privacy Act.*

In the Landmarks case, a group of terrorists led by Sheikh Omar Abdel Rahman (the "Blind Sheikh") and including some of his supporters, who also were involved in the World Trade Center bombing, similarly traveled on fraudulent documents and then committed serial immigration fraud in order to stay in the country; others were married to Americans.

For example, Rahman was issued several visas on different passports to travel to the United States, although he was a known radical in Egypt. He was later granted legal permanent residency as a "Special Immigrant, Religious Teacher." This status was later revoked on grounds of polygamy. Rah men then filed an application for asylum, which was also denied after the attack on the World Trade Center (see text box on the Blind Sheikh). Siddig Ibrahim Siddig Ali, the mastermind of the plot, married an American. Mohammed Saleh, who provided fuel from his Yonkers gas station to make bombs, obtained legal permanent residency by marrying an American. Ibrahim Ilgabrowny passed messages between conspirators and obtained five fraudulent Nicaraguan passports for his cousin, El Sayyid Nosair, and his family.[19] Nosair, convicted of conspiracy, married an American in 1982 and became a citizen in 1989. He was also convicted of a gun charge in the killing of Rabbi Meir Kahane in 1990. Amir Abdelgani picked up fuel and helped determine targets; he, too, was married to an American. His cousin,

Fadil Abdelgani, mixed explosives; he overstayed his 1987 tourist visa and obtained legal residency by marrying an American. Others who had married Americans included Tarig Elhassan, who also mixed explosives, and Fares Khallafall, who bought fertilizer for the bombs.[20] Biblal Alkaisi initially filed an application for temporary protected status, using what turned out to be a fake Lebanese birth certificate. He then filed an application for political asylum but failed to appear for the interview.[21] Matarawy Mohammed Said Saleh was supposed to get stolen cars for the plot; he married two American women in an effort to gain legal permanent residency.[22]

THE CASE OF THE BLIND SHEIKH

Appearances can be deceiving. One consular officer remarked, "Now he looked like a sweet old man. I can tell you that he did not look like a terrorist. He was a charming, little old man."[23] But Sheikh Omar Abdel Rahman regularly preached jihad at mosques in New York and New Jersey to individuals who participated in the February 26, 1993, bombing of the World Trade Center building.[24] He himself was convicted on charges that he was "a leader" of their criminal organization and was sentenced on January 17, 1996, to life in prison.[25] Subsequent investigation revealed that Rahman entered the United States and remained in the country owing to a series of exceptional failures in the border security system, some with eerie parallels to the 9/11 hijackers.[26] For example:

- Rahman used multiple passports to structure his visa applications and travel over a four-year period from 1986 to 1990.

- In 1986, Rahman was issued a visa in Khartoum, Sudan, even though there arguably was sufficient information about him in the U.S. embassy in neighboring Egypt as early as 1981 to justify denying that visa.[27] Before he ever applied for a visa, Rahman was well known to U.S. officials in Egypt as a "high-profile" opponent of secular Egyptian regimes accused of issuing a fatwa that resulted in the 1981 assassination of Egypt's president, Anwar Sadat. This knowledge was not conveyed to officials in Khartoum. The officer who approved it later stated that he may have done a poor job of scrutinizing Rahman's application.[28]

- In April 1987, Rahman received a visa in Cairo, Egypt, after providing formal documentation that Islamic Brotherhood, Inc., in

Brooklyn, New York, was sponsoring him as their spiritual leader during the upcoming holy month of Ramadan, and would be financially responsible for him. The officer "knew who the Sheikh was, but after receiving the needed documents decided to issue the visa because of his understanding that the Sheikh had not been convicted of any crime."[29] In fact, Rahman's applications "were incomplete and misleading" and questions were possibly "answered falsely," since he had been convicted of passing bad checks.[30] Further, by 1987, the Cairo embassy's political section had a biographical file on Rahman and his subversive activities "that would make him ineligible for a visa."[31] However, this derogatory information was not shared with the Consular Section, which issued visas.

- Even though Rahman had been placed on an internal State Department watchlist on August 7, 1987,[32] his watchlisting was not discovered by consular officials when he applied for another visa in 1988. The visa, which was initially granted, was "canceled" on the same day under the intending immigrant provision when a local staff member pointed out that Rahman was a leading radical in Egypt. If the denial had instead been based on his presence on the watchlist, that fact also would have been recorded in the INS database. Then he could have been denied entry by the INS if he somehow later managed to obtain a U.S. visa.[33]

- In fact, on May 10, 1990, the Sheikh did receive another visa—his third—in Khartoum, Sudan, after a State Department foreign service national who processed the application falsely indicated that he had checked the watchlist on microfiche. He later stated that he had decided not to check because of Rahman's age, his physical appearance, and his success in receiving previous U.S. nonimmigrant visas.[34] The consular officer who issued this visa did not know that on May 2 and May 3, 1990, Embassy Cairo alerted Embassy Khartoum by cable that Egypt's "leading radical" had left Egypt for Sudan, possibly to seek exile in the United States, and asked Khartoum to provide information on his activities.[35] By this point, U.S. officials knew that Rahman had been arrested repeatedly in Egypt between 1985 and 1989 for attempting to take over mosques, inciting violence, attacking police officers, and demonstrating illegally, and that he had been imprisoned and placed under house arrest until he left Egypt for Sudan in early 1990.[36]

- On November 26, 1990, about six months after it first learned it had issued the visa, the State Department revoked Rahman's visa and sent a notice to the INS for entry in their National Automated Immigrant Lookout System (NAILS), which was done on December 10, 1990.[37]

However, Rahman had already used the visa to enter the United States on July 18 and November 15, 1990.

- Even though he was finally on the NAILS watchlist, Rahman used the visa to enter the United States again on December 16, 1990. He avoided detection at the port of entry by using on his entry form (I-94) a variation of the name in his passport: to identify potential terrorists, the INS watchlist needed an almost exact name match.

- Even though the INS office in New York had begun an investigation of Rahman by January 1991 to determine if he had made material misstatements on his visa application that could subject him to prosecution, deportation, or both, on January 31, 1991, he filed an application for Permanent Residence with the Newark INS office as a Special Immigrant, Religious Teacher. The agency was unaware that it had two files on Rahman, one in New York and one in Newark, or that he had been watchlisted; and on April 8, 1991, the Newark office granted him permanent resident status. His change of status enabled Rahman to successfully use his valid I-551 green card to enter the United States after he was detected and detained at JFK Airport on July 31, 1991.

- On March 6, 1992, the INS rescinded Rahman's permanent resident status on grounds he was a polygamist, had been convicted of bad check charges in Egypt, and had failed to disclose these facts in his application.[38] However, he avoided being removed from the United States by filing an application for asylum and withholding of deportation to Egypt on August 27, 1992. An immigration judge held a hearing on Rahman's claim on January 20, 1993, shortly before his followers bombed the World Trade Center, killing six people and injuring 1,042. On March 16, 1993, an immigration judge denied Rahman's application.[39]

The important factors in Rahman's success in traveling freely can be found in the cases of many other terrorists who have targeted the United States, including some of the 9/11 hijackers:

- Rahman's visa applications were incomplete.
- Rahman's visa applications contained lies.
- Rahman used multiple passports to structure visa applications and travel.
- Prior visa approvals helped Rahman avoid close scrutiny when he sought again to come to the United States.
- Uncertainty in visa law played a role in the Rahman's getting his visas.
- Failure by a local staff member to do his job—by checking microfiche—allowed Rahman to defeat the watchlist.
- Information on Rahman's subversive activities that should have been shared within the government was not, a failure that repeatedly played a role in his acquiring visas.
- Even after Rahman was placed on two terrorist watchlists, he was not detected and stopped, because those using the lists lacked an effective search engine and the technology they needed.
- Failure by the State Department to promptly watchlist Rahman played a role in his gaining entry to the United States.
- Poor coordination between INS computer systems allowed Rahman to gain lawful permanent residency and thus remain in the United States.
- Rahman committed fraud on his benefits applications.
- Rahman abused the asylum system to remain in the United States.

Atlantic Avenue Subway Plot, July 1997—Gazi Ibrahim Abu Mezer committed serial immigration fraud during his planning to destroy the Atlantic Avenue subway in Brooklyn with explosives in 1997.[40] Mezer was arrested on his third illegal entry into the United States along the northwest border with Canada. He asked to be deported to Canada, but Canada refused to accept him. He then filed a political asylum claim in the United States and was released on bond. Mezer withdrew the application, claiming he had returned to Canada when in fact he was in Brooklyn. His co-conspirator, Lafi Taisir Mufleh Khalil, was originally issued a C-1 transit visa; but upon his arrival at JFK Airport in New York, the immigration inspector incorrectly treated him as a tourist, which allowed Khalil to stay in the United States for six months. Khalil overstayed his visa and was arrested along with Mezer on July 31, 1997, the morning of the planned attack.[41]

The East Africa Bombings, August 1998—Although the attacks were carried out on foreign soil, the bombings of the U.S. embassies in Dar es Salaam, Tanzania, and Nairobi, Kenya, featured al Qaeda operatives linked to the United States. Ali Mohamed, an Egyptian national, married an American woman he had met on the airplane on his first visit to the United States in 1985. He entered the United States as a lawful permanent resident in San Francisco in June 1986, and his affiliation with al Qaeda dated to 1991. In 1993, Mohamed traveled to Kenya to conduct surveillance against American, British, French, and Israeli targets, including the U.S. embassy. Another operative, Khalid Abu al Dahab, was granted permanent residency after his third marriage to an American and later became a naturalized citizen. During his 12 years in the United States, he reportedly provided money and fraudulent travel documents to terrorists around the globe; he was thereby implicated in multiple terrorist attacks, including the East Africa bombings. Wadi el Hage studied in the United States in the late 1970s and mid-1980s; in between, he went to Pakistan to aid in the fighting against the Soviets in Afghanistan. He served as a personal secretary to Usama Bin Ladin and gained permanent residency when he married an American.[42]

The East Africa embassy bombings provided further evidence that terrorists used particular tactics when traveling. Had they been analyzed, they would have provided investigators with additional information about the techniques that terrorists would continue to use until the 9/11 attacks.

The Millennium Plot, December 1999—Following a familiar terrorist pattern, Ahmed Ressam and his associates used fraudulent passports and immigration fraud to travel. In Ressam's case, this involved flying from France to Montreal using a photo-substituted French passport under the name of Tahar Medijadi. Under questioning, Ressam admitted that the passport was fraudulent and claimed political asylum. He was released pending a hearing, which he failed to attend, his political asylum claim was denied. He was arrested again, released again and given another hearing date. Again, he did not show. He was arrested four times for thievery, usually from tourists, but was never jailed nor deported. He also supported himself selling stolen documents to a friend who was a document broker for Islamist terrorists.[43]

Ressam eventually obtained a genuine Canadian passport through a document vendor who stole a blank baptismal certificate from a Catholic church.[44] With this document he was able to obtain a Canadian passport under the name of Benni Antoine Noris. This enabled him to travel to Pakistan, and from there to Afghanistan for his training, and then return to Canada.[45] Impressed, Abu Zubaydah, one of al Qaeda's leading travel facilitators, asked Ressam to get more genuine Canadian passports and send them to him for other terrorists to use.[46]

Another conspirator, Abdelghani Meskini, used a stolen identity to travel to Seattle on December 11, 1999, at the request of Mokhtar Haouari, another conspirator. Haouari provided fraudulent passports and visas to assist Ressam and Meskini's planned getaway from the United States to Algeria, Pakistan, and Afghanistan.[47] One of Meskini's associates, Abdel Hakim Tizegha, also filed a claim for political asylum, though in the United States rather than Canada, on the grounds that he was being harassed by Muslim fundamentalists.[48] He was released pending a hearing, which was adjourned and rescheduled five times. His claim was finally denied two years after his initial filing.[49] His attorney appealed the decision, and Tizegha was allowed to remain in the country pending the appeal. Nine months later, his attorney notified the court that he could not locate his client and a warrant of deportation was issued.[50]

The unraveling of the millennium plot to blow up Los Angeles International Airport in December 1999, which began with the arrest of operative Ahmed Ressam, was yet another opportunity to focus on the importance of travel to successful terrorist operations. This plot demonstrated that difficulties with travel documents restricted terrorist movement.[51] Investigators also confirmed that terrorists had bought genuine blank baptismal certificates and filled them in with personal data.[52]

Thus, despite evidence that difficulties with travel documents restricted terrorist movement, no agency of the U.S. government was analyzing terrorist travel patterns or immigration abuses before 9/11.[53] Because the government simply did not know what it knew, it missed opportunities to disrupt terrorist mobility and, therefore, terrorist operations. Conversely, by 2000, when al Qaeda began inserting participants in the September 11 plot into the United States, their operational knowledge of our immigration, visitor, and border systems was considerable.

3.3 Al Qaeda's Organizational Structure for Travel and Travel Tactics

The ability of terrorists to travel clandestinely—including to the United States—is critical to the full range of terrorist activities, including training, planning, communications, surveillance, logistics, and launching attacks. A body of intelligence indicates that al-Qa'ida and other extremist groups covet the ability to elude lookout systems using documents with false identities and devoid of travel patterns that would arouse suspicion.[54]

TERRORIST TRAVEL TACTICS IN THE 1990S

By the time of the 9/11 attacks, available information suggested that terrorists could use up to 21 different entry and embedding tactics:

- Operatives typically traveled on fake passports and often had more than one passport.[55]
- Terrorists' passports were sometimes photo-substituted.[56]
- Terrorists were trained in passport forgery, including erasing and adding visas.[57]
- Document forgers altered stolen or borrowed passports.[58]
- Searches of homes of terrorists and their associates turned up travel documents and blank visas.[59]
- Travel facilitators, some of whom were identified or known to investigators, provided terrorists with fraudulent passports.[60]
- Genuine blank passports and visas could be purchased for a price and filled in with personal data.[61]
- Terrorists traveled extensively.[62]
- Operatives attempted to keep evidence of travel to and from Pakistan out of their passports.[63]
- Smugglers were used to sneak operatives into Afghanistan.[64]
- Terrorists reported their passports lost, stolen, or damaged in order to acquire new, "clean" new passports and to avoid revealing previous travel indicated in the old passport.[65]
- Terrorists' passports contained fake travel cachets.[66]
- Document forgers created fraudulent passports and travel cachets, or visas.[67]
- Corrupt government officials facilitated travel at border points.[68]
- Operatives tried to acquire sophisticated graphics software to assist them in forging documents.[69]
- Terrorists and their supporters committed serial immigration fraud.[70]
- Terrorists overstayed their visas.
- Terrorists requested political asylum.
- Terrorists studied in the United States.
- Terrorists traveled under aliases.
- Terrorists entered the United States without an immigration inspection.

Like their terrorist predecessors, members of al Qaeda clearly valued freedom of movement as critical to their ability to plan and carry out attacks prior to September 11. It is equally clear that al Qaeda relied heavily on many of the same basic travel tactics associated with these earlier groups to satisfy its substantial travel requirements. What distinguished al Qaeda's tactics was its heavy reliance on travel facilitators and document forgers, as well as its ability to adapt its techniques to defeat screening mechanisms, such as visa issuance systems.

Much of what is known about al Qaeda's travel tactics was learned after 9/11. Recall that there was no comprehensive analysis of terrorist travel methods after the Redbook ceased publication in 1992.

Lack of Travel Documents Disrupts Operations. Significantly, there is evidence that the lack of appropriate travel documents delayed or interrupted terrorist operational plans. For example, scrutiny in the United Arab Emirates of the travel documents of Ahmad al Darbi, who was involved in a plan to attack oil tankers in the Straits of Hormuz, caused him to divert the ship he was escorting away from port in Yemen to Somalia. Immigration officials in the UAE strongly suspected that Darbi was the same person as someone on their watchlist traveling on an alias; he feared he might also be watchlisted in Yemen.[71] The plan never came together after that.

In August 2001, two operatives were instructed by Khalid Sheikh Mohammed (KSM) to return to Saudi Arabia on September 15, 2001, to renew their passports in preparation for an unspecified operation. They were instructed to obtain new photos of themselves clean shaven to be used in applying for visas to the Philippines. After getting their passports they were to travel to the United Arab Emirates, where they would be met and informed of a suicide operation in the Philippines. But because of problems with one of their passports the operation was not carried out.[72]

In yet another case, in mid-2002, the senior al Qaeda operative Abd al Rahim al Nashiri scheduled an operational planning trip to Saudi Arabia. He was delayed for more than a month while document facilitators tried to get him a new passport.[73]

Conversely, the ability of operatives to travel easily to certain countries often determined the location of operational and planning meetings. Malaysia, for example, was viewed by both Usama Bin Ladin and KSM, the mastermind of the 9/11 plot, as an "excellent" venue for meetings because "Muslims could enter without a visa, including those with Saudi and Gulf passports."[74]

Organization and Training. Underscoring the high premium placed on travel, two senior al Qaeda operatives, KSM and Abu Zubaydah, played key roles in facilitating travel for the group's terrorist operatives. In addition, al Qaeda had a division of passports and host country issues under its security committee. The office was located at the Kandahar airport and was managed by Muhammed Atef, al Qaeda's chief of military operations and the number two man in the organization. According to a detainee, the committee altered papers, including passports, visas, and identification cards.[75] Following the U.S. invasion of Afghanistan in late 2001, the office moved to Pakistan.[76]

Certain al Qaeda members were charged with organizing passport collection schemes to keep the pipeline of fraudulent documents flowing. To this end, al Qaeda required jihadists to turn in their passports before going to the front lines in Afghanistan. If they were killed, their passports were then recycled for use by others.[77] Its operational mission training course, as well as an urban warfare course and a four-month explosives course, taught operatives how to forge documents.[78] Certain passport alteration methods, including photo substitution as well as erasing and adding travel cachets, were also taught. Manuals demonstrating how to "clean" visas were reportedly circulated among operatives.[79]

The purpose of all of this training was twofold: to develop an institutional capacity for such techniques and to enable operatives to make necessary adjustments in the field. It was well-known, for example, that if a Saudi traveled to Afghanistan via Pakistan, his passport, showing a Pakistani stamp, would be confiscated upon his return to Saudi Arabia. Operatives thus either erased the Pakistani visas from their passports or traveled through Iran, which did not stamp visas directly into passports.[80] Mohamed Atta, the presumed pilot on American Airlines Flight 11, was reported to have been trained in passport alteration techniques.[81]

Travel Facilitators. Despite the activities of the passport office and its various training programs, al Qaeda relied heavily on a small cadre of operatives and their assistants to facilitate travel for the network.[82] Chief among them were Abu Zubaydah, a facilitator we will call "the African facilitator," and Riyadh. Broadly speaking, a terrorist travel facilitator assisted operatives in obtaining fraudulent documents, arranging visas (real or fake), making airline reservations, purchasing airline tickets, arranging lodging and ground transportation, and taking care of any other aspect of travel in which his expertise or contacts were needed.[83] The following profiles illustrate how the al Qaeda network organized and carried out these activities.

Abu Zubaydah. Al Qaeda's most seasoned travel facilitator was Abu Zubaydah. A Palestinian national, he was born in the early 1970s in Riyadh,

Saudi Arabia, where his father worked as a teacher.[84] He attended a computer school in India, although he considered studying in the United States before and after this training.[85] He is suspected of having illegally entered Pakistan during the Afghan war against the Soviets. After the war he remained in Pakistan; in 1992 he moved to Peshawar, where he set up a honey-trading business.[86]

Abu Zubaydah began his work as a travel facilitator in Peshawar, living and working at the Martyr's House, where he aided mujahideen coming to and going from Afghanistan. He provided them with false passports and visas until about 1994, when he went to the al Faruq camp in Afghanistan to train Tajiks. He remained there for seven to eight months, returning to the Martyr's House to continue his work as a travel facilitator.[87]

In 1996, he helped al Qaeda members move from Sudan to Afghanistan. By 1997, Usama Bin Ladin asked him to continue his facilitation work for the organization.[88] For recruits at the Khaldan training camp he opened the first of three safehouses in Rawalpindi, on the outskirts of Islamabad, Pakistan, in the spring of 1998. There, Zubaydah and his assistants doctored passports and visas.[89] In 2000, Usama Bin Ladin put him in charge of foreign communication, or external relations, for al Qaeda.[90]

Abu Zubaydah considered himself an expert at moving people.[91] Indeed, he went beyond the technicalities of altering documents to prepare operatives and mujahideen to travel undetected.[92] Zubaydah told travelers to cut their hair, to shave their beards and mustaches, and to always be polite. He told them what kinds of clothes to wear, what kinds of airline tickets to purchase, how to alter their appearances, and what to carry in order to avoid attracting suspicion from border authorities. He tried to recruit operatives who spoke the language of the country whose travel documents he provided them. Zubaydah said he spared no expense on operational travel.[93]

Abu Zubaydah described the activities of another facilitator who we will call **The African Facilitator.** Sometime in his late teens, The African Facilitator left his native country and joined the fight against the Soviets in Afghanistan.[94] In the early to mid-1990s, he used a photo-substituted Saudi passport to travel to the Sudan with Usama Bin Ladin.[95] He and a companion were subsequently arrested in an African country for entering without a visa. His fraudulent passport also was discovered, and he spent time in a Saudi prison.[96]

After his release, The African Facilitator traveled to Pakistan.[97] In 1996, he met Abu Zubaydah and the two began collaborating. According to Zubaydah, The African Facilitator would send him copies of passports and tickets and Zubaydah would get exit permits to match, either legally or by bribing officials. He also asked Zubaydah to provide him with passports, although sometimes he would buy them from vendors in Peshawar and Islamabad.[98] He tasked Zubaydah with examining the passports of all new arrivals at his safehouse and with copying and passing to him any new visas and entry and exit stamps in the arrivals' passports.[99]

The African Facilitator soon became al Qaeda's man in Pakistan, with responsibility for overseeing its logistical network in the country. Indeed, according to a senior detainee, he was "famous" for his ability to arrange whatever one needed in Pakistan, as well as for his work with the al Qaeda document committee in Afghanistan.[100] For a few months in 1999, four assistants worked for him, buying tickets for Yemeni and Saudi family members who wanted to return home after visits to Afghanistan and Pakistan.[101]

As noted above, the document committee altered passports for mujahideen in Afghanistan. In 2000, The African Facilitator reportedly had a house in the al Qaeda compound at the Kandahar airport. Although he was not himself skilled in the methods of passport forgery, he supervised Kenyans who performed this work.[102] From this base, he facilitated the movement of mujahideen who attended one of al Qaeda's terrorist training camps, providing them with the necessary passports, stamps, and visas to travel; greeting them when they arrived; and sending them home after their training was completed.[103] He also kept track of the passports used by fighters on the front lines. When one of them was killed, he would cross their name off of his list and make that passport available for reuse.[104]

Riyadh, an al Qaeda Facilitator. Riyadh reportedly joined the al Qaeda organization in 1998 after stints fighting in Bosnia and Burma.[105] Based in Yemen, he facilitated the travel of mujahideen to the training camps in Afghanistan.[106] Riyadh and his assistant worked out of the al Jaziri hotel providing Yemeni passports; Egyptian, Pakistani, or Saudi visas; money; plane tickets; contact numbers; and transportation to the airport for travelers. They reportedly had contacts in the Pakistani and Yemeni governments who helped them by providing necessary travel documents.[107] In recognition of his wide range of contacts, in 1999 Usama Bin Ladin gave Riyadh the responsibility of organizing the travel of Muslim youth.[108]

Sometime in 2000, Riyadh left for Afghanistan.[109] After receiving additional training in the camps, he moved to Karachi, Pakistan, and resumed his activities facilitating the travel of Yemeni mujahideen to Afghanistan.[110]

Riyadh was well-known in Karachi under the name Aziz and did little to protect his security. He also may have facilitated the flow of funds to al Qaeda, allegedly passing $500,000 in late 2001 from Saudi donors to extremists and their families in Pakistan.[111]

Reliance on Outsiders. As these profiles make clear, in addition to its own travel facilitators, al Qaeda relied on outsiders to help move operatives around the world. Al Qaeda relied on hundreds of these vendors of fraudulent documents, corrupt government officials, travel agencies, and human smugglers.[112]

Document vendors provided al Qaeda with a wide range of bogus and genuine documents and were valued for their forgery skills. Through these vendors, al Qaeda operatives had access to an "impressive range of fraudulent travel, identification and other documents," including passports from countries in almost every region of the world, travel cachets, blank visas, foils, stamps, seals, laminates, and other material.[113] Some of these forgers are dedicated to al Qaeda's cause and tend to be located along main travel routes; others are interested only in profit.[114]

Corrupt government officials have facilitated terrorist travel by selling genuine travel documents. Ramzi Yousef, convicted of attempting to blow up a tower of the World Trade Center in 1993, claimed he bought an Iraqi passport from a Pakistani official for $100.[115] Two of the 9/11 hijackers, Waleed and Wail al Shehri, reportedly received new Saudi passports from a relative in the passport office.[116] Al Qaeda also relied on bribery to get passports and the special plastic used inside them to protect biographical information.[117] Moreover, corrupt officials have been known to take bribes at the border from a terrorist lacking proper documentation.[118]

Travel agencies have sometimes supported terrorist travel. Many travel agencies will work with anyone who is willing to pay. For example, Abu Zubaydah said that in Peshawar, it was generally understood that local Arabs were training in the camps in Afghanistan, but the travel agencies they used never asked any questions. In addition, Zubaydah said that he did business with several travel agencies in Pakistan, depending on which one offered him the best deal.[119]

There is also evidence that terrorists used *human smugglers* to sneak across borders.[120] Smugglers were typically paid to make all logistical arrangements, including mode of travel and lodging, and to pay off corrupt officials if necessary.[121] A typical smuggling scheme aided jihadist youth wanting to travel through Iran to Afghanistan to train in al Qaeda's camps. They would first travel to Jeddah, Saudi Arabia, to meet with a facilitator, who would then contact a second facilitator, who would buy plane tickets. When the jihadists arrived in Iran they contacted the first facilitator again and told him the name of their hotel. He would then tell an associate in Iran to meet them and smuggle them into Afghanistan.[122]

Because the penalties for these crimes tend to be inadequate, they have not been vigorously prosecuted. Laws against document fraud, for example, are generally weak and punishment light.[123] For example, in Spain, police officers assigned to the Foreigners Division have told Department of Homeland Security agents that crimes involving the possession and use of stolen or altered documents are not worth pursuing once the suspect is in the country.[124]

This lax legal environment, coupled with the need for clients, allows facilitators to operate only semi-clandestinely. In addition, travel facilitators operate in loose business networks; many are based in countries allied with the United States in the global war against Islamist terrorists.[125] Cracking down on these accomplices of terrorists thus appears to be not only practical from a law enforcement perspective but also a way to impede a wide range of terrorist activities, including planning, communicating, conducting surveillance, and carrying out attacks. If terrorists' travel options are reduced, they may be forced to rely on means of interaction which can be more easily monitored, and to resort to travel documents which are more readily detectable.[126]

Travel Documents. For the first time in more than a decade, in 2003 an effort was made to systematically study terrorist travel tactics. This study, as well as our earlier plot-by-plot analysis of terrorist travel tactics, clearly demonstrates that terrorist operatives employed certain repetitive travel practices that were ripe for disruption. In addition to their use of facilitators, numerous other patterns were identified. For example, operatives carefully selected the passports they used for operational travel, often using fraudulent ones. They also regularly used fraudulent travel stamps, especially to cover up travel to Afghanistan or Pakistan.[127] They studied visa and entry requirements for countries they transited or traveled to and structured their travel to avoid appearing suspicious.[128] Al Qaeda also adopted several techniques designed to mask travel and identity, including traveling under an alias.[129] Terrorists appeared to exercise particular caution with regard to

Western travel. Their main purposes in so doing were to eliminate the possibility of being detained on fraudulent document charges, a goal that became especially important when an operative was traveling to participate in an attack, and to avoid the suspicions raised by indicators of travel to Afghanistan. Terrorists, including al Qaeda, clearly expended considerable effort thinking about travel and engaging in methods intended to facilitate their movement around the globe.

Reliance on Saudi Passports. Al Qaeda favored Saudi passports. KSM estimated that 70 percent of the mujahideen in the al Qaeda training camps in Afghanistan before 9/11 were Saudi. Irregularities in the Saudi passport issuance system made Saudi passports more readily available.[130] As many as 10,000 Saudi passports may have been lost or stolen in recent years.[131] Saudis also enjoyed visa waiver status as visitors to most Middle Eastern countries and, until September 2002, to Canada.[132] An added attraction of Saudi passports was that reporting a Saudi passport stolen that later turned up in someone else's possession was not a crime.[133] Moreover, several document forgers specialized in altering Saudi passports.[134]

Furthermore, blank Saudi passports lacked a document control number to track their disposition before they were issued.[135] In practical terms, this meant that a blank passport that was stolen lacked any number to put on a watchlist that might catch a person trying to use it. In late 2001, Saudi Arabia began issuing new passports that incorporated enhanced security features. Problems in the issuance regime persist, however.[136]

Types of Passport Alteration. There are four main ways in which al Qaeda altered passports: substituting photos, adding false cachets and visas, removing visas and bleaching stamps, and counterfeiting passports and substituting pages.[137] The organization used advanced computer graphics programs, such as Paintshop Pro, Adobe Photoshop, and Adobe Printshop to copy and alter passports. Skilled members also used software to scan and make copies of travel stamps, visas, and passport security features. Raids in 2002 and 2003 indicate that fraudulent material was shared among terrorists.[138]

But not all counterfeiting efforts were high quality. For example, terrorists often cleaned and reused Pakistani sticker visas, sometimes leaving tell-tale evidence of fraud.[139] Other attempts at forgery resulted in obvious fakes. Thus, officials who know what to look for can identify terrorists who present travel documents with these suspicious indicators.

EXPLORING THE LINK BETWEEN
HUMAN SMUGGLERS AND TERRORISTS

In July 2001, the CIA warned of a possible link between human smugglers and terrorist groups, including Hamas, Hezbollah, and Egyptian Islamic Jihad.[140] Indeed, there is evidence to suggest that since 1999 human smugglers have facilitated the travel of terrorists associated with more than a dozen extremist groups.[141] With their global reach and connections to fraudulent document vendors and corrupt government officials, human smugglers clearly have the "credentials" necessary to aid terrorist travel.

We have already seen that documents are critical to terrorists—they are needed by those wishing to plan and carry out attacks. Documents are similarly critical to human smugglers, who have access to document vendors able to obtain genuine passports and visas from corrupt government officials.[142] Corrupt officials are also paid off to allow illegal migrants to pass through travel and security checkpoints.[143]

These connections combine with lax immigration and border security in many countries to make human smuggling an attractive avenue for terrorists in need of travel facilitation.[144] Following the September 11 attacks, additional information surfaced linking al Qaeda to human smugglers. Following the coalition attack on Tora Bora, human smugglers assisted fighters fleeing Afghanistan and Pakistan. In January 2002, smugglers helped about 400 fighters in Taftan, Pakistan, to escape to Iran.[145] Finally, there are uncorroborated law enforcement reports suggesting that associates of al Qaeda used smugglers in Latin America to travel through the region in 2002 before traveling onward to the United States.[146]

To date, only one human smuggler with suspected links to terrorists has been convicted in the United States.[147]

4

IMMIGRATION AND BORDER
SECURITY EVOLVE:
1993 TO 2001

4.1 The Intelligence Community

As we have seen in chapter 3, prior to September 11, 2001, the intelligence community did not organize to disrupt terrorist travel except when targeting individual terrorists. It also failed to fully use the one tool it supported to prevent terrorist entry—the terrorist watchlist.

Overall, intelligence community guidance about terrorist travel was limited. Recognizing the importance of freedom of movement to international terrorist groups, the Annual Strategic Intelligence Review for Counterterrorism, issued in October 1995, called for additional intelligence information on terrorist "travel procedures," "surveillance/targeting capability regarding modes of transportation and facilities," and "training."[1] The same review released two and a half years later, in April 1998, pointed to the need for more information on terrorist "travel procedures" and "operational tactics and tradecraft capabilities."[2]

Such calls for additional intelligence regarding terrorist travel in its broader context seem to have had no result. A likely explanation for this inaction is that in the context of the Lockerbie experience, "travel procedures" were interpreted to mean access to transportation and reservation systems. But the previous existence of the Redbook, whose purpose was to assist frontline border officials in disruption and law enforcement operations, suggests that the phrase might have been more broadly understood. In any case, as we noted earlier, there was certainly no lack of raw data concerning terrorist travel methods. During the 1990s, the FBI's numerous terrorist law enforcement investigations provided a cache of information, obtained in part from raids and seized hard drives, on the travel tactics of terrorists as they moved around the globe—planning, surveilling targets, and carrying out attacks.[3]

This information apparently remained stovepiped at the FBI, drawn on only when needed for a particular law enforcement case. It was not shared with the CIA unit that published the Redbook. The CIA as a whole simply did not engage in analysis of terrorist travel information at this time.[4] The closest it came to doing so was through a program called the Personal Identification Secure Comparison and Evaluation System, or PISCES, started by the CIA in 1997.[5]

PISCES initially assisted foreign countries in improving their watchlisting capabilities. It provided a mainframe computer system to facilitate immigration processing in half a dozen countries. Foreign authorities used the technology to watchlist and share information with the CIA about terrorists appearing at their borders. The CIA used the information to track and apprehend individual terrorists, not for wide-ranging analysis of terrorist travel methods.[6]

Thus, despite some intelligence community guidance and the availability of considerable information from investigations, as well as work done in producing the Redbook, no agency of the U.S. government undertook what was so desperately needed: a comprehensive analysis of how terrorists exploit weaknesses in travel documents and international travel channels to commit deadly attacks. In practical terms, this meant the United States denied itself the ability to disrupt terrorist operations and prevent undetected terrorist entries by disrupting operatives' ability to travel.

Meanwhile, as we have already noted, al Qaeda had established a passport office under the leadership of one of Usama Bin Ladin's deputies, Mohammed Atef. It also was training operatives in document forgery and expanding its links with a wide variety of travel facilitators, corrupt government officials, and document forgers to enhance its ability to travel throughout the world undetected.

4.2 The State Department

Beyond playing a critical role in maintaining the terrorist watchlist, the State Department also administered U.S. immigration laws abroad; it therefore handled applications for both immigrant and nonimmigrant visas.[7] Nonimmigrant visas are issued to temporary visitors to the United States; immigrant visas are for those who intend to become permanent residents. For the State Department, visa policy was a powerful tool to achieve larger U.S. foreign policy goals.[8]

Background

U.S. national security interests depend not just on military and intelligence personnel overseas but also on diplomats. Most of them are members of the

Foreign Service, serving at American overseas diplomatic and consular posts and at the Department of State in Washington. One of the duties these overseas diplomats perform with support from Washington is to adjudicate the issuance of visas to foreign citizens seeking to come to the United States.

Congress first charged consular officers with the responsibility of issuing visas to certain aliens in 1884.[9] In 1917, all aliens seeking to enter the United States were required to obtain visas. This requirement has been continued since that time under successive immigration laws.[10] With certain exceptions, therefore, aliens wanting to come to the United States before September 11, 2001, needed to obtain appropriate visas from U.S. consular officers stationed at one of the 230 visa-issuing diplomatic posts around the world.[11]

From October 1, 2000, through September 31, 2001, the State Department adjudicated approximately 10 million nonimmigrant visa applications worldwide, approving 7.5 million. An integral part of this process was a "name check," which involved checking the name and other biographical identifiers of an applicant against existing records— including lists of known or suspected terrorists—to see if the he or she should be given additional scrutiny or be denied a visa.

What Is a Visa and Who Needs One?

Because there are many common misunderstandings about the role of the State Department in border security, it is useful to review basic facts about visas.

A visa does not authorize entry to the United States.[12] It simply indicates that an application has been reviewed by a U.S. consular officer at an American embassy or consulate overseas, and that the officer determined the applicant's eligibility to travel to the United States for a specific purpose. Only a U.S. immigration officer has the authority to permit entry into the United States.[13] That decision is made at the port of entry, when the immigration officer also decides how long any given stay can last.

Prior to September 11, 2001, a visa was not required of every one of the approximately 500 million people seeking to enter the United States each year. Indeed, most who crossed U.S. borders did not need a visa to present themselves at a U.S. port of entry. These "visa waiver" entrants included U.S. citizens and lawful permanent residents, citizens of Canada, and citizens of 27 other countries, most in Europe.

As might be obvious, U.S. citizens need not obtain visas to travel to the United States from abroad.[14] In addition, U.S. citizens and legal permanent residents (LPRs) are not required to have a passport to enter or depart the

United States when traveling between the United States and Canada, Mexico, or the Caribbean.[15] These two groups—citizens and LPRs—constitute more than half the total number of people seeking to enter the United States.

Citizens of Canada also are not required to present a Canadian passport or a visa if they are visiting the United States from Canada.[16] In fiscal year 2001, about 13 million Canadians presented themselves at U.S. ports of entry.

Similarly, citizens of the 27 countries participating in the Visa Waiver Program can simply board an aircraft or drive to a land border and ask permission to enter the United States without a visa.[17] They are screened by an immigration inspector at a port of entry before admission. In 2000, about 17 million individuals entered the United States under the Visa Waiver Program, which applies only to temporary visitors traveling to the United States for business or pleasure who are staying 90 days or less.[18] Persons traveling to the United States from these countries for other purposes—for example, to study or to work—must have a visa.

The remaining approximately 203 million people seeking entry to the United States in 2000 needed some form of a visa. Of these, approximately 117 million were Mexican citizens who used visa/border crossing cards (BCCs). These special visas in the form of cards include both a fingerprint and a photograph. Thus, out of the approximately 500 million people seeking entry in the year before 9/11, only approximately 86 million, or 17 percent, were required to have visas and were from countries other than Mexico.

As noted above, there are two types of visas: immigrant and nonimmigrant. The number of immigrant visas available each year to citizens of a particular country, and in particular categories, is strictly controlled by statute, and the number of prospective applicants for U.S. immigrant visas often exceed these caps. People applying from an oversubscribed country are registered on waiting lists. In 2000, the State Department issued about 400,000 immigrant visas worldwide.[19]

By contrast, the availability of nonimmigrant visas available is controlled not limited by a quota system rather by the qualifications of the individual applicant for the particular type of visa being sought. It is also influenced by the resources the State Department is able to allocate to visa processing. In 2000, about 1,000 State consular officers processed 10 million applications for nonimmigrant visas, issuing about 7 million.[20]

There are several categories of nonimmigrant visa. Most common are B or business/tourist visas, 3.5 million of which were issued in 2000.[21] Next, with 1.5 million issued that year, are the BCCs used by Mexicans seeking to cross the border temporarily (for example, to commute every day to the United States). Some 300,000 F visas were issued to foreign students, and 290,000 H visas to temporary workers or trainees.[22]

All 19 of the 9/11 hijackers entered the United States on nonimmigrant visas. Eighteen entered on B visas, and one—Hani Hanjour—entered on an F visa.[23]

Visas are governed by reciprocal agreements with other countries regarding their duration and cost. Prior to September 11, although it was not mandatory, nonimmigrant visas were issued "incorporating the most liberal provisions possible with respect to validity period and fees on the basis of reciprocity, that is, the treatment accorded by the applicant's country to U.S. citizens."[24] In other words, if a given country granted U.S. citizens seeking to travel there a visa valid for five years—as did Egypt, Mohamed Atta's country—then the United States ordinarily reciprocated and provided its citizens a five-year visa.

A visa can be single entry, allowing its holder to enter the United States only once, or multiple entry. The length of time during which the visa holder could apply for entry to the United States was also determined by negotiation on a country-by-country basis. Before 9/11, Saudi citizens received multiple-entry B visas valid for two years; citizens of the United Arab Emirates, multiple-entry ten-year B visas; and citizens of Egypt and Lebanon, multiple-entry five-year B visas.

Obtaining a U.S. Visa

Prior to September 11, 2001, the basic process for applying for a U.S. visa was the same worldwide, but the precise guidelines followed at each visa-issuing embassy or consulate were often different. Though the law was uniform, the State Department gave individual visa-issuing posts broad latitude in establishing procedures for visa application and processing.[25]

On matters of border security, the State Department derives its authority from the Immigration and Nationality Act of 1952 (INA), the primary body of law governing immigration and visa operations.[26] Among other functions, the INA defines the powers in this area given to the attorney general, the secretary of state, immigration officers, and consular officers.[27] It delineates categories of and qualifications for immigrant and nonimmigrant visas, and it provides a framework of operations through which foreign citizens are allowed to enter and immigrate to the United States. It defines the terms used in immigration law, including *alien*, which means "any person not a citizen or national of the United States."[28] It also sets forth the grounds for refusing someone a visa.

Consistent with the INA, aliens began the visa process by presenting a valid passport and completed visa application, along with a photograph, to a State Department consular, or visa, section at an embassy or consulate abroad.[29] Visa applicants paid a nonrefundable application fee of $65 and submitted their application either in person, indirectly (by mail or by drop box at the embassy where applicants could leave their completed applications), or through a third party such as a travel agent.

After the application and passport arrived at the consular section, it was reviewed by a consular officer who decided whether or not to issue a visa. Many of these adjudicators were in their first overseas tours as Foreign Service officers, and many moved on to other kinds of work within the State Department after fulfilling their consular rotation. The consular section reports to the ambassador in that country and to the Bureau of Consular Affairs within the State Department.[30] The consular officer's decision to grant or deny the visa cannot be challenged or reviewed in court.[31]

Three aspects of this adjudication process are particularly noteworthy. First, there was a mandatory computerized name check done of every visa applicant. This requirement had been in place since 1995, when all visa-issuing posts worldwide gained access to a centralized, computerized name-check database.[32] Specifically, the applicant's essential information was checked against a large database called the Consular Lookout and Automated Support System (CLASS), which included a number of data-bases containing such derogatory information on individuals as prior visa refusals and federal arrest warrants, before the visa was physically issued. One of the databases in CLASS was a watchlist of known and suspected terror-ists called TIPOFF. When a check of the CLASS database revealed derogatory information on the applicant, the consular officer could refuse the visa if there were sufficient legal grounds to do so.[33] A consular officer who received a response of "00" when querying CLASS—an indication of a potential, serious ineligibility, including terrorism—was required to request a security advisory opinion from the State Department before considering the case further.[34]

Second, the law required all applicants for nonimmigrant visas to appear for a personal interview.[35] However, the law also provided for a waiver of this requirement if it was deemed to be in the "national interest." Prior to September 11, 2001, State Department policy encouraged waiving the interview.[36] Understanding why personal appearances were so routinely waived in the pre-9/11 era is critical to understanding the State Department's view of its role in border security; this issue will be discussed in greater depth below, particularly with regard to visa policy in Saudi Arabia at the time the hijackers received their visas.

The third point worth noting concerns the grounds for denying a visa. In the year 2000, there were more than 50 different grounds to refuse someone a nonimmigrant visa under the INA.[37] Three that are of particular importance to understanding the visa applications of the 9/11 hijackers and their co-conspirators are discussed below.

Section 214(b)—The Intending Immigrant Presumption. Under immigration law before 9/11, all foreigners applying for a nonimmigrant visa were presumed to be intending immigrants.[38] Section 214(b) of the Immigration and Naturalization Act provided that "Every alien . . . shall be presumed to be an immigrant until he establishes to the satisfaction of the consular officer, at the time of application for a visa, and the immigration officers, at the time of application for admission, that he is entitled to a nonimmigrant status[.]" Thus, the law placed the burden of proof squarely on the applicant to demonstrate that he or she had no desire to reside in the United States. A finding that the applicant had not met this burden under section 214(b) was "the basic and most frequent reason for an NIV [nonimmigrant visa] denial."[39] In fiscal year 2001, these were the grounds on which about 2.2 million applicants were refused a nonimmigrant visa, totaling about 80 percent of all nonimmigrant visa denials.[40]

Section 221(g)—Lack of Documentation. Under section 221(g) of the INA, consular officers were obligated to deny a visa if the alien failed to comply with the application requirements or was otherwise legally ineligible for a visa. This catchall provision, in effect before September 11, prohibits the issuance of a visa to an applicant if it appears from the application or its supporting documents that he or she is not entitled to a visa or if the consular officer "knows or has reason to know" the applicant is ineligible to receive a visa.[41] For example, this section was used to deny a visa to hijacker Hani Hanjour in September 2000 when he failed to attach to his application documentation supporting his request for a student visa.

In fiscal year 2001, about 600,000, or about 20 percent of all nonimmigrant visa denials, fell under this provision. Thus, almost all visas that were denied before 9/11 were denied under either 214(b) or 221(g).[42]

Denial on Grounds of Terrorism. The INA in effect before September 11 also allowed a consular officer to deny a visa to a foreigner who engaged in, or was deemed likely to engage in, terrorist activity after entry.[43] This included an individual acting alone or as a member of a group who committed an act of terrorism, or who provided material support to any individual, organization, or government conducting a terrorist action.[44] These provisions, explicitly providing for the exclusion of foreign visa applicants based on their involvement in terrorism, were added to the law in 1991.[45] Prior to that time, foreigners could be excluded if there was a more general conclusion that they might endanger the security of the United States.[46]

Few aliens were ever denied a nonimmigrant visa on grounds of terrorism in the pre-9/11 era—only 83 in fiscal year 2001.[47]

Issuing the Visa

If the application was approved, then a visa—a piece of paper or "foil" with various security features on it, including a digitized photograph of the applicant—was printed out and affixed to the applicant's passport. By the mid 1990s, this visa could be read by a machine at a U.S. port of entry (the so-called machine-readable visa), enabling the immigration inspector to input the visa data quickly into the immigration database.[48]

If the application was refused, then the passport was returned to the applicant. The fact of and reasons for the refusal were noted in the State Department's computerized CLASS database used by consular officers. If the person reapplied using the same or similar biographical information—name, date of birth, place of birth, passport number—the earlier refusal would automatically pop up as part of the name-check process. However, if the applicant's visa was approved, the record of the prior approval would not automatically be brought to the attention of the consular officer. Similarly, as discussed earlier, consular officers had no access to the immigration records of a particular visa applicant when evaluating his or her case.

The Bureau of Consular Affairs

In order to understand how consular officers working for the State Department handled the visa applications of the 19 September 11 hijackers and their co-conspirators, it is necessary to understand how the branch of the department overseeing those officers—the Bureau of Consular Affairs—worked.[49] Assistant Secretary of State for Consular Affairs Mary Ryan has told the Commission that she always viewed Consular Affairs (CA) as the "outer ring of border security."[50] Under Ryan's leadership in the 1990s, CA increased its focus on border security by providing greater resources to the development of secure passport and visa technology, improving computer name-check capability, and creating a worldwide real-time consular communication system.[51]

Visas were not the only responsibility of Consular Affairs during the 1990s, but rather were a subset of one of its three primary strategic goals:

- protecting the safety and security of Americans who travel abroad, by means that included issuing travel warnings;
- meeting the demands of American travelers in a timely and professional manner, by means that included issuing passports to U.S. citizens; and
- facilitating travel to the United States by foreign visitors and immigrants, while enhancing border security to deter entry by those who abuse or threaten our system.[52]

As discussed above, before the Department of Homeland Security was created, consular officials administered the immigration law abroad in partnership with the Immigration and Naturalization Service (INS). Recall that INS inspectors made an independent determination at a port of entry regarding the admissibility of a person who presented a visa. If the visa holder was admitted, INS inspectors also decided the length of his or her stay.[53] Perhaps surprisingly, State officials overseas had very limited contact with the INS before 9/11, and most consular officials never spoke to an INS officer in the ordinary course of their duties.[54] In general, consular officials received little feedback from the INS about their visa-issuing decisions. The INS did not collect or disseminate information to consular officials about either the rejection rate of visa holders at ports of entry or the rates at which citizens from particular countries overstayed their time of admission granted by the INS. Thus, although consular officers made some efforts on their own to validate their visa decisions—for example, they called visa recipients to see whether they had returned from their trips and not remained in the United States—the lack of accurate data from the INS left them little to go on.[55]

The State Department Budget in the 1990s
The State Department, like much of the federal government in the early 1990s, made do with fewer resources. As the department itself described the situation, "The years of the Clinton administration coincided with a decline in the Department of State's resources, leading to cuts and streamlining throughout the agency."[56] This seems an accurate assessment. Both the Clinton White House and the Congress—particularly after the Republican takeover in 1994—were determined to hold the line on the federal government's growth.[57] The under secretary of state for management during this

time, Richard Moose, recalled, "We were in a very tight bind in our operating accounts."[58]

Compounding these tough budget conditions were what Moose termed "some serious unfunded mandates" associated with the State Department's decision—made in the administration of President George H. W. Bush—to build new embassies and consulates in the countries of the former Soviet Union without an additional revenue stream.[59] As part of a broad reevaluation of its overseas presence during this time, the State Department identified 42 diplomatic posts that could be closed. Many of these were small consulates, while many of the 40 new overseas posts were new embassies, including 14 embassies in the newly independent nations of the former Soviet Union, 4 in the new states of the former Yugoslavia, 2 in Southeast Asia, and 2 in Africa.[60] The net increased cost of these buildings was in the hundreds of millions of dollars.[61]

Embassy security also received greater resources during this time. The bombings of three U.S. facilities in Beirut, Lebanon, in 1983 awakened the United States to the destructive power of explosive-laden trucks and car bombs. Following the attacks, Secretary of State George Shultz formed a commission—the Advisory Panel on Overseas Security—headed by retired admiral Bobby Inman.[62] The Inman Commission recommended $3.5 billion to meet security needs overseas, and Congress appropriated $5 billion for security from fiscal year 1987 to fiscal year 1998.[63] However, progress in improving embassy security was slow. When al Qaeda bombed the U.S. embassies in Dar es Salaam, Tanzania, and Nairobi, Kenya, on August 7, 1998, neither embassy met Inman standards, and their threat levels were considered medium to low.[64]

The Accountability Review Boards tasked with gathering lessons learned from the August 1998 embassy bombings—chaired by retired admiral William Crowe—recommended in January 1999 that $1.4 billion be spent annually over the next ten years to improve embassy security.[65]

In response to these renewed concerns about embassy security, Congress appropriated additional funds. In all, the United States spent about $2.4 billion to upgrade security at our overseas posts before the attacks of September 11, 2001.[66] But these vast sums were not directed at increasing State's workforce, already strained by personnel cuts, nor were they used to upgrade the ability of consular officers to combat terrorism. In its proposed fiscal year 1995 budget, the State Department requested 366 fewer positions than in the previous year.[67] Position cuts were recommended under every heading in diplomatic and consular programs.[68] Downsizing proceeded in 1995 with the implementation of five buyout programs. Encouraged by delayed buyouts approved for 1996 and 1997, more than 600 employees voluntarily left the Department of State.[69] The number of Foreign Service personnel thus fell from 5,071 in 1993 to 4,061 in 1996. Civil service positions at State showed a similar decline.[70]

These shrinking budgetary resources disproportionately affected the Bureau of Consular Affairs because of The State Department's organizational structure, employee hiring, and the deployment scheme in the 1990s. Traditionally, many Foreign Service officers spend their first overseas tour of duty performing consular work. With the State Department budget crunch, the Bureau of Consular Affairs could not hire replacements for officials lost to attrition; it was forced to extend the length of tours for consular officers and was unable to promote qualified personnel to more senior consular positions.[71] The result was a high burnout rate for consular officials, and a flight of senior qualified personnel to other portions of the State Department or to the private sector. According to Assistant Secretary of State for CA Mary Ryan, "The slogan was to do more with less, to the point where we were doing everything with nothing."[72]

The Visa Waiver Program

One recent innovation that initially helped CA adjust to its budget crunch during this period was the Visa Waiver Program. Its growth led to a drop in demand for nonimmigrant visas, because citizens of the participating countries were no longer required to obtain a U.S. visa for short-term visits.[73] Established in 1986, the Visa Waiver Program enabled citizens of participating countries to travel to the United States for tourism or business for 90 or fewer days without first obtaining a visa.[74] Criteria for inclusion in the program included a low nonimmigrant visa refusal rate (below 2 percent) for nationals of the country, a high volume of visa applications for nationals of the country, and the offer of reciprocal treatment for U.S. citizens.[75] The departments of State and Justice established processes intended to determine a country's eligibility for the program under the statutory criteria. They also evaluated the country's political and economic stability. By 9/11, about 17 million travelers per year were admitted to the United States under this program, which played a significant role in 1990s' border security policymaking at the State Department. Most important, in participating countries it significantly reduced the workload (and thus the staffing needs) of consular personnel, who would otherwise have been tasked with processing visas.

THE VISA WAIVER PROGRAM

The Immigration Reform and Control Act of 1986 provided for the establishment of a nonimmigrant visa waiver pilot program for nationals of up to eight countries.[76] Its two main objectives were to save U.S. government resources for higher-priority activities and to encourage travel to the United States.[77] State was eager to implement the system in part because it wished to reallocate resources then devoted to visa processing in countries eligible for the program.[78]

The statute required the secretary of state and the attorney general to certify that an automated data arrival and departure system was in place before the program was implemented.[79] State expressed concern that the INS could not meet this requirement since its inspectors lacked the necessary equipment to "allow for a real time electronic name check of all incoming passengers."[80] State also noted that because the forms filled out by departing visitors to record their departures (the I-94) were still being collected by the airlines, not government officials, it was very difficult to collect accurate, automated exit data.[81]

Notwithstanding these initial worries, the program was certified by Attorney General Ed Meese in 1988 and commenced operation for passengers traveling from the United Kingdom over the July Fourth weekend.[82] It was expanded to include Japan in December 1988; by July 30, 1989, Germany, Switzerland, France, Sweden, Italy, and the Netherlands were participating.[83] Justice Department concerns about entry to the United States by Mafia members, terrorists, and drug traffickers from the six additional countries were allayed when State provided to the INS (for use by their inspectors at ports of entry) "all information on nationals of participating countries found in the visa lookout system"[84] by sharing the TIPOFF terrorist watchlist.

The State Department realized an immediate benefit from the Visa Waiver Program. Instead of an expected 20–25 percent increase in applications at posts in countries that otherwise would have been subject to the visa requirement, there were reductions "of up to 80 percent."[85] However, this reduced demand for nonimmigrant visas meant that a higher percentage of visas were being adjudicated and issued in posts where rates of fraud were higher.[86] In addition, these savings could not be fully realized—and CA resources reprogrammed—unless the pilot program were made permanent.[87]

The State Department lost no time in urging that such action be taken.[88]
On October 30, 2000, the Visa Waiver Permanent Program Act was signed
into law (P.L. 106-396).

Consular Affairs—Technology and Watchlists

Although Consular Affairs saw itself and its administration of the visa function as the "outer ring of border security" during the 1990s, State's
technology in the early 1990s was anything but state-of-the-art.[89]

Indeed, the State Department began the 1990s with a patchwork of
information technology systems serving about 230 diplomatic posts worldwide.[90] The development in early 1990 of a machine-readable visa
(MRV)—containing a laser-printed digital photograph of the visa applicant
that could be read by a machine used by INS inspectors at ports of entry,
thereby making possible an automatic download of visa information into
the INS database—seemed to promise a brighter future.[91] But by the time
of the World Trade Center attack three years later, the MRV system was not
installed worldwide because it had not been funded.[92]

In the early 1990s, State's watchlisting efforts were similarly stymied by
a lack of modern technology. In 1993, visa applicants were screened using
one of three systems: a real-time interface with the State Department in
Washington (where the TIPOFF watchlist was maintained—see text box),
a check against the watchlist contained on a computer disk distributed to
posts every two months or so, or a check against the watchlist on a microfiche distributed to posts approximately every six months. Almost half of all
diplomatic posts received these updates by microfiche, which was cumbersome and time-consuming to use.[93]

Fortunately, State's main counterterrorism tool, the TIPOFF terrorist
watchlist, did receive much-needed funds to improve its capabilities.
Beginning in 1990, State received funding from the Technical Support
Working Group (TSWG) to hire a computer consultant to design a robust
computer architecture for TIPOFF.[94] However, TIPOFF, and State's system
of identifying ineligible visa applicants generally, was only as effective as the
system used to access it, and the system in 1993 was antiquated.

In 1991, on the eve of the Gulf War, State was asked by the White House
to use TIPOFF to help prevent the infiltration into the United States of Iraqi
intelligence agents. This request provided the impetus to broaden access to
the TIPOFF system to include immigration inspectors at U.S. ports of entry.
The expansion made sense, since immigration inspectors determined the

admissibility of all individuals seeking entry to the United States, including those who came from countries where no visa was required.

By design, the database of names available to inspectors at ports of entry was smaller than that available to consular officials. Because the INS needed to process travelers quickly, it used only that portion of the TIPOFF database containing specific information on a person, such as date of birth. The State Department, which had more time to evaluate a visa applicant's papers submitted at an embassy or consulate, could call an applicant back in for an interview to clarify data needed for positive identification. Thus, the INS sought access to only about two-thirds of all TIPOFF entries at ports of entry.

By September 11, 2001, the consular database, CLASS, contained the TIPOFF terrorist watchlist, which then contained about 60,000 names. It also included some 10 million records of individuals denied visas previously, individuals wanted by federal authorities, and individuals who for some other reason should not be issued a visa.

BORDER COMMUNITY AND WATCHLISTING

Before 1987, there was no automated terrorist watchlist systematically used by border security officials. Instead, hardbound books created and used by intelligence agencies contained names of known or suspected terrorists.

After a Palestinian terrorist acquired a U.S. visa in 1987, an enterprising State Department employee named John Arriza was asked by his supervisor to "do something" about terrorism. Arriza created TIPOFF, an interagency data-sharing program designed to prevent known or suspected terrorists from entering the United States. The State Department's Bureau of Intelligence and Research (INR), where Arriza worked, would collect information on suspected terrorists from all sources, including other members of the intelligence community and the media, and enter it into a searchable database.[95]

Arriza persuaded intelligence community agencies to allow the declassification of four data fields pulled from a classified document with terrorist identity information: the individual's name, date of birth, country of birth, and passport number. This limited declassification enabled consular and immigration officials, who operated in an unclassified environment and who daily scrutinized travel documents containing applicants' biographical information, to check applicants against a larger classified list of terrorists. On June 18, 1991, State signed a Memorandum of Understanding (MOU) with the INS and the U.S. Customs Service making the four unclassified data fields in TIPOFF available to them. The data would be entered into the National Automated Immigrant Lookout System (NAILS) maintained by the INS and available to officials working at ports of entry. The MOU also provided a mechanism for State/INR to pass classified information about an individual to an INS duty officer, using secure communications lines. The INS duty officer would then communicate an admissibility determination to the INS officer at the port of entry without divulging to that officer the classified information supporting it.

The MOU gave State/INR eight hours to provide information to be used by INS in making its decision to permit or deny an applicant admission to the United States. Under this first MOU, Customs officials used the INS as their point of access to TIPOFF.

In 1997, State signed an agreement to share the TIPOFF watchlist with Canada (TIPOFF U.S.–Canada, or TUSCAN). Like the MOU with U.S. immigration officials, the Canada MOU required State/INR to respond to Canadian inquiries within a set period of time—10 to 15 working days for a visa application hit, and one hour for a hit at a port of entry.[96]

In March 1999, State signed a new MOU with the INS and U.S. Customs Service that broadened access to TIPOFF data by Customs and added a database that included individuals watchlisted because of their connection to organized crime syndicates.

THE FBI AND WATCHLISTING

Prior to September 11, 2001, the FBI did not provide written guidance to its employees on how to collect and disseminate information on terrorists' identities for inclusion in watchlists.

The FBI's focus was on investigating and prosecuting particular cases. It was not oriented toward producing finished intelligence products, or culling identifying information out of case files for inclusion in terrorist watchlists. Indeed, an FBI employee who was not working on a particular case—even a counterterrorism analyst at headquarters—would generally not have been able to gain access to data gathered in other investigations, though his or her purpose might be to collect information for inclusion in a watchlist.

While some employees working in the FBI's counterterrorism sections, such as the Usama Bin Ladin and Radical Fundamentalists units, did routinely submit names to the State Department for inclusion in the TIPOFF watchlist—and participated in State's efforts to clarify the nature of any derogatory information after a lookout hit—this cooperation was ad hoc, and not the result written FBI policy. FBI watchlisting policy also reflected the pre-9/11 view of the division of labor between the FBI and CIA: terrorists out of the country were the CIA's problem, and there was no reason to watchlist any terrorists who were already in the country.

The statistics are telling. In 2001, the CIA provided 1,527 source documents to TIPOFF; the State Department, 2,013; the INS, 173. The FBI, during this same year, provided 63 documents to TIPOFF—fewer than were obtained from the public media, and about the same number as were provided by the Australian Intelligence Agency (52).

The Effect of the World Trade Center Bombing on the State Department

The bombing of the World Trade Center on February 26, 1993, was a tipping point for change at the State Department, particularly within Consular Affairs. Shortly after that attack, it was learned that a participant in the plot who was the spiritual leader of the group that carried it out— Sheikh Omar Abdel Rahman—had obtained a visa to enter the United States at the U.S. embassy in Khartoum, Sudan. As we discussed in the previous chapter, this blind cleric's application was successful even though he was a known Islamic extremist in Egypt whose name was on a watchlist— on microfiche—at the Khartoum embassy. A subsequent investigation revealed a series of problems, spanning several years, involving visas issued to Rahman. In the case of his last application, the State Department local employee tasked with checking the microfiche to see if Rahman's was watchlisted had not done so, because he believed that the aged cleric was unlikely to present a risk. He told the consular officer who issued the visa that he had performed the name check. The "Blind Sheikh episode"— notorious in the minds of State Department policymakers in the 1990s—led to a reexamination of visa-processing procedures.

One change in policy was the Visas Viper program, created in August 1993.[97] The Viper program, managed by State, was designed to improve interagency communication about terrorists whose names should be on a watchlist. The State Department directed all diplomatic and consular posts to form committees, to meet quarterly, that included members from State, as well as representatives from law enforcement and intelligence agencies.[98] Agencies were asked to supply terrorist identity information directly to State personnel at the post or, if there were concerns about classified or sensitive information, to State INR from their respective headquarters. Yet the Viper program was hampered by a lack of cooperation from intelligence and law enforcement agencies, which were reluctant to provide sensitive information to consular officials for fear that doing so would compromise sources and methods of collection.[99] Thus, while Viper submissions accounted for a significant percentage of the records added to TIPOFF during the period from 1993 through 2001, not all the information on terrorists' identities made its way into TIPOFF, because not all was shared with the State Department.[100]

Another significant outcome of this reexamination was the passage of a bill enabling the State Department to retain funds received from the issuance of nonimmigrant machine-readable visas.[101] Beginning in 1994, when MRV fees totaled less than $10 million, the amount collected grew steadily; by 1999, it exceeded $300 million annually. State used these funds to automate its consular visa-issuing systems, develop secure passport and visa technology, improve computer name-check capability, and create a worldwide real-time consular communications system. By April 1995, State had spent $32 million dollars upgrading its computer systems.[102]

The results were impressive. Whereas in February 1993, 111 State visa-issuing posts relied on microfiche for their name checks, by the end of 1995 none did. Instead, all visa-issuing posts had direct telecommunications access to the Department's CLASS lookout system, with a backup name-check system available on CD-ROM in case the automated system went down. This meant that TIPOFF, which existed as a file within CLASS, was always available to consular officers performing name checks. State also implemented Congress's statutory requirement that no visa be issued unless the consular officer first performed the CLASS name check.

Furthermore, State developed language algorithms to improve CLASS's name-check capability. The first language algorithm State developed, for Arabic, was implemented in December 1998. This enabled the system would search its records for all variant spellings of, for example, the name

"Mohammed." A second algorithm, for Russian/Slavic names, was added in December 2000.[103]

Another technological advance funded by MRV revenue was the creation of a worldwide, real-time database, known as the Consular Consolidated Database (CCD). The CCD for the first time allowed visa data entered in any embassy or consulate to be transferred automatically and immediately to a central location in the United States. For example, if an individual applied for a visa in Athens, Greece, a consular officer in Seoul, South Korea, could see the record of that application within minutes. The CCD also contained all aspects of the visa application, including the digitized photograph of the applicant.[104]

Nonimmigrant visa records were loaded into the CCD beginning in 1999 in Frankfurt, Germany.[105] All other posts were phased in between February 1999 and January 2001. By January 2001, every visa-issuing post sent its data to the CCD in real time.[106] On September 11, 2001, the State Department's CLASS contained the TIPOFF terrorist watchlist as well as 10 million records of individuals denied visas previously (with the grounds for their denial), individuals wanted by federal authorities, and individuals who for some other reason should not be given a visa.

Visa Policy Generally in the 1990s

While new technology helped prevent the issuance of visas to terrorists during the 1990s, aspects of State's approach to visa policy during the 1990s had a more mixed effect on its ability to counter terrorism.

During the period from 1993 to 2001, the State Department's visa operations focused primarily on screening applicants to determine whether they were intending immigrants: that is, intending to work or reside illegally in the United States.[107] Although visa and passport fraud have long been an integral part of terrorist travel practices, terrorists were not a major concern of consular officers. They were not trained in how to interview visa applicants to ascertain whether they had terrorist connections—or even criminal ones— nor were they supplied with the training or technology needed to detect an applicant's use of fraudulent travel document practices long associated with terrorism. In fact, consular officers were discouraged from using either section 214(b) or section 221(g) of INA to deny a visa to an applicant suspected of being a terrorist. Instead, to prevent terrorists from obtaining visas, consular officers were instructed to rely on the name-check function—including the TIPOFF terrorist watchlist check—and evaluation of potential terrorists' cases by officials in Washington.

The State Department's policy guidance to visa officers prior to September 11 concentrated on facilitating travel. This guidance consisted of the *Foreign Affairs Manual* (FAM), instruction telegrams sent to posts, informal communications such as email and oral history provided to officers arriving at posts, the *Consular Management Handbook*, and the *Consular Best Practices Handbook*.[108]

The FAM contained regulations, policies, and procedures for the department's operations and provided interpretive guidance to visa officers on the sections of the Immigration and Nationality Act and the Code of Federal Regulations related to the visa process. A confidential appendix to the FAM focused on security checks and individuals suspected of membership in terrorist groups.

Before 9/11, the FAM encouraged consular officers to expedite visa processing as a means of promoting travel to the United States. In the section dealing with the most common type of visa—issued to temporary visitors for business and pleasure—the FAM stated that it was the U.S. government's policy to facilitate and promote travel and the free movement of people of all nationalities to the United States.[109] The FAM called for consular officers to speed applications for the issuance of visitor visas, so long as the consular officer was satisfied that the issuance was in accordance with U.S. immigration law and the applicant had overcome the presumption of intending immigration. For while the law placed the burden of proof on the applicants to establish that they are eligible to receive a visa, "it is the policy of the U.S. government to give the applicant every reasonable opportunity to establish eligibility."[110]

Although always a priority for reasons of commerce and foreign policy, the streamlining of the visa process increased steadily during this period. CA focused extensively on "reinventing consular functions" to make them "work better, cost less, and get meaningful results by putting customers first, cutting red tape, empowering employees, and cutting back to basics."[111] Two additional factors helped drive this change. First, Consular Affairs became a "reinvention lab" in April 1993 as part of Vice President Gore's initiative to reinvent government.[112] Second, while resources devoted to the consular function remained flat or decreased, as discussed above, visa demand was rising. The number of U.S. visa applications worldwide grew from about 7.7 million in fiscal year 1998 to 10.6 million in fiscal year 2001, an increase of 37 percent. Staffing did not keep pace with visa demand, leading to gaps in coverage at posts that lacked a consular officer to adjudicate visas, unusually long work hours for consular staff, and "staff burnout."[113] Something had to give.

The result was the *Consular Best Practices Handbook*,[114] a collection of business process improvements gathered from a series of 49 cables sent to posts between 1997 and 2000 that were intended to help "improve customer satisfaction, improve decision-making, and increase efficiency."[115] The *Handbook* urged improvement of processes to "support the three key goals that every consular manager should strive to achieve: high quality decision making, more efficient processes, and improved customer service." By introducing new processes that improved efficiency, and outsourcing activities that "do not have to be performed by government employees," the consular managers were directed by officials in Washington to "focus the majority of your . . . decision-making resources on the most difficult cases."[116]

Best Practices cable number 6 listed "the four top goals of the visa process as efficient processing, high quality decisions, people-friendly services and sharing of all pertinent information within the US Government."[117] The cable acknowledged that the first two goals—efficient processing and high-quality decisions—"express a basic conflict in our traditional approach to visa processing. Quality decisions can make the process less efficient, and, in the context of declining staff, posts have often been forced to choose efficiency over quality."[118]

This cable also provided an excellent synopsis of the rationale underlying the push to save resources in the late 1990s and the environment in which the hijackers received their visas, under the title "Reconciling Efficiency and Quality":

> For many years growing work and static personnel resources have led us to search for areas we can eliminate or place last in our scale of priorities. But, with a few minor exceptions, everything we do in consular work is too important to cut, either because of its impact on the public or because of its impact on quality. For example, postponing or slowing down NIV (Non-Immigrant Visa) services is like squeezing a balloon—the demand pops up someplace else, either at another post, through the referral system or through pleas for exceptions. Similarly, cutting out anti-fraud work harms our entire effort and leads to poor decision-making. Giving inadequate information results in applicants arriving for an interview without necessary documentation.
>
> The consequences of cutting out or slowing down any discrete function are unacceptable. But viable alternatives exist, namely to cut out the parts of all of our processes that contribute the least to good decision making and to outsource or automate the parts that don't need to be done by

government employees. Several cables in this series have offered suggestions on how to replace certain functions with automated or contracted-out approaches. Where feasible, these approaches work and posts should adopt them.

Although much of our approach to visa work can be streamlined, the most pertinent example of a part of the process that can be cut back successfully is the nonimmigrant visa interview. This doesn't mean that interviews should be shorter; it means that interviews should be fewer.[119]

Finally, because these practices were considered by CA to be "integral to effective consular operations," implementing best practices was "a mandate, not an option."[120]

In chapter 5 we explore how this aggressive effort to cut back on resources devoted to screening individual visa applicants, a reduction in interviews, and a heavy reliance on a Washington-based watchlist system played out as the 9/11 hijackers began applying for their visas in April 1999. First, we examine the Immigration and Naturalization Service's activities before September 11.

4.3 The Immigration and Naturalization Service

Those who should get in, get in; those who should be kept out, are kept out; and those who should not be here will be required to leave.

—Barbara Jordan, chair,
U.S. Commission on Immigration Reform,
February 24, 1995

The Immigration and Naturalization Service has the statutory responsibility under the Immigration and Nationality Act to determine who may enter, who may stay, and who must be removed from the United States.[121] Thus, U.S. border inspectors and Border Patrol agents remain the last physical barrier between terrorists and their entry into the United States. This section discusses INS functions and provides an analysis of how well the agency operated prior to September 11 in the context of counterterrorism.

Background

The Constitution gave Congress plenary power over immigration, and the first federal laws addressing immigration issues were passed in 1790.[122] Not until the 1880s, however, did Congress make the "supervision over the business of immigration to the United States" a federal responsibility.[123] In 1891, Congress created an immigration office in the Treasury Department and in 1895 assigned its most senior post the title of commissioner.[124] Part of the Bureau of Immigration's purpose was to administer and create the rules necessary to facilitate land border inspections for "ordinary" travelers, including the classes of persons to be denied entry.[125]

Although the nation's growth depended on successive waves of immigrants, the Bureau of Immigration never seemed quite important enough to become its own department, with its own secretary reporting directly to the president of the United States. In fact, the bureau was something of an administrative orphan. Over the century its name and bureaucratic home changed repeatedly, and increasing numbers of confusing statutes created conflicting jurisdictions in both immigration services and enforcement.[126]

In addition, the agency never received adequate support from its parent department, Justice, the Congress, the White House, or the intelligence community. It is therefore not surprising that the INS entered the 1990s as a badly organized agency with a poor self-image and a troubled public reputation. Despite its mandate to secure America's borders, it was not held in high enough regard to be given an active role in counterterrorism efforts. Thus, a few creative INS employees struggled to keep our borders safe from terrorists while the rest of the agency, and the government in general, remained mostly oblivious to this mission. As we will see, the INS was a border security agency without a recognized role in counterterrorism and without the vision and resources to enforce its own laws.

The INS Structure

The INS was charged with welcoming U.S. citizens, immigrants, visitors, students, and others deemed beneficial to the nation while denying entry to those judged undesirable. Its employees performed three different functions. Immigration inspectors at land, air, and sea ports of entry processed applicants for admission to the United States, determining who should be admitted and who should not. The Border Patrol and special agents enforced immigration law at the border and within the United States against those who violated it.[127] Immigration services officers adjudicated benefits for temporary visitors, immigrants, asylum seekers, and refugees. In 2000, all three of these functions reported to two separate chains of command, one for headquarters and one for the field.

The field was renowned for its independence from Washington and for the range of leadership skills found there. As one former employee told the Commission, "the mountains were high and the emperor far."[128] Indeed, the budget and policy planning offices were literally far away in Washington. Together, they were responsible for all INS budget decisions, including those supporting field operations, as well as a significant part of the policy that guided work in the field. But they reported to an executive office different from the regional field offices.[129] As former deputy commissioner Mary Ann Wyrsch told the Commission, this structure helped ensure that people were confused about their job descriptions, operating without communication or direction and often duplicating efforts at more senior levels.[130] The result was low morale, unclear goals, inefficiency, and difficulty moving forward on the policies and programs needed.

Compounding the management problem, the INS commissioner reported to the deputy attorney general (DAG) in the Justice Department. The DAG managed the Criminal Division, the United States Attorneys, the FBI, the Drug Enforcement Agency, and the INS.[131] Although the INS was closely scrutinized on those issues important to the attorney general, which recently had included naturalization, the Southwest border, and Cuban migration, it was largely ignored on other issues such as interior immigration enforcement and systematic development of technology.[132] The INS commissioner also had to answer to Congress, in its oversight role, and the White House, which set policy. Thus, the commissioner spent much time dealing with institutional actors who often had different agendas and only in rare instances envisioned a role for the INS in counterterrorism.[133]

The multiple demands, lack of oversight focused on counterterrorism from the Justice Department, growing demands to stem the tide of illegal immigration, an overburdened immigration benefits system, and growing number of visitors to the United States at ports of entry were weaknesses and pressures that left the INS wholly unprepared to fulfill its statutory obligations. It is therefore not surprising that when Doris Meissner, who had served in the INS from 1981 to 1986, returned as Commissioner in 1993, she found an agency in disarray.[134] Border Patrol agents were still using manual typewriters,[135] inspectors at ports of entry were using a paper watchlist, the asylum system did not detect or deter fraudulent applicants, and policy development was inadequate.[136] The explosive growth that followed congressional appropriations to upgrade INS technology and human resources to respond to illegal entries over the Southwest border—the agency grew 40 percent overall from 1997 to 1998, as Border Patrol and inspection resources increased 94 percent and the immigration services budget increased an astounding 150 percent between 1996 and 1998[137]— represented a major new administrative challenge. Only a small group of forward-thinking midlevel employees quietly worked counterterrorism issues. These employees were scattered throughout the agency in investigations, the Joint Terrorism Task Forces (JTTFs), intelligence, legal counsel, inspections, and budget; others worked on one of the many technology initiatives such as student tracking.[138]

The INS, clearly, was struggling.

The Many Facets of the INS Mission

The INS was responsible for enforcing the immigration and nationality law in three general areas: inspecting applicants and adjudicating admissions at the ports of entry; enforcing immigration law by patrolling the border to prevent and detect illegal entry and investigating, detaining, and removing illegal and criminal aliens already in the country; and adjudicating applications to change a person's immigration status. While each of these roles is critical, the immigration inspection and immigration benefits adjudications functions are most relevant to the 9/11 story.

Inspections at Ports of Entry. INS immigration inspectors are located at ports of entry along the land and sea borders and at international airports. They are responsible for determining who may legally enter the United States.[139] They also set the conditions for temporary stays in the United States.

Indeed, the stated mission of immigration inspectors is to "control and guard the boundaries and border of the United States against the illegal entry of aliens."[140] In practical terms, this means determining the admissibility and length of stay of aliens applying for admission into the United States at ports of entry. As discussed in the previous chapter, some of these aliens must have visas issued by State Department consular officers at U.S. embassies and consulates abroad. Tourists from countries that require a visa to enter the United States receive a mandatory six-month length of stay. All of the 19 September 11 hijackers presented visas (18 of 19 were tourist visas) in their 33 successful entries, as none was from a visa waiver country.[141]

Those aliens from visa waiver countries who seek to visit for pleasure or business must only present a passport and a departure ticket to an immigration inspector upon their arrival in the United States.[142] These "visa waiver" passport holders are granted a mandatory three-month stay.

Screening at Airports. Prior to September 11, all persons seeking admission to the United States through any of the 220 international U.S. airports had to submit to an initial or "primary" screening by immigration inspectors.[143] Many airports required the screening to take place in an average of

45 seconds—30 seconds for U.S. citizens and one minute for foreign citizens—during which immigration inspectors had to sort the bona fide from the mala fide travelers. This brevity was forced on inspectors by a 1991 congressional mandate that each flight be processed within 45 minutes.[144]

In primary immigration inspection the traveler was asked a series of questions in order to learn the identity, purpose, and duration of his or her visit and the validity of the visa. Travel documents—the passport and visa— were reviewed for potential fraud. When visitors had machine-readable passports, like those issued by Saudi Arabia, the lookout checks were automatically performed as the document was optically scanned. For others, the inspector would enter the information manually. He or she would check the security features of the document, relying on fraud training and on specialized equipment, including ultraviolet lights and magnifying glasses. Arrival and customs forms were reviewed for completeness. A name check was conducted along with a passport number search to determine if the traveler was on a watchlist or if the passport had been reported lost or stolen.[145]

A primary inspector was also trained to use behavioral cues to determine whether the traveler might be mala fide. In such instances, the inspector could ask to see travel itineraries, looking for a last-minute ticket purchase, a one-way ticket, or unusual routing. Such indicators, along with a visitor's limited English, insufficient funds for travel, or questionable behavior, could also be the basis for a referral to a secondary immigration inspector.

If documents, database checks, interviews, and demeanor raised no questions, the visitor was admitted into the United States. If the immigration inspector was suspicious about the visitor, he or she had the discretion to make a referral to a secondary immigration inspection for further scrutiny. Such suspicions led to the secondary referral of Mohamed Atta, Marwan al Shehhi, and Saeed al Ghamdi and to the removal of Mohamed al Kahtani.

When a primary inspector received a hit against the watchlist, the inspector was required to escort the visitor to a secondary immigration inspection area for an interview.[146] At that time, travel documents were again reviewed for potential fraud. "Pocket litter"[147] might be inspected. Unlike the case with the primary immigration inspection, the secondary inspection had no time constraints. Multiple investigative resources were available to the inspector, who might check one of a couple of dozen INS databases, call the FBI or a translator, review travel document fraud alerts and manuals produced by the INS Forensic Document Lab, and access a biometric system called IDENT, which contained digital fingerprints and photos. Only in Kahtani's case were any of these tools used.[148]

Only a single INS employee at INS headquarters was permitted to liaise with the State Department, which managed the TIPOFF terrorist watchlist, when there was a watchlist hit. This liaison officer would attempt to get the supporting documentation and then relay what unclassified information he or she could to the inspector determining admissibility.[149] Denials required supervisory approval.[150] Before 9/11, local members of Joint Terrorism Task Forces, composed of individuals in federal, state, and local law enforcement, would occasionally assist in the interview of a suspect individual.

If an arriving traveler was sent back to his or her home country, then a photograph and fingerprints were taken and added to an electronic file opened on the individual. This file was part of a database called IDENT (Automated Biometric Identification System), which was initially implemented on the Southwest land border to try to reduce the recidivism of those violating immigration law.[151]

Inspection Practices Specific to Counterterrorism. As the one successful exclusion of a potential September 11 hijacker, Kahtani, makes clear, the screening tools, training, and procedures available to immigration officials are critical to making admissions decisions. Generally the inspectors at the ports of entry were not asked and were not trained to look for terrorists. Indeed, most inspectors interviewed by the Commission were not even aware that the automated watchlist against which they checked the names of incoming passengers was a terrorist watchlist. Their ignorance was largely a function of a technological approach to terrorist screening that relied almost exclusively on a mechanical, computerized name check at the primary immigration inspection.[152]

Behavior was also a substantial consideration in referring a traveler to secondary inspection. Yet no inspector interviewed by the Commission received any operational training in the types of behavior that might be exhibited by terrorists. Nor were they instructed on the types of travel documents known to be carried by terrorists. As noted in chapter 3, the CIA's Redbook, which contained information on terrorist travel documents, was discontinued in 1992; inspectors were thus left without specific information on terrorist travel practices. Few inspectors were aware of the existence of its successor, the Passport Examination Manual, which treated generic fraudulent documents and travel stamps.[153] Today, there is still on electronic version of such a manual.

At headquarters and in the field, the INS did organize a few scattered offices and programs to aid its inspectors in identifying suspect individuals, especially terrorists.

THE INS TERRORIST WATCHLIST

The National Automated Immigration Lookouts System contained the TIPOFF terrorist watchlist and was the most valuable tool for identifying terrorists that INS and Customs inspectors had until September 11, 2001.[154] TIPOFF first became available to the INS in 1991 by way of a Memorandum of Understanding between the State Department, Customs Service, and INS.[155] This name-based system provided key unclassified biographical information about aliens reasonably suspected to be involved or closely associated with terrorist activity. The database was checked by the inspector at the primary immigration inspection as he or she was determining admissibility.

By September 11, TIPOFF contained about 80,000 records on terrorists and terrorism-related criminals. The State Department's criteria for creating a file in the database included reasonable suspicion that the alien engaged in or might engage in terrorism, otherwise known as "derogatory information" and sufficient biographical information for positive identification.[156] Because the INS had a slightly higher standard for including information in NAILS, not all State Department TIPOFF records made it into the INS database.[157] If the INS considered the State Department's supporting intelligence insufficient, the referral would be stricken from consideration, at least until further information was provided by State.[158]

Thus, the INS was wholly dependent on the State Department for both the referrals to TIPOFF and the supporting intelligence for the nomination. The INS did not seek intelligence to support the referrals from elsewhere in the agency or from any outside intelligence agency.[159]

In 1998, the INS excluded three people as a result of TIPOFF watchlist hits. The State Department claimed there were 97 such exclusions or arrests. This inconsistency was due to poor INS recordkeeping and the inclusion of arrest data in State Department but not INS statistics.[160] By 2003, the ports with the largest number of TIPOFF hits corresponded to the ports through which the hijackers entered: JFK in New York, Miami, Atlanta, Dulles near Washington, D.C., Orlando, Los Angeles, Newark, Tampa, and Cincinnati. The nationalities of those excluded also corresponded to the nationalities of the hijackers—Saudi, Emirati, Egyptian, and Lebanese—though they did not constitute the greatest number of those flagged by TIPOFF.[161]

Terrorist Watchlisting at U.S. border ports of entry

Intel community submits derogatory information and alien biographical data to State Dept.

→

State inputs data into TIPOFF and sends a weekly CD of "referrals" to INS Lookout Unit.

→

Lookout Unit reviews referrals for sufficient (1) derogatory information and (2) biographical identifiers.

↓

Terrorist lookout database automatically queried. If a "00" hit, mandatory referral to secondary inspection.

←

Applicant applies for admission at U.S. port of entry.

←

Referrals with sufficient derogatory information entered into INS terrorist lookout database.

↓

At secondary, inspector works with INS Lookout Unit to determine admissibility, copies all pocket litter, and photographs and fingerprints alien.

→

Inspector has discretion to notify FBI of hit and has final discretion to admit or exclude.

→

Intel community receives a copy of alien's pocket litter, photograph, and fingerprints.

The INS Lookout Unit. The INS tried to support primary and secondary immigration inspectors in their search for terrorists through its Lookout Unit. Initially created to liaise with the State Department in order to share terrorist information with those at ports of entry, it took on more duties, which included working with the airlines to detect improper travel documents.

The Carrier Consultant Program, initiated under 1996 changes to immigration law, trained foreign airlines to recognize fraudulent documents used by those seeking admission to the United States. The purpose of the program was to prevent aliens with improper documents from boarding airplanes in the first place.[162] If an airline failed to detect such mala fide travelers, it was subject to fines from the INS National Fines Office.[163]

The Lookout Unit also tried to ease the burden on primary inspectors by reviewing the incoming passenger manifests every morning and notifying the port of entry if a suspected terrorist was scheduled to arrive there.[164] Although Customs had access to the airline carriers' reservation system, these manifests were not required to be submitted to INS by law; most airlines provided them voluntarily, however.

Forensic Document Lab. Immigration inspectors also relied on the considerable expertise of forensic document examiners at the INS to help them detect fraudulent travel documents. Indeed, beginning in the early 1980s, the use of such documents was a growing problem. The INS responded by creating the Forensic Document Laboratory. The lab supported officers in the field, primarily immigration inspectors and benefits adjudicators, with training and manuals on legitimate and illegitimate travel and identification documents.[165] The laboratory was the only federal crime lab dedicated almost entirely to the forensic examination of documents, and its archives contained more than 20 years' worth of identification and travel documents.[166] Its extensive scientific expertise and reference library enabled the lab to provide authoritative analysis of all types of identification and travel documents— counterfeit, altered, and impostor. The lab also supported the FBI and CIA.[167]

But in the decade prior to September 11, the Forensic Document Laboratory did not focus on terrorists. Nor did it have access to terrorist travel intelligence. Therefore, although terrorist organizations dedicated significant resources to producing and acquiring passports, visas, cachets, and secondary identification, the lab was unaware of their efforts.[168]

Office of International Affairs. The Office of International Affairs considered itself an office of international law enforcement, "a critically important, cost-effective, and integral part of the Administration's comprehensive strategy to deter illegal immigration."[169] The INS began placing officers overseas in the 1950s; their work focused on bringing those displaced by World War II to the United States from Europe and the Pacific. As immigration law changed in the 1960s, INS overseas officers shifted into U.S. consulates, mainly to process immigrant visa and refugee applications and to troubleshoot issues arising abroad concerning U.S. citizens and their relatives. This work was focused in the Near East, Mexico, and Europe, with management responsibilities in district offices in Rome, Beijing, Mexico City, and Ottawa. Asylum applications filed domestically also were housed in the Office of International Affairs. These functions continued through September 11, 2001.[170]

By the 1990s, the emphasis turned to two areas of enforcement, deterring illegal entry and combating alien smuggling. In 1995, with fewer than 100 INS employees overseas, "Operation Global Reach" was coordinated with the State Department and the Justice Department's Office of National Security to train nearly 12,000 host-country law enforcement officials, airline personnel, and foreign consular officers to detect fraudulent travel documents. The training was aimed at intercepting alien smugglers, and it succeeded beyond anyone's expectations. Statistics provided by the INS indicate that there was a 5,500 percent jump in fraudulent document intercepts by INS officers and their trainees from 1994 to 1995.[171] Regrettably, none of the document training was intended to catch terrorists. The International Affairs Office also never developed leads or investigated cases with foreign governments or U.S. Attorneys offices for the purpose of pursuing counterterrorism cases, although they did so for alien smuggling.

Although the Lookout Units, the Forensic Document Laboratory, and the International Affairs Office were doing important work, the INS initiated but failed to bring to completion two efforts that would have provided inspectors with information relevant to counterterrorism—a proposed system to track foreign student visa compliance and a program to establish a way of tracking travelers' entry to and exit from the United States. These programs would have been substantially helpful to inspectors in accurately determining the admissibility of travelers, including the September 11 terrorists.

A system to monitor foreign student compliance. As early as 1972, the INS was concerned that some foreign students could pose a threat to national security. They were particularly worried about student sympathizers to Yasir Arafat's Palestinian terrorist organization; in 1974, INS agents found 154 students associated with the organization were in the United States.[172] The issue of foreign students as security risks reemerged during the 1984 Libyan crisis when intelligence indicated that Libyan leader Muammar Qadhafi might have planted assassins in the United States under student cover. Thus began the first national foreign student registration program. Libyan students were registered and fingerprinted, and regulations were put in place to "immediately terminate the studies of Libyan nationals engaged in flight training and nuclear-related education."[173]

The INS first established a comprehensive national system to keep track of students in the late 1980s—the Student/School System—but its information was routinely out of date or lacking.[174] In 1994, the Department of Justice, pointing out that a key conspirator in the first World Trade Center bombing had been a student who had overstayed his visa, asked Commissioner Meissner how the INS could better track students.[175] The following year, an interagency task force led by a former General Accounting Office investigator recommended that the INS start over with a new system built around a biometric student identification card that could be issued at the time of the visa application and used for the duration of his or her studies in the United States.[176] With real-time technologies and biometrics, the task force believed that the new systems would act as a true compliance mechanism for both students and schools.[177] FBI Director Louis Freeh's concerns about foreign students seeking U.S. studies not necessarily being in the national security interests of the United States were also not lost on the task force. Interest in tracking terrorists and criminal aliens "linked to student visas" was stated as a guiding principle of the task force.[178]

In 1996, Congress required the creation of a system to track students from countries designated as state sponsors of terrorism.[179] Although the deadline for the system's implementation was just two years away, Congress did not appropriate specific funds for the program.[180] The INS scraped together $10 million in seed money and launched a successful pilot program in June 1997.[181] The program enrolled 21 schools of different types and sizes (including Duke, Clemson, and Auburn), technical schools, two-year community colleges, and a flight school. It was the test case for the development of a national student tracking system and included the latest biometric smart card and scanners available.[182] The project drew the interest of White House Counterterrorism Coordinator Richard Clarke, who held meetings with both the INS Commissioner and its project managers.[183] He successfully proposed including the completion of the project in a 1998 presidential directive.[184] There was congressional interest as well.[185] By August 1998, managers of the project deemed it ready for national development.[186] It was considered a success.[187]

These initial successes were achieved despite the orders the program manager received in early 1998 to stop work.[188] Providing education for foreign students is a multi-billion-dollar business, and the higher education community vigorously resisted the system. They argued that the program was unduly burdensome and costly.[189] The 1996 law was strictly interpreted by INS management to require educational institutions, not the government, to collect the government fee that was to fund the program.[190] These groups then argued that this fee-based method of funding was unfair to the schools and would deter foreign students from U.S. study.[191] In August 1998, a senior group of policy managers at the INS decided to defer the testing of the biometric student card. Within a year, they fired the project manager over concerns that he had gone outside of his chain of command in soliciting support for the project.[192] A new manager, unfamiliar with the project, was brought in. Progress stalled.[193]

By 2000, powerful members of the Senate were pressuring the INS to stop the fee-based funding approach, thereby jeopardizing its existence.[194] The Senate appropriations committee chairman apparently sought repeal of the law authorizing the program.[195] Although the law stayed on the books, there was still no congressional funding for the student tracking program, and INS management was growing increasing reluctant to continue internal funding.[196] Although the program's supervisor found other money to keep minimal development alive, these efforts were insufficient to complete the system.[197]

Thus, when the September 11 hijackers began entering the United States in 2000 to attend flight school, there was no student tracking system available. If there had been, immigration authorities might well have been alerted to the fact that Mohamed Atta, the plan's ringleader, had made false statements about his student status and therefore could have been denied entry into the United States.

An Entry-Exit System. The INS also was unable to enforce the rules regarding the terms of admission of visitors to the United States because there was no national tracking system designed to match a person's entry with that person's exit. Inspectors were similarly unaware of whether a visitor had overstayed a previous visit.

In 1996, expressing frustration at the apparent number of overstays in the United States and the inability of INS to enforce the law, Congress took action. It passed a law requiring the attorney general to develop an automated entry-exit program to collect records on every arriving and departing visitor.[198] Congress provided about $40 million over four years to fund the development of such a system.[199] By contrast, Congress provided nearly $1 billion to increase the Border Patrol's presence in the Southwest in order to stem the flow of illegal immigration from Mexico.[200] Countering terrorist entry was not a rationale for the system.

Leaders of border communities along the Canadian and Mexican borders, where more than a million people move back and forth daily, denounced the system. They argued that it would inhibit border trade.[201] Some members of Congress, along with senior INS managers, agreed and decided to automate only the entry process.[202] Prior to September 11, even these efforts were unsuccessful.[203] Thus, while the hijackers were preparing for the planes operation in the United States, immigration authorities had no way to determine whether any of them had overstayed their visas or had reliable information regarding their travel in and out of the country. The lack of an entry-exit system was especially significant for Satam al Suqami and Nawaf al Hazmi, as we saw in chapter 2.

The INS Intelligence Unit. Further hampering the ability of the INS to track terrorists was the unfortunate state of its intelligence unit.[204] The quality of its work was considered so poor by Commissioner Meissner that she never requested the daily intelligence brief common in other federal agencies.[205] In fact, only once in her eight-year tenure did she receive a briefing on the threat posed by radical fundamentalist terrorists.[206] In her interview with us, Meissner did not recall that 1995 briefing.[207] She also told us she never heard of Usama Bin Ladin until August 2001, nearly 10 months after she left the INS.[208]

In reality, the INS operated in a virtual intelligence vacuum. The intelligence unit was wholly dependent on the CIA, the National Security Agency, the FBI, and the State Department's Intelligence and Research section for terrorist information.[209] In stark contrast, its parent, the Justice Department, routinely received intelligence information on terrorism cases and surveillance intercepts, mostly from investigations conducted from the FBI.[210] In 1996, there were only five analysts at INS headquarters and none in the field.[211] By 1998, fewer than 100 part-time intelligence officers in the field were providing the bulk of information used by the unit, but the apparent increase in personnel is misleading. All of the part-time officers were special agents whose main responsibility was enforcement of immigration law; they would also write up "intelligence" reports to forward to headquarters, but doing so was optional. Neither they nor any of the 2,000 special agents, 4,500 inspectors, and 9,000 Border Patrol agents had a mandate to report information gathered in the field back to the intelligence unit in Washington.[212] Instead, the unit was dependent on reporting voluntarily forwarded by supervisors in the field, where lookouts could be posted without the knowledge of the intelligence unit.[213]

Indeed, the unit was unable even to regularly gather information on terrorists from its own employees assigned to work as liaisons to other government agencies. A total of 24 intelligence unit employees were assigned to Interpol (the international law enforcement agency), the CIA's Counterterrorism Center, the FBI Counterterrorism Center, and the Joint Terrorism Task Forces throughout the country. All potentially had access to counterterrorism information. The intelligence unit was not interested, and chose instead to remain focused on its primary assignment from INS leadership: alien smuggling.[214]

However, some of these detailees did prove valuable. For example, the INS detailee to the CIA helped streamline the declassification process for the INS so that the intelligence unit could receive intelligence from the intelligence community and make it available to the field more quickly. He also helped create the 1980s counterterrorism training film for border inspectors, "The Threat Is Real," and designed and implemented CIA-based counterterrorism training classes for law enforcement personnel.[215]

Enforcement of Immigration Law within the United States
We know that in the terrorist plots of the 1990s, terrorists exploited the U.S. immigration system to enter and stay in the United States. The public prosecutions of the conspirators in the World Trade Center and Landmark cases in the early 1990s often brought to light violations of immigration law. The INS therefore had the potential to play a significant law enforcement role in counterterrorism. Under the Immigration and Nationality Act, immigration attorneys, special agents, immigration inspectors, and Border Patrol agents were all capable of enforcing the law. However, the INS and the government institutions that controlled much of its agenda—Congress, the Justice Department and the White House—acknowledged only a small role for the agency in counterterrorism. They failed to connect the facts of terrorist exploitation of immigration border and benefits policies and the need for the INS to act to prevent terrorist abuse of the immigration system. The prevailing view was that the INS was valuable in counterterrorism only insofar as it supported the FBI in its Joint Terrorism Task Force investigations.

Nevertheless, a few midlevel INS employees took counterterrorism seriously. They often had difficulty getting things done.

The Special Agents in the Field. The first problem encountered by those concerned about terrorists was an almost complete lack of enforcement resources. Neither the White House, the Congress, the Department of Justice, nor the INS leadership ever provided the support needed for INS enforcement agents to find, detain, and remove illegal aliens, including those with terrorist associations. Throughout the 1990s, about 2,000 immigration special agents were responsible for dealing with the millions of illegal aliens and related immigration crimes in the United States.[216] Because of these resource constraints, they focused on aliens involved in criminal activity.

Enforcement of U.S. immigration law violations inside the country is referred to as "interior enforcement." It is governed by a set of extraordinarily complex laws, rules, and regulations that are adjudicated in its own administrative court system. The law and procedures governing these courts were geared toward giving the benefit of doubt to the alien. Appearance bonds were low and often not required. Aliens were granted multiple hearings, often resulting in lengthy delays. This system was easy to exploit. Because the immigration attorneys representing the INS in cases against aliens worked solely from paper files, they were often unable to properly track cases or access the necessary files to present their cases efficiently and knowledgeably. For much of the 1990s, case backlogs were considerable. Terrorists knew they could beat the system—and, as we have seen, they often did.

Recognizing the deficiencies in the system, in April 1997 Congress directed the INS to devise an interior enforcement strategy. The plan was delivered nearly two years later and only after much congressional prodding. Meanwhile, three national counterterrorism strategies had been produced—in 1986, 1995, and 1997. They called for the addition of more JTTF positions, the creation of a robust intelligence network within the intelligence community, and acceptance of a role for the INS and its immigration authority in counterterrorism efforts.[217] These recommendations were not implemented by INS senior management.

The Creation of the National Security Unit. The INS did take one important step to enhance its counterterrorism enforcement capability. In 1997, it established a National Security Unit to oversee national security work in the field, including that of the JTTF representatives. In addition, the unit produced security alerts for ports of entry and worked with the Justice Department on national security issues; this collaboration included case referrals to the newly created Alien Terrorist Removal Court, discussed below.

Here as in much of the INS, key employees worked long hours with inadequate resources.[218] The unit's manager produced a comprehensive strategy, which called for increased interagency cooperation on watch-listing and a more active role for enforcement in counterterrorism cases.[219] The unit began to determine which immigration laws could be used as counterterrorism tools. For instance, it sought unsuccessfully to require that the CIA complete its security checks before naturalization benefit applications were adjudicated. According to the NSU manager, these efforts were not supported by INS senior management, who believed such checks would be prohibitively time-consuming and add to an already immense backlog of applications.[220]

For the reasons discussed above, the National Security Unit relied not on the in-house Intelligence Unit but on INS personnel at the FBI and the CIA for its understanding of the terrorist threat.[221] However, when Usama Bin Ladin was indicted for the August 1998 bombings of the U.S. embassies in Tanzania and Kenya, the two INS units did cooperate. Drawing on information supplied by the Justice Department, they directed inspectors in the field to be on a heightened security alert. Inspectors were also instructed to give extra scrutiny to travelers born or residing in certain

Middle Eastern countries, including Saudi Arabia, Egypt, Lebanon, and the United Arab Emirates.[222] These national-security-related cases came to be known within the INS as "special interest" cases.[223] All of the hijackers' countries of citizenship were named in this 1998 alert.

In 2001, the National Security Unit had four staffers at headquarters, and three at the FBI, as well as about 50 INS special agent detailees at the JTTFs.[224] It generally did not receive information on the heightened threat in the summer of 2001 from the INS intelligence unit, the intelligence community in general, or from the JTTFs. However, two staffers were sent to the White House on July 5 for a briefing by the CIA at the request of the Richard Clarke, but both felt that it was "over their heads." One staffer wrote a memo noting the main points raised at the meeting, but the other apparently took no action, returning to his job as the manager of the JTTF detailees. The acting INS Commissioner never learned of the meeting or the threat.[225]

INS Detailees to the Joint Terrorism Task Forces. In the absence of other efforts, the Joint Terrorism Task Forces became the focus of INS counterterrorism enforcement activity. Interest in bringing INS agents into the JTTFs grew as the FBI, with INS agents' help, began investigating the conspirators in the 1993 World Trade Center bombing and revealing that they were aliens who had used travel document fraud to enter the United States and immigration benefit fraud to stay here. When a criminal case on terrorism grounds could not be brought, a charge relating to visas or admission might be available. Therefore, the FBI soon learned how important the INS could be in developing a case. An alien terrorist's immigration violation was easily proved, while the evidence relating to terrorist acts was often classified or arguably insufficient.[226]

The INS did not initially embrace a role in these counterterrorism investigations.[227] In 1993, its Investigations Division asked for five positions in the newly created Joint Terrorism Task Forces. The INS did not approve this modest budget request. The highest-ranking official for field operations argued that he was "unable to concur" that INS would "benefit" from participation in the JTTFs.[228] Four years later, Investigations tried again, this time asking for 29 positions in the JTTFs. Commissioner Meissner wrote in support to the Department of Justice, citing the value of INS agents to the World Trade Center prosecutions and the agency's commitment to the JTTFs.[229] The Justice Department did not approve Meissner's request. Congress split the difference and added 18 positions.[230]

New Legal Tools against Terrorism. In 1996, the Antiterrorism and Effective Death Penalty Act and the Illegal Immigration Reform and Immigrant Responsibility Act also provided new immigration enforcement tools relevant to counterterrorism. One of them was expedited removal. For the first time, border authorities were permitted to deny entry, without a hearing, to those failing to qualify for admission.[231] This provision could be used to deny suspected terrorists the opportunity to enter the United States and stay.[232] In the first months of 1997, 1,200 travelers a week were subject to expedited removal, mostly over the Southwest border.[233] Despite this success, the INS never expanded expedited removal to include persons attempting to enter illegally across the expansive physical borders between ports of entry.[234] As a result, it was not used against Gazi Ibrahim Abu Mezer, who was able to stay in the United States despite being apprehended three times for illegal entries along the Canadian border. He later became known as the "Brooklyn Bomber" for his plan to blow up the Atlantic Avenue subway in Brooklyn.[235] The INS never did seek to expand expedited removal to illegal entries along U.S. borders.[236]

The 1996 Antiterrorism Act also created the Alien Terrorist Removal Court, expressly designed to remove alien terrorists by using classified evidence to support a terrorist allegation and staffed by counsel possessing the security clearances necessary to review classified evidence. Although the Justice Department considered the creation of the court one of its top counterterrorism legislative priorities in the mid-1990s, the court still has never been used.[237] Judges were appointed and rules made,[238] but by 1998, Justice attorneys in the Terrorism and Violent Crime Section had led a department review of 50 cases for possible application to the ATRC, but they were all rejected.[239] Over the following two years, another 50 cases were rejected.[240]

A major reason for the lack of use of the ATRC was that new immigration laws permitted the use of classified evidence in traditional deportation hearings, making recourse to a special court unnecessary.[241] Moreover, many "special interest" cases became stalled by internal Justice Department deliberations regarding sharing of information, alien rights, and sufficiency of evidence.[242] At times, differences of opinions arose between INS Commissioner Meissner, who wanted to proceed with these cases, and the Attorney General, who resisted.[243] Conflicts also arose between the INS, which had the expertise and legal authority to bring the cases, and the FBI, which possessed the classified information but did not always make it available to the INS. Thus cases stagnated or, in some cases, were never brought at all.[244]

A National Security Law Division was established in the INS to try to handle the procedural complexities that soon overwhelmed these terrorist cases. By 1998, a handful of the aliens affiliated with terrorist activity that were known to the INS and the Justice Department were successfully removed by the INS using both traditional immigration law and classified evidence.[245] None was known to be affiliated with al Qaeda.

Immigration Benefits

Terrorists in the 1990s, as well as the September 11 hijackers, needed to find a way to stay in or embed themselves in the United States if their operational plans were to come to fruition. As already discussed, this could be accomplished legally by marrying an American citizen, achieving temporary worker status, or applying for asylum after entering. In many cases, the act of filing for an immigration benefit sufficed to permit the alien to remain in the country until the petition was adjudicated. Terrorists were free to conduct surveillance, coordinate operations, obtain and receive funding, go to school and learn English, make contacts in the United States, acquire necessary materials, and execute an attack.

We thus come to the third significant function of the INS relevant to the September 11 story: immigration benefits. They are a vast system of laws and regulations that control the status both of aliens within the United States and of those outside the United States who wish to come and stay in the country. Every immigration benefit has its own set of rules, regulations, and procedures. Many are complex and time-consuming to adjudicate. Some are so difficult to process that specialists must handle them. The Immigration and Nationality Act, which is in fact a miscellaneous collection of federal laws, is the controlling authority concerning aliens and the benefits available to them.

Before 9/11, immigration benefits allowed tourists, for example, to extend their length of stay or to change their immigration status from tourist to student after arriving in the United States. Visitors who married Americans could petition for legal permanent residency status. Other classes of persons who could ask for a benefit from the INS were aliens seeking permanent legal residency, immigrants wishing to be naturalized, asylum seekers ("asylees"), and refugees.[246] A number of terrorists discussed in chapter 3 abused the asylum system. Commissioner Meissner spent much of her time in the 1990s honing it, creating what was considered a model program that balanced humanitarian and security interests.

But the benefits process overall was vulnerable to fraud and poorly managed. Each of the five immigration benefit service centers had its own computer system. It was therefore not uncommon for one alien to have multiple benefits files, sometimes as a result of a fraudulent attempt to win approval from one office after an application was denied by another. As early as 1991, terrorists exploited this deficiency. Mir Amal Kansi, who in 1993 fatally shot two CIA employees and wounded three others, had already legally entered the United States when he applied for legalization as an illegal alien as part of a class action lawsuit; he falsely claimed that he had entered the United States through Mexico in 1981.[247] Mohamed and Mahmud Abouhalima, conspirators in the 1993 World Trade Center bombing, were granted green cards (i.e., legal permanent resident status) under the Special Agricultural Program (SAW) program.[248] SAW was an amnesty program created under the Immigration Reform and Control Act of 1986.[249] In 1999, the INS general counsel, Paul Virtue, testified before the House Judiciary Subcommittee on Immigration that amnesty programs were "subject to widespread abuse."[250]

In fact, INS benefits adjudicators did not have a recognized counterterrorism role. As the INS struggled, its inability to adjudicate applications quickly or with adequate security checks made it easier for terrorists to wrongfully enter and remain in the United States throughout the 1990s.

The Border Patrol and Illegal Entry into the United States

The INS Border Patrol monitors the 9,500 miles of shared borders with Canada and Mexico that exist between ports of entry.[251] Throughout the 1990s, the priority was to control the vast illegal immigration from Mexico along the Southwest border.[252] About 1.6 million illegal aliens a year were being apprehended from Texas to California.[253] In San Diego alone, there were 2,000–3,000 arrests daily. The Border Patrol clearly lacked the resources to stem the tide. In the early 1990s, they were still using manual typewriters.[254]

Nevertheless, the Border Patrol received the most attention from Congress and Attorney General Reno of any INS section.[255] Congressionally approved budget requests between 1994 and 1998 doubled the number of agents on the Southwest, from 4,000 to 8,000. By 2000, there were 9,000 Border Patrol agents.[256]

Even after the arrests in Washington state of Abu Mezer (who was plotting to blow up the Brooklyn subway) in August 1997 and Ahmed Ressam (the "millennium bomber") in December 1999, the patrol's attention remained on the Southwest border. Neither the Border Patrol, the Commissioner, nor the Justice Department considered revising its strategy to include counterterrorism initiatives. Only the White House, through

Richard Clarke, seemed interested in pursuing a more aggressive strategy on the Northwest border after Ressam's attempted entry.

While Congress and the Clinton administration required the Border Patrol's coverage along the border with Mexico to double to one agent every quarter mile by 1999, the Canadian border had only one agent for every 13.25 miles.[257] Despite examples of terrorists' entering from Canada, awareness of terrorist activity in Canada and its more lenient immigration laws, and an Inspector General's report recommending that the Border Patrol develop a northern border strategy, the only positive step was that the number of Border Patrol agents was not cut any further.[258]

The failure of the Border Patrol to make any significant efforts in counterterrorism was predictable. Because the INS's relationship with the intelligence community was minimal, any valuable information these agencies might have gleaned on migrant flows or alien smuggling did not routinely reach Border Patrol agents. They also lacked access to the terrorist watchlist databases, TIPOFF and NAILS. And lookouts with terrorist watchlist information available at border stations were not routinely used or checked by the patrol.[259]

Another factor hampering any unified counterterrorism effort by the Border Patrol was that it lacked a direct chain of command from its chief, based in Washington, to the field. The chief therefore had no control over the field, as well as limited input on policy and budget within the INS. As agents were rotated and the Border Patrol reacted to the everchanging locations at which aliens attempted to enter the United States illegally, regional directors were in constant competition with each other for human and technical assistance.[260]

State and Local Law Enforcement Support

Both administration regulations and criminal statutes apply to immigration enforcement. The majority of alien offenders are handled through the immigration administrative court system, which consists of judges, attorneys, and immigration detention facilities.[261] Criminal violations are handled by the U.S. Attorney's office and the federal court system.[262] In most cases, an alien committing an administrative violation is at the same time violating federal law. The federal government deports most immigration violators from the United States rather than prosecuting them as criminal defendants.

Many state and local law enforcement agencies worked closely with federal immigration authorities before 9/11. They contacted INS when they arrested aliens on criminal charges and assisted in the investigation, arrest, and detention of illegal aliens. In return, INS special agents, with their specialized training and resources, assisted other law enforcement agencies fighting violent crime and drug trafficking.[263] Their cooperation— and their knowledge of aliens' languages, cultures, and religions—was particularly valuable in ethnic communities. However, these state and local enforcement agencies never had access to terrorist watchlists.

Friction also existed in these relationships. It mainly arose from the INS's inability to respond to all requests for assistance, ambiguity regarding the role of state and local law officers in enforcing immigration regulations, and the discomfort many various immigrant advocacy groups had with local enforcement of immigration law. Despite these difficulties, many police officers continued officially and sometimes unofficially to work with the INS by identifying criminal aliens and turning them over to the INS. Many county officials sought to prevent criminal aliens from returning to the streets, and frequently pressured their congressional representatives to force local INS offices to deport them.

Still, the problem of getting in contact with INS enforcement persisted. While the understaffed INS investigations offices kept bankers' hours, the police operated around the clock and often needed assistance when the INS offices were closed.[264] Many INS investigations offices did not even have a computer link to their state's Criminal Justice Information System, making it was difficult for the police simply to communicate with them.

Recognizing the problem Congress attempted to get the INS to address it. The Law Enforcement Support Center (LESC) evolved out of the 1988 antidrug law that required the INS to maintain a 24/7 hotline to identify individuals arrested as aggravated felons.[265] The initial objective was to assist state and local law enforcement in identifying criminal aliens, to locate and prosecute criminal aliens who had been deported after being convicted of felonies, and to act as a control point for INS arrest warrants. The LESC was not established until 1994.

The center was available to all state and local law enforcement officials who encountered a suspected alien during routine police work.[266] The LESC provided timely information regarding the status and identities of aliens suspected of, arrested for, or convicted of criminal activity, but it offered no specific information on aliens associated with terrorism.[267]

In 1996, a new law enabled the INS to enter into agreements with state and local law enforcement agencies through which the INS would provide training and the local agencies would exercise immigration enforcement authority.[268] Terrorist watchlists would not be made available to them. Such agreements were voluntary, and only Salt Lake City—unsuccessfully—

attempted to take advantage of the law. Moreover, in prior years mayors of cities with large immigrant populations sometimes imposed limits on city employee cooperation with federal immigration agents.[269]

• • •

Prior to September 11, immigration inspectors were focused on facilitating the entry of travelers to the United States. Special agents were focused on criminal aliens and alien smuggling, and those handling immigration benefits were inundated with millions of applications. Thus, on the eve of the 9/11 attacks, the INS found itself in a state of disarray. Although a few offices were attempting to carry out counterterrorism initiatives, their efforts were severely limited by a lack of recognition, both national and local, of the connection between border security and national security. As we will see in chapter 5, the failure to link available information with government action unwittingly facilitated the entry of the September 11 hijackers.

5

PLANNING AND EXECUTING ENTRY FOR THE 9/11 PLOT

5.1. The State Department

Overview

After the 9/11 attacks, as the country struggled to comprehend the enormity of the tragedy, one question was asked over and over: "How did these people get in?" In the search for government officials potentially responsible for failing to prevent the attacks or, worse, enabling them, the spotlight turned on the State Department. The hijackers needed visas to apply for entry to the United States, and it was the State Department that supplied the hijackers with those visas: 15 in Saudi Arabia, 2 in the United Arab Emirates, and 2 in Germany. But for State's actions, critics argued, the 9/11 attacks could not have taken place. When the visa applications of the hijackers were scrutinized, and some were disseminated in the media, State drew fire for approving incomplete applications, particularly for the 15 Saudi hijackers. The department's officials were also criticized for speeding the process of issuing visas and interviewing few if any applicants in Saudi Arabia and the UAE, where 17 of the 19 hijackers acquired their visas. With its reputation as a friend of foreigners, State was an easy target.

Our investigation has determined that some of the criticism leveled against the State Department was warranted. State officials did approve incomplete visa applications and did expedite the issuance of visas, requiring few interviews of Saudi and Emirati applicants during a time of rising extremism in Saudi Arabia and, during the summer of 2001, heightened threat reporting in the Middle East generally. However, the reasons for the State Department's adoption of these visa policies in Saudi Arabia, the UAE, and Germany have never been adequately explained. More specifically, no one has discussed the differences in visa policy between the Jeddah and

Riyadh visa posts in Saudi Arabia, the extent to which individual consular officers in were actually aware of the extremist threat, and the true effect on visa issuance of the ill-named Visa Express Program. We explore these topics in this section.

As noted in the previous chapter, the basis for immigration law applied by the State and Justice Departments before 9/11 was the Immigration and the Nationality Act (INA) and its accompanying regulations. To comply with the portions of these laws regarding visa applications, the Department of State created a form to be completed by all applicants. Form OF-156 consisted of 35 questions covering each applicant's biography, visa and travel history, purpose for visiting the United States, intended destination, means of financial support, and occupation. Applicants were also asked if they fell within certain categories of persons who are inadmissible to the United States, including those afflicted with a communicable disease "of public health significance" and those who "seek to enter the United States to engage in export violations, subversive or terrorist activities, or any unlawful purpose."

Visa Policy in Berlin

September 11 hijacker, ringleader, and pilot Mohamed Atta and his fellow pilot hijacker Ziad Jarrah received their visas in Berlin, Germany, in May 2000.[1] Conspirator Ramzi Binalshibh tried and failed to obtain a visa in Berlin around the same time. German citizens do not need a visa to come to the United States for business or pleasure, because they qualify for the Visa Waiver Program (VWP). All three 9/11 conspirators, however, were so-called third country nationals (TCNs)—that is, persons living in a country other than their own. Thus, because they did not hold passports from another VWP country, they were required to apply for a visa to come to the United States.

With rare exceptions, TCNs applied for a U.S. visa by mail or through a drop box at the embassy in Berlin. In addition to the application, they were required to submit their passport, some proof of residence status from the local German police district where they lived, and documents indicating their source of income. This was more documentation than was typically required of Emirati or Saudi Arabian citizens applying in their home countries, as the discussion of those countries, below, will make clear. The application papers would be reviewed by a State local employee who would categorize them according to their qualifications for a visa.

Consular officers working in Berlin at that time told us that if the papers indicated that the applicant "might be an intending immigrant we would interview that person. Our focus was on stopping intending immigrants."[2] The basic criteria used to screen out intending immigrants centered on the applicant's ties to Germany. In general, all TCNs with "less than 18 months to two years of residence were interviewed," a consular officer told us. If they met this threshold, then the consular officer would look to additional factors—including nationality, family, job, and school status—to see whether applicants presented a good visa risk.[3] These criteria were not put in writing but rather were conveyed to officers orally in training when they arrived at the Berlin post to perform consular work.

Individuals who clearly demonstrated they were qualified for a visa were put into a "routine processing" pile. Applicants who clearly did not qualify were put into a "high-risk" pile.[4] The Consular Lookout and Support System (CLASS)—State's automated lookout and watchlist system—was checked early in the process as part of the data input for each applicant, and any derogatory information was taken into account.[5] For example, a prior refusal for a visa would "kick someone out instantly."[6]

Applicants in the high-risk pile were sent a letter alerting them of the need to schedule an interview. If the interview confirmed the officer's initial suspicion, then they were denied a visa, and that denial was recorded in the CLASS system. Applications considered routine were processed in a number of ways. As a consular officer described it to us, if the application was strong—that is, if the applicant had submitted all the necessary paperwork and had overcome the presumption of being an intending immigrant—then he or she was issued a visa. If, however, the application was in some way incomplete, consular staff would do one of two things. Sometimes, they would call up the applicant to get the missing data.[7] In other cases, when they believed the applicant had not yet met the INA's statutory burdens, they would send the applicant a letter stating that the application had been denied under INA section 221(g) and inviting the submission of additional supporting information.

A consular officer we interviewed told us that by putting the ball back into the court of the visa applicant, they reduced their workload. They described the technique as a "quasirefusal in order to avoid interviewing" some visa applicants.[8] An applicant who wanted to continue the visa application had one year within which to submit additional documentation and seek an interview. If this supplemental material succeeded in persuading the officer that the original 221(g) denial was in error, then this denial could be "overcome" and a visa issued.

If, on the other hand, the applicant's interview failed to demonstrate to the officer that he or she qualified for a visa, then the applicant could be denied a visa as an intending immigrant under INA section 214(b), a denial with far greater significance. Although such a denial could be overcome, its presence in an applicant's electronic records made consular officers adjudicating future applications regard them more closely. A denial under the more general 221(g) did not carry the same weight, since it could be based merely on an applicant's failure to submit necessary paperwork. Because of the way they used 221(g)—as a delaying tactic when applications were questionable—Berlin consular officials considered it "one case" when an applicant applied, received an initial denial on 221(g) grounds, and then pursued his or her application through to an interview followed by a denial under 214(b).

Citizens of countries that were relatively advanced economically stood a better chance of obtaining a visa. Conversely, applicants whose home countries were more impoverished were more likely to be seen as potential economic immigrants to the United States. In this respect, Berlin visa policy toward third country nationals mirrored the policy toward citizens of those countries in their own countries.[9]

But TCNs who were long-term German residents were basically treated like German citizens. As participants in the Visa Waiver Program, German citizens did not fill out visa applications or apply for visas to travel to the United States. All they needed was a passport. Berlin considered third country nationals who were successful students in Germany to be good visa risks.[10] Their view was that German was a difficult language and matriculation in a German university was a major accomplishment, both factors that provided TCNs with an incentive to return to Germany.[11]

Visa Policy in the United Arab Emirates

Two of the 9/11 hijackers—Marwan al Shehhi, the pilot of United Airlines 175, and Fayez Banihammad, a hijacker on the same flight—acquired their visas in the United Arab Emirates.

Beyond the visa law contained in the INA and Department of State regulations, visa policy in the UAE was not codified in writing; rather, it was conveyed to incoming consular officers by their colleagues and supervisor.[12] Like their colleagues serving in other posts around the world, consular officers in the UAE were not trained to use the visa application to screen for terrorists or to conduct visa application interviews to discover terrorists. They were also not familiar with al Qaeda.[13]

There had never been a terrorist attack in the UAE, nor had any UAE national been a terrorist before 9/11, one consular officer told us.[14] Consequently, consular officials did not consider UAE nationals to be security risks before 9/11, although there were some concerns with their passport issuance regime.[15] UAE passports, while of "excellent quality," often contained inaccurate information.[16] For example, the year of birth often reflected the person's vanity rather than reality, and before 1970 births in the country were not recorded. In addition, people were issued UAE passports that falsely listed the UAE as their birthplace.[17] Passports also were issued through patronage from tribal sheikhs.[18]

Nevertheless, UAE nationals generally enjoyed a high standard of living and were not considered likely economic immigrants. One consular officer told us that Emiratis were considered "low-risk applicants who had lots of money, left the UAE to escape the summers, and were Western-oriented [people] who simply wanted to visit the U.S. There was little fear of Emiratis overstaying their visits."[19] Emirati nationals had "an incredibly low refusal rate."[20] Indeed, before 9/11, consular officials in the UAE had tried on at least two occasions to have the UAE included in the Visa Waiver Program, pointing to the applicants' strong economic status and low refusal rate. Officials believed the only reason these attempts failed was that the UAE was unwilling to reciprocate and allow Americans to enter it without a visa, one of the program's requirements.[21] The INS provided no negative feedback about Emiratis from encounters with them at ports of entry.[22] State thus considered the UAE a de facto visa waiver country, and concentrated on facilitating the issuance of visas to them.[23]

One result of this attitude was a very low interview rate before 9/11. One consular officer observed, "I would guess that about 95 percent of the Emiratis . . . were not interviewed"; they were "almost never interviewed unless we got a 'hit' on the CLASS lookout system indicating derogatory information about the applicant."[24] Said another, "Virtually all UAE nationals were the beneficiaries of personal appearance waivers."[25] This officer, who served in the consular section for more than a year before 9/11, told us that they "did not do one interview of an Emirati during my time."[26] UAE nationals submitted their applications through a travel agency referral program akin to Saudi Arabia's Visa Express Program (discussed below) or through a drop box at the embassy. Their applications were almost always approved.[27]

Another result was consular officers' lack of interest in carefully scrutinizing all aspects of the visa application. In the view of a number of officers, questions regarding occupation, financial support, address in the United States, and purpose of visit "shed little light on the applicant's intentions," and were "not important" because "the UAE looks after the financial needs of its nationals."[28]

Visa Policy in Saudi Arabia

This place really is Wonderland.

—Tom Furey,
consul general in Riyadh, Saudi Arabia,
June 2001

Fifteen of the 9/11 hijackers acquired their visas in Saudi Arabia at either the U.S. consulate in Jeddah or the U.S. embassy in Riyadh, the only two visa-issuing posts in Saudi Arabia. Because visa policy in Saudi Arabia has been the focus of much controversy and criticism since the 9/11 attacks, we explore it as some length. Though visa policy in Saudi Arabia is in many ways similar to that in other Persian Gulf countries, including the UAE, Saudi policy and practices also exhibit some unique aspects.

Visa policy in Saudi Arabia derived from several sources. The law—the INA and its accompanying regulations—applied in every foreign post. In addition, each country's policy was shaped by larger U.S. foreign policy interests. One high-ranking U.S. diplomat who served in Riyadh described the U.S-Saudi relationship as having "very deep roots; it was a close relationship rooted in common interests." Pertinent facts included Saudi Arabia's status as the world's largest oil producer and the largest market for U.S. goods and services in the Middle East, as well as the U.S. and Saudi interest in a stable Middle East.[29]

These common interests resulted in what one senior consular official serving in Saudi Arabia described as "a culture in our mission in Saudi Arabia to be as accommodating as we possibly could."[30] Another explained that the "liberal visa policy" supported U.S. policy goals, such as encouraging good relations with wealthy future leaders of Saudi Arabia.[31] When we asked consular officials whether they felt pressure from their superiors or others to issue visas, they answered that pressure was applied from several sources, including the U.S. ambassador, Saudi government officials or businesspeople, and members of the U.S. Congress.[32] Some officials told us, however, that this pressure was no different from what they experienced at other posts and did not affect them.

Visa applicants in Saudi Arabia fell into two distinct groups who applied in roughly equal numbers: Saudi citizens and third country nationals.[33] Because the socioeconomic profiles of these groups were perceived differently by State consular personnel, visa policies for the groups differed.[34] Although none of the September 11 hijackers were third country nationals, the TCN policy is relevant for understanding visa policy applied to Saudi citizens.

Third Country Nationals. TCN visa applicants were considered a high risk of becoming intending immigrants. Prior to June 2001, they were generally required to apply for their visas in person, and about 75 percent were interviewed.[35] Indeed, consular officials we interviewed uniformly said that they interviewed most TCN nonimmigrant visa applicants, who sought to come to the United States for pleasure, business, or school. Officers said this policy was due to TCNs' low social and economic status in Saudi Arabia.[36] TCN applicants were often servants of Saudi citizens—maids, butlers, or "tea boys" whom the Saudis sought to bring with them to the United States.[37] Much of the work in Saudi Arabia was performed by third country nationals brought to Saudi Arabia specifically for that purpose, who needed a Saudi sponsor to enter or leave the country.[38] If TCNs did not present letters from their Saudi employer in support of their application, then they were, in the words of a consular officer, a "clear refusal."[39] Consular officials also requested that TCNs supply proof of ties to their home country, bank statements, and clear evidence of their intended destination in the United States.[40] Consular officials described attempts by Saudi citizens to help their servants acquire visas in order to aid their illegal immigration to the United States.[41]

In fact, some of the most egregious examples of consular officials being pressured to issue visas concerned the applications of TCNs who were servants of the Saudi royal family or of Saudi diplomats. In one case, U.S. Ambassador Wyche Fowler ordered a consular officer to issue a visa to a diplomat's servant even though the diplomat refused to provide proof he was paying his servants minimum wage as required by U.S. law. The diplomat was "a Saudi . . . a Saudi!" Fowler said, adding, "they never pay them what they say anyway."[42] In a more serious incident, Fowler, frustrated with the consul general's insistence that servants of the Saudi royal family come in for visa interviews, ordered him to leave Saudi Arabia within 24 hours. Fowler then gave him a poor performance rating, on the grounds that he was not cooperating with embassy policies.[43] The consul general apparently retired to avoid having the negative performance rating made a permanent part of his record.[44]

Generally, TCNs would apply for a U.S. visa using a passport from their birth country; but during the 1990s, evidence of fraud by TCNs in the visa process grew. Non-Saudis who are not employed have no lawful permanent residence status in the Kingdom, and the Saudi government's stated policy was to replace foreign workers with Saudi nationals.[45] In addition, the government began a campaign in 1997 to expel millions of illegal aliens living within its borders.[46] As a result, TCNs began fraudulently applying for U.S. nonimmigrant visas to avoid being sent back to their countries of origin. According to memos and cables prepared by consular officers in the year 2000,

> Some Saudi businessmen have provided assistance to illegal employees in the form of false employment letters or even passports. Saudi VIPs have included unqualified TCNs in their entourage when applying for visas. *Fraudulent Saudi passports have become a concern.* Saudi Arabia issues Saudi travel documents to non-citizens with the only difference being an Arabic notation on page six of the passport. *In addition, it appears that Saudi citizens have sold their passports containing valid NIVs [nonimmigrant visas].* Several have been detected being used as far afield as Mali. Both Jeddah and Riyadh have detected photo-substituted Saudi passports being submitted by TCNs with NIV applications.[47]

When a TCN was detected using a Saudi passport, one consular official said, "we'd cull those out" and give them greater scrutiny.[48]

These cases in which TCNs were involved in passport and visa fraud demonstrated that the TCNs were significant risks for becoming intending immigrants. However, more systematic attempts by consular officials to investigate whether a representative sample of TCN visitor visa applicants stayed in compliance and returned to Saudi Arabia were unsuccessful, "since most employers did not cooperate with consulate survey efforts."[49] One official described an "informal tickler system, though, especially for servants of Saudis," to make sure they did, in fact, return as their visas required.[50]

Evidence that we reviewed suggests that the concerns expressed above about the fraudulent use of Saudi passports did not significantly influence visa policy as it applied to Saudi citizens.

Saudi Citizens. Prior to September 11, 2001, it was State Department policy that Saudi citizens, *as a group*, had overcome the presumption under section 214(b) of the INA that every alien is to be considered an immigrant "until he establishes to the satisfaction of the consular officer, at the time of application for a visa ... that he is entitled to nonimmigrant status."[51] This presumption applied to any concern that Saudi citizens were at risk of becoming *economic* immigrants to the United States. One consular officer who issued a visa to a 9/11 hijacker said, "It was factual, as far as our statistics showed, that they just weren't economic immigrants, they went, they spent a lot of money, they went on their vacations, they loved to go to Florida and then they came back."[52]

Consular officers were not given written guidance that the 214(b) presumption had been overcome,[53] although the policy was recognized in written materials about consular work produced in Saudi Arabia before September 11.[54] Consular officers in Saudi Arabia were advised of this policy orally when they arrived at the post.[55] They were told that Saudi Arabia met the criteria for inclusion in the Visa Waiver Program because of its citizens' low visa refusal rates and that the country had applied for inclusion in the program. But, like the UAE, the Saudis refused to reciprocate and allow U.S. citizens to travel to Saudi Arabia without a visa.[56] Thus, although Saudi Arabia was not technically a part of the VWP, consular officers were told it was unwritten State Department policy to consider Saudi Arabia a "virtual visa waiver" country.[57]

This virtual visa waiver policy led to a number of outcomes. First, since most Saudi applicants were presumed to be eligible for a visa, consular officers did not generally demand that they fully complete their visa application forms.[58] Second, unlike applicants from Middle Eastern countries who applied in Germany, Saudis generally were not required to present supporting documentation such as proof of financial means, proof of academic standing, or proof of home address. Third, most Saudi citizens were not required to appear for a personal interview.

According to one high-ranking consular official in Riyadh, the State Department's Bureau of Consular Affairs (CA) and the Visa Office leadership within CA were well aware of this policy and tacitly agreed that personal appearances generally could be waived for Saudi citizens.[59] As discussed earlier, consular officers relied on a check of the TIPOFF terrorist watchlist to prevent terrorists from obtaining visas. Thus, under this policy, a Saudi citizen who was a terrorist not included in the TIPOFF watchlist stood a very good chance of acquiring a U.S. visa without ever having a face-to-face encounter with a U.S. consular official and without presenting a fully completed visa application or any supporting documentation.

Implicit within the policy decision to consider Saudi Arabia a virtual visa waiver country was an assumption that Saudi citizens were not security risks. Inclusion in the *actual* Visa Waiver Program before 9/11 required that both the State and Justice department weigh not only visa overstay and refusal rates but also the security risks posed by citizens of the particular country being considered for inclusion in the program. By treating Saudi Arabia as if it were in the Visa Waiver Program, State arguably had arrogated to itself that portion of the visa waiver calculation. And even before 9/11, evidence was accumulating that this assumption was in error. The CIA had analyzed and reported on Saudi Arabia's Islamic awakening as early as 1993.[60]

Beyond this judgment that Saudis were not security risks was a determination that they were not economic risks either. INS records show little evidence that Saudi citizens overstayed their visas or tried to work illegally in the United States. For example, out of a total of 1,387,486 deportable aliens located by the INS in fiscal year 2001, only 36 were Saudi nationals.[61] Nevertheless, there were significant signs of economic stagnation in Saudi Arabia before September 11, 2001. As early as 1991, consular officers noted that "while many Saudis are well off[,] . . . a surprising number of the younger generation [are] scraping by on incomes which cannot support the large families and high prices typical of Riyadh."[62] Indeed, studies indicate that Saudi per capita income peaked at $16,700 in 1981 (when U.S. per capita income was $13,960), and had dropped to around $8,000 by 2000.[63] Furthermore, the Saudis had a "youth bulge," with a significant percentage of their population under 30 years of age and unemployed.[64]

Consular officers who adjudicated the visas of the 9/11 hijackers said they were aware of these strains. One testified that there was a growing concern about Saudis "because, with the economic problems of Saudi Arabia and the population explosion, you've got the potential . . . that . . . people . . . might not, you know, want to stay in Saudi Arabia. . . . We realized that Saudi Arabia has big economic problems, it's getting worse, because they've got an unbelievable population growth. And so, therefore, we need to keep that in mind as we're looking at Saudi applicants."[65]

Nevertheless, most consular officials in Saudi Arabia did not regard unemployment as an impediment to getting a visa, since "they have a terrible unemployment problem in Saudi Arabia, and a lot of people have money but they don't have jobs."[66] At other posts, an applicant's lack of employment would have been significant; but according to consular officials in Saudi Arabia, there it was not, because Saudis were not actually looking for jobs. Said one consular officer, "It's their choice to be unemployed."[67] Another was more blunt: "The Saudis do not work."[68] Though this viewpoint was widespread it was not universal. One consular officer in Saudi Arabia before September 11, concerned about issuing visas to people with no apparent economic prospects, recalled, "We were issuing visas to people who, if you just covered the 'nationality' block on the application form with your thumb, we would deny in any other country."[69]

Saudis were not completely excused from visa interviews. Formal communications between the Riyadh embassy and the Department of State described the policy as one of "interview by exception."[70] This term was borrowed from the title of a cable in the *Consular Best Practices Handbook*, which urged visa-issuing posts to calibrate visa policy so as to interview only those applicants who truly needed to be interviewed.[71]

In general, "interview by exception" meant that Saudi citizens were interviewed only if their applications contained something out of the ordinary or an indication of visa ineligibility, such as an applicant failing to include the necessary INS form (I-20) to support a request for a student visa. An interview might also be triggered by an applicant indicating a desire to stay beyond the ordinary six-month period authorized by the INS for tourists, or, as in one instance described to the Commission, an applicant stating on his application that the purpose of his visit was "terrorism" when he meant "tourism."[72] In the specifics of this approach, there were some significant differences between the two visa-issuing posts, Riyadh and Jeddah.

The Difference between Jeddah and Riyadh. Our investigation has revealed a lack of uniformity in Saudi interview policy. It changed over time according to personnel changes at Jeddah and Riyadh, security threats to the embassy and consulate, and difference in consular management. We also found that some consular officers serving in Jeddah believed before 9/11 that Saudi citizens posed potential security risks to the United States and that they therefore more carefully scrutinized Saudi visa applicants.

Despite the disparities in the accounts of consular officers, there is strong evidence that for several years prior to September 11 a more aggressive policy of interviewing visa applicants was in place at the consulate in Jeddah than at the embassy in Riyadh. Many pilgrims arrived and passed through Jeddah, sometimes called "Gateway to the Hajj," on their way to the Muslim holy sites; a rich assortment of individuals entered the consulate, some of whom applied for visas. Partly for these reasons, consular officers serving in Jeddah were particularly sensitized to the possibility that Saudis could be security threats to the United States. This sensitivity in turn led to a policy— more or less in evidence at various times—under which Jeddah consular officers were "tougher" than those in Riyadh on Saudi applicants.[73]

A consular officer who served in Jeddah in 1996 estimated that they interviewed 50–60 percent of Saudi visa applicants.[74] A consular officer in Jeddah two years later told us that they interviewed "a majority" of male Saudi visa applicants between the ages of 16 and 40. When we asked why, the latter officer said that they knew who Usama Bin Ladin was, they knew that he was dangerous, and they were concerned about the possibility that

Saudi visa applicants might be intending to go to the United States to participate in terrorist attacks.[75] When we asked this consular officer if State Department personnel in Saudi Arabia lacked any reason to believe that Saudi citizens were security threats to the United States, he responded, "That's absurd; that's patently ridiculous."[76] He pointed out that the U.S. embassies in East Africa had been attacked days before his arrival in Jeddah. Security concerns were high.[77]

Their practice, according to this officer, was to look for potential extremists: Saudi applicants who had long beards, a short robe, or other indicators of fundamentalism and fundamentalist Muslim clerics who were seeking a visa to chant the Qur'an in a U.S. mosque around the time of Ramadan would receive greater scrutiny. In addition, even an applicant who did not look like an extremist who was from a location known to have produced extremists, such as al Qassim Province, "and he doesn't have a good explanation, and he wants to go to the U.S. for an extended stay, that person didn't get a visa."[78] Though these individuals would be denied visas for security reasons, the officer told us he would use 214(b)[79]—that is, the section of the INA that states, "Every alien . . . shall be presumed to be an immigrant until he establishes to the satisfaction of the consular officer, at the time of application for a visa, and the immigration officers, at the time of application for admission, that he is entitled to a nonimmigrant status[.]"

Another officer corroborated the existence of an interview policy in Jeddah in 1998 that focused on potential Muslim extremists. He said it was instituted "in about August 1998, a month after I arrived," and described the policy somewhat differently. He said they would interview 100 percent of Saudi citizens who were first-time student visa applicants, 80 percent of all students, and 5 percent of all other Saudi applicants.[80]

By contrast, officers in Riyadh at that time seem not to have displayed the same level of concern about Saudi visa applicants posing a potential security risk. As discussed earlier, Saudis were generally seen as good visa risks, exempt from the presumption of intending immigrants under INA section 214(b). Riyadh consular officers, including those who issued visas to the September 11 hijackers, said that they reviewed the visa applications of Saudi citizens and interviewed them "if something was unusual or indicated that we had a concern,"[81] such as an applicant answering "yes" rather than "no" to one of the ineligibilities on the visa form.[82] Another officer said they would interview the applicant if the application "looked odd" or "funny," or the applicant "hadn't been clear about where he was going."[83]

Although officers in both posts appear to have scrupulously used the State Department's CLASS name-check system to screen visa applicants for any connections to terrorism, the evidence suggests that consular officers in Riyadh apparently did not pursue potential terrorists beyond that system as assiduously as did the officers in Jeddah. Their approach may have contributed to the creation of the Visa Express Program, discussed below.

The 1998 interview policy in Jeddah apparently continued, though somewhat less aggressively, into the early fall of 2000. According to one officer, whom we will call "Tom," when he arrived in August 2000 they were interviewing a significant percentage of Saudi citizen visa applicants and all first-time students.[84] "Tom" told us that they were suspicious of Saudi citizens who were from locations where they knew extremists lived and who had only a vague notion of where they were headed in the United States.[85] They further believed that previous assumptions about the eligibility of Saudis for visas needed to be rethought because of the downturn in the Saudi economy.[86] For these reasons, this officer who processed visa applications on a part-time basis in Jeddah turned down a significant percentage of Saudi visa applicants as well as third country applicants.[87]

The other consular officer at Jeddah during this time period, whom we will call "Steve," took a different approach to adjudicating visa applicants. "Steve"—who worked full-time and processed most of the approximately 30,000 applications handled in Jeddah every year—told us he was "never really afraid of Saudis." Moreover, they never made the connection between the known presence of al Qaeda members in Saudi Arabia and the possibility that the Saudis applying for visas were terrorists.[88] "Steve" sought to adhere to the "tougher" Jeddah visa policy, and he interviewed all first-time student visa applicants.[89] However, he believed that "Tom"—whose approach led to large numbers of rejections—was denying Saudi applicants "for the wrong reasons."[90]

Documents supplied to us by the State Department corroborate "Tom's" contention that his refusal rate for Saudi citizens was higher than "Steve's" while they served together in Jeddah.[91] Apparently because, as "Steve" put it, some of "Tom's" denials to visa applicants were made "for the wrong reasons," "Tom" was rebuked by the Consul General in Jeddah for denying too many Saudi visa applicants.[92] "Tom" and his supervisor told us that notwithstanding this criticism, "Tom" did not alter his approach to visa adjudication during his time in Jeddah, and that his approach was "validated" by the events of September 11.[93] "Steve" issued visas to 11 of the 9/11 hijackers.

This disagreement between consular officers in Jeddah reflected a disagreement we observed in a number of locations about the proper use of INA section 214(b)—the intending immigrant provision. "Tom"—and other consular officers stationed in Jeddah whose views were discussed earlier—believed that suspicions about an applicant that caused the officer to view the individual as a security concern were sufficient under INA section 214(b) to deny him or her a visa. "Steve" and others, in contrast, were uncomfortable with this approach and believed it was inconsistent with the proper interpretation of INA section 214(b). This lack of clarity about the proper interpretation of section 214(b) was noted as well by the General Accounting Office in their study of visa issuance to the 9/11 hijackers.[94]

Thus, although Saudi visa policy before 9/11 was that Saudi citizens as a group had overcome the presumption of Section 214(b) that all visa applicants they were *economic* immigrants, some consular officers in Jeddah nevertheless sought to give Saudi citizens greater scrutiny because of *security* concerns, which arose from their knowledge of extremist activity in Saudi Arabia and the connections between Saudi citizens and the al Qaeda terrorist organization.

Such was the situation when Thomas Furey arrived in late 2000 to take over management of all consular functions in Saudi Arabia as Consul General in Riyadh. As will become clear, the opinions of consular officers who were concerned about Saudi citizens as terrorists did not reach Furey's ears before the 9/11 attacks.

Visa Express. When Thomas Furey became the Consul General on September 11, 2000, his initial impressions were that the Riyadh visa operation was "chaotic"[95] and "dysfunctional."[96] Morale was low. Because visa applications were increasing by about 5 percent per year, consular officers were overworked, often processing applications until 8 P.M. The waiting room could not hold the masses of applicants who came each day; sometimes there were fistfights between Saudi citizens and third country nationals.[97] Meanwhile, large crowds caused problems for the Saudi and U.S. guards both inside and outside the embassy compound.

A consular officer serving in Riyadh at that time agreed with Furey's general observations, describing the atmosphere as "total chaos, which you cannot imagine."[98] "The crowds were unbelievable," he said.[99] The consular operation in Jeddah was similarly overworked. One officer and one part-time officer received about 30,000 visa applications a year. During the busy summer season, the section routinely processed 450 applicants every day.[100]

At the same time that Furey made these observations about the state of visa processing in Riyadh, he also came to several other conclusions based on his discussions with other embassy personnel:

- Saudis, and all other citizens of the countries who form the Gulf Cooperation Council, had overcome the presumption of INA section 214(b) because they did not overstay their visas, did not work in the United States, were not deported by the INS, and did not commit crimes in the United States.[101]
- Saudis often did not submit their applications in person.
- Saudis had a very low interview rate.
- Saudis had a very low refusal rate (below 2 percent).
- There were many security threats to the embassy and consulates in Saudi Arabia.
- Saudis were not security risks.[102]

Furey was adamant in his interview with the Commission that he did not think Saudis were security risks when he arrived in Riyadh, or at any time before 9/11.[103] It is difficult to understand how the strong views of consular officers in Jeddah about the security risk posed by Saudi citizens—views informed by growing intelligence supporting their outlook and by commonsense conclusions from recent events, such as the East Africa bombings—could apparently be unknown to the most senior State Department official making visa policy in Saudi Arabia. A number of factors seem to have been at work.

First, Consul General Furey believed, as did Assistant Secretary of State for Consular Affairs Mary Ryan, that if there was intelligence information he needed to know about possible terrorism threats, he would have received it. However, he apparently did not receive any such information from either intelligence or consular officials. Furey told the Commission that had he been told Saudis were a security risk—something he said he learned on September 11, 2001—he would not have established the Visa Express Program. Second, Furey, like most others in the State Department, apparently believed that border security should be addressed primarily through improved automated consular systems and reliance on the TIPOFF terrorist watchlist. And third, Furey seems not to have solicited the views of his consular staff on this topic.

Before serving in Riyadh, Furey had been Ministerial Counselor for Consular Affairs (1997–2000). In Mexico City, Furey supervised the largest consular operation in the world: 150 consular officers and 350 Foreign Service nationals, or local staff, handling 2 million nonimmigrant visa applications in 2000.

Furey discussed the problems he observed in Riyadh with officials in the Bureau of Consular Affairs in Washington. His superiors made clear to him that his troubles did not justify having more consular officers; rather, the difficulties were caused by a lack of efficiency.[104] Furey, determined to address the problems he was observing, consulted with embassy staff and his predecessor in the Riyadh post. He also turned to the *Consular Best Practices Handbook* for guidance.[105] In seeking ways to improve visa processing in Saudi Arabia, Furey drew heavily on the "mandate" contained in cable number 6 of the handbook to use "waiver of personal appearance programs, drop boxes and prescreening approaches to cut down on the number of applicants who have a full interview."[106]

As an initial matter, Furey sought to set up an appointment system for Saudi visa applicants as directed by cable 10.[107] Unfortunately, Furey said, the appointment system outlined there relied on a "900 number"—a fee-for-service phone reservation system—whose use was illegal in Saudi Arabia. Furey examined the possibility of accepting visa applications through the Saudi postal system, but learned that it was considered too unreliable for transporting passports.[108]

Furey then pursued the recommendation in cable 7 of the *Best Practices Handbook*: "Drop Box and Personal Appearance Waiver (PAW) Programs." This cable addressed the core advice of handbook—reducing resources consumed by reducing the number of interviews: "Elimination of the personal interview clearly saves time and resources and spares applicants the inconvenience of appearing in person."[109] Although the cable refers to a "drop box," the term is clearly used loosely. For example, two approved forms of "drop boxes" discussed were "mail-in applications" and "third-party screening," which included travel agency referral of visa applications.[110]

First, in the fall of 2000 Furey installed a literal drop box on the Riyadh embassy wall through which people could submit their visa applications. This alone could not address all the inefficiencies associated with visa adjudication in Saudi Arabia. For example, information still had to be entered into a computer by consular personnel after the applications and passports were dropped off at the embassy.[111]

Furey then worked to develop a program combining several "best practices." He combined a form of drop box with the personal appearance waiver for certain classes of applicants, third-party screening by travel agencies who would receive the applications, "interviews by exception," remote data entry, and off-site fee collections.[112]

The concept was simple. Instead of going to the U.S. consulate to apply for a U.S. visa, the person would fill out an application at one of ten approved travel agencies. The travel agency would collect the application, the visa application fee, and the applicant's passport and deliver these documents to the embassy in Riyadh or to the consulate in Jeddah; it would then pick up the package of documents on the following day. If the application was approved, the agency would be responsible for returning the passport, now containing a visa, to the applicant. If the consular officials determined that an interview was necessary, the travel agency would be responsible for providing the applicant with a letter of notification from the consular section. Applicants were rejected only after an in-person interview.

The consular officers developing Visa Express solicited proposals from more than 20 travel agencies seeking to participate in the program.[113] Consular officials screened them in ten major categories, including experience, computer capability, commitment to advertising, office security, geographic breadth of branch networks, and general reputation nationally or regionally.[114] According to the official overseeing the program's development, the prospective participants were vetted by "all elements of the embassy."[115] The agencies selected signed memoranda of understanding with the U.S. government.[116] Once the ten agencies were chosen, consular officials spent seven months developing and implementing a training program for them.[117] Visa Express was mandated to begin Kingdom-wide on June 1, 2001, for all Saudis and for TCNs who had previously traveled to the United States.

The cable heralding its arrival described why this program was adopted in Saudi Arabia:

> Embassy Riyadh, in coordination with consulates general in Jeddah and Dahran, has launched a new, mandatory service for processing nonimmigrant visas. Naming the new program "U.S. Visa Express," Embassy Riyadh established the service to reduce the number of public visitors entering the posts. The program draws on CA Best Practices—travel agencies as NIV reception agents, remote data entry, and interview by exception. As a result, the workload on the consular sections' staff has been made manageable, customer service to NIV applicants has improved, and general post security has improved. The program has transformed the U.S. consular scene throughout Saudi Arabia.[118]

The cable makes clear that security concerns played a significant role in the creation of the Visa Express Program. However, these concerns were connected not to Saudi citizens with terrorist ties. but to the physical security of posts in Saudi Arabia and the Middle East generally. Nor were they entirely new. The drive to alter visa policy had grown significantly following the embassy bombings in Kenya and Tanzania in August 1998.[119]

As we mentioned in chapter 4, after the 1998 embassy attacks, Accountability Review Boards were established by Secretary of State Madeleine Albright to examine the facts and circumstances surrounding the bombings.[120] One of their recommendations was that the Department of State should increase the number of posts with full-time regional security officers (RSOs), who should be trained in "terrorist methods of operation" and provided "with the ability to examine their areas of responsibility from the offensive point of view, to look for vulnerabilities as seen through the eyes of the attacker."[121]

From August 2000 through the summer of 2001, the RSO in Riyadh looked at the embassy and saw the large crowds congregating outside and inside as a security threat. He was "very much in favor of ideas to minimize people coming into the embassy unnecessarily." One RSO in Riyadh during this time told the Commission that "people were very sensitive to the fact that we were the most targeted embassy on Earth." During the height of the travel season, as 800 people a day came into the embassy in Riyadh to apply for visas. When Furey suggested there might be a way to significantly lower this number through the Visa Express Program, the RSO said he "jump[ed] at the opportunity to lower it to 50 [a day]."[122]

On June 26, 2001, Furey wrote to Mary Ryan touting the security virtues of the program:

> The number of people on the street and coming through the gates should be only 15 percent of what it was last summer. The RSO is happy, the guard force is happy, the public loves the service (no more long lines and they can go to the travel agencies in the evening and not take time off from work), we love it (no more crowd control stress and reduced work for the FSNs) and now this afternoon [we] discovered the most amazing thing—the Saudi Government loves it.[123]

Thus, in late June 2001, when intelligence indicated that al Qaeda was planning a major attack against U.S. interests in the near future, the Visa Express Program in Saudi Arabia was expanded to include all applicants in Saudi Arabia.[124]

This extension generated some controversy in Jeddah. The consular officer processing most applications believed it created havoc with the visa workflow in the busy summer months of 2001.[125] It also established uniform procedures in the two visa issuing posts. In so doing, the program largely ended the differences in visa and interview policy between Jeddah and Riyadh.[126]

At the same time, Visa Express eliminated an important aspect of visa work that had existed before its creation: the ability of consular officers and staff to eyeball visa applicants when they presented their applications. It also became impossible for the consular officer to select an individual for an interview on the basis of some concern—including one related to security—without drawing attention to the decision. In other words, the Visa Express Program removed the element of surprise from visa interviews. Whereas previously a consular officer could decide to interview an applicant for any reason, or—as one said they sometimes did—for no reason, after the program's implementation, the consular officer was required to send formal notice to the applicant via a travel agency that an interview was requested.[127]

Visa Express required those making visa decisions to rely heavily on paper. One consular officer in Jeddah in the summer of 2001 worried that the program created a built-in bias to issue a visa to an applicant whose documents looked good and even to someone whose application was borderline.[128] He worried that applying this program, with its over reliance on the paper application, to third country nationals—as was mandated in late June 2001—would allow someone who should be denied a visa under 214(b), the intending immigrant provision, to slip through.[129]

Although Visa Express did lessen the intelligence that might be gleaned from the physical presence of particular applicants in the embassy or consulate, Saudi citizens often did not submit their applications in person even before the program began. The precise percentage who formerly submitted their applications via third parties before the implementation of Visa Express cannot be determined, because the State Department did not collect the relevant data. Consul General Furey said he believed that a "majority" of Saudis submitted their applications through third parties before Visa Express.[130] A consular officer in Jeddah believed that a "significant percentage" of Saudis did not submit their applications in person.[131] This officer also pointed out that some groups had expediters who worked for them. For example, one individual routinely came into the Jeddah consulate to expedite visas for all members of the air crews of Saudi Arabian Airlines. In addition, "all 15,000" members of the Saudi royal family used a designated expediter.[132]

Officials involved in adjudicating visas in Saudi Arabia during and after the implementation of Visa Express have stated emphatically that the program did not change the frequency with which people were interviewed or the approval rates of Saudi applicants.[133] One officer in Riyadh stated that they interviewed "the same people that we were looking at before."[134] The General Accounting Office similarly concluded that the Visa Express Program "did not affect the likelihood that Saudi applicants would be interviewed."[135] Others, however, including one officer who served in Jeddah and who saw Saudi citizens as potential security threats, told the Commission that drop box programs were a "bad idea" because they removed most Saudi visa applicants from the view of consular officers evaluating their cases.

We have not found any evidence that the Visa Express program increased the approval rates for either Saudi or TCN visa applicants in Saudi Arabia between June 2001 and September 11, 2001. In general, it lengthened by at least one day the time needed to process visa applications.[136]

While Visa Express may not changed the quantity or quality of the interviews conducted in Riyadh, the same was not true in Jeddah. Specifically, it eliminated the program to interview first-time student visa applicants; more generally, the Jeddah consulate's more aggressive interview policy came to an end.

Four of the 9/11 hijackers were issued their visas in June 2001, during the Visa Express program, and all applied in Jeddah: Saeed al Ghamdi, Khalid al Mihdhar, Abdul Aziz al Omari, and Salem al Hazmi. In addition, 9/11 mastermind Khalid Sheikh Mohammed acquired a visa in Jeddah in July 2001 using an alias.

Armed with their visas, all that stood between the hijackers and the United States was an immigration inspection.

5.2 The Immigration and Naturalization Service

Overview

A review of the entries and immigration benefits sought by the hijackers paints a picture of conspirators who put the ability to exploit U.S. border security while not raising suspicion about their terrorist activities high on their operational priorities. Evidence indicates that Mohamed Atta, the September 11 ringleader, was acutely aware of his immigration status, tried to remain in the United States legally, and aggressively pursued enhanced immigration status for himself and others.

Despite their careful efforts to understand and operate within the legal requirements, however, the hijackers were not always "clean and legal." For example, they utilized fraudulent documents and alias names as necessary. And when the hijackers could, they skirted the requirements of immigration law. Ziad Jarrah, for example, failed to apply to change his immigration status from tourist to student, and Satam al Suqami failed to leave the country when his length of stay expired. They thus were vulnerable to exclusion at ports of entry and susceptible to immigration law enforcement action. In this section, we explore how the hijackers succeeded in making it through U.S. airports of entry in 33 of 34 attempts, drawing on interviews of the immigration and customs inspectors who had contact with the hijackers, immigration law, port of entry policy, training, and resources available to inspectors in primary and secondary inspections.

Commission Interviews

To more fully understand how and why the hijackers were permitted entry on 33 occasions and refused entry only once, the Commission interviewed 26 of the 38 inspectors involved in 28 of the attempted entries.[137]

One inspector told the Commission that the FBI interviewed her in regard to her deferred inspection of Atta on May 2, 2001, but never followed up with a promised second interview, which might have provided the FBI with an identification of at least one of Atta's companions that day.[138]

Eight of the 11 inspectors who had contact with Atta and Shehhi in their seven entries and one deferred inspection, including the one mentioned above, were interviewed previously by the Department of Justice's Office of the Inspector General (DOJ OIG) during late 2001 and early 2002 in preparation for Justice's May 2002 report, "The Immigration and Naturalization Service's Contacts with Two September 11 Hijackers." A few of the inspectors were interviewed by the inspector general's office multiple times. The Commission has copies of these DOJ OIG interviews.

To our surprise, many of the inspectors we interviewed, almost two and a half years after September 11, had never been interviewed by the FBI or the DOJ OIG and were often unaware that they had admitted a hijacker. Thus, except in a few cases, memories were lost. Nevertheless, it is possible to note some common themes.

In general, these interviews underscored a critical lack of counterterrorism training, a lack of standard operating procedures at airports, and wide variations in inspectors' understanding and application of immigration law to travelers seeking entry.

Hijacker Immigration

Inspections in Context. Prior to 9/11, immigration inspections were not considered a counterterrorism tool. Rather, they were viewed in the context of travel facilitation. As a result, inspectors often did not have the tools, training, or clear guidance in immigration law that they required in order to properly do their jobs. They were unable, for example, to verify that the identity of the person seeking admission was the same as that of the person who acquired a U.S. visa, because they did not have access to the photo each visitor was required to submit along with his or her visa application at a U.S. embassy or consulate overseas.[139]

Nor were immigration inspectors given any information about terrorist indicators in documents that could have enabled them to recognize the anomalies we know existed in some of the hijackers' passports. After the early 1990s, inspectors, senior INS management, and the intelligence community collectively did not associate terrorists with fraudulent documents.[140] As a result, inspectors looked for generic document fraud about which they had information, while they remained oblivious to some fairly obvious terrorist alterations and indicators.

Inspectors were mainly concerned about three types of travelers: intending immigrants, criminals, and drug couriers, all of whom were known to present fraudulent documents. Most inspectors interviewed by the Commission said that they relied on equipment such as black lights to help them detect certain types of passport fraud, but it was often broken. One inspector said he was so frustrated with equipment being out of order that he bought his own to use on the job. Travel stamps were reviewed merely to determine whether a prior visitor had overstayed or was intending to overstay the terms of the visa. Marwan al Shehhi, for example, was referred to a secondary immigration inspection out of concern that he was an intending immigrant.

Equally problematic was the immigration inspectors' lack of discretion in determining a tourist's length of stay. Tourists in the United States on visas, such as the hijackers, were automatically allowed to stay in the country for six months and were not required to present a return ticket. Even if a tourist asked for only a two-week stay, the inspector was legally required to grant six months. Indeed, it was this six-month stay rule that enabled 13 muscle hijackers to legally remain in the United States from the spring and early summer of 2001 until September 11.

In contrast, an inspector had complete discretion to determine the length of stay for a business traveler. Individual airports, and even inspectors at those airports, had different standards for allotting time to these business visitors. For example, most but not all of the inspectors from JFK in New York and Miami International thought that one month was the standard length of stay for a business visitor. At Newark, however, one inspector gave business travelers one month, another 90 days, and another up to six

TOP—*Mohamed Atta's U.S. visa issued in Berlin, Germany on May 18, 2000, 10 days after he acquired a new passport.* BOTTOM—*A partly-burned copy of Ziad Jarrah's U.S. visa recovered from the Flight 93 crash site in Somerset County, Pennsylvania.*

Ramzi Binalshibh's May 17, 2000 visa application with handwritten notes of U.S. consular officials. This visa application was denied July 18, 2000 under INA section 214(b), the "intending immigrant" provision.

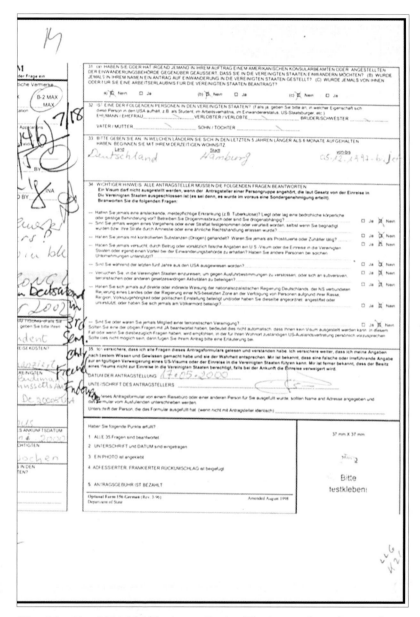

The right side of Binalshibh's visa application. The images shown here overlap to completely display the oversized form.

First page of Hani Hanjour's Sept. 10, 2000 visa application. The handwritten notes of a U.S. consular official (top right) indicate concern about Hanjour's desire to stay in the United States for three years. This application was incomplete; Hanjour did not specify the name and address of the school he claimed to be attending.

31. (a) HAVE YOU OR ANYONE ACTING FOR YOU EVER INDICATED TO A U.S. CONSULAR OR IMMIGRATION EMPLOYE DESIRE TO IMMIGRATE TO THE U.S.? (b) HAS ANYONE EVER FILED AN IMMIGRANT VISA PETITION ON YOUR BEHALF? HAS LABOR CERTIFICATION FOR EMPLOYMENT IN THE U.S. EVER BEEN REQUESTED BY YOU OR ON YOUR BEHA?

(a) ☑ No ☐ Yes   (b) ☑ No ☐ Yes   (c) ☑ No ☐ Yes

32. ARE ANY OF THE FOLLOWING IN THE U.S.? (If YES, circle appropriate relationship and indicate that person's status in t U.S., i.e., studying, working, U.S. permanent resident, U.S. citizen, etc.)

HUSBAND/WIFE ___no___   FIANCE/FIANCEE ___no___   BROTHER/SISTER ___no___

FATHER/MOTHER ___no___   SON/DAUGHTER ___no___

33. PLEASE LIST THE COUNTRIES WHERE YOU HAVE LIVED FOR MORE THAN 6 MONTHS DURING THE PAST 5 YEARS. BEGIN WITH YOUR PRESENT RESIDENCE.

Countries	Cities	Approximate Dates
ARZona	Phnor	

34. IMPORTANT ALL APPLICANTS MUST READ AND CHECK THE APPROPRIATE BOX FOR EACH ITEM:

A visa may not be issued to persons who are within specific categories defined by law as inadmissible to the United States (except when a waiver is obtained in advance). Are any of the following applicable to you?

- Have you ever been afflicted with a communicable disease of public health significance, a dangerous physical or mental disorder, or been a drug abuser or addict? . . . . ☐ Yes ☑ No

- Have you ever been arrested or convicted for any offense or crime, even though subject of a pardon, amnesty or other such legal action? . . . . ☐ Yes ☑ No

- Have you ever been a controlled substance (drug) trafficker, or a prostitute or procurer? . . . . . ☐ Yes ☑ No

- Have you ever sought to obtain or assist others to obtain a visa, entry into the U.S., or any U.S. immigration benefit by fraud or willful misrepresentation? . . . . ☐ Yes ☑ No

- Were you deported from the U.S.A. within the last 5 years? . . . . ☐ Yes ☑ No

- Do you seek to enter the United States to engage in export control violations, subversive or terrorist activities, or any unlawful purpose? . . . . ☐ Yes ☑ No

- Have you ever ordered, incited, assisted, or otherwise participated in the persecution of any person because of race, religion, national origin, or political opinion under the control, direct or indirect, of the Nazi Government of Germany, or of the government of any area occupied by, or allied with, the Nazi Government of Germany; or have you ever participated in genocide? . . . . . . ☐ Yes ☑ No

A YES answer does not automatically signify ineligibility for a visa, but if you answered YES to any of the above, or if you have any question in this regard, personal appearance at this office is recommended. If appearance is not possible at this time, attach a statement of facts in your case to this application.

35. I certify that I have read and understood all the questions set forth in this application and the answers I have furnished on this form are true and correct to the best of my knowledge and belief. I understand that any false or misleading statement may result in the permanent refusal of a visa or denial of entry into the United States. I understand that possession of a visa does not entitle the bearer to enter the United States of America upon arrival at port of entry if he or she is found inadmissible.

DATE OF APPLICATION ___10___   1 0 SEP 2000

APPLICANT'S SIGNATURE _____

If this application has been prepared by a travel agency or another person on your behalf, the agent should indicate name and address of agency or person with appropriate signature of individual preparing form.

SIGNATURE OF PERSON PREPARING FORM _____
(if other than applicant)

DO NOT WRITE IN THIS SPACE

OPTIONAL FORM 156 (Rev 6-93) PAGE 2
Department of State

Second page of Hanjour's visa application.

A–5

U.S. Department of Justice
Immigration and Naturalization Service

Application to Extend/ChangeNonimmigrant Status

START HERE - Please Type or Print

FOR INS USE ONLY

Part 1.   Information about you.

Family Name	ALSHEHHI	Given Name	MARWAN	Middle Initial YOUSEF

Address - In Care of:

Street # and Name   516 W LAUREL RD.   Apt #

City NOKOMIC   State FL.

Zip Code 34275

Date of Birth (month/day/year) 05/09/1978   Country of Birth UNITED ARAB EMIRATIS

Social Security # (if any)   A# (if any)

Date of Last Arrival Into the U.S. 06/03/2000   I-94#

Current Nonimmigrant Status   R   B1/B2   Expires on (month/day/year) 01/17/2010

Returned / Receipt / Resubmitted / Date / Reloc Sent / Date / Reloc Rec'd / Date / Date
□ Applicant Interviewed

Part 2.   Application Type.   (See Instructions for fee.)

1. I am applying for: (check one)
   a. □ an extension of stay in my current status
   b. □ a change of status. The new status I am requesting is: M-1
2. Number of people included in this application: (check one)
   a. □ I am the only applicant
   b. □ Members of my family are filing this application with me.
      The Total number of people included in this application is
      (complete the supplement for each co-applicant)

19 SEP '00

□ Extension Granted
   to (date):
X Change of Status/Extension Granted
   New Class: M-1   To (date): 10-1-20

If denied:
□ Still within period of stay
□ V/D to:
□ S/D to:
□ Place under docket control

Remarks

Part 3.   Processing Information.

1. I/We request that my/our current or requested status be extended until (month/day/year)   09/01/01
2. Is this application based on an extension or change of status already granted to your spouse, child or parent?
   ☒ No   □ Yes (receipt #   )
3. Is this application being filed based on a separate petition or application to give your spouse, child or parent an extension or change of status?
   ☒ No   □ Yes, filed with this application □ Yes, filed previously and pending with INS
4. If you answered yes to question 3, give the petitioner or applicant name:

   If the application is pending with INS, also give the following information.
   Office filed at_____ Filed on_____ (date)

Action Block

APPROVED
AUG 09 2001
SSC

Part 4.   Additional Information.

1. For applicant #1, provide passport information:
   Country of issuance UNITED ARAB EMIRATS   Valid to (month/day/year) 01/01/2005
2. Foreign address:
   Street # and Name   ALNaKil   Apt#
   City or Town   State or Province Ras Al Khaimah
   Country UNITED ARAB EMIRATIS   Zip or Postal Code

To Be Completed by Attorney or Representative, if any
□ Fill in box if G-28 is attached to represent the applicant
VOLAG#

ATTY State License #

Form I-539 (Rev. 12-2-91)   Continued on back.

Marwan al Shehhi's Sept. 15, 2000 application to change his immigration status (I-539) from tourist to vocational student in order to legally attend flight training school. The application was approved on August 9, 2001. Also on Sept. 15, 2000, Atta submitted a substantially similar I-539 to change his status from tourist to student. Both Atta and Shehhi were assisted by the same student coordinator at Huffman Aviation in filing the I-539, and were approved for their applications by the same INS benefits adjudicator. The applications used the same bank statement and lease, and nearly identical statements of financial support (although the handwriting is different on each application).

Part 4. Additional Information. *(continued)*

Answer the following questions. If you answer yes to any question, explain on separate paper.

	Yes	No
a. Are you, or any other person included in this application, an applicant for an immigrant visa or adjustment of status to permanent residence?		X
b. Has an immigrant petition ever been filed for you, or for any other person included in this application?		X
c. Have you, or any other person included in this application ever been arrested or convicted of any criminal offense since last entering the U.S.?		X
d. Have you, or any other person included in this application done anything which violated the terms of the nonimmigrant status you now hold?		X
e. Are you, or any other person included in this application, now in exclusion or deportation proceedings?		X
f. Have you, or any other person included in this application, been employed in the U.S. since last admitted or granted an extension or change of status?		X

If you answered YES to question 3f, give the following information on a separate paper: Name of person, name of employer, address of employer, weekly income, and whether specifically authorized by INS.

If you answered NO to question 3f, fully describe how you are supporting yourself on a separate paper. Include the source and the amount and basis for any income.

Part 5. Signature. *Read the information on penalties in the instructions before completing this section. You must file this application while in the United States.*

I certify under penalty of perjury under the laws of the United States of America that this application, and the evidence submitted with it, is all true and correct. I authorize the release of any information from my records which the Immigration and Naturalization Service needs to determine eligibility for the benefit I am seeking.

Signature	Print your name	Date
Marwan Alshehhi	*Marwan Yousef Alshehhi*	09/15/2000

Please Note: If you do not completely fill out this form, or fail to submit required documents listed in the instructions, you cannot be found eligible for the requested document and this application will have to be denied.

Part 6. Signature of person preparing form if other than above. *(Sign below)*

I declare that I prepared this application at the request of the above person and it is based on all information of which I have knowledge.

Signature	Print Your Name	Date

Firm Name
and Address

(Please remember to enclose the mailing label with your application)

Page 2 of al Shehhi's I-539.

Mohand al Shehri's Oct. 23, 2000 visa application. This application was incomplete. He claimed to be a student (#24), but failed to clearly state the name and address of his school (#10). He also claimed to be supporting himself during his proposed 6-month visit to the United States. This application was approved.

31. (a) HAVE YOU OR ANYONE ACTING FOR YOU EVER INDICATED TO A U.S. CONSULAR OR IMMIGRATION EMPLOYEE A DESIRE TO IMMIGRATE TO THE U.S.? (b) HAS ANYONE EVER FILED AN IMMIGRANT VISA PETITION ON YOUR BEHALF? (c) HAS LABOR CERTIFICATION FOR EMPLOYMENT IN THE U.S. EVER BEEN REQUESTED BY YOU OR ON YOUR BEHALF?

(a) ☑ No ☐ Yes   (b) ☑ No ☐ Yes   (c) ☑ No ☐ Yes

32. ARE ANY OF THE FOLLOWING IN THE U.S.? (IF YES, circle appropriate relationship and indicate that person's status in the U.S., i.e., studying, working, U.S. permanent resident, U.S. citizen, etc.)

HUSBAND/WIFE _____ FIANCE/FIANCEE _____ BROTHER/SISTER _____

FATHER/MOTHER _____ SON/DAUGHTER _____

33. PLEASE LIST THE COUNTRIES WHERE YOU HAVE LIVED FOR MORE THAN 6 MONTHS DURING THE PAST 5 YEARS. BEGIN WITH YOUR PRESENT RESIDENCE.

Countries	Cities	Approximate Dates

34. IMPORTANT: ALL APPLICANTS MUST READ AND CHECK THE APPROPRIATE BOX FOR EACH ITEM.

A visa may not be issued to persons who are within specific categories defined by law as inadmissible to the United States (except when a waiver is obtained in advance). Are any of the following applicable to you?

- Have you ever been afflicted with a communicable disease of public health significance, a dangerous physical or mental disorder, or been a drug abuser or addict? ☐ Yes ☑ No

- Have you ever been arrested or convicted for any offense or crime, even though subject of a pardon, amnesty, or other such legal action? ☐ Yes ☑ No

- Have you ever been a controlled substance (drug) trafficker, or a prostitute or procurer? ☐ Yes ☑ No

- Have you ever sought to obtain or assist others to obtain a visa, entry into the U.S., or any U.S. immigration benefit by fraud or willful misrepresentation? ☐ Yes ☐ No

- Were you deported from the U.S.A. within the last 5 years? ☐ Yes ☐ No

- Do you seek to enter the United States to engage in export control violations, subversive or terrorist activities, or any unlawful purpose? ☐ Yes ☑ No

- Have you ever ordered, incited, assisted, or otherwise participated in the persecution of any person because of race, religion, national origin, or political opinion under the control, direct or indirect, of the Nazi Government of Germany, or of the government of any area occupied by, or allied with, the Nazi Government of Germany; or have you ever participated in genocide? ☐ Yes ☐ No

A YES answer does not automatically signify ineligibility for a visa, but if you answered YES to any of the above, or if you have any question in this regard, personal appearance at this office is recommended. If appearance is not possible at this time, attach a statement of facts in your case to this application.

35. I certify that I have read and understood all the questions set forth in this application and the answers I have furnished on this form are true and correct to the best of my knowledge and belief. I understand that any false or misleading statement may result in the permanent refusal of a visa or denial of entry into the United States. I understand that possession of a visa does not entitle the bearer to enter the United States of America upon arrival at port of entry if he or she is found inadmissible.

DATE OF APPLICATION _3/10/2000_

APPLICANT'S SIGNATURE _____

If this application has been prepared by a travel agency or another person on your behalf, the agent should indicate name and address of agency or person with appropriate signature of individual preparing form.

SIGNATURE OF PERSON PREPARING FORM *
(if other than applicant) _____

DO NOT WRITE IN THIS SPACE

Are you a member/representative of a terrorist organization? ☐ Yes ☑ No

OPTIONAL FORM 156 (Rev. 6-93) PAGE 2
Department of State

Ahmad al Haznawi's Nov. 12, 2000 visa application. Although he claimed to be a student (#24), he left blank the name and address of his school (#10). He also claimed to be supporting himself while in the United States. This application was approved.

A–10

4. (a) HAVE YOU OR ANYONE ACTING FOR YOU EVER INDICATED TO A U.S. CONSULAR OR IMMIGRATION EMPLOYEE A DESIRE TO IMMIGRATE TO THE U.S.? **(b)** HAS ANYONE EVER FILED AN IMMIGRANT VISA PETITION ON YOUR BEHALF? **(c)** HAS LABOR CERTIFICATION FOR EMPLOYMENT IN THE U.S. EVER BEEN REQUESTED BY YOU OR ON YOUR BEHALF?

(a) ☐ No   ☐ Yes   (b) ☑ No   ☐ Yes   (c) ☑ No   ☐ Yes

32. ARE ANY OF THE FOLLOWING IN THE U.S.? (If YES, circle appropriate relationship and indicate that person's status in the U.S., i.e., studying, working, U.S. permanent resident, U.S. citizen, etc.)

HUSBAND/WIFE _____   FIANCE/FIANCEE _____   BROTHER/SISTER _____

FATHER/MOTHER _____   SON/DAUGHTER _____

33. PLEASE LIST THE COUNTRIES WHERE YOU HAVE LIVED FOR MORE THAN 6 MONTHS DURING THE PAST 5 YEARS, BEGIN WITH YOUR PRESENT RESIDENCE.

Countries	Cities	Approximate Dates
No Thom		

34. IMPORTANT. ALL APPLICANTS MUST READ AND CHECK THE APPROPRIATE BOX FOR EACH ITEM:

A visa may not be issued to persons who are within specific categories defined by law as inadmissible to the United States (except when a waiver is obtained in advance). Are any of the following applicable to you?

- Have you ever been afflicted with a communicable disease of public health significance, a dangerous physical or mental disorder, or been a drug abuser or addict? . . . . ☐ Yes   ☑ No

- Have you ever been arrested or convicted for any offense or crime, even though subject of a pardon, amnesty, or other such legal action? . . . . ☐ Yes   ☑ No

- Have you ever been a controlled substance (drug) trafficker, or a prostitute or procurer? . . . . . ☐ Yes   ☑ No

- Have you ever sought to obtain or assist others to obtain a visa, entry into the U.S., or any U.S. immigration benefit by fraud or willful misrepresentation? . . . . ☐ Yes   ☑ No

- Were you deported from the U.S.A. within the last 5 years? . . . . ☐ Yes   ☑ No

- Do you seek to enter the United States to engage in export control violations, subversive or terrorist activities, or any unlawful purpose? . . . . ☐ Yes   ☑ No

- Have you ever ordered, incited, assisted, or otherwise participated in the persecution of any person because of race, religion, national origin, or political opinion under the control, direct or indirect, of the Nazi Government of Germany, or of the government of any area occupied by, or allied with, the Nazi Government of Germany; or have you ever participated in genocide? . . . . . . ☐ Yes   ☑ No

A YES answer does not automatically signify ineligibility for a visa, but if you answered YES to any of the above, or if you have any question in this regard, personal appearance at this office is recommended. If appearance is not possible at this time, attach a statement of facts in your case to this application.

35. I certify that I have read and understood all the questions set forth in this application and the answers I have furnished on this form are true and correct to the best of my knowledge and belief. I understand that any false or misleading statement may result in the permanent refusal of a visa or denial of entry into the United States. I understand that possession of a visa does not entitle the bearer to enter the United States of America upon arrival at port of entry if he or she is found inadmissible.

DATE OF APPLICATION _____

APPLICANT'S SIGNATURE _____

If this application has been prepared by a travel agency or another person on your behalf, the agent should indicate name and address of agency or person with appropriate signature of individual preparing form.

SIGNATURE OF PERSON PREPARING FORM _____
(if other than applicant)

DO NOT WRITE IN THIS SPACE

Page 2 of Haznawi's visa application.

PLEASE TYPE OR PRINT YOUR ANSWERS IN THE SPACE PROVIDED BELOW

1. SURNAMES OR FAMILY NAMES *(Exactly as in Passport)* 1 3 NOV 2000
Al-Gamdi

2. FIRST NAME AND MIDDLE NAME *(Exactly as in Passport)*
SAEED AbdullAH

3. OTHER NAMES *(Maiden, Religious, Professional, Aliases)*

4. DATE OF BIRTH *(Day, Month, Year)*
5.5.1981

8 PASSPORT NUMBER
B331951

5. PLACE OF BIRTH City, Province   AL-HAL Country
BalgurShi   S.A

DATE PASSPORT ISSUED *(Day, Month, Year)*
16.10.1420

6. NATIONALITY
S.A

7. SEX
☒ MALE
☐ FEMALE

DATE PASSPORT EXPIRES *(Day, Month, Year)*
28.11.2004

9. HOME ADDRESS *(Include apartment no., street, city, province, and postal zone)*
AL-TLAIA - Hira

10. NAME AND STREET ADDRESS OF PRESENT EMPLOYER OR SCHOOL *(Postal box number unacceptable)*
SAEED . JEDDAH

11. HOME TELEPHONE NO.
6545050

12. BUSINESS TELEPHONE NO.
—

13. COLOR OF HAIR
Black

14. COLOR OF EYES
Brown

15. COMPLEXION

16. HEIGHT
cm 165

17. MARKS OF IDENTIFICATION
Nic

18. MARITAL STATUS
☐ Married ☒ Single ☐ Widowed ☐ Divorced ☐ Separated
If married, give name and nationality of spouse.

19. NAMES AND RELATIONSHIPS OF PERSONS TRAVELING WITH YOU *(NOTE: A separate application must be made for a visa for each traveler, regardless of age.)*
Nic

20. HAVE YOU EVER APPLIED FOR A U.S. VISA BEFORE, WHETHER IMMIGRANT OR NONIMMIGRANT?
☒ No
☐ Yes Where? _____
When? _____ Type of visa? _____
☐ Visa was issued ☐ Visa was refused

21. HAS YOUR U.S. VISA EVER BEEN CANCELED?
☒ No
☐ Yes Where? _____
When? _____ By whom? _____

22. Bearers of visitors visas may generally not work or study in the U.S.
DO YOU INTEND TO WORK IN THE U.S.? ☒ No ☐ Yes
If YES, explain.

23. DO YOU INTEND TO STUDY IN THE U.S.? ☒ No ☐ Yes
If YES, write name and address of school as it appears on form I-20.

DO NOT WRITE IN THIS SPACE

B-1/B-2 MAX   B-1 MAX   B-2 MAX
OTHER _____ MAX
Visa Classification
MULT OR _____
Number Applications
MONTHS _____
Validity
L.O. CHECKED _____
ISSUED/REFUSED
ON _____ BY _____
UNDER SEC. _____ INA
REFUSAL REVIEWED BY _____

To stay one year
no job got
studented
graduated from
H.S. last year
he has SR10000
only + staying
one year !

not working

24. PRESENT OCCUPATION *(If retired, state past occupation)*
Nic

25. WHO WILL FURNISH FINANCIAL SUPPORT, INCLUDING TICKETS?
FATHER

26. AT WHAT ADDRESS WILL YOU STAY IN THE USA?
carlivonly

27. WHAT IS THE PURPOSE OF YOUR TRIP?
TOURING

28. WHEN DO YOU INTEND TO ARRIVE IN THE USA?
3 months

29. HOW LONG DO YOU PLAN TO STAY IN THE USA?
12 months

30. HAVE YOU EVER BEEN IN THE USA?
☒ No
☐ Yes When? _____
For how long? _____

NONIMMIGRANT VISA APPLICATION

COMPLETE ALL QUESTIONS ON REVERSE OF FORM

OPTIONAL FORM 156 (Rev 6-93) PAGE 1
Department of State
50156-108
PREVIOUS EDITIONS OBSOLETE
NSN 7540-00-139-0053

Nov. 13, 2000 visa application for Saeed al Ghamdi (not the hijacker of the same name). Handwritten notes (upper right) of a consular officer indicate that his visa was denied because he was unemployed, lacked sufficient finances to support his trip and told officials that he planned to stay one year in the United States.

31. (a) HAVE YOU OR ANYONE ACTING FOR YOU EVER INDICATED TO A U.S. CONSULAR OR IMMIGRATION EMPLOYE DESIRE TO IMMIGRATE TO THE U.S.? (b) HAS ANYONE EVER FILED AN IMMIGRANT VISA PETITION ON YOUR BEHALF? HAS LABOR CERTIFICATION FOR EMPLOYMENT IN THE U.S. EVER BEEN REQUESTED BY YOU OR ON YOUR BEHA

(a) ☑ No ☐ Yes　　　　(b) ☑ No ☐ Yes　　　　(c) ☑ No ☐ Yes

32. ARE ANY OF THE FOLLOWING IN THE U.S.? (If YES, circle appropriate relationship and indicate that person's status in t U.S., i.e., studying, working, U.S. permanent resident, U.S. citizen, etc.)

HUSBAND/WIFE _____　　FIANCE/FIANCEE _____　　BROTHER/SISTER _____

FATHER/MOTHER _____　　SON/DAUGHTER _____

33. PLEASE LIST THE COUNTRIES WHERE YOU HAVE LIVED FOR MORE THAN 6 MONTHS DURING THE PAST 5 YEARS. BEGIN WITH YOUR PRESENT RESIDENCE.

Countries	Cities	Approximate Dates
	JEDDAH	*illegible handwriting*

34. IMPORTANT. ALL APPLICANTS MUST READ AND CHECK THE APPROPRIATE BOX FOR EACH ITEM:

A visa may not be issued to persons who are within specific categories defined by law as inadmissible to the United States (except when a waiver is obtained in advance). Are any of the following applicable to you?

- Have you ever been afflicted with a communicable disease of public health significance, a dangerous physical or mental disorder, or been a drug abuser or addict? . . . . ☐ Yes ☑ No

- Have you ever been arrested or convicted for any offense or crime, even though subject of a pardon, amnesty, or other such legal action? . . . . ☐ Yes ☑ No

- Have you ever been a controlled substance (drug) trafficker, or a prostitute or procurer? . . . . . ☐ Yes ☑ No

- Have you ever sought to obtain or assist others to obtain a visa, entry into the U.S., or any U.S. immigration benefit by fraud or willful misrepresentation? . . . . ☐ Yes ☑ No

- Were you deported from the U.S.A. within the last 5 years?. . . . . ☐ Yes ☑ No

- Do you seek to enter the United States to engage in export control violations, subversive or terrorist activities, or any unlawful purpose?. . . . . ☐ Yes ☑ No

- Have you ever ordered, incited, assisted, or otherwise participated in the persecution of any person because of race, religion, national origin, or political opinion under the control, direct or indirect, of the Nazi Government of Germany, or of the government of any area occupied by, or allied with, the Nazi Government of Germany, or have you ever participated in genocide? . . . . . ☐ Yes ☑ No

A YES answer does not automatically signify ineligibility for a visa, but if you answered YES to any of the above, or if you have any question in this regard, personal appearance at this office is recommended. If appearance is not possible at this time, attach a statement of facts in your case to this application.

35. I certify that I have read and understood all the questions set forth in this application and the answers I have furnished on this form are true and correct to the best of my knowledge and belief. I understand that any false or misleading statement may result in the permanent refusal of a visa or denial of entry into the United States. I understand that possession of a visa does not entitle the bearer to enter the United States of America upon arrival at port of entry if he or she is found inadmissible.

DATE OF APPLICATION ___1/3/2001___

APPLICANT'S SIGNATURE ___*signature*___

If this application has been prepared by a travel agency or another person on your behalf, the agent should indicate name and address of agency or person with appropriate signature of individual preparing form.

SIGNATURE OF PERSON PREPARING FORM (if other than applicant) _____

DO NOT WRITE IN THIS SPACE

OPTIONAL FORM 156 (Rev. 6-93) PAGE 2
Department of State

Page 2 of al Ghamdi's denied visa application. To our knowledge he was the only potential Saudi hijacker denied a U.S. visa.

Ahmed al Nami's April 23, 2001 visa application. The presence of notes in the upper right suggests that he was briefly questioned by consular officials. This was his second visa application even though his previous visa had not expired. Nami submitted this application with a new passport perhaps in order to hide travel to Afghanistan in the old passport.

☑ NO ☐ YES

HAS A LABOR CERTIFICATION FOR EMPLOYMENT IN THE U.S. EVER BEEN REQUESTED BY YOU OR ON YOUR BEHALF?

☑ NO ☐ YES

27. ARE ANY OF THE FOLLOWING IN THE U.S., RESIDE IN THE U.S., OR HAVE U.S. LEGAL PERMANENT RESIDENCE?
(Circle YES or NO and indicate that person's status in the U.S., i.e., studying, working, permanent resident, U.S. citizen, etc.)

YES NO Husband/ Wife _____   YES NO Fiance/ Fiancee _____   YES NO Brother/ Sister _____

YES NO Father/ Mother _____   YES NO Son/ Daughter _____

28. WHERE HAVE YOU LIVED FOR THE PAST FIVE YEARS? DO NOT INCLUDE PLACES YOU HAVE VISITED FOR PERIODS OF SIX MONTHS OR LESS.

Countries	Cities	Approximate Dates
saudi	*Abha*	
saudi	*Jeddh*	

29. IMPORTANT: ALL APPLICANTS MUST READ AND CHECK THE APPROPRIATE BOX FOR EACH ITEM.

A visa may not be issued to persons who are within specific categories defined by law as inadmissible to the United States (except when a waiver is obtained in advance). Are any of the following applicable to you?

- Have you ever been afflicted with a communicable disease of public health significance, a dangerous physical or mental disorder, or been a drug abuser or addict? [212(a)(1)]   ☐ YES ☑ NO

- Have you ever been arrested or convicted for any offense or crime, even though subject of a pardon, amnesty or other similar legal action? Have you ever lawfully distributed or sold a controlled substance (drug), or been a prostitute or procurer for prostitutes? [212(a)(2)]   ☐ YES ☑ NO

- Do you seek to enter the United States to engage in export control violations, subversive or terrorist activities, or any other unlawful purpose? Are you a member or representative of a terrorist organization as currently designated by the U.S. Secretary of State? Have you ever participated in persecutions directed by the Nazi government of Germany; or have you ever participated in genocide? [212(a)(3)]   ☐ YES ☑ NO

- Have you ever been refused admission to the U.S., or the subject of a deportation hearing, or sought to obtain or assist others to obtain a visa, entry into the U.S., or sought to obtain a visa or any U.S. immigration benefit by fraud or willful misrepresentation? Have you attended a U.S. public elementary school on student (F) status, or a public secondary school without reimbursing the school after November 30, 1996? [212(a)(6)]   ☐ YES ☑ NO

- Have you ever departed or remained outside the United States to avoid military service? [212(a)(8)]   ☐ YES ☐ NO

- Have you ever violated the terms of a U.S. visa, or been unlawfully present in, or deported from, the United States? [212(a)(9)]   ☐ YES ☑ NO

- Have you ever withheld custody of a U.S. citizen child outside the United States from a person granted legal custody by a U.S. court, voted in the United States in violation of any law or regulation, or renounced U.S. citizenship for the purpose of avoiding taxation? [212(a)(10)]   ☐ YES ☑ NO

A YES answer does not automatically signify ineligibility for a visa, but if you answered YES to any of the above, or if you have any question in this regard, a personal appearance at this office is recommended. If an appearance is not possible at this time, attach a statement of facts in your case to this application.

30. I certify that I have read and understood all the questions set forth in this application and the answers I have furnished on this form are true and correct to the best of my knowledge and belief. I understand that any false or misleading statement may result in the permanent refusal of a visa or denial of entry into the United States. I understand that possession of a visa does not entitle the bearer to enter the United States of America upon arrival at port of entry if he or she is found inadmissible.

DATE OF APPLICATION *(mm-dd-yyyy)* _____

APPLICANT'S SIGNATURE _____

If this application has been prepared by a travel agency or another person or name and address of agency or person with appropriate signature of individual.

SIGNATURE OF PERSON PREPARING FORM
(If other than applicant) _____

DO NOT WRITE IN THIS SPACE

OPTIONAL FORM 156   PAGE 2
REV. 10-1999
Department of State

ehmai

Page 2 of Nami's visa application.

*Mohamed Atta's revised immigration arrival record (I-94) for his January 10, 2001
entry at Miami International Airport created on May 2, 2001 at the Miami INS
district office. Atta had gone to the office seeking a length of stay for a colleague—
possibly Ziad Jarrah—equal to the eight months he had received. Tourists were not
normally granted a length of stay of more than six months. The INS officer in Miami
refused to grant eight months to Atta's colleague. Instead, the inspector rolled-back
Atta's length of stay to the standard six months, until July 9, 2001. Atta departed
the United States on July 7 and returned on July 19, at which time he was granted
another six month length of stay. Jarrah would depart for the final time on July 25,
2001, and would be the last hijacker to return to the United States on August 5, 2001.*

18. Occupation	19. Waivers.
20. INS File A -	21. INS FCO
22. Petition Number	23. Program Number
24. ☐ Bond	25. ☐ Prospective Student

26. Itinerary/Comments

I-94 WAS Issued AT MIA
I.I. 1903, I.94 WAS Issued
IN Error, New I 94 WAS Issued
AT DEF-MIA. Same Validity of Time

Handwritten notes of the immigration official at the Miami district office, explaining the roll-back Atta's length of stay.

State of Florida
Department of Highway Safety and Motor Vehicles
FOR USE ONLY AS AUTHORIZED BY DHSMV
DRIVER LICENSE

DL/ID number
A300-540-68-321-0   Class E

Name
MOHAMED ATTA

Address
10001 W ATLANTIC BLVD
CORAL SPRINGS, FL 33071-0000

Date of birth   Sex   Height
09-01-68   M   5-08

Restrictions   Endorsements

Fingerprint on file
None

Issue date   Issue time
05-02-01   15:36:28

Expiration date   Duplicate date
09-01-07   00-00-00

Form number
R010105020258

Copy of Mohamed Atta's Florida state driver's license. Several other hijackers obtained Florida state identification including Hani Hanjour, Marwan al Shehhi, Nawaf al Hazmi, Ziad Jarrah, Waleed al Shehri, Hamza al Ghamdi, Ahmed al Nami, Ahmed al Haznawi, Saeed al Ghamdi, Mohand al Shehri, and Fayez Banihammad.

Immigration arrival record (I-94) for Saeed al Ghamdi with a stated destination as "hotel" in Orlando, Florida. The failure of Ghamdi to state a specific address made this primary immigration inspector concerned that Ghamdi did not seem to know where he was going in the United States.

Saeed al Ghamdi's Customs Declaration presented at arrival. The primary immigration inspector who reviewed this customs declaration was concerned Ghamdi had insufficient funds to support himself while in the United States as a tourist.

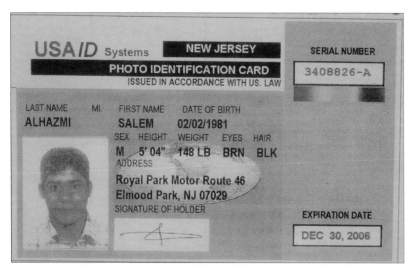

TOP—*Identification obtained by Salem al Hazmi. In addition, Ahmed al Ghamdi, Nawaf al Hazmi, Majed Moqed, and Abdul Aziz al Omari obtained similar USA identification cards. BOTTOM—Identification obtained by Khalid al Mihdhar. The address listed is for a hotel.*

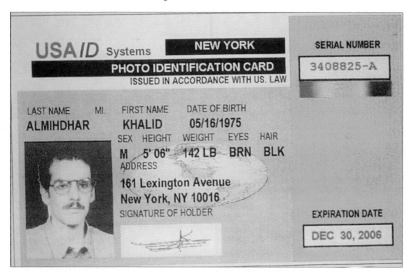

PLEASE TYPE OR PRINT YOUR ANSWERS IN THE SPACE PROVIDED BELOW EACH ITEM

2 3 JUL 2001

DO NOT WRITE IN THIS SPACE

| B-1-B-2 MAX | B-1 MAX | B-2 MAX |

1. SURNAMES OR FAMILY NAMES (Exactly as in Passport)
AL-GHAMDI

2. FIRST NAME AND MIDDLE NAME (Exactly as in Passport)
ABDUL RAHMAN A.A.

OTHER _____ MAX
Visa Classification

3. OTHER NAMES (Maiden, Religious, Professional, Aliases)
N'

MULT OR _____
Number Applications

4. DATE OF BIRTH (mm-dd-yyyy)
09-24-1965

8. PASSPORT NUMBER
C-174152

MONTHS _____
Validity

5. PLACE OF BIRTH
City, Province   Country
RAGHDAN   K.S.A.

DATE PASSPORT ISSUED (mm-dd-yyyy)
06-17-2000

L.O. CHECKED
ON _____ BY _____
ISSUED/REFUSED

6. NATIONALITY
SAUDI

7. SEX
☑ MALE
☐ FEMALE

DATE PASSPORT EXPIRES (mm-dd-yyyy)
04-23-2005

ON _____ BY _____

9. HOME ADDRESS (Include apartment no., street, city, province, and postal zone)
P.O. Box - 1843, MADINA, KSA
MADINA AIRPORT ROAD

UNDER SEC. 214(b) 221(g)

OTHER _____ _____ INA

10. NAME AND STREET ADDRESS OF PRESENT EMPLOYER OR SCHOOL (Postal box number unacceptable)
AL-GHAMDI EST. (OWNER)
AIRPORT RD MADINA, KSA

REFUSAL REVIEWED BY _____

11. HOME TELEPHONE NO.
8484214

12. BUSINESS TELEPHONE NO.
053198224

13. MARITAL STATUS
☑ Married ☐ Single ☐ Widowed ☐ Divorced ☐ Separated
If married, give name and nationality of spouse
1) ZAINAB AL-GHAMDI SAUDI

14. NAMES AND RELATIONSHIPS OF PERSONS TRAVELING WITH YOU
(NOTE: A separate application must be made for a visa for each traveler, regardless of age.)
N'

15. HAVE YOU EVER APPLIED FOR A U.S. NONIMMIGRANT VISA?
☑ NO ☐ YES

HAVE YOU EVER APPLIED FOR A U.S. IMMIGRANT VISA?
☑ NO ☐ YES
WHERE? _____
WHEN? _____
VISA WAS ISSUED ☐ VISA WAS REFUSED ☐

16. HAS YOUR U.S. VISA EVER BEEN CANCELED?
☑ NO ☐ YES
WHERE? _____
WHEN? _____
BY WHOM? _____

17. Bearers of visitors visas may generally not work or study in the U.S.
DO YOU INTEND TO WORK IN THE U.S.? ☑ NO ☐ YES
If YES, explain.

18. DO YOU INTEND TO STUDY IN THE U.S.? ☑ NO ☐ YES
If YES, write name an address of school as it appears on form I-20.

19. PRESENT OCCUPATION (if retired, state past occupation)
MERCHANT

20. WHO WILL FURNISH FINANCIAL SUPPORT, INCLUDING TICKETS?
MYSELF

21. AT WHAT ADDRESS WILL YOU STAY IN THE U.S.A.?
NEW YORK
(ANY HOTEL)

22. WHAT IS THE PURPOSE OF YOUR TRIP?
TOURIST

23. WHEN DO YOU INTEND TO ARRIVE IN THE U.S.A.?
25-7-2001

24. HOW LONG DO YOU PLAN TO STAY IN THE U.S.A.?
MULTIPLE ENTRY

25. HAVE YOU EVER BEEN IN THE U.S.A.?
☑ NO ☐ YES
WHEN? _____
FOR HOW LONG? _____

COMPLETE ALL QUESTIONS ON REVERSE OF FORM

NONIMMIGRANT VISA APPLICATION

NSN 7540-00-139-0053

OPTIONAL FORM 156   PAGE 1
REV. 10-1999
Department of State

60156-109
PREVIOUS EDITIONS OBSOLETE

Visa application submitted on behalf of Khalid Sheikh Mohammed. Although KSM was on a terrorist watchlist, this application was submitted under an alias name. The application was approved but there is no evidence that KSM used this visa to enter the United States.

26. HAVE YOU OR ANYONE ACTING FOR YOU EVER INDICATED TO A U.S. CONSULAR OR IMMIGRATION EMPLOYEE A DESIRE TO IMMIGRATE TO THE U.S., OR HAVE YOU EVER ENTERED A U.S. VISA LOTTERY?

☑ NO ☐ YES

HAS ANYONE EVER FILED AN IMMIGRANT VISA PETITION ON YOUR BEHALF?

☑ NO ☐ YES

HAS A LABOR CERTIFICATION FOR EMPLOYMENT IN THE U.S. EVER BEEN REQUESTED BY YOU OR ON YOUR BEHALF?

☑ NO ☐ YES

27. ARE ANY OF THE FOLLOWING IN THE U.S., RESIDE IN THE U.S., OR HAVE U.S. LEGAL PERMANENT RESIDENCE? (Circle YES or NO and indicate that person's status in the U.S.; i.e., studying, working, permanent resident, U.S. citizen, etc.)

YES (NO) Husband/Wife _____ YES (NO) Fiance/Fiancee _____ YES (NO) Brother/Sister

YES (NO) Father/Mother _____ YES (NO) Son/Daughter _____

28. WHERE HAVE YOU LIVED FOR THE PAST FIVE YEARS? DO NOT INCLUDE PLACES YOU HAVE VISITED FOR PERIODS OF SIX MONTHS OR LESS

Countries   Cities   Approximate Dates

29. IMPORTANT: ALL APPLICANTS MUST READ AND CHECK THE APPROPRIATE BOX FOR EACH ITEM

A visa may not be issued to persons who are within specific categories defined by law as inadmissible to the United States (except when a waiver is obtained in advance). Are any of the following applicable to you?

- Have you ever been afflicted with a communicable disease of public health significance, a dangerous physical or mental disorder, or been a drug abuser or addict? [212(a)(1)] ☐ YES ☑ NO

- Have you ever been arrested or convicted for any offense or crime, even though subject of a pardon, amnesty or other similar legal action? Have you ever lawfully distributed or sold a controlled substance (drug), or been a prostitute or procurer for prostitutes? [212(a)(2)] ☐ YES ☑ NO

- Do you seek to enter the United States to engage in export control violations, subversive or terrorist activities, or any other unlawful purpose? Are you a member or representative of a terrorist organization as currently designated by the U.S. Secretary of State? Have you ever participated in persecutions directed by the Nazi government of Germany, or have you ever participated in genocide? [212(a)(3)] ☐ YES ☑ NO

- Have you ever been refused admission to the U.S., or the subject of a deportation hearing, or sought to obtain or assist others to obtain a visa, entry into the U.S., or sought to obtain a visa or any U.S. immigration benefit by fraud or willful misrepresentation? Have you attended a U.S. public elementary school on student (F) status, or a public secondary school without reimbursing the school after November 30, 1996? [212(a)(6)] ☐ YES ☑ NO

- Have you ever departed or remained outside the United States to avoid military service? [212(a)(8)] ☐ YES ☑ NO

- Have you ever violated the terms of a U.S. visa, or been unlawfully present in, or deported from, the United States? [212(a)(9)] ☐ YES ☑ NO

- Have you ever withheld custody of a U.S. citizen child outside the United States from a person granted legal custody by a U.S. court, voted in the United States in violation of any law or regulation, or renounced U.S. citizenship for the purpose of avoiding taxation? [212(a)(10)] ☐ YES ☑ NO

A YES answer does not automatically signify ineligibility for a visa, but if you answered YES to any of the above, or if you have any question in this regard, a personal appearance at this office is recommended. If an appearance is not possible at this time, attach a statement of facts in your case to this application.

30. I certify that I have read and understood all the questions set forth in this application and the answers I have furnished on this form are true and correct to the best of my knowledge and belief. I understand that any false or misleading statement may result in the permanent refusal of a visa or denial of entry into the United States. I understand that possession of a visa does not entitle the bearer to enter the United States of America upon arrival at port of entry if he or she is found inadmissible.

DATE OF APPLICATION (mm-dd-yyyy) ___07 _ 23 ___2001___

APPLICANT'S SIGNATURE _____

If this application has been prepared by a travel agency or another person on your behalf, the agent should indicate name and address of agency or person with appropriate signature of individual preparing form.

SIGNATURE OF PERSON PREPARING FORM (if other than applicant) _____

DO NOT WRITE IN THIS SPACE

OPTIONAL FORM 156 PAGE 2
REV. 10-1999
Department of State

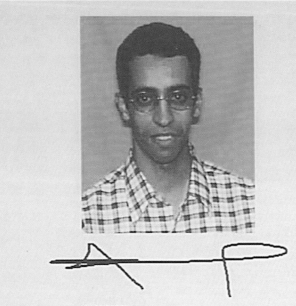

CUSTOMER#: A69600380
CUST. NAME: AL GHAMDI,AHMED,SALEH S
ISSUE DATE: 2001/08/02 12:32
PRINT DATE: Sun Sep 23 10:26:25 EDT 2001

This is to certify, in accordance with section 46.2-215 of the Code of Virginia,
that this machine produced digital image, transmitted by electronic means to
iso/dmv/dana snead is an accurate depiction of the digital image for customer number
A69600380 as maintained by the Virginia Department of Motor Vehicles as
of the date printed above.

Richard D. Holcomb
Commissioner

This ends transmission.

Ahmed al Ghamdi's photo as it appeared on his state of Virginia identification card. Hani Hanjour, Khalid al Mihdhar, Ziad Jarrah, Abdul Aziz al Omari, Majed Moqed, and Salem al Hazmi also obtained Virginia state identification cards. All these identifications were obtained fraudulently.

months. Most thought that these policies were port-specific, but some believed them to be national.[141] These local variations explain why on January 10, 2001, Atta was initially granted a one-month business stay by an inspector at the Miami airport, but on February 25, 2001, Jarrah was granted a six-month business stay by an inspector at Newark.[142]

The four pilots, who went into and out of the United States 17 times, were admitted on business four times. Only one muscle hijacker, Suqami, was given a one-month stay as a business traveler when he entered at Orlando on April 23, 2001, with Waleed al Shehri. Both hijackers had filled out their Customs declarations stating that they intended a 20-day stay. The immigration arrival record did not require information about the length of stay, however; and since immigration inspectors checked the Customs declarations only for completeness and not for substance, the 20-day stay request was ignored—to their advantage, in fact.

Indeed, the 30-year INS veteran inspector who admitted both hijackers told the Commission that the Customs declaration had no bearing on the length of stay he gave Suqami, which was based solely on Suqami's answer regarding the purpose of his visit.[143] That Suqami was limited to a business instead of a tourist stay meant that he and Nawaf al Hazmi (who overstayed his tourist visa despite filing for an extension of his stay in July 2000) were the only operatives who had overstayed their authorized lengths of stay as of September 11.

Particularly significant for the 9/11 story is the lack of secondary training for inspectors. As we detailed in the chronology, the hijackers (and Kahtani) were referred to a total of six secondary inspections, four by immigration and two by Customs. Inspectors interviewed by the Commission all said they learned the criteria for secondary inspections at their assigned airport. Because of the lack of standardized training and guidance in this area, each inspector looked for different red flags for referrals to secondary. For example, some inspectors were adamant that a traveler's apparent lack of adequate funding for a certain length of stay was a "bread-and-butter" case of referral to secondary; others did not consider this set of facts to be noteworthy. Insufficient funding was part of the basis of referral for Saeed al Ghamdi, but was not seen as significant by the inspector who admitted him.

Most, however, agreed that a pattern of entries and exits from the United States that looked like the traveler was actually living in the United States would be cause for a more in-depth interview. Such a pattern was exhibited by Atta on his last entry into the United States on July 19, 2001. The inspector that admitted him told us that upon reviewing Atta's travel history, he likely would have asked Atta more questions to determine if he was in fact living in the United States.[144] Assuming that these questions were asked, Atta's answers must have satisfied the inspector that he was admissible, since he was not referred to secondary.

All of the inspectors agreed that failure to have the proper visa for the stated purpose was a solid basis for referral to secondary. Thus, when Atta entered on January 10, 2001, and told the immigration inspector that he was still a student while he was traveling on a tourist visa, he was referred to secondary. Some inspectors added that in the pre–September 11 atmosphere of facilitation at the ports, Atta most likely would have been admitted with a waiver for a fee or a deferred inspection, even if he did not technically qualify for the admission. Admitting Atta as a tourist, however, should not have been an option for the secondary inspector. In addition, every inspector said that giving a tourist a stay of more than six months required a supervisor's approval. Atta was given an eight-month length of stay without such approval.

Immigration inspectors also agreed that forms—the immigration arrival record called an I-94 and the customs declaration—were always checked for completeness. Immigration inspectors checked the I-94 but not the Customs declaration for substance: the latter was the responsibility of the customs inspectors. The forms were also not always compared for consistency. Thus, Fayez Banihammad got away with using two completely different names on his I-94 ("Fayez Rashid Ahmed Hassan") and his customs declaration ("Banihammad"). In addition, inspectors differed significantly on what constituted a "complete" I-94 form. Some wanted a full address. Others accepted "Hotel Orlando FL," which was used by Saeed al Ghamdi and resulted in a secondary inspection; it satisfied the secondary inspector, however, who admitted him.

Customs Inspections of the Hijackers. At airports, about 5 percent of travelers were subject to a customs inspection of their personal effects, which occurred only after their admission through the immigration inspection line. The customs inspectors were required to report declared amounts of currency greater than $10,000. Majid Moqed and Ahmed al Ghamdi, who arrived together at Washington Dulles International Airport on May 2, 2001, were the only hijackers whose surviving customs declarations[145] reported an amount in excess of $10,000.[146] There is no record of the required electronic report that should have been generated about Ghamdi's declaration. On 4 of the 13 hijacker Customs declarations available to the Commission, the question was left blank. While our focus is on the admission of the hijackers through immigration, this evidence suggests that Customs inspections of the hijackers were, at best, incomplete.

Customs, unlike INS, had access to advanced passenger manifests before a flight arrived. They reviewed these for criminal indicators, mostly with an eye to preventing narcotics trafficking. Five different hijackers' names were on advanced passenger manifests voluntarily provided by the airlines and reviewed by Customs prior to the hijackers' reaching U.S. soil.[147] None of these hijackers was on a watchlist, so their names did not set off any alarm bells.

Pressures to Facilitate Travel

It is important to note that the hijackers' entries occurred in an environment of "travel facilitation." Much pressure was placed on immigration inspectors to process travelers rapidly. Individuals were refused entry only rarely, with many airports permitting "waivers" or "deferrals" of documents normally required for admission. In some cases, such as entries by Atta on January 10, 2001, at Miami International Airport and Shehhi on January 18 at Newark International Airport, the inspectors did not recall nor did records indicate that they asked either hijacker to provide any documentation to support their stories about attending school and acquiring additional pilot training.[148]

Pressure was applied by embassies and by members of Congress who wrote letters requiring INS to justify decisions to deny entry in specific cases. The travel industry—and, according to inspectors, the airlines in particular—loudly insisted on efficient passenger processing. Most inspectors said that their supervisors would monitor processing times and "remind" inspectors to keep within 45 seconds for each passenger. One inspector stated that if processing times were not kept to a minimum, a supervisor would threaten to send the inspector back to training. Indeed, immigration inspectors were graded on how fast airline passengers were processed and how many "nonfrivolous" referrals to secondary immigration inspections they made.[149]

Driving this emphasis on speed was a 1990 congressional guideline that limited the total amount of time for a visitor to disembark from a plane and be processed through immigration inspection to 45 minutes, regardless of the number of passengers on the flight.[150] Supervisors were expected to calibrate the number of staff to the number of arriving passengers. The practical effect of this guideline was that inspectors, depending on the port of entry, generally had between 30 seconds and one minute to decide whether a visitor was admissible, and if so, how long that visitor was legally allowed to stay in the country. Both determinations by the inspector were important, as a violation either of the terms of admission or of length of stay would render the visitor's status in the United States illegal.

The prevailing view at the time was that the role of immigration was to facilitate the rapid entry of visitors to the United States. With few exceptions, speed was everything. Neither the INS nor others in government ever viewed the agency as having a pivotal role in preventing terrorist entry into the United States.

Inspector Training

The problems of the environment of facilitation in which the inspectors worked were compounded by a weak training regime. Indeed, the deficiencies in the immigration inspection process that we have discussed stem largely from inadequate training. Throughout the 1990s, immigration inspectors such as those the Commission interviewed were often hired on a temporary basis. They worked long hours for a year and more without any formal training in immigration law or policy and received no information about terrorists.[151] Only when an inspector was hired as a full-time INS employee did he or she receive the standard four-month immigration inspector training at the Federal Law Enforcement Training Center (FLETC) in Glenco, Georgia. A few inspectors received further training when promoted or given special operations assignment.

These inspectors all similarly characterized their training, which occurred from the 1970s through 2000. The inspectors did not recall substantial differences in training as the 1990s progressed, although information had become available that terrorists had entered, stayed, and committed violent acts in the United States. The focus was on passing tests. One inspector who received his training in 2000 said that "at FLETC, it is not about how much you learn—it was learn this now and pass the test, and then get rid of it. It was expected you would learn what you needed to at the port."[152]

Counterterrorism Training. The counterterrorism mission that seems so obvious today was barely acknowledged then. For example, although non-Spanish speaking inspectors received five weeks of Spanish-language instruction—which was important—there were only a few hours devoted to terrorism; these focused on Usama Bin Ladin after the 1998 bombings of the American embassies in Dar es Salaam, Tanzania, and Nairobi, Kenya.[153] Indeed, no inspector interviewed by the Commission, whether a 30-year veteran or a student of multiple trainings, ever recalled receiving any operational guidance on the role of the immigration inspector in counterterrorism. None recalled seeing "The Threat Is Real," a film intended to educate border inspectors on the travel document tactics of terrorists, which was produced by the CIA in the early 1980s.[154] The film, as noted above, was based on the

Redbook, the terrorist document manual last published in 1992 (discussed in chapter 3). Three inspectors were aware of the Redbook's existence, but only one had ever seen it.[155]

Primary and Secondary Inspection Training. Significantly, only about a half-day over the four-month course was devoted to conducting mock primary inspections. Inspectors did not receive any training in secondary inspections until they reached their assigned airport. All received training in land border inspections. The lack of training in conducting primary immigration inspections is somewhat surprising, for it is this initial inspection that identifies potentially inadmissible travelers.

Document Fraud Training. Course materials were offered on document fraud generally, including training from the Forensic Document Lab on anomalies and security features to look for in travel documents. None of this training was specific to known terrorist document fraud. Most inspectors thought this limited training was valuable, but the critical continuing education on document fraud was rare. Instead, most ports left it up to the inspectors to review the binders of fraudulent document alerts issued by the Forensic Document Lab on an as-needed basis. The task was so cumbersome and the numbers of passengers awaiting processing so great that the inspectors rarely had a free moment to assimilate new information on fraud, let alone review binders of fraud alerts that contained information on passports and visas in every language in the world.

The Commission did learn that a dedicated Arabic-speaking inspector at JFK Airport in New York in the mid-1990s produced a "bluebook" that translated into English commonly used Arabic, Farsi, Yemeni, and Saudi travel documents and stamps.[156] This bluebook was never disseminated outside of JFK, however, although it was appreciated by the inspectors we interviewed who were familiar with it.

Database Training. Similarly, although there was training in the existence of the 20-plus databases available in primary and secondary immigration and customs inspection, immigration inspectors were not taught the content and value of these databases. Thus most inspectors who had contact with the hijackers did not know that suspected terrorists were included in these databases and that they should be looking for them. All the inspectors said INS databases, including lookouts, were learned on the job,. There was also only limited behavioral training and no cultural training to help inspectors better discriminate between legitimate and mala fide travelers.

The Preferential Treatment of Saudis[157]

Inspectors from Orlando, Los Angeles, and Dulles International airports all recalled an unwritten policy of preferential treatment enjoyed by Saudis prior to September 11. In these airports, which admitted eight hijackers and refused one, Saudi travelers generally received less scrutiny. They were often escorted to the front of the immigration lines by airline personnel.

In Orlando, one inspector recalled being presented with the travel documents of an entire Saudi family by his supervisor and asked to process them all even if he personally interviewed only one or two of the family members. This, he said, happened on multiple occasions. Another inspector remembered being told he had "better be careful" in seeking to refuse entry to Saudis, since the pressure from the port, the Saudi embassy, and Congress was strongly in favor of facilitating their admission. Upon request, female Saudis would be interviewed by female inspectors, in deference to Saudi culture. Another inspector from Los Angeles International Airport recalled an incident prior to September 11 when he was required to board an arriving private Saudi 727 jet and process all the travel documents in the back of the jet, and to do so quickly and without a thorough examination of the travelers. He reluctantly complied.

At other ports that admitted hijackers, inspectors reported no preferential treatment of Saudis. No inspector considered Saudis a threat to national security. Almost all the Saudis they screened could speak English. In fact, most shared the common perception that Saudis were U.S. allies, spent a lot of money in the United States, did not overstay their visas, did not work here, and were generally good travelers to admit. The only problem that might have occurred was an occasional overstay of a student visa, for which waivers would be given "95 percent of the time."

IMMIGRATION VIOLATIONS COMMITTED BY THE HIJACKERS IN THE UNITED STATES

Once a non-U.S. citizen is admitted to the United States, he or she remains subject to U.S. immigration laws and may be deported if any are violated. The hijackers violated many laws while gaining entry to, or remaining in, the United States.

- **Every hijacker** submitted a visa application falsely stating that he was not seeking to enter the United States to engage in terrorism. This was a felony, punishable under 18 U.S.C. § 1546 by 25 years in prison and under 18 U.S.C. § 1001 by 5 years in prison, and was a violation of immigration law rendering each one inadmissible under 8 U.S.C. § 1182(a)(6)(c).

- **The hijackers**, when they presented themselves at U.S. ports of entry, were terrorists trained in Afghan camps who had prepared for and planned terrorist activity to further the aims of a terrorist organization—al Qaeda—making every hijacker inadmissible to enter the United States under 8 U.S.C.§ 1182(a)(3)(b).

- At least two (**Satam al Suqami** and **Abdul Aziz al Omari**) and possibly as many as seven of the hijackers (**Suqami, Omari, Mohand al Shehri, Hamza** and **Saeed al Ghamdi, Ahmed al Nami,** and **Ahmad al Haznawi**) presented to State Department consular officers passports manipulated in a fraudulent manner, a felony punishable under 18 U.S.C. § 1543 by 25 years in prison and a violation of immigration law rendering them inadmissible under 8 U.S.C. § 1182(a)(6)(c).

- At least two hijackers (**Suqami** and **Omari**) and as many as eleven of the hijackers (**Suqami; Omari; Waleed, Wail,** and **Mohand al Shehri; Hani Hanjour; Majed Moqed; Nawaf al Hazmi; Haznawi;** and **Hamza** and **Ahmed al Ghamdi**) presented to INS inspectors at ports of entry passports manipulated in a fraudulent manner, a felony punishable under 18 U.S.C. § 1543 by 25 years in prison and a violation of immigration law rendering them inadmissible under 8 U.S.C. § 1182(a)(6)(c).

- **Ziad Jarrah** attended flight school in June 2000 without properly adjusting his immigration status, thereby violating his immigration status and rendering him inadmissible under 8 U.S.C. § 1182(a)(7)(B) each of the subsequent six times he reentered the United States between June 2000 and August 5, 2001.

- **Hanjour** did not attend school after entering on a student visa in December 2000, thereby violating his immigration status and making him deportable under 8 U.S.C. § 1227(a)(1)(B).

- **Mohamed Atta** failed to present a proper M-1 (vocational school) visa when he entered the United States in January 2001. He had previously overstayed his tourist visa and therefore was inadmissible under 8 U.S.C. § 1182(a)(7)(B).

- **Nawaf al Hazmi** and **Suqami** overstayed the terms of their admission, a violation of immigration laws rendering them both deportable under 8 U.S.C. § 1227(a)(1)(B).

Were the Hijackers' Legal Violations Detectable?

As the accompanying text box clearly indicates, all of the hijackers violated some aspect of immigration U.S. law. The key question is whether these violations could have been detected by U.S. border security officials at the time the hijackers presented themselves for review and inspection. We know the following:

- At least three of the hijackers (**Khalid al Mihdhar** and **Nawaf** and **Salem al Hazmi**) were in the information systems of the intelligence community and thus potentially able to be watchlisted. Had they been watchlisted, their terrorist affiliation could have been exposed at the time they applied for a visa (in the case of Mihdhar and Salem al Hazmi) and applied for admission at a port of entry (in the case of all three) a decision could have been made to deny them entry or to track them in the United States.

- At least two of the hijackers, and possibly as many as seven, presented travel documents to the State Department manipulated in a fraudulent manner that indicated possible association with al Qaeda. We do not believe that the consular officers who reviewed these documents were aware of this manipulation or were told to be on the lookout for evidence of it.

- Three of the hijackers had passports that contained an indicator of Islamist extremism and thus were worthy of additional scrutiny. We do not believe that the consular officers who reviewed these documents were aware of this indicator of extremism or were told to be on the lookout for it.

- Two of the hijackers made false statements about prior visa and travel history on their visa applications during the course of the plot. These lies were potentially detectable. The State Department did have the ability to determine whether an applicant had applied previously for a nonimmigrant visa. However, prior to September 11, because its computer system did not automatically display this information in connection with a visa application, the consular officer would have had to specifically look for it.

5.3 Finding Fair Verdicts

The State Department

The State Department began the 1990s with a consular corps largely untrained to address the threat of transnational terrorism. It used outdated and insecure technology to produce visas, with a patchwork of name-check technology systems at 230 visa-issuing posts overseas, and with an innovative but funding- and information-starved terrorist watchlist known as TIPOFF. Moreover, the budget picture was bleak, as resources declined and demand for visas was expected to grow. State's Bureau of Consular Affairs suffered disproportionately from these budget cuts because many consular positions were customarily filled by junior Foreign Service officers—and they simply were not being hired. The only positive news was the temporary decline in visa demand in the early 1990s caused by growth of the Visa Waiver Program.

The State Department received a wake-up call when it was discovered that it had issued visas to come to the United States to the terrorists involved in the World Trade Center bombing in 1993, and that the spiritual leader of the group—Sheikh Omar Abdel Rahman—obtained a visa despite being on a watchlist. State's outdated technology and poor controls over watchlist screening had allowed the visa to be issued.

In response to the shock of that attack, the State Department took some significant steps during the 1990s to improve its ability to counter terrorism. Specifically, the department

- established the Visas Viper Program to force better interagency information sharing on known or suspected terrorists;
- improved the security of its visa technology;
- modernized its name-check technology by establishing a real-time connection to the watchlist located in Washington and by creating several language algorithms; and
- made available TIPOFF terrorist data to the INS—for use at the ports of entry—and to foreign partners Canada and Australia.

Many of these changes were accomplished because of the 1994 law that allowed State to fund its border security initiatives with fees collected from applicants for the machine-readable visa (MRV). For example, State used MRV fees to fund antifraud programs in the Bureau of Diplomatic Security. Unfortunately, these funds did not arrive quickly enough to prevent damage to State's counterterrorism capabilities from the continued budget shortfalls.

In response to the 1998 East Africa embassy bombings, State spent more than $3 billion to improve overseas embassy security. And while overseas embassy security had been in desperate need of improvement—a fact well-known since the Beirut bombings a decade earlier—the $3 billion spent after the 1998 bombings and before 9/11 to improve U.S. facilities appears in hindsight to demonstrate that we were fighting the last war. While embassy security was being improved, State took steps to streamline its work processes in ways that cut back on the scrutiny given individual visa applicants. Posts were encouraged to reduce interviews and speed processing of applications. Reducing face-to-face contact with visa applicants through programs such as Visa Express was even seen as enhancing security by reducing the crowds that potentially threatened our overseas facilities.

Despite its acknowledgment that consular officers were the "outer ring" of border security, during the 1990s State strongly resisted the notion that consular officers were responsible for ferreting out terrorists in visa interviews. State never sought to increase the training for consular officers to identify terrorists or unravel their travel trails by carefully examining their often-fraudulent documents. State also refused to give consular officers the latitude to deny visas to individuals they suspected might be terrorists, fearing that this discretion would be abused. Instead, consular officers were trained to spot intending economic immigrants, not terrorists, and to leave decisionmaking about potential terrorists to officials in Washington.

Faced with increasing demand for visas and pressure to improve customer service, State began to rely too much on technology and a terrorist watchlist name check to prevent terrorists from obtaining visas. Senior State officials trusted intelligence community agencies to provide data on terrorist identities for inclusion in the watchlist, but no law required that this information be given to State. Assistant Secretary of State for Consular Affairs Mary Ryan was naïve about the willingness of the intelligence community to supply this critical information, believing that it was being provided to State when in fact, for at least three hijackers, it was not.

Citizens of wealthy Persian Gulf nations or third country nationals from the Middle East with established lives in Germany were seen by State as good visa risks because they rarely overstayed their terms of admission or sought to work in the United States. The U.S. foreign policy interest in stable relations with the oil-rich Gulf countries also played a role. Even though al Qaeda leader Usama Bin Ladin had held Saudi citizenship, Saudi funding for terrorism was well established, and CIA personnel working shoulder to shoulder with State consular officials were well aware of the presence of Saudi extremists in Saudi Arabia, State Department personnel in Saudi Arabia and in Washington never acted to increase the scrutiny given Saudi visa applicants.

Indeed, it was not until July 2002 that the State Department reversed course and ordered that all visa applicants be interviewed. Today, consular training for interviewing techniques to spot terrorists is still in its infancy, and State still has not fully operationalized knowledge of terrorist travel practices.

Ultimately, the individual consular officers who adjudicated visas for the 9/11 hijackers were following State Department policy. They were not trained to spot terrorists. They were told not to give great scrutiny to applicants with the hijackers' socioeconomic backgrounds. They believed their job was to deny visas to intending immigrants and to check all applicants against the terrorist watchlist, and they did these tasks scrupulously. It is difficult to blame them for acting according to and within the discretion of policies provided them by their superiors. However, it is striking that they and their superiors—senior consular officials in Washington and in Saudi Arabia—did not recognize the yawning disconnect between the increasing terror threat in Saudi Arabia, which reached a peak in the summer of 2001, and their actions in response to that threat, which reduced the number of face-to-face encounters with Saudi visa applicants.

In all aspects of State's approach to counterterrorism—its successes and its failures, its improvements and its lapses—Congress was directly complicit. State officials told us that prior to 9/11, members of Congress rarely if ever questioned consular officers' decisions to issue visas. In fact, they told us, consular officers' most frequent correspondents were members of Congress advocating on behalf of constituents seeking the issuance of visas. It was Congress (with White House support) that starved the State Department of resources and that, persuaded that border security deserved greater attention, provided the lifeline of MRV fee collection.

In any case, though the decisions to issue visas now seem questionable, in every case State consular officers followed their standard operating procedures and adhered to the visa policy as they understood it. For the five conspirators and would-be hijackers who were denied visas, in every case those denials appear to have been grounded in concerns other than terrorism—usually the fear that they were intending immigrants. Those 9/11 hijackers and co-conspirators not pulled from the stream of visa applicants and interviewed were spared because consular officers believed they satisfied the legal requirements for obtaining a visa. In each case, consular officials performed a name check using their lookout database, including the TIPOFF watchlist. At the time these people applied for visas, none of them—or at least none of the identities given in their passports—was in the database.

The Immigration and Naturalization Service

The INS has no articulated counterterrorism policy.

—Senate Judiciary Committee report (1998)

Under the Immigration and Nationality Act, the INS has always had the statutory responsibility to determine who may enter, who may remain, and who must be removed from the United States. However, neither INS leadership nor any other entity in government ever fully recognized that within INS's overall responsibility to determine admission for all travelers was an important responsibility to exclude and remove terrorists, a task that no other agency could perform.

The failure of the INS to recognize the value of its immigration authority in identifying and removing terrorists was manifested throughout the agency. It stemmed from a general lack of a counterterrorism strategy. As we have seen, the fledgling INS counterterrorism activities of the late 1990s were carried out by a handful of dedicated employees in middle management whose resources were minimal and whose strategies and recommendations were mostly ignored. But the INS was not alone in failing to identify a counterterrorism role for itself. The White House was concerned in the 1990s with human smuggling and trafficking, illegal entries, naturalization backlogs, refugee crises, employer sanctions, criminal alien deportations and detention space, and INS restructuring. Even when presidential decision directives assigned a role to the INS in countering terrorism, the INS was not sent those directives. Attorney General Reno and her deputies, along with Congress, made their highest priorities shoring up the Southwest border to prevent the migration of illegal aliens and selectively upgrading technology systems. And while some parts of the Justice Department were preoccupied with counterterrorism investigations, its leadership never saw a significant role for INS in counterterrorism other than to support the FBI.

Programs initiated by Congress with a counterterrorism capability, notably foreign student tracking and an entry-exit system at the ports of entry, never received adequate support from the Congress or the INS leadership and so never materialized. Financial and human resources were also lacking. The budget for interior enforcement remained static in the face of millions of immigrants outside the legal framework. Many INS agents were overwhelmed and disheartened.

Immigration benefits applications were backlogged for months and even years. Technology moneys were spent, but often for stand-alone computer systems that lacked essential information. As a result, the officers adjudicating these applications did not have access to immigration or law enforcement histories of applicants requesting extended stays or naturalization or to intelligence information. Thus, immigration benefits were obtained by many terrorists in the 1990s even when they were being investigated or prosecuted as terrorists by other personnel in the Justice Department.

These immigration cases against suspected terrorists were often mired for years in bureaucratic struggles over alien rights and the adequacy of evidence. The quality of intelligence within the agency was low; Commissioner Meissner had never heard of Usama Bin Ladin until after she left government service.

The verdict for the INS as an institution is that a poorly organized agency with a poor public image and low self-esteem never received adequate support from within its own leadership, its parent Justice Department, the Congress, or the White House to take itself seriously or be taken seriously as having a key role in counterterrorism. Thus no one at the White House or in the Justice Department noticed that INS leadership was unaware of the White House after-action work on the northern border in 2000 or of the heightened state of threat under which the rest of the government was operating during the summer of 2001. Meanwhile, the hijackers were seeking entry into the United States— and succeeding in an atmosphere in which the priority was neither enforcement nor counterterrorism.

Given the lack of a defined counterterrorism role for the INS, it should not be surprising that training for inspectors at ports of entry lacked a counterterrorism component. That training did not, for example, include information on terrorists' use of fraudulent travel documents, which forensic specialists stopped examining in the early 1990s, or the critical role of the inspector in preventing terrorists' entry. Our study also suggests that training in immigration law, procedures, and regulations was similarly insufficient. Indeed, immigration law was, and remains, so intricate and confusing that some inspectors lacked a clear understanding of issues of admissibility, and therefore mistakenly admitted some hijackers into the country. Other inspectors were simply worn down by the culture of facilitation, in which travelers with questionable admissibility were almost inevitably given the benefit of the doubt and admitted.

Different conclusions can be drawn regarding a few of the immigration inspections of some of the hijackers. Most immigration inspectors, operating under severe time constraints and an expectation of facilitation, and lacking standard operating procedures and basic visitor information, conducted fair adjudications. The primary immigration inspectors who referred Atta, Shehhi, Saeed al Ghamdi, and Kahtani to secondary inspection to be questioned further used the tools available to them and their training to make good decisions.

But the secondary inspectors for the first three men failed to ask the kinds of questions that might have elicited information that the hijackers could not substantiate. For example, Atta's secondary inspector misjudged him as a tourist, even though Atta presented him with a student/school form as a basis for entry. Rather than admit him as a tourist, which he did, this inspector could have given Atta a deferred inspection to gather his school papers and return to an INS district office in 30 days to verify his status. Atta would have been unable to do so, since he had received his pilot's license a month earlier. The inspector also violated length of stay requirements by giving Atta an eight-month stay without a supervisor's approval. It took an astute inspector at the Miami INS District Office to roll back his length of stay to July 9, 2001, after Atta unwittingly made a mistake in seeking a longer length of stay for a fellow hijacker. When Kahtani was refused entry, the secondary inspector had a weaker legal basis for denial than existed for Atta. But he took the time to determine mala fide intent and, basing his decision on evidence Kahtani intended to immigrate to the United States, he denied him entry, thereby preventing at least one hijacker from participating in the plot.

6

CRISIS MANAGEMENT AND RESPONSE:
POST-SEPTEMBER 11

6.1 The Intelligence Community

> The main thing now is security, do you understand? We must be most
> careful above all with documents and identities, because without them . . .
> we're lost.
>
> —al Qaeda operative

The attacks of 9/11 did what policy guidance and evidence had failed to
do: it focused at least one intelligence agency, the CIA, on the critical need
for terrorist travel information.

CIA's Directorate of Science and Technology set up a Passport
Analysis Program. Its mission is to identify terrorists according to the
documents they use. The program looks for individuals whose passports
incorporate indicators of terrorist affiliation; develops automated detection tools that identify in near real-time the bearers of fraudulent foreign
passports, and helps to verify the citizenship of individuals attempting to
enter the United States.

Integration of the Passport Analysis Program's proven methods is
languishing. No government component responsible for interdicting illegal
travelers has incorporated the automated detection tools at the front end of
its screening process where the tools would have the greatest utility for
consular officers and immigration inspectors.

A second program was created in October 2001, when most of the
CIA's Office of Transnational Issues (OTI) moved to the Office of Terrorism
Analysis (OTA) of the Counterterrorism Center (CTC) to form a new
Terrorist Transportation and Travel Branch. The unit was later renamed the
Terrorist Mobility Branch.[1] Before its creation there was no programmatic

effort at CTC—or anywhere else in government—that focused on broad trends and methodologies of terrorist travel.

The goal of the Terrorist Mobility Branch has been to identify key groups and individuals that facilitate terrorist travel, such as travel agencies, corrupt government officials, fraudulent document vendors, and document forgers, as well as patterns of document fraud and other travel tactics associated with al Qaeda and other terrorists.[2] In order to "operationalize" the intelligence produced by the Terrorist Mobility Branch, in the fall of 2002 a new branch was formed in the Directorate of Operations.[3] Since January 2002, 17 facilitators have been disrupted in coordinated CTC-law enforcement efforts.[4]

Yet anecdotal evidence suggests that much of the analysis being generated by the Terrorist Mobility Branch is failing to reach critical audiences whom it would greatly benefit. An informal survey indicates that border inspectors at primary immigration stations at ports of entry do not receive it systematically because of classification and security issues.[5] It is not hard to see why. There is no electronic dissemination system capable of sending highly classified reports to field units who need them. The clearances of INS officers are insufficient to allow the transfer of important and relevant information to them. And some agencies are culturally opposed to sharing information.[6]

For its part, the FBI did not endeavor to analyze terrorist travel information and does not include such analysis as a terrorist disruption technique. Generally speaking, there is no systematic and centrally directed collection and analysis of suspect travel documents.

6.2 The Department of State

In the immediate aftermath of 9/11, the State Department responded to requests for information from the FBI and other law enforcement agencies investigating the 9/11 attacks.[7] When it was discovered that two of the 9/11 hijackers were known to the CIA in 1999 but this information had not been passed to State for watchlisting purposes, Assistant Secretary for Consular Affairs Mary Ryan requested a meeting with CIA Director George Tenet at which she expressed her outrage over this failure to share information.[8] Tenet promised Ryan there would be changes; shortly thereafter, CIA contributions to the TIPOFF watch list increased dramatically.[9]

Initially, the State Department did not begin to reevaluate its visa-issuing processes. Instead, investigations of visa-issuing policies and how they related to the 9/11 attacks were launched by the General Accounting Office

(GAO), Congress in its oversight capacity, and the State Department Inspector General. Consular officers in the field became frustrated by the lack of direction on visa policy from Washington. Dissatisfaction ran especially high in Saudi Arabia, where 15 of the 19 hijackers had acquired their visas. Consular officials in Jeddah believed that it was "business as usual," with the consulate continuing "to waive interviews for the vast majority of Saudi applicants."[10] They were chastised by the State Department for publicly stating this view.[11]

The period from 9/11 to 2003 was spent responding to law enforcement needs regarding the 9/11 attacks, tightening up visa issuance procedures at the margins, and implementing a number of programs in cooperation with the Justice Department and other agencies. These included the 20-day hold and Condor name-check programs developed in the interagency process, the NSEERS (National Security Exit and Entry Registration System) program, and the relevant provisions of the USA PATRIOT Act, the Enhanced Border Security Act, and the Homeland Security Act, discussed in the next section.

Following 9/11, State also expanded its Terrorist Interdiction Program (TIP) to include 60 priority countries. This foreign assistance program is designed to enhance border security around the globe by providing state-of-the-art border control technology to specific nations.[12] The system has been installed in approximately ten countries.

By 2003, State's approach for the future was coming into focus. It included making dramatic changes in visa processing, retooling consular work for counterterrorism, supporting the development of U.S. and international biometric border and travel document standards, and enhancing the security of the U.S. passport system. State established the Vulnerability Assessment Unit to systematically review issued visas for patterns that might indicate malfeasance, and began checking the database of issued visas against any new terrorist watch list information.

On August 1, 2003, State issued new regulations that limited the waiver of personal appearances for nonimmigrant visa (NIV) applicants to only a few categories of exceptions, among whom were diplomats, children, and the elderly.[13] This was a major change from the era before 9/11, when State policies encouraged consular managers to decrease the frequency of visa interviews in order to save resources. Beginning on October 17, 2003, State also lengthened its basic consular course, also known as ConGen, from 26 to 31 days, in order to add material on visa security, counterterrorism awareness, and interviewing techniques. The new training included a two-day course on ways to identify deception by applicants, a half-day program on counterterrorism at CIA headquarters, and a module on terrorist travel patterns. State also expanded intranet resources for consular officers to assist them in reading and verifying entry/exit cachets in Arabic or Persian script.[14]

On September 22, 2003, State began the worldwide deployment of biometric nonimmigrant visa (NIV) software that provided for the collection of fingerprints in the NIV application process.[15] State is on schedule to have all visa-issuing posts collecting biometrics for all applicants by October 26, 2004, the statutory deadline. A few months later, on December 1, 2003, the TIPOFF terrorist watchlist, created by State in 1987, was transferred to the Terrorist Screening Center (TSC) for integration with other government watchlists. The TSC maintains watchlist information—including intelligence on foreign persons and information from FBI terrorism investigations into U.S. persons—from all sources, and through the National Crime Information Center (NCIC) it provides a link to state and local law enforcement.

State is working with countries eligible for the Visa Waiver Program and with the International Civil Aviation Authority to meet the requirement that those countries incorporate biometric identifiers in their passports by October 2004, as mandated by the Enhanced Border Security Act. State recently asked for an extension to November 30, 2006.

With the passage of the Homeland Security Act—which transferred the task of setting visa policy from State and to the Department of Homeland Security (DHS)—State entered into a memorandum of understanding with DHS formalizing the division of responsibility on visa policy. State now coordinates visa determinations with DHS's Immigration and Customs Enforcement officers in some overseas posts, including Saudi Arabia.

6.3 The Department of Justice

Immediately after September 11, Attorney General John Ashcroft developed an antiterrorism plan with two strategic goals: to develop intelligence to identify and apprehend terrorists, and to undertake law enforcement operations to disrupt terrorist planning and operations.[16] Thereafter, the Department of Justice, on its own and through the interagency process, created a number of programs that singled out for greater scrutiny aliens from predominantly Muslim or Arab countries, both those inside the United States and those outside the United States who were seeking visas.

These programs—in roughly chronological order—were the Interview Project, the 20-day hold, the Absconder Apprehension Initiative, Visas

Condor, and NSEERS. In addition, beginning on September 11 throughout this period, the Justice Department directed its subcomponents, the FBI and the INS, in actions that led to the detention of 768 individuals, mostly Muslims and Arabs, considered by Justice to be of investigative interest following the September 11 attacks.[17]

The Interview Project

On November 9, 2001, the Attorney General announced that the Department of Justice would interview several thousand nonimmigrant aliens from countries with an al Qaeda terrorist presence about their knowledge of terrorist elements within the United States,[18] an undertaking known as the Interview Project. Ashcroft described the purposes of the project as threefold: (1) the department wanted to have law enforcement presence in the community, (2) it wanted the agents "off their duffs," and (3) it was hoping to get some investigative leads.[19] The interviews were voluntary, although in some cases interviewees may have felt they had no choice but to participate. Between November 9 and February 26, 2002, law enforcement officers under the direction of U.S. Attorneys conducted 2,261 interviews out of FBI and INS database searches that had identified 4,793 potential interviewees.[20]

In March 2002, the Attorney General started a second phase of interviews of 3,189 nonimmigrant aliens from 26 countries—the same as the Condor countries (discussed below)—and from a broader age range than was represented in the first phase.[21] Although data from all the interviews conducted were entered into a database maintained by the Justice Management Division, they were never analyzed by the Justice Department. We asked Justice to provide us with documents summarizing the origin, mission, and results of the Interview Project, including the "intelligence, counterterrorism, and law enforcement benefits which resulted from the program," but we received no documents prepared after February 2002, shortly before the second phase began.[22]

Justice asserts that the project met its two goals, intelligence gathering and disruption, a judgment based mostly on anecdotal reporting and speculation.[23] However, as the GAO pointed out, there has been no analysis of the value of the law enforcement leads it yielded, and law enforcement officials differed on whether the interview project helped build ties to the communities involved or created greater hostility within them. The GAO concluded that without such analysis, it was difficult to draw lessons from the project. We agree, and add that the system was never designed to allow its results to be analyzed. Under guidance provided to officers conducting interviews, any valuable counterterrorism leads from interviews in the field were to be forwarded directly to FBI agents in the field for follow up.[24] Thus, the centralized database simply served the interests of management and oversight and aided little in assessing the program's benefit to counterterrorism.

Twenty-Day Hold

Effective November 14, 2001, the State Department—at the urging of Justice—issued a blanket 20-day hold before any visa could be issued to males 16 to 45 years old from 26 countries in the Middle East and North Africa, plus Bangladesh, Malaysia, and Indonesia. This program was discontinued on October 18, 2002. Records we have reviewed suggest it yielded no useful antiterrorist information and led to no visa denials.[25]

The Absconder Apprehension Initiative (AAI)

Under U.S. immigration law, absconders are noncitizens who willfully fail to depart the United States after receiving a final order of deportation from an immigration judge. They may be prosecuted for a federal felony.[26] After September 11, INS Commissioner James Ziglar proposed that the names of 314,000 absconders be placed in the Wanted Persons file in the National Crime Information Center database accessible by state and local law enforcement.[27] To meet NCIC standards, every absconder entry had to be supported by a full set of fingerprints and a photograph so that the INS Law Enforcement Support Center (LESC) could electronically transmit those identifiers to the querying law enforcement official within ten minutes.[28] If the absconder's identity was confirmed, then the INS could place a federal detainer—requiring that the alien already in custody only be released into federal custody—or arrange for an INS agent to take the individual into custody and proceed with removal. Finding terrorists was not a focus of the program.[29] Attorney General Ashcroft liked the idea, and Commissioner Ziglar announced it on December 5, 2001.[30] Shortly thereafter, the initiative was recast as a counterterrorism program.[31]

Deputy Attorney General Larry Thompson on January 25, 2002, provided guidance for the newly renamed Absconder Apprehension Initiative (AAI). He explained that the object of the initiative was to deport the 314,000 alien fugitives in two phases. The first phase would focus on several thousand priority absconders "who come from countries in which there has been al Qaeda terrorist presence or activity . . . because some of them have information that could assist our campaign against terrorism."[32] The second phase would locate and deport the remaining absconders.[33]

The Deputy Attorney General directed the FBI's Foreign Terrorist Tracking Task Force to remove any names that were subjects of active terrorist investigations.[34]

At the INS, the National Security Unit (NSU) was tasked with the project.[35] The AAI effort was a massive undertaking for this small unit, which was the INS's primary counterterrorism unit.[36] The NSU developed a special project staff of its own agents and INS intelligence analysts from the Office of Intelligence, and it detailed agents from the INS field offices, as many as ten at a time, to develop the project.[37] For each absconder case in which a last known address could be found, the NSU created a work file and sent it to a designated supervisory special agent in the INS field office located in that geographic area for follow-up. The administrative tasks associated with the AAI priority cases required that many field officers be assigned to the NSU headquarters unit, leaving fewer special agents available to investigate the AAI priority cases in the field.[38]

Phase 1 of the AAI covered 5,932 cases.[39] In order to help immigration authorities locate these absconders, some of their records were entered into the National Crime Information Center database.[40] In addition, criminal record checks were conducted on all AAI cases.[41] A total of 863 absconders had a criminal history, but in many cases the final disposition of these criminal cases was not recorded in the NCIC database. As a result, case agents had to obtain additional court documents to determine what action was appropriate in each of these cases.

NCIC hits resulting from routine record checks conducted by law enforcement agencies led to the location of 95 absconders.[42] In these cases, the LESC placed a detainer on the alien and referred the case to the local Immigration and Customs Enforcement field office for follow-up.[43]

A total of 191 absconders turned out to be U.S. legal permanent residents. Another 80 had been naturalized and were now U.S. citizens. Together, these groups accounted for 5 percent of priority absconders. Naturally, this statistic raises the question of how an alien absconder could be granted either legal residency or citizenship. The reasons for this error are many. Foremost is the problem of INS recordkeeping, which has always been unreliable. Individual immigration files are actually paper files. Each is created from an alien's name and is not linked to a biometric identifier, such as a photograph or a fingerprint. Thus one person could easily have multiple immigration files, enabling him or her to apply for various immigration benefits at the same time.[44] Aliens so inclined could use a variety of name variations or an alias to commit immigration fraud or to avoid deportation. In some cases, the final order of deportation had been issued years previously. Because of the overall poor state of INS recordkeeping, some aliens were able to return to the United States without being arrested on the deportation order at the port of entry.

Ultimately, 4,074 cases were closed.[45] The 1,858 remaining cases either were still under investigation or lacked a final report. The total number of absconder cases that were actually closed because the subject was determined to be *no longer an absconder* was 2,267, or approximately 38 percent of the original number.

AAI Phase 1

5,932	Total initial cases
2,267	Cases closed after investigation verified departure or immigration status
1,807	Cases closed after investigation, unable to locate or verify immigration status
704	Absconders located and removed from U.S. during Phase 1
1,858	Cases remain open
14	Cases referred to FBI for further investigation relating to possible terrorist links
0	Cases prosecuted or removed on terrorism grounds

By early 2003, 1,139 of the designated absconders had been apprehended, 704 had removed from the country, and 224 were in custody and awaiting removal. In addition, U.S. Attorneys had criminally prosecuted 45 individuals, 41 of whom for criminal immigration violations.[46] Although the INS had referred 14 cases to the FBI on the grounds of their possible links to terrorism, no absconders who were removed as part of phase 1 were deported under a terrorism statute or prosecuted for terrorism-related crimes.

Thus, even though extensive investigative resources were committed to the effort, only 38 percent of the priority absconders could be located or their immigration status verified. The immigration records system was so poor that approximately 5 percent of the absconders had, in fact, become legal residents or naturalized citizens of the United States. The INS's difficulty in locating absconders is consistent with the difficulty generally faced by immigration authorities attempting to locate aliens inside our country, whether they came in legally through a port of entry or illegally across an unguarded border. It is very difficult to find alien absconders without extraordinary effort or pure luck.

The Commission believes the remaining absconders who were not apprehended in the first phase of the program no longer receive special attention from immigration enforcement personnel. Indeed, DHS has absorbed phase 2 of the AAI into its current fugitive operations unit.

The Visas Condor Program

The Visas Condor Program was initiated on January 26, 2002. It mandated additional security screening by the FBI and other agencies for certain visa applicants from 26 predominantly Muslim countries. However, neither the FBI nor the CIA was able to process these visa applicants in a timely fashion, because their other responsibilities burgeoned after the September 11 attacks. In July 2002, the FBI acknowledged it could not meet the agreed-on 30-day target for name checks, and on July 20, 2002, the State Department agreed to place these visa applicants on indefinite hold until the FBI responded. In September 2002, the CIA withdrew from the program because it had uncovered no significant information from these visa applicants. The CIA was already placing all important information into the TIPOFF terrorist watchlist, used by the State Department to screen these same visa applicants when they submitted their applications. On October 2, 2003, the Condor criteria were changed and more narrowly focused.[47] As of April 2004, approximately 130,000 Condor name checks had been completed.[48] No individual subject to a Visas Condor name check has had his or her visa application turned down on grounds of being a terrorist.

NSEERS

In May 2002, the Attorney General directed the INS to develop an entry-exit registration system at selected ports of entry, and on September 11, 2002, the INS implemented the National Security Exit and Entry Registration System.[49] The program had a number of components. It mandated the photographing, fingerprinting, and interviewing of certain individuals from certain predominantly Arab and Muslim countries upon their arrival in the United States, and required the same kind of registration for such individuals already inside the United States. It also mandated that these individuals be reinterviewed 30 days after their entry to the United States, that they notify the INS if they changed their address, that they present themselves for an annual interview if they remained inside the United States, and that they have an interview when they departed the United States. Finally, the program provided for enforcement measures against those who were found to be in violation of immigration or other laws when they sought to register or who violated program rules by, for example, failing to register at all.[50]

NSEERS was imposed in phases. Beginning on September 11, 2002, inspectors of the INS (now Customs and Border Protection, or CBP) were required to register nonimmigrant aliens applying for admission to the United States who were citizens or nationals of the state sponsors of terrorism: Iran, Iraq, Sudan, Libya, and Syria.[51]

Beginning October 1, 2002, when all ports of entry were to have the new alien registration database and equipment installed,[52] inspectors were also required to register nonimmigrant males between the ages of 16 and 45 years of age who were citizens of Pakistan, Saudi Arabia, and Yemen.[53] A discretionary component allowed State Department consular officials and INS inspectors to order the registration of aliens from any country if they determined such action to be in the interests of national security.[54]

The registration at ports of entry worked as follows. All aliens applying for admission to the United States were screened against the Interagency Border Inspection System (IBIS) by inspectors at ports of entry. If an alien applying for entry was identified in IBIS as being subject to NSEERS registration, the alien was referred to secondary inspection for enrollment in NSEERS. In the secondary inspection area, the registrant was placed under oath and asked predefined questions that covered, among other things, biography, employment, school, intended address in the United States, points of contact, and credit card information.[55] The registrant's photograph and two index fingerprints were captured digitally. The applicant's biometric and textual data were then stored in a database administered by the Bureau of Immigration and Customs Enforcement (ICE).[56]

The biometric data were checked against four databases containing information on convicted aggravated felons, known or suspected terrorists, people wanted on criminal warrants, and criminal alien recidivists.[57] If there was a hit from one of these database checks, or if another immigration law violation was uncovered as part of the routine border screening, the person could be denied entry. If there was no derogatory information discovered, then the alien was enrolled in NSEERS and admitted to the United States.[58]

As of May 2, 2004, there had been 352,385 NSEERS registrations at ports of entry involving 141,168 individuals,[59] and 1,352 enforcement actions taken at ports of entry.[60] These actions often involved denial of entry, because, for example, the alien had failed to comply with NSEERS requirements when previously in the United States. Some denials related to more serious conduct involved such violations of criminal law as document fraud, espionage, crimes involving moral turpitude, and willful misrepresentations of fact.[61]

Once admitted into the United States, NSEERS registrants were required to report to an INS/DHS field office for a 30-day interview between the 30th and 40th day of their admission and within 10 days of the one-year anniversary of that admission. As of May 2, 2004, a total of 30,490 30-day and 172 annual interviews had been conducted.[62] DHS has estimated that 400 to 2,000 individuals were referred to ICE for investigation following the 30-day interview.[63]

Registrants also were directed to report to designated ports of departure for an interview on the date they left the United States.[64] As of May 22, 2003, there had been 34,439 departure interviews.[65] However, the departure interviews were conducted at an immigration office and not at the airport terminal, so it is "quite possible that a registrant could be given a departure interview by CBP, and then fail[] to depart."[66] Significant changes in the infrastructure of airports would be required for NSEERS exit procedures to occur at the actual point of departure.[67]

NSEERS domestic call-in registration began on November 15, 2002, and ended on April 25, 2003. Four call-in notices were announced through publication in the *Federal Register* setting forth the countries and conditions under which certain nonimmigrants were required to register. Male citizens or nationals 16 years of age or older from Iran, Iraq, Libya, Sudan, Syria, Afghanistan, Algeria, Bahrain, Eritrea, Lebanon, Morocco, North Korea, Oman, Qatar, Somalia, Tunisia, the United Arab Emirates, Yemen, Pakistan, Saudi Arabia, Bangladesh, Egypt, Indonesia, Jordan, and Kuwait who were admitted as nonimmigrants on or before September 30, 2002, were directed to register in NSEERS at their local immigration offices.[68] The registration process was the same as that at the ports of entry, described above. As of May 2, 2004, a total of 83,909 individuals were registered pursuant to call-in registration.[69] If the domestic registrant was not in violation of any law and there was no hit in any of the four databases, he was told to report for an annual interview, but not for a 30-day interview.[70]

A significant number of domestic registrants were in violation of some law. According to DHS records, about 13,000 call-in registrants, or 16 percent, were found to be in violation of immigration laws when they appeared; they were registered, arrested, and processed for removal from the United States.[71] The call-in registration process had considerable problems, caused by a flood of applicants in the last week of the call-in period, the failure to provide sufficient computer terminals to quickly handle the processing, and the INS's lack of preparation for handling the approximately 13,000 individuals who were arrested.[72]

Estimates of the number of NSEERS violators—individuals who failed to register initially, failed to show up for the 30-day or annual interview, or failed to register their departure through a designated port of departure—vary, in part because the database used to produce this information has been error-prone and unreliable.[73] As of May 22, 2003, the Department of Homeland Security put the figure at 12,670 "potential NSEERS violators."[74] By May 2, 2004, DHS reported it had begun 1,883 investigations: 132 NSEERS violators were arrested, 372 were determined to have left the country, and 457 were found to be in compliance with NSEERS regulations.[75]

There was significant opposition to the NSEERS program from some U.S. government officials, who feared the program would offend countries that were U.S. allies in the global war on terror.[76] State personnel we interviewed said that NSEERS did harm our relations with foreign countries whose citizens were subject to its registration requirements. FBI Director Mueller said it came at a cost.[77] Documents we reviewed, including correspondence from foreign countries' representatives, indicate that some foreign governments were strongly opposed to having their nationals subject to NSEERS registration.[78]

On March 31, 2003, apparently in response to these concerns, the White House sent out a "global message" on NSEERS from the Homeland Security Council to the executive secretaries of State, Justice, Homeland Security, the National Security Council, the Office of Management and Budget, the White House Domestic Policy Council, the Office of the Vice President, and the President's Chief of Staff. The purpose of this message was "to explain responsibilities and ramifications of NSEERS to foreign governments" and avoid misunderstandings with foreign partners.[79]

As of May 5, 2004, individuals from 170 countries had been registered in NSEERS.[80] The country with the largest number of NSEERS registrants—38,000—was Indonesia, followed by Pakistan with 29,000, and Iran with 15,000.[81]

According to the Department of Homeland Security, the US VISIT (Visitor and Information Status Indication Technology) program—which captures the fingerprints and photographs of nonimmigrant visa holders upon entry and exit—"will ultimately subsume the functions of the NSEERS program."[82]

DHS asserts that 11 persons out of approximately 140,000 registrants have been shown to have a connection to terrorism.[83] Of these, six were NSEERS call-in registrants, though it is not clear from information we have received whether the registration process led to their arrest; two were denied entry at the port of entry following a hit in the TIPOFF watchlist, and thus their identifications were not attributable, in other words, to the NSEERS program; one failed to appear for a call-in registration and was encountered and arrested in the field on grounds that are not clear to us; one was arrested, and we have no information whether he was required to participate in the NSEERS program; and one is currently "at large."[84]

The counterterrorism benefits from the NSEERS program are unclear. The Department of Homeland Security asserts that arresting and processing for removal the approximately 12,000 individuals "who appeared for call-in registration and were found to be illegally in the U.S." had a *deterrent effect* because it "signaled a clear message to those 'sleeper' terrorists embedded in U.S. communities, that U.S. immigration law would be enforced."[85] DHS also claims that NSEERS had a *disruptive effect* because it "forc[ed] would be terrorists to comply with the terms and conditions of their admission to the United States or run the risk of being removed from the United States. This additional pressure may make the job of carrying out a terrorist mission much more difficult, therefore disrupting the mission."[86] But one witness who testified before the Commission maintained that the call-in registration component of NSEERS may have diminished the willingness of immigrant communities to supply the government with intelligence.[87]

It is difficult to gauge the counterterrorism benefit from these programs because information on how they have affected terrorists is not always easy to come by. Our analysis of the 9/11 plot and the actions taken by the hijackers while inside the United States suggests that the conspirators worked diligently to manipulate the U.S. immigration system to enable them to remain inside the United States long enough to commit the attack. They appear to have been aware of U.S. immigration laws and regulations, and to have structured their travel and entries to the United States with those constraints in mind. As we have noted, the enforcement of immigration laws might have disrupted the plot if it had led, for example, to the removal of Mohamed Atta from the United States when he attempted to enter in January 2001 with the wrong visa. Likewise, the lack of an entry-exit system hampered the efforts of intelligence and law enforcement officials to locate Nawaf al Hazmi when he was finally placed on the watchlist in August 2001. Thus, the proposition that these programs had the potential to disrupt and perhaps to deter terrorist plots forming inside the United States after 9/11 certainly has some support. Ultimately, it is difficult to measure the success of operations whose goals included deterrence. However, our research demonstrates that terrorists often need to break laws in order to successfully complete their operations, undertaken in the United States and elsewhere.

They routinely commit immigration and document fraud, and often sustain their operations with petty crime. The routine enforcement of laws, including those not specifically related to terrorism, can therefore raise obstacles for and in some cases have a deterrent effect on individuals intending to commit terrorist attacks.

Perhaps significantly, a senior al Qaeda detainee has stated that after the 9/11 attacks, U.S. government efforts to more closely monitor the American homeland through such actions as, as he termed it, reviewing Muslims' immigration files and deporting nonpermanent residents made al Qaeda operations more difficult.[88] The detainee cited problems in obtaining tourist visas without interviews and instances in which visa applications were turned down even when the visa documents and passport documentation were complete.[89] If this detainee's account is credible, these programs may have had some deterrent effect on al Qaeda planning and operations in the United States and may have required terrorists to consider other tactics for entering and remaining inside the United States or to attack elsewhere.

6.4 Response at the Borders, September 11–20, 2001

In the days immediately following the attacks, the immigration and customs services undertook a number of measures, independently and in cooperation with one another and other agencies in the government, to better secure America's borders. The counterterrorism role so long ignored was finally getting the attention it deserved, although these measures taxed the limited human resources and technology then in place on U.S. borders.

"Level One" Border Security Measures

At about 10:00 on the morning of the attack, the new INS commissioner, Jim Ziglar, received a call from the acting commissioner of the Customs Service, Chuck Winwood.[90] He recommended that the two services implement their most stringent "Level One" inspections of travelers and goods seeking admission into the United States at land, sea, and air ports of entry.[91] No one knew if a second wave of attacks was coming. Ziglar agreed, and an order was issued throughout both the Customs and INS system.[92]

In addition, both INS and Customs immediately activated their command and control centers to monitor and provide directives for border operations. For both services, these centers collected the incoming information that by the evening of September 11 helped identify most of the hijackers and retrieve their arrival/departure records,[93] information that was immediately provided to the FBI. As the week wore on, the centers also processed information concerning security and trade at the borders, lists of visitors who were not permitted to leave the United States, and the arrests of possible terrorists who had immigration violations, and they helped review international airline passenger manifests for arriving travelers.[94]

Airport Inspections. On the morning of September 11, airports across the country initially were preoccupied with devising ways to clear out passengers from airport terminals, while the FAA diverted incoming international flights to Canada and Mexico. As a no-fly ban was put into effect, some airport immigration inspectors were temporarily reassigned to help with the mounting traveler backups at the land borders. On the following day, airport immigration inspectors, many of whom were still conducting security at their assigned airports, were given permission to carry a firearm.[95]

By the time the flight ban was lifted on September 13, the INS had deployed 318 Border Patrol agents to nine airports—about as many agents as were working the entire northern border.[96] The INS had suggested this deployment to the Attorney General, and Ashcroft had relayed the request to President Bush, who approved it.[97]

On September 13, both airspace and airports reopened under tight security. However, "Level One" procedures did not affect admission procedures or wait times at airports as dramatically as they had those at land borders, which technically never shut down. The difference between the two was that airports always had processed all international travelers, whereas land ports of entry scrutinized travelers and vehicles randomly. The heightened threat alert placed a tremendous strain on their human and technological resources.

Land borders. Given the tremendous volume of people and commerce that cross U.S. land borders every day, a shift from random to comprehensive and thorough immigration and customs inspections caused an urgent problem. Land borders process about four times as many travelers as airports, and have about three times as many immigrant entries.[98] In addition, the United States and Canada have the largest trading relationship in the world, worth hundreds of billions of dollars per year.[99]

Under Level One, nearly every commercial or passenger vehicle was to be thoroughly checked—under the car, under the hood, in trunks, and in glove compartments. People also were checked more carefully. Dedicated cross-border commuter programs and remote inspection reporting systems were suspended.[100] Ambassador Bridge in Detroit saw its normal 20-minute wait grind to a 12-hour crawl on September 12. The bridge normally handles 6,000 trucks per day, and 25 percent of the total trade from Canada. Commercial traffic was paralyzed. Automobile plants in Detroit dependent on just-in-time deliveries shut down.[101] The Customs and INS commissioners were inundated with phone calls from distressed business leaders whose financial lifeblood was free interchange with trading partners on the other side of the border.[102] All this occurred despite inspectors working 12 to 16 hours a day, sometimes seven days a week.[103]

With the pressure building on the borders and repercussions being felt in the private sector, it became critical to border authorities to minimize wait times with Level One procedures in place. Additional primary inspection lanes were opened where the infrastructure of the port permitted. While in line, arriving cargo vehicles were prescreened by roving inspectors, nonintrusive technologies, and canine enforcement teams.[104] In full cooperation with each other, the INS and Customs, along with additional support from airport inspectors temporarily reassigned to help at the land borders, the National Guard, the Canadian Customs and Revenue Agency, local law enforcement, and the private sector, reduced wait times almost to pre–September 11 norms by September 17, although the heightened alert was never lifted.[105]

Support to the FBI. On the afternoon of September 11, Jim Ziglar participated in a meeting called by the Attorney General and attended by Deputy Attorney General Thompson and the new FBI director, Robert Mueller, among others. Its purpose was to discuss the Justice Department's strategy to prevent a second wave of attacks while investigating the September 11 attack itself. Ziglar was told that the FBI was in charge of the investigation and that the INS was expected to support them. Ziglar quickly reassigned 1,000—or nearly half—of his special agents to the FBI, which dramatically diminished the ability of the INS to exercise its immigration enforcement mission. This meeting also laid the foundation for the Attorney General's subsequent use of INS immigration authority as a tool in the war on terror.[106]

Transit without Visa Suspended. Within days of September 11, the INS and Customs suspended "in-transit" processing for air passengers.[107] Traditionally, in-transit processing allowed passengers whose final destination was in the United States to enter the country and catch a connecting flight to that destination before undergoing immigration and customs inspections. The suspension of the program required all flights from abroad to be inspected at their first arriving port of entry.[108] The same procedures were to apply at technical stops for refueling.[109] All passengers and crew had to exit the aircraft with all carry-on baggage and then be escorted by airline personnel to the INS, Customs, and the Animal and Plant Health Inspection Service for full inspection.[110]

Defense Department Assistance. On September 12, Customs leadership placed a call to Michigan Governor John Engler requesting the help of Michigan's National Guard at land ports of entry.[111] During this time, the President also asked state governors to provide extra security at airports with National Guard personnel. As a result, 7,000 National Guard members were activated to supplement security at 421 airports.[112] Six months later, the INS and Department of Defense signed an agreement lending National Guard personnel for six months for specific duties at land borders.[113]

6.5 The Department of Homeland Security

September 11 brought border security to the forefront of the President's counterterrorism agenda. One result was to sweep the Immigration and Naturalization Service and U.S. Customs into the Department of Homeland Security, where they were reconfigured in a manner that hinted of past debates about restructuring the INS into its immigration services and immigration enforcement functions. Approximately 60,000 employees working at U.S. borders, interior enforcement, and immigration benefit services were divided into separate agencies for the purpose of "minimizing duplication of efforts, improving coordination, and combining functions that are currently fragmented and inefficient."[114] In addition, about 40,000 Coast Guard officials, who interdict about 5,000 illegal aliens at sea per year, were also moved into DHS. While the President initially sought to pull the State Department's Consular Affairs visa issuance function into DHS, in the end DHS was given responsibility only for determining visa issuance policy.[115]

> In his message of support to Congress in 2002, the President articulated a strategic purpose for the Department's Border and Transportation Directorate, which has responsibility for immigration: "Terrorism is a global threat and we must improve our border security to help keep out those who mean to do us harm. We closely monitor who is coming into and out of our country to help prevent foreign terrorists from entering our country and bringing instruments of terror. At the same time, we must expedite the legal flow of people and goods on which our economy depends."[116]

The directorate is working hard to develop policies and programs that will create the foundations of the vigorous information network necessary to prevent terrorist entry. For example, DHS is attempting to incorporate new elements of enforcement into overseas operations at consulates and in airports with U.S.-bound air carriers. The first phase of the new border screening and entry-exit system, USVISIT, although based on an antiquated technology platform, is working now to capture a photograph and two fingerprints from travelers originating in countries where visas are issued, and it has had some success in catching fraud. Verification systems such as the Student and Exchange Visitor Information System (SEVIS) and the lost and stolen passport database housed by Interpol are now available to inspectors who refer travelers to a secondary inspection; to be truly helpful, these systems must be integrated into USVISIT in the primary lines. And the National Targeting Center, assisted by the new Terrorist Screening Center, provides information support to inspectors at ports of entry so that they can make more informed decisions about potential terrorists and harmful cargo attempting to enter the United States.

• • •

But while the rhetoric continues to focus on the critical mission of preventing terrorist entry, virtually no attention is being given to the most recent information available about terrorist travel and to the mission, at least equally important, of preventing terrorists who get in from staying in. All elements of terrorist border activity—travel facilitation, border inspections, compliance issues, and immigration benefits—are part of a continuum of terrorist planning and activity on both sides of the U.S. border, requiring a coordinated response within the national counterterrorism strategy. This has yet to be fully recognized and implemented.

The merging of immigration and customs border functions within the Department of Homeland Security, together with the initial construction of a biometric entry-exit system at the airports, has addressed some of the glaring deficiencies highlighted by the September 11 attacks. However, border inspectors today still do not have basic intelligence and operational training to aid them in detecting and preventing terrorist entry, or adequate access to databases important to determining admissibility, or even viable options to prevent documents known to be fraudulent from being returned to travelers denied entry into the United States. There is no programmatic effort to focus on terrorist travel facilitators, and special agents lack the resources and authority to pursue visitors for immigration violations associated with terrorist activity. Similarly, immigration benefits adjudicators do not have effective and efficient tools to conduct background security checks on applicants. Each immigration encounter with an alien should be treated as both an opportunity and an obligation to verify the individual's identity and legitimate purpose in seeking to enter or to stay in the United States. Yet border officials still do not have access at every contact, whether overseas or within the United States, to a visitor's full U.S. travel and immigration history.

Finally, immigration law remains immensely complex. This unnecessary complexity affects inspectors, special agents, prosecutors, and immigration benefit adjudicators alike who struggle to interpret and implement it every day.

APPENDICES

APPENDICES

APPENDIX A:
TRAVEL AND IDENTIFICATION DOCUMENTS DIGITAL IMAGES

See full-color pictorial insert.

ILLUSTRATIONS IN APPENDIX A

- Mohamed Atta's visa   A-1
- Ziad Jarrah's charred visa recovered in Somerset County, Penn.   A-1
- Ramzi Binalshibh's visa application   A-2
- Hani Hanjour's visa application   A-4
- Marwan al Shehhi's application to change his immigration status   A-6
- Mohand al Shehri's visa application   A-8
- Ahmad al Haznawi's visa application   A-10
- Saeed al Ghamdi's visa application   A-12
- Ahmed al Nami's visa application   A-14
- Mohamed Atta's revised immigration arrival record   A-16
- Handwritten notes of immigration official re: Atta's record   A-17
- Mohamed Atta's Florida state driver's license   A-18
- Saeed al Ghamdi's Immigration arrival record   A-19
- Saeed al Ghamdi's Customs declaration   A-20
- Salem al Hazmi's USAID identification card   A-21
- Khalid al Mihdhar's USAID identification card   A-21
- Khalid Sheikh Mohammed's alias visa application   A-22
- Ahmed al Ghamdi's state of Virginia identification card photo   A-24

APPENDIX B:
THE SAUDI FLIGHTS

AT 9:45 A.M. ON SEPTEMBER 11, 2001, the Federal Aviation Administration (FAA) Air Traffic Control System Command Center (ATCSCC) issued verbal direction for all airborne aircraft to land at the nearest destination or as soon as practical.[1] A notice to all airmen (NOTAM) was issued at 10:39 closing all operations at all airports; at 11:06, ATCSCC suspended operations in the national airspace.[2]

While the national airspace was closed, decisions to allow aircraft to fly were made collaboratively with the departments of Defense and State, the U.S. Secret Service, the FBI, and the FAA.[3] The Department of Transportation reopened the national airspace to commercial flights effective 11 A.M. on September 13, 2001, provided the airport had implemented the new security measures dictated by the FAA Civil Aviation Security Office.[4] The reopening for commercial flights included hired charter flights, but so-called general aviation flights by individuals flying for pleasure continued to be restricted at some airports.[5]

A number of flights with Saudi nationals departed the United States for domestic and international destinations after airspace was reopened. Our investigation revealed 11 such flights between September 13 and September 24, 2001.

We have determined that the airports involved in these 11 Saudi flights were open when the flights departed.[6] We have found no credible evidence that any of these flights of Saudi nationals flew within the United States or departed from the United States before the reopening of the national airspace.

Although the airspace and airports were open when these flights left, we have investigated the process by which these individuals were able to leave the United States. It began with a phone call around September 13, 2001. Fearing reprisals against Saudi nationals, Rihab Massoud, deputy chief of mission of

171

the Kingdom of Saudi Arabia in Washington, D.C., called Dale Watson, the FBI's assistant director for counterterrorism, shortly after the attack and asked for help in getting some of the Kingdom's citizens out of the country.[7]

At about the same time, Michael Rolince, the FBI section chief of the International Terrorism Operations Section (ITOS), learned about a proposed flight of Saudi nationals intending to depart the country from Newark, New Jersey.[8] Rolince told FBI officials in the field that the Saudis should not be allowed to leave until the names on their passports had been matched to their faces, and their names had been run through various databases—including some watchlists—to see whether the FBI had derogatory information on them.[9] The next morning, Watson and Rolince briefed FBI Director Robert Mueller about the issue.[10]

The Saudi government was advised of the requirements the FBI wanted met before the flights could leave: identification and name check. The Saudi government agreed to this policy, and in most cases provided a flight manifest to the FBI in advance of the flight's proposed departure.[11] In the FBI Special Intelligence and Operations Center (SIOC), Rolince took on responding to matters related to the Saudi flights as part of his duties.[12] Other U.S. government agencies played a role as well—often by video teleconference. The FAA had a representative assigned to the FBI SIOC who worked to ensure that the FBI was aware of flights of Saudi nationals and was able to screen the passengers before they were allowed to depart.[13] The State Department was involved in flights involving Saudi royalty and diplomats because in some circumstances diplomatic flights are accorded special privileges.[14]

At the White House, Counterterrorism Security Coordinator Richard Clarke participated through the Counterterrorism Security Group (CSG) process.[15] Clarke told the Commission that he approved the release of these flights subject to the FBI's approval.

> So, I was told that the Saudi embassy wanted to get people out of the country who were royal family members, and who were Bin Ladin family members. I asked the FBI, Dale Watson, who was the senior number two, I think person at the FBI at the time, to handle that, to check to see if that was all right with them, to see if they wanted access to any of these people, and to get back to me. And if they had no objections, it would be fine with me. . . .
>
> Now your next question is going to be, who in the White House did I clear it with, or did I clear it with anybody in the White House. And I have no recollection of clearing it with anybody in the White House. I may have. But it's more than likely, when the FBI said it was all right with

them, I told whoever had asked me that it was all right with me. And again, I don't, I have no idea who asked me.

Contextually here, this is coming at a time when we were being hit with information and requests for decisions on matters that normally we would take weeks to decide, and we're deciding them in about two minutes. And this was one in a flow of hundreds, if not thousands, of decisions that we made during the course of those first 72 hours. . . .

This is the kind of thing that I have done many, many times on the other side of the request. It is very frequently the case that when there is an emergency situation in another country, we approach that country and ask for extraordinary help in evacuating our people. And I've done that a lot. And so I had sympathy with their request.[16]

Clarke appears to be the highest-ranking official in the White House involved with the decision to approve the departure of the Saudi flights. There is no evidence of involvement by senior political officials.

President Bush and Vice President Cheney told the Commission that they did not speak with Saudi government officials about the flights before their departure. The President told the Commission that the first he knew about the issue was when he read about it in the newspaper. Although White House Chief of Staff Andrew Card remembered someone telling him about the Saudi request shortly after 9/11, he said he had not talked to the Saudis and did not ask anyone to do anything about it.[17]

Thus, decisions about these flights—including how much screening of the passengers should be done and whether they should be allowed to depart—appear to have been delegated from more senior officials at the FBI and by Richard Clarke at the White House to midlevel officials of the FBI, FAA, and State Department participating in the interagency decision-making process centered in the FBI SIOC.[18]

We pause to caution against overemphasizing the issue of authorizing the flights' departure, because such a focus reveals ignorance of two key facts: first, prior to 9/11, there was virtually no screening of individuals seeking to leave the United States;[19] and second, under U.S. law, the legal authority to prevent the departure of someone wishing to leave the United States is unusual and, we believe, seldom utilized. The first point is important because it answers people who have assumed, incorrectly, that some kind of authorization was required before the Saudi flights, or any others, could depart the United States in the wake of 9/11. The second underscores that assumptions about the FBI's ability to detain all Saudis on these flights are misplaced as well. Unless the FBI developed facts justifying a detention, such as reason to believe the individual was in violation of their immigration status,[20] had committed a crime, or was a material witness to a crime, it is not clear that actions to prevent any individual's departure would have had a lawful basis.[21]

The more important question is, Did any terrorists escape from the U.S. on one of these flights? Our research to date leads us to believe the answer is no. Screening for flights, including the "Bin Ladin" flight carrying members of Usama Bin Ladin's extended family, was done by FBI officials in the field according to a policy set by FBI headquarters personnel and in a process coordinated among agencies. The purpose of this screening was to ensure that the people on these flights did not pose a threat to national security and that no one of interest to the FBI in connection with the 9/11 investigation was allowed to leave the country. We believe that the FBI interviewed all persons of interest on these flights prior to their departures. The FBI has concluded that none of the passengers was connected specifically to the 9/11 attacks or to terrorism generally.

Because it was not clear to the Commission whether all departing passengers' names were checked against the definitive source for terrorist identity information—the TIPOFF terrorist watchlist—at our request, prior to our hearing in April 2004, the Terrorist Screening Center (TSC) checked the names of individuals on the flight manifests of these six Saudi flights against the current TIPOFF watchlist. There were no matches.[22] Also at our request, drawing on additional information—including information collected by journalists researching this issue—the TSC in June and July 2004 rechecked the names of individuals believed to be on these six flights and on four more flights identified by 9/11 Commission staff since our April hearing as having one or more Saudi nationals as passengers.[23] Again, there were no matches. Finally, we asked the TSC to check the names of 160 Saudi nationals listed on a Web site as having left the United States between September 11 and September 15, 2001.[24] There were no matches.

It is our view that the FBI handled the screening of these flights in a professional manner consistent with the other pressing duties they faced after September 11, particularly the need to prevent the future terrorist attacks that many then feared were imminent.

The Flights

In April 2004, we reported that after U.S. airspace reopened, six chartered flights with 142 people, mostly Saudi nationals, departed from the United States between September 14 and 24. Since our initial report, we have found evidence of four more flights between September 14 and 23 containing two or more Saudi nationals. We also researched one flight that flew within the United States on September 13, 2001, a topic we were in the process of researching in April. Finally, we looked into departures of Saudi nationals on commercial flights after 9/11 that journalists had described as suspicious. We have identified the following flights:

1. *The Phantom flight.* A Hop-A-Jet flight with three Saudis, including a Saudi prince, that flew from Tampa, Florida, to Lexington, Kentucky, on September 13, 2001.
2. *The Providence flight.* A Northstar Aviation flight with four Saudis, including a Saudi sheikh, that departed from Providence, Rhode Island, for Paris, France, on September 14, 2001.
3. *The Newark flight.* A Saudi Arabian Airlines flight with 116 individuals, including the Saudi deputy defense minister, that departed from Newark Airport on September 14, 2001.
4. *The Lexington flight.* A Jetlease chartered luxury Boeing 727 with 14 people, including a Saudi prince, that departed from Lexington, Kentucky, for an unknown city in England during the evening hours on September 16, 2001.
5. *The Universal Weather flight.* A Universal Weather & Aviation, Inc., flight with four Saudi nationals that departed from Boston's Logan Airport for Gander, Newfoundland, at 12:30 P.M. on September 18, 2001.
6. *The First Las Vegas flight.* Flight DC-8-73, a chartered Republic of Gabon airplane with 46 people, including several members of the Saudi royal family, that departed from Las Vegas, Nevada, for Geneva, Switzerland, on September 19, 2001.
7. *The "Bin Ladin" flight.* Ryan International Flight 441, a Boeing 727 with 26 passengers, most of them relatives of Saudi fugitive Usama Bin Ladin, that departed the United States from Boston, Massachusetts, for Goose Bay, Newfoundland, at 2:05 A.M. on September 20, 2001 (after making stops in Los Angeles, Orlando, Washington Dulles, and Boston).
8. *The Second Las Vegas flight.* Chartered Flight B 727-21, with 18 people, members of a single Saudi royal party, that departed from Las Vegas, Nevada, for Stanstead, England, on September 20, 2001.[25]
9. *The VIP flight.* A flight from New York's JFK Airport with four members of the Saudi royal family that departed from New York for Paris, France, on September 22, 2001.

10. *The Hanscom flight.* A Gulfstream 3, jet tail number N706JA, with two Saudi nationals that departed from Hanscom Airfield in Bedford, Massachusetts, on September 23, 2001.[26]

11. *The Third Las Vegas flight.* American Trans Air Flight L-1011, with 34 members of the party of Saudi Prince Turki, that departed from Las Vegas, Nevada, for Paris, France on September 24, 2001.

We address each flight in the order they flew, and then turn to the departures of Saudis on commercial flights.

The "Phantom Flight."[27] Much has been made of the Tampa flight, nicknamed the "Phantom flight" because of claims in media accounts, attributed to government officials at the FAA and FBI, that the flight had not in fact taken place. Our conclusion is that the flight definitely took place, and that there was nothing improper or unusual about it.

On September 13, 2001, Tampa police officers were providing security to three young Saudi nationals at an apartment in Tampa, Florida.[28] One of the three was Prince Sultan Fahad bin Salman bin Abdulaziz, whose father, Prince Ahmed bin Salman bin Abdulaziz, was in Lexington, Kentucky, attending a horse auction. The Tampa Police Department was in contact with the Lexington Police Department about this security because the elder Prince Salman was concerned about his son's safety and had contacted the Lexington police.[29] At approximately 11 A.M., the Tampa police were told by the Saudis they were protecting that a plane had become available to fly them to Lexington.[30] Tampa police were asked to provide two officers who could act as security guards for the three by accompanying them on the plane scheduled to leave the afternoon of September 13, 2001.[31] The Tampa police chief declined to let his officers fly on the plane.[32]

The Tampa sergeant handling the security arrangements then contacted Dan Grossi, a recently retired Tampa police detective and private investigator, and asked if he was interested in providing security services by flying to Lexington with the Saudis.[33] Grossi agreed, and called another private investigator—Manuel Perez, a retired FBI agent—to accompany him on the flight.[34] Tampa police officers drove the three Saudi nationals to the Tampa International Airport in unmarked police vehicles.[35] The Tampa officers, accompanied by the three Saudi nationals, met Dan Grossi in the lobby of Raytheon Aircraft Services, a separate terminal at the Tampa airport.[36] A Tampa police officer described seeing a plane that looked like a "cream-colored Learjet" on the tarmac outside the Raytheon facility.[37] The Tampa officers waited with Grossi and the three young Saudis until Manuel Perez arrived, and then they left.[38]

Grossi, Perez, the three Saudi nationals, and the two pilots then boarded the chartered plane, a Learjet model LJ35.[39] The pilot of the Learjet was Christopher Steele, an employee of the plane's owner, Hop-A-Jet, Inc.[40] The plane's unique identification number, based on the name of the company, was "HPJ32."[41] For Steele, there was "nothing unusual whatsoever" about the flight other than that there were few planes flying that day.[42] Barry Ellis, Hop-A-Jet's president and director of operations agreed, saying that "it was just a routine little trip for us" and that he would have heard if there had been anything unusual about it.[43] Steele said he followed standard procedures and filed his flight plan with the FAA prior to the flight, noting, "I was never questioned about it."[44]

FAA records show Steele filed his flight plan at 3:30 P.M. on September 13, 2001, indicating the plane was flying from Tampa to Lexington, and then back to Tampa.[45] According to FAA records, the plane took off from Tampa bound for Lexington at 4:38 P.M. on September 13, 2001.[46] Witnesses, including security guards Grossi and Perez, recall the flight leaving at around 4:30.[47] Tampa airport's aircraft flight tracking system, which captures the jet noise made by arriving and departing aircraft, recorded the plane's departure at 4:37.[48] At the time this charter flight took off, both the national airspace and Tampa Airport were open.[49] In fact, Tampa records show that 10 aircraft arrived at Tampa and 12 departed before Steele's plane left.[50] The FAA has stated they have "no record" of any special authorization for this flight.[51]

At approximately 6 P.M., the plane landed at Lexington Blue Grass Airport and taxied to the Truman Arnold Corporation or TAC Air facility, separate from the main airport terminal.[52] Lexington Blue Grass Airport had been open since 12:50 P.M. that day.[53] The three Saudi nationals disembarked from the plane and were met by Captain Mark Barnard of the Lexington, Kentucky, Police Department, the same person who had been in contact with Tampa police officers earlier in the day.[54] Grossi and Perez were paid for their work by the Saudis, and were given money with which to pay the off-duty Tampa police officers.[55] Barnard escorted the three Saudi nationals to a hotel where the prince joined his father.[56] The plane refueled at the TAC Air facility and, according to FAA records, departed Lexington for Tampa at 6:43 P.M.[57] On board were the two pilots, Dan Grossi, and Manuel Perez.[58] The three Saudis on the Tampa–Lexington flight stayed in Lexington until September 16, 2001, when they departed the United States on a flight described below.

Thus, there does not appear to be anything unusual about the so-called Phantom Flight other than that it was one of the earlier charter flights flown after airspace reopened.[59]

The Providence Flight. On September 14, 2001, a Northstar Aviation flight to Paris, France, departed from Providence, Rhode Island.

- There were four Saudi nationals on board.
- According to the FBI, all four passengers "were interviewed and their identity confirmed."
- The FBI made copies of the passengers' passports.[60]
- According to the FBI, the FBI and INS checked the four individual's names against FBI and INS databases "with negative results."
- The FBI also reported that the U.S. Customs Service and Rhode Island State Police searched their luggage "with negative results."[61]
- It is not clear whether these individuals were checked against the State Department's TIPOFF terrorist watch list prior to their departure, but a check of their names in April 2004 produced no matches.
- According to the Transportation Security Administration, Providence Airport was open when this flight departed.[62]

The Newark Flight. A Saudi Arabian Airlines flight with 116 individuals, including the Saudi deputy defense minister, Prince Abdul Rahman bin Abdul Aziz, departed from Newark International Airport on September 14, 2001, at approximately 9:25 P.M. We do not know its immediate destination.[63]

- FBI agents received a flight manifest for this flight containing the names, dates of birth, and country of citizenship or residency of all passengers in advance of its departure.
- FBI records indicate that these individuals were checked against four databases: IIIA (containing FBI analysts' reports), TECS (the U.S. Customs Service watchlist system), ACS (the FBI's Automated Case System), and Rapid Start (containing FBI leads, including those related to the 9/11 investigation, known as PENTTBOM).[64]
- Based on these checks, at least one of the crew members was interviewed extensively. His answers apparently satisfied the FBI and he was allowed to depart.[65]

- At our request, the Terrorist Screening Center in July 2004 checked the names of the passengers on this flight against the TIPOFF watchlist; there were no matches.
- At the time this flight departed, Newark Airport was open.[66]

The Lexington, Kentucky, Flight. On September 16, 2001, a chartered luxury Boeing 727 departed from Lexington, Kentucky, for England.

- There were 14 individuals on board, the majority of whom were Saudi nationals, including Saudi Prince Ahmed Bin Salman Bin Abdulaziz and his son Prince Sultan Bin Fahad Bin Salman Abdulaziz; the latter had flown to Lexington from Tampa, Florida, on September 13, 2001.[67]
- The FBI copied the passports of all 14 passengers prior to their departure and made sure that those who boarded the plane were the same individuals whose passports they had collected.[68]
- The FBI and U.S. Customs Service inspected the plane before it departed.
- Although they did speak with one passenger prior to the plane's departure, and records show the passengers were checked against the Security Directive List (an FBI watchlist created shortly after 9/11), there is no evidence that the FBI interviewed these 14 individuals or checked their names against other terrorist watchlists prior to their departure.[69]
- Lexington Blue Grass Airport was open at the time this flight took off.[70]
- One individual on this flight—Ahmad A. M. al Hazmi—has the same last name as hijackers Nawaf and Salem al Hazmi. However, the FBI determined that he was not on any watchlists associated with the 9/11 attacks.[71]
- The Terrorist Screening Center checked the names of the passengers on this flight in April 2004 with no matches.
- We found no evidence to support the allegation that Prince Ahmed Bin Salman, a passenger on the flight, had ties to al Qaeda operative Abu Zubaydah and may have had advanced knowledge of the 9/11 attacks. This claim was allegedly made by Zubaydah after his capture when he was interrogated by the CIA.[72] We have seen no evidence of any such statement, and the CIA has stated they have "no intelligence reporting to support" this assertion.[73]

The Universal Weather Flight. A Universal Weather & Aviation, Inc., flight with four Saudi nationals departed from Boston's Logan International Airport at 12:30 P.M. on September 18, 2001.

- We learned of this flight while reviewing FBI documents in preparation for our April 13, 2004, hearing.
- We were not able to determine the destination of this flight from the documents we reviewed.
- FBI records of this flight included a flight manifest with the names and other biographical information of four Saudi nationals.
- Because we were not able to determine whether the names of these four individuals had been checked against TIPOFF, at our request in April the Terrorist Screening Center checked these four individuals against TIPOFF with negative results.
- Boston's Logan Airport was open when this flight departed.[74]

The Las Vegas Flights. The FBI reports that it "conducted extensive investigation prior to the departure" of the three Las Vegas flights based on a lead it received about the presence of Saudis in Las Vegas on September 11, 2001.[75] Two of these flights, one September 19, 2001 and one on September 20, 2001, contained members of the entourage of Saudi Prince Abdulmajeed Bin Abdulaziz.[76]

- *Republic of Gabon–Flagged DC-8-73*

  - On September 19, 2001, Flight DC-8-73, tail number TR-LTZ, a chartered Republic of Gabon airplane, departed Las Vegas, Nevada, for Geneva, Switzerland. This flight contained members of the party of Prince Abdulmajeed bin Abdulaziz.[77]
  - There were 69 people aboard this flight, 46 of whom were Saudi nationals, according to the FBI.[78]
  - Before the flight took off, the FBI acquired the name, date or year of birth, passport numbers, and copies of passports for all 69 people scheduled to board.
  - The FBI checked their names against "the current FBI Watch List and ran for IIIA reports. No Watch List matches were discovered."[79]
  - FBI records state that agents interviewed three of the passengers based on nonderogatory information in its IIIA database, but found nothing suspicious.[80]

- The FBI also reported that "Additional interviews were conducted by INS and USCS [the U.S. Customs Service]."[81]
- Before the flight was allowed to leave, the plane was searched and FBI agents and agents of the U.S. Customs Service matched all passengers to the flight manifest and to photocopies of their passports.[82]
- Although FBI records indicate that Customs personnel assisted in the investigation of this flight, it is not clear from FBI records whether the names of passengers on this flight were checked against the Customs–TECS database, which included the TIPOFF terrorist database, prior to its departure.
- The Terrorist Screening Center ran the names of all passengers on this flight against TIPOFF in April 2004; there were no matches.
- Las Vegas Airport was open when this flight departed.[83]

- *Chartered Flight B 727-21, Tail Number N727PX*

On September 20, 2001, 18 members of the party of Saudi Prince Abdulmajeed Bin Abdulaziz departed from Las Vegas, Nevada, for Stanstead, England.[84] They underwent the same vetting process as the 69 people on the flight the day before.

- The FBI checked the 18 names against "the current FBI Watch List and ran for IIIA reports. No Watch List matches were discovered."[85]
- FBI records state that agents interviewed one passenger based on nonderogatory information in its IIIA database, but found nothing suspicious.[86]
- Before the flight was allowed to leave, the plane was searched and FBI agents and agents of the U.S. Customs Service matched all passengers to the flight manifest and to photocopies of their passports.[87]
- Although FBI records indicate that Customs personnel assisted in the investigation of this flight, it is not clear from FBI records whether the names of passengers on this flight were run against the Customs–TECS database, which included the TIPOFF terrorist database, prior to its departure.
- At our request, the Terrorist Screening Center ran the names of all passengers on this flight against TIPOFF in April 2004; there were no matches.
- Las Vegas Airport was open when this flight departed.[88]

Ryan International Flight 441 (the "Bin Ladin Family Flight"). On September 20, 2001, at 2:05 A.M., Ryan International Flight 441, a Boeing 727 contracted by the Saudi embassy, departed the United States from Boston, Massachusetts, for Newfoundland.

- The screening of this flight was directed by an FBI agent in the Baltimore Field Office who was also a pilot.[89] This agent, coordinating with FBI headquarters, sent an electronic communication to each of the field offices within whose jurisdiction the Bin Ladin flight was scheduled to land; it including the proposed flight manifest and directions regarding what screening should occur.[90] The communication directed agents in those offices to verify the identities of the passengers and ensure "that the flight did not pose a threat to US security."[91] The Baltimore agent monitored the flight as it moved around the country—from St. Louis to Los Angeles to Orlando to Washington Dulles and to Boston Logan—correcting for any changes in itinerary to make sure there was no lapse in FBI screening.[92]
- The flight manifest indicates that when the flight departed the United States, there were 26 individuals on board other than the flight crew: 23 passengers and 3 security guards.[93]
- Most of the 23 passengers were Saudi nationals. Most of the Saudis were relatives of Usama Bin Ladin, and 12 had the last name Bin Ladin.[94]
- The FBI interviewed 19 of the 23 passengers on Flight 441, some of them more than once.[95] The interviews took place in a number of locations, including the passengers' homes, in automobiles, and at the airport; some were done over the telephone. FBI agents also spoke with the flight crew of Flight 441 and the three security guards who accompanied the passengers prior to the flight's departure.
- Records of the interviews the FBI conducted of Bin Ladin Flight passengers—which amount to 39 single-spaced typed pages—indicate that the FBI interviewed many of these individuals at some length.[96] They were questioned, for example, about their personal biographical information; where they lived; which of their relatives lived in the United States and where; what relationship, if any, they had with Usama Bin Ladin; when, if ever, they had seen Usama Bin Ladin; their knowledge of terrorist groups or activity; whether they had ever traveled to

Afghanistan or Pakistan; whether they knew any of the 9/11 hijackers; and whether they had any information about the attacks. Many family members told the FBI that they had lived or traveled in the West for years. Some of the Bin Ladins declared that they were U.S. citizens. None of the passengers claimed to have had any recent contact with Usama Bin Ladin or any knowledge about terrorist activity.

- Two of the passengers on the Bin Ladin flight had been the subjects of preliminary investigations by the FBI; both their cases had been closed, in 1999 and March 2001, respectively, because the FBI had uncovered no derogatory information on either person linking him to terrorist activity. Their cases remained closed as of September 11, 2001; they were not reopened before they departed the country on this flight and have not been reopened since.[97]

- The flight originated in St. Louis on September 18, 2001. It acquired its passengers as follows: in Los Angeles, one passenger embarked, and the flight departed on September 19, 2001; in Orlando, Florida, three passengers embarked, and the flight departed September 19, 2001; in Washington, D.C., five passengers embarked, and the flight departed September 19, 2001; in Boston, fourteen passengers embarked and the flight departed at 2:05 A.M. on September 20, 2001.[98]

- FBI agents verified the names of passengers on Flight 441 in Los Angeles, Orlando, and Boston.[99]

- FBI agents searched the airplane and luggage in Los Angeles and Orlando. The FBI searched the plane prior to its departure in Boston.[100]

- "At each airport, passengers were processed through immigration and customs as well as security checks."[101]

- In Boston, the FBI photographed all 14 individuals boarding the aircraft.

- "Record checks were conducted" of the passengers.

- One claim that has been made is that the FBI helped shuttle Bin Ladin family members to this flight. We found that in two cases, when the FBI called members of the Bin Ladin family in connection with their plans to depart the country, the Bin Ladins asked the FBI agents to accompany them to the airport because they were afraid for their and their family's safety.[102] In one instance, the FBI agent agreed that there was the potential for danger to someone with the last name "Bin Ladin."[103] That agent, in Florida, provided an escort to the airport for three Bin Ladin family members because of their fears and took the opportunity to interview one of the family members during the drive.[104] In a second case, Usama Bin Ladin's sister, who lived in Los Angeles, requested an escort on September 19, 2001 to the airport in Los Angeles because she was concerned about her safety. An FBI agent agreed to and did accompany her to the airport.[105]

- The four Ryan Air flight 441 passengers who were not interviewed were Maria Bayma, apparently the sister-in-law of Khalil Bin Laden, Usama Bin Ladin's brother; Sultan Bin Ladin, the "17- to 18"-year-old son of Khalil Bin Ladin; a female Saudi national who embarked in Boston; and an Indonesian maid who worked for one of the Saudi passengers.[106] There is strong evidence that the first three individuals, although they were not interviewed separately, "were present during interviews" of others.[107]

- The FBI has stated, on the basis of their investigation of the individuals on the Ryan Air Flight, that there were "no siblings of UBL's with ties to Militant Islamic Fundamentalists aboard the flight."[108]

- The FBI maintains that "no persons received FBI approval to depart the US without being determined to be of no investigative interest to the PENTTBOM investigation."[109]

- At our request, in April 2004 the Terrorist Screening Center ran the names of all the passengers on the Bin Ladin flight against the TIPOFF list; there were no matches.

- Each of the airports through which the Bin Ladin flight passed was open and no special restrictions applied that were lifted to accommodate its passage.

The VIP Flight. A flight from New York's JFK Airport with 12 people, including four members of the Saudi royal family, apparently departed for Paris on September 22, 2001.

- From a story that surfaced in the media, we learned of a flight that apparently departed from New York's JFK Airport on September 22, 2001.[110]

- We obtained a copy of the alleged flight manifest from an Internet Web site.[111]

- Although we found evidence of a VIP flight that involved FBI screening, we have not been able to determine definitively whether this is the flight involved.[112]
- Because it was not clear to us whether the individuals on this flight had been checked against terrorist watchlists, we asked the Terrorist Screening Center in June 2004 to run the names of all passengers against the TIPOFF terrorist watchlist; there were no matches.
- New York's JFK Airport was open when this flight departed.[113]

The Hanscom Flight. A Gulfstream 3, jet tail number N706JA, with two Saudi nationals departed from Hanscom Airfield in Bedford, Massachusetts, on September 23, 2001.

- We learned of this flight while reviewing FBI documents in preparation for our April 13, 2004, hearing.
- FBI records of this flight included a flight manifest with the names of two Saudi nationals and other biographical information.
- Because we were not able to determine whether the names of these two individuals had been checked against TIPOFF, at our request in June 2004 the Terrorist Screening Center checked these two individuals against TIPOFF; there were no matches.
- Hanscom Airfield was open when this flight departed.[114]

American Trans Air Flight ATA L-1011. On September 24, 2001, 34 members of the party of Saudi Prince Turki departed on Flight American Trans Air (ATA) L-1011 from Las Vegas, Nevada, to Paris, France.[115]

- These 34 individuals underwent the same vetting process as the Saudis on flights that had left Las Vegas earlier. The FBI checked the 34 names against "the current FBI Watch List and ran for potential IIIA reports. Both checks met with negative results."[116]
- There were 19 Saudi citizens on board.[117]
- The plane was searched before the flight was allowed to leave.
- FBI agents and agents of the U.S. Customs Service matched all passengers to the flight manifest and to photocopies of their passports.[118]
- From our review of FBI records, it appears that none of the 34 people on this flight was interviewed.

- FBI records indicate that U.S. Customs Service personnel assisted in the investigation of this flight; however, it is not clear from FBI records whether the names of passengers on this flight were run against the Customs-TECS database, which included the TIPOFF terrorist database, prior to its departure.
- The Terrorist Screening Center ran the names of all passengers on this flight against TIPOFF in April 2004; there were no matches.
- Las Vegas Airport was open when this flight departed.[119]

Commercial flights of Saudi Nationals out of the United States. In February 2004, the advocacy group Judicial Watch obtained through a Freedom of Information Act Request documents showing that 160 Saudi nationals departed the United States on 55 flights on September 11, 2001, and from September 13 to September 15, 2001.[120] These documents, released by the Department of Homeland Security, Bureau of Customs and Border Protection, do not include the names of the individuals. They do include each person's country of citizenship, class of admission, date of departure, port of departure, and flight number. The records indicate that these 160 individuals departed from Atlanta, Washington Dulles, JFK Airport, Boston, Houston, Chicago, and many other airports.

The FBI subsequently obtained from DHS the complete biographical information—including name and passport number—of the individuals dealt with in this FOIA request.[121] At our request, in June 2004 the Terrorist Screening Center checked the names of these individuals against the TIPOFF terrorist watchlist. There were no matches.[122]

The fact that 160 Saudi nationals departed our country on commercial flights on September 11, 2001 and after airspace reopened on September 13, 2001, is not particularly remarkable. After the 13th, thousands of individuals departed on flights from the United States, as they do every day that our airspace is open. As we noted above, the United States did not have departure controls in the period immediately before and after the 9/11 attacks.

APPENDIX C:
IMMIGRATION HISTORIES OF CERTAIN INDIVIDUALS WITH TERRORIST CONNECTIONS

The following analysis is based on information obtained primarily from reviewing immigration files, court documents and government reports. Individual INS immigration files were reviewed unless otherwise noted. The individuals whose immigration histories are discussed here are either known terrorists, or individuals with connections to terrorist attacks, including the 9/11 attacks, whose backgrounds are not discussed extensively in either the 9/11 Commission Report or Chapter 3 of this Staff Report.

CIA ATTACK JANUARY 25, 1993

Mir Aimal Kansi aka Kasi[1]
Place of birth: Pakistan
Date of birth: February 10, 1964

12/4/90   Using the alias of Mir Aimal Kasi, Kansi was issued a B-1 business visa at the U.S. Consulate in Karachi, Pakistan.

2/27/91   Kansi, still using the name Kasi, arrived in New York on Pakistani passport G399099. He was permitted to stay for one month, but remained in the country for a year without the permission of the Immigration and Naturalization Service, in violation of INA 237(a)(1)(A). This was grounds for deportation.

3/19/91   He was issued a new Pakistani passport at the Pakistani Embassy in Washington, D.C. in the name of Kansi.[2] The new passport had a notation that it replaced Pakistani passport D398086, which was not the number of the passport he used to enter the U.S. a month earlier.

2/7/92   Kansi filed a claim for political asylum, claiming he illegally
            entered the United States on March 3, 1991 at New York City
            without inspection by the INS. He received permission from
            the INS to work in the United States while his application was
            pending. He obtained a Virginia driver's license and began
            working for a courier service in the Washington, D.C. area. This
            political asylum claim was denied.

            Kansi didn't give up. He applied for legalization under the
            Immigration Reform and Control Act of 1986. One of the
            requirements of this amnesty program was that the applicant
            must have entered the United States illegally prior to January 1,
            1982.[3] Kansi claimed he entered the United States from
            Mexico and had lived here illegally from April 1981 to June
            1987, a contradiction to his assertions in his political asylum
            petition. To support this claim, Kansi presented two leases, four
            letters of employment and one letter from a friend in Pakistan
            verifying a visit to that country. An examination of copies of
            these documents indicated that they all were typed on the
            same typewriter.[4]

            Kansi, however, missed the statutory filing deadline for this
            program. He then joined a class action lawsuit, *Catholic Social
            Services v. INS,* involving aliens who also missed the filing dead-
            line or who had left the United States for a brief period of
            time.[5] With his application pending, Kansi again applied for
            and received authorization to work in the United States.

4/15/92   The INS renewed Kansi's work authorization.[6]

1/25/93   Armed with an AK-47 assault rifle, Kansi opened fire on five
            male CIA employees while they sat in their cars at a stoplight
            in front of CIA headquarters in Langley, Virginia, killing Frank
            Darling and Lansing Bennett and seriously injuring three
            others. The following day Kansi fled to Pakistan.

2/16/93   The State of Virginia charged Kansi with murder, malicious
            wounding and five counts of using a firearm in the commission
            of a felony.[7]

6/15/97   The FBI, working with Pakistani intelligence, arrested Kansi in
            a hotel.[8]

11/10/97 After trial in Fairfax County, Virginia, Kansi was guilty of all counts, and sentenced to death for capital murder, life in prison for first degree murder, 20 years on each of the five counts of malicious wounding, two years in prison on one firearms charge and four years in prison on each of the other four firearms charges. Kansi was executed in 1998.

WORLD TRADE CENTER BOMBING, FEBRUARY 26, 1993

Eyad Mahmoud Ismail aka Ismoil[9]
Place of birth: Kuwait
Country of citizenship: Jordan
Date of birth: January 26, 1964

10/3/89 The U.S. consulate in Kuwait issued Ismail an F-1 student visa to study English in the United States.

10/9/89 He entered the United States at Honolulu and enrolled at Wichita State University in Kansas where he attended the English language program.

11/21/90 Ismail received approval from the INS to work part-time for one year while he was in school. He dropped out and eventually made his way to Texas. Because he was no longer a student, Ismail was in violation of the terms of his visa.

2/21/93 Ismail flew from Texas to New York City.

2/26/93 The World Trade Center was bombed. Ismail drove the van containing the bomb. That night he fled to Jordan.

9/12/94 Ismail was indicted on 10 counts for his role in the World Trade Center bombing.[10]

8/3/95 Ismail was extradited from Jordan for prosecution in the United States.

11/13/97 Ismail was convicted and sentenced to 240 years in federal prison and ordered to pay restitution of $10 million.

Mohammed Abouhalima aka Abo Halima[11]
Place of Birth: Egypt
Date of Birth: 2/23/64

7/22/85   Abouhalima entered the United States at New York on a B-2 tourist visa and was granted permission to remain in the country until Aug. 15, 1985.

11/6/85   Abouhalima asked the INS to extend his length of stay but his request was denied. He was ordered to voluntary depart the country before Dec. 5, 1995. He failed to comply and became in violation of immigration laws, subject to deportation.

9/30/87   Abouhalima filed for and received temporary residence under the Seasonal Agricultural Worker (SAW) program claiming to have picked beans in Florida. This program involved 1.3 million applications from aliens claiming to have worked for at least 90 days in agriculture from 1985 to 1986.

7/15/92   His application was denied after it was determined that he had never worked in agriculture.[12]

2/26/93   After the World Trade Center attack, Abouhalima was indicted as an accessory after the fact under 18 USC § 3, for his assistance to the first World Trade Center bombing terrorists. The indictment charged that he drove his brother, Mahmoud Abouhalima, to the airport knowing that he was involved in the bombing plot.

11/24/98   He was found guilty at trial and sentenced to 96 months in prison.

4/23/02   Based on his felony conviction Abouhalima was ordered deported following the service of his sentence. Abouhalima is in federal prison and scheduled for release on August 25, 2005.[13]

Biblal A. Alkaisi aka Bibal Elqisi
Place of Birth: Jordan[14]

11/5/90   Alkaisi attended a rally held by Rabbi Meir Kahane. He accompanied El Sayyid Nosair, who shot and killed Kahane at the event. Alkaisi was questioned about the shooting but released by the police.

8/20/91   The Islamic Brotherhood, Inc. in Brooklyn, New York wrote a letter in support of Bilal El Qisi's application for temporary protected status. In their letter they used the same address as the Al-Farouq Mosque and the Alkifah Refugee Center, both locations since linked Islamist extremist activity.[15]

9/21/91   Still using the name of Bilal El Qisi, Alkaisi filed an application for temporary protected status (TPS) at the Cleveland, Ohio INS office.[16] He stated that he was born in Lebanon on September 6, 1965 and that he entered the United States at New York City on September 25, 1988.[17] He supported these claims with a Lebanese birth certificate and an INS Form I-94 (Arrival and Departure Record), which was later determined to have been altered to show a different country of birth.

3/11/92   The Cleveland INS office initiated an investigation into a number of suspected fraudulent TPS applications, including Alkaisi's.

3/19/92   The INS Forensic Document Laboratory completed an examination of Alkaisi's Lebanese birth certificate and concluded it was produced by a color copier. The English translation of the Arabic document was also incorrect. In addition, the INS I-94 Record of Entry and Departure that Alkaisi submitted with his application was altered to change the country of birth.

5/22/92   Bibal El Qisi filed a request for political asylum, now claiming he was born in Jordan on December 20, 1965 and had entered the United States on October 10, 1987 in New York via Jordan Airlines. He claimed he was not inspected by the INS and said that he lived in Brooklyn, New York. The INS assigned him a new case file. INS recordkeeping did not connect this application with his previous one.

7/13/92   El Qisi failed to appear for his political asylum interview.

7/28/92   As a result of his failure to appear the INS terminated action on his political asylum claim.

2/26/93   The World Trade Center was bombed.

3/25/93   A known associate of the conspirators, El Qisi was arrested by
            the FBI office in Newark, New Jersey. He told the agents that
            his name was Bilal Salem Alkaisi and that he was born on
            December 25, 1965 in Jordan. The ensuing investigation
            revealed that all of the residences and employments that Alkaisi
            had listed on his political asylum claim were false.

8/8/93   Under the name El Qisi, Alkaisi was indicted with five other
            co-conspirators for his part in the bombing. The U.S. Attorney
            for the Southern District of New York later severed Alkaisi
            from the indictment due to a lack of evidence.

5/9/94   Alkaisi plead guilty to making false statements to the INS.[18]

5/19/94   The INS certified that there was no record of an entry of
            Alkaisi under that name or any of his other aliases.

7/123/94   Alkaisi was sentenced to 20 months in prison for making false
            statements in his political asylum claim.

11/7/94   He was released from federal prison and deported to Jordan the
            following day.

Nidal Abderrahman Ayyad
Place of birth: Kuwait
Country of citizenship: Jordan
Date of birth: July 17, 1967

7/15/85   Abderrahman Yousif Ayyad, a legal permanent resident, petitioned
            the INS to bring his son Nidal to the United States.

10/10/85   His petition was granted and Nidal Ayyad entered the United
            States at New York City as the unmarried son of a lawful
            permanent resident.

2/21/91   Nidal applied for naturalization at the INS office in Newark,
            and swore allegiance to the United States.

3/7/91   Nidal became a naturalized citizen in a ceremony in Newark.

2/26/93   The World Trade center was bombed. The following day Nidal called the *New York Times*, proclaiming the bombing to be the work of the "Liberation Army."

5/24/94   Nidal was charged and convicted as part of the World Trade Center plot, and was sentenced to 240 years in prison for conspiracy to destroy buildings with an explosive device, explosive destruction of property, destruction of a motor vehicle, assault of a federal officer and using or carrying a destructive device during a crime of violence.

5/28/96   The INS Newark office recommended that Nidal's citizenship be revoked based on his membership in a terrorist group before and after his naturalization. The recommendation is based on INA 340 (a)(2) "withholding of a material fact," section 340(c) "reopening of naturalization proceedings" and 313(3) "membership in groups advocating the violent overthrow of the government of the United States."[19] It does not appear that action was taken to formally revoke his citizenship. The Commission was not provided access to his immigration file, and the Department of Homeland Security advised that his file was protected by the Privacy Act, which covers citizens, legal permanent residents and naturalized citizens. Ayyad is scheduled for release on April 3, 2095.

Mohammed Salameh[20]
Place of birth: Jordan
Date of birth: September 1, 1967

4/8/84   The Jordanian Passport office in Amman issued passport #B468365 to Mohammad Amin Abdel-Rahim Salameh. Ramzi Yousef's fingerprints were later found on this passport.[21]

11/5/90   Rabbi Meir Kahane was shot to death by El Sayyid Nosair. Salameh was arrested that night at one of Nosair's addresses and admitted that he was with Nosair at the shooting. However, the next day Salameh was released for lack of evidence.

9/22/92   Salameh submitted a fraudulent Seasonal Agricultural Worker (SAW) application in an attempt to become a legal permanent resident. He claimed that he planted tomatoes, and weeded and picked green beans for Oak Valley Farms in Crawford, Texas.

2/26/93   Salameh drove a rented Ryder van containing a bomb into the World Trade Center.

3/4/93   Salameh was arrested trying to obtain a $400 refund on the rented truck. He was later charged with criminal violations of the immigration laws and prosecuted on charges related to the bombing.

3/4/94   Salameh was convicted in Federal court of all charges including 8 USC § 1546(a) ("fraud and misuse of visas, permits and other documents") and was sentenced to 240 months in federal prison. His projected release date is January 2, 2024.

Mahmud Abouhalima aka "Mahmud the Red"[22]
Place of birth: Egypt
Date of birth: November 17, 1959

1985   Abouhalima and his German wife, Marianne Weber, entered the United States on tourist visas. They were admitted for six months but overstayed their authorized length of stay.

1987   Abouhalima applied for amnesty under the Special Agricultural Program (SAW) program claiming that he worked seven months on a South Carolina farm. There were indications that this claim was fraudulent, namely that Abouhalima was in New York and never worked on a farm. Nevertheless, he received his legal permanent resident alien status (green card).

11/5/90   Abouhalima was supposed to drive the getaway taxi from the Marriott Eastside Hotel after Nosair's assassination of Rabbi Meir Kahane. While he waited for Nosair, an employee at the hotel ordered him to move his car, which was blocking the hotel entrance. That night Abouhalim was arrested along with Mohammed Salameh and others. However, like Salameh, he was released for lack of evidence.

2/23/93   Abouhalima filed Form I-131, Application for a Travel
           Document, listing an expected departure on March 6, 1993 for
           Egypt. This allowed him to remain abroad for more than one
           year without losing his legal resident status.

2/26/93   The World Trade Center was bombed. Abouhalima drove
           behind the Ryder rental truck carrying the bomb. He then
           drove the group away from the scene.

3/2/93   Abouhalima fled to Sudan via Jeddah, Saudi Arabia.

6/93   One of Abouhalima's fingerprints was found in one of the
           bomb-making manuals seized from another bombing conspirator,
           Ahmad Ajaj, when Ajaj had entered the United States at JFK
           airport in New York on September 1, 1992. Another fingerprint
           belonging to Ramzi Yousef, the mastermind of the plot, was
           found on the same manual. After a worldwide search, he was
           arrested by FBI agents in Egypt and returned to the United
           States where he was tried on terrorism charges. He was
           convicted and sentenced to 1,300 months in prison. He is
           scheduled for release on September 2, 2087.

PLOT TO DESTROY NEW YORK CITY LANDMARKS
JUNE 24, 1993

Matarawy Mohammed Said Saleh[23]
Place of birth: Egypt
Date of birth: March 4, 1956

1/31/86   Using the alias Wahid Mohamed Ahmed, Saleh married Evelyn
           Cortez, a United States citizen.[24] Based on this marriage, Cortez
           filed INS form I-130, Petition to Classify Status of Alien Relative
           in INS New York City.[25] This application started the process of
           acquiring legal permanent residency for Saleh. In the petition,
           Saleh claimed to be a self-employed scuba diver. It also claimed
           both he and his wife lived at the same address in the Bronx.

5/14/86   The INS denied the petition on the ground that Cortez failed to
           submit a divorce decree from her previous marriage. The denial
           was sent by certified mail but was returned marked "unclaimed."

10/4/87   Still married to Cortez, Saleh married Leslie Sonkin, also a
            United States citizen, in a ceremony in Egypt. They then filed
            an immigrant visa petition for Saleh claiming Saleh had never
            been previously married.

12/12/87   Saleh entered the United States at New York City as a condi-
            tional resident alien based on his marriage to Sonkin. This
            status allowed him to remain in the United States legally for
            two years after which time he could file to permanently remain
            in the United States.[26]

8/11/88   Saleh was convicted in federal court for selling heroin in
            Detroit and sentenced to five years' imprisonment.[27] He was
            paroled after two and a half years and turned over to the INS
            for deportation on the basis of his conviction.

12/18/90   The INS initiated deportation proceedings while Saleh was
            detained in Oakdale, Louisiana. One month later, Sultan El
            Gawly posted an $8,000 bail with the INS to secure Saleh's
            release. The deportation order was still pending.

3/31/93   Saleh's conditional residence status was terminated by the INS.

7/16/93   The FBI interviewed Saleh's wife Evelyn Cortez, who claimed
            she had re-married Ashraf Mohammed. She claimed that she
            had a son by Saleh six years earlier.

7/22/93   Saleh was arrested by a joint INS-FBI team in Wildwood,
            New Jersey.

12/15/95   Saleh was convicted of conspiracy to bomb various targets in
            New York City.[28] He was sentenced to time served and placed
            on supervised release for three years despite his outstanding
            deportation order, despite his illegal immigration status, heroin
            conviction, violation of probation, assault of his ex-wife
            Cortez, assaults on his current wife, and involvement in credit
            card fraud and theft.[29]

6/4/96   The INS Philadelphia office issued an arrest warrant for
            Saleh for his violation of immigration laws. Shortly thereafter

he was arrested by INS Special Agents at the Federal Probation office in Wilkes-Barre, Pennsylvania, and placed in INS custody.

6/27/96   Based on his terrorism conviction, Saleh was placed in administrative deportation proceedings as an aggravated felon. This procedure did not involve a deportation hearing.[30]

9/25/96   Saleh was served with a final notice of deportation. Egypt issued a temporary travel document allowing Saleh to travel only to Egypt.

11/19/96   Saleh was released from prison and deported to Egypt.

El Sayyid Nosair[31]
Place of birth: Egypt

1981   Nosair entered the United States at an unknown time and place. He obtained legal permanent residence status based on his marriage to a United States citizen.

1985   Nosair moved to New Jersey and became a regular visitor at the Alkifah Refugee Center in Brooklyn where he contacted Sheik Rahman, an Egyptian radical cleric also known as the Blind Sheik.

9/27/89   Nosair was naturalized in Newark, New Jersey. Prior to his naturalization he was observed, while under surveillance by the FBI, shooting a variety of weapons with other suspected Muslim militants at a firing range. The INS was not aware of this fact.

11/5/90   Nosair shot and killed radical Jewish Rabbi Meir Kahane in front of a crowd of followers at the Marriott Eastside Hotel in New York City. He also shot an elderly man who tried to stop him. He accidentally got into the wrong taxi, believing it was the getaway car driven by Mahmud Abouhalima. Realizing his mistake, he jumped out of the taxi with his gun still in his hand. He was confronted by an off-duty postal inspector. Both were shot in the ensuing gun fight.

11/8/90   The FBI raided Nosair's apartment. They found numerous military documents from Ft. Bragg, North Carolina. The documents were traced to Ali Mohammed, a sergeant in the Army Special Forces. Mohammed, an FBI informant, was later convicted for his role in the bombings of the U.S. embassies in Kenya and Tanzania in 1998.

12/21/91   At trial, Nosair was found not guilty of murder and attempted murder. He was convicted of carrying a weapon and of assault. He was sentenced to eight years' imprisonment.

2/26/93   The World Trade Center was bombed.

3/4/93   FBI agents obtained a search warrant for Ibrahim el Gabrowny's apartment in connection with the bombing investigation. There, FBI agents found Nosair's U.S. passport, five Nicaraguan passports issued in July 1991 and five Nicaraguan birth certificates for Nosair, his wife and his three children as well as Nicaraguan drivers' licenses. The foreign documents were in alias names.[32]

5/8/96   The INS recommended revoking Nosair's naturalization based on his lack of "good moral character," required for naturalization. He was also subject to a violation of 18 USC § 1425 for having unlawfully obtained naturalization.[33] We have found no evidence that further action has been taken with regard to this recommendation. Nosair is currently serving a life sentence in federal prison. His projected release date is September 2, 2087.

Abdel Rahman Yasin

Yasin was born in Indiana to Iraqi parents. His father was a graduate student. Yasin left the United States and grew up in Baghdad. Later he returned to the United States to live with his mother in Jersey City, New Jersey.

6/21/92   Yasin applied for a new U.S. passport in Amman, Jordan, to replace one he claimed to have lost.[34]

            Ramzi Yousef, the mastermind of the 1993 bombing of the World Trade Center, stayed at Yasin's apartment before the bombing. They also mixed the chemicals for the bomb. During this process, Yasin's leg was burned by chemicals.

2/26/93   The World Trade Center was bombed. As part of the investiga-
          tion the FBI questioned Yasin whom they encountered while
          executing a search warrant. He provided information on
          Ramzi Yousef, who had fled the United States. He also took the
          agents to the apartment where the bomb chemicals were
          mixed. Yasin appeared helpful and open and was released by the
          FBI. He immediately disappeared.

5/23/02   CBS news reporter Lesley Stahl located Yasin, then living in
          Baghdad, and interviewed him. Yasin remains a fugitive, his
          whereabouts unknown.

THE LANDMARKS CONSPIRATORS

*A number of conspirators in the June 1993 plot to blow up the Federal building,
the FBI office, the Lincoln and Holland Tunnels, and the George Washington
Bridge, obtained legal permanent residency or were naturalized citizens. The Privacy
Act prevented our review of their files.*[35] *They are:*

- **Amir Abdelghani.** Currently in federal prison, projected release date
  of August 13, 2019.[36]
- **Fadil Abdelghani.** Currently in federal prison, projected release date
  of April 5, 2015.[37]
- **Tarig El Hassan.** Currently in federal prison, projected release date of
  December 21, 2023.[38]
- **Fares Khallafalla.** He obtained legal permanent residency immigration status through the Special Agricultural Worker (SAW) provision of
  the Immigration Reform and Control Act of 1986. Currently in
  federal prison, projected release date of August 13, 2019.[39]
- **Siddig Ibrahim Siddiq Ali.**

PLOT TO DESTROY THE NEW YORK CITY SUBWAY

*In this plot two illegal immigrants conspired to blow up the Atlantic Avenue subway in
Brooklyn, New York. The plot was discovered shortly before five bombs were planted.*

Mohamed Mustafa Khalil[40]
Place of birth: Amman, Jordan
Date of birth: October 5, 1974

7/6/96   Khalil was issued Jordanian passport E925402 in Amman, Jordan. He applied for and received a Canadian tourist visa.

11/19/96 Khalil traveled to Toronto. He was permitted to study English in Canada.

1/14/97   Khalil was arrested by INS Border Patrol officers at a Greyhound Bus station in Bellingham, Washington during routine patrol duties. Khalil told the Border Patrol that he had crossed the Canadian border with co-conspirator Abu Mezer (See chapter 3) in a taxi but was not inspected by the INS. Khalil had violated immigration law by failing to obtain a visa to visit the United States. He was detained without bond until his detention hearing.[41]

1/29/97   Immigration Judge Anna Ho set bail at $10,000.

2/27/97   At the deportation hearing, Khalil said he wanted to apply for political asylum. His bond was reduced to $5,000 It was posted by Kamal Hourani, an acquaintance. Khalil told the judge that upon release from INS custody he planned to live in Centreville, Virginia.

7/4/97   Khalil told the INS that he had married Sofina Assaf, a United States citizen residing in Canada.

8/1/97   Khalil was arrested in New York City during the investigation of the New York subway bombing plot.[42]

11/12/97 Khalil was released from prison and deported to Jordan.[43]

THE MANILA AIR PLOT

In 1994, KSM accompanied Ramzi Yousef to the Philippines, and the two of them began planning what is now known as the Manila air or "Bojinka" plot—the intended bombing of 12 U.S. commercial jumbo jets over the Pacific during a two-day span.

Abdul Hakim Murad aka Ahmed Saeed
Place of birth: Pakistan; raised in Kuwait
Date of birth: January 4, 1968

Late in 1994, KSM sent $3,000 to Ramzi Yousef in the Philippines to fund the plot. Another conspirator, Murad, transported the money.[44]

1/6/95   Murad was arrested by the Philippine police in Manila after he returned to the scene of a small fire at the Dona Josefa Apartments where he had been building bombs with Ramzi Yousef. Murad had wanted to retrieve his laptop. Following 67 days of interrogation he disclosed the substance of the plot—planting bombs aboard U.S. airliners and a related plan to fly an explosives-laden plane into the CIA. At the time of his arrest, Murad used the alias of Ahmed Saeed.

4/12/95   Murad was transported to the United States where he testified at the trial of Ramzi Yousef, who had been extradited from Pakistan. Murad was charged with terrorist acts in Federal court and was sentenced to life imprisonment. Murad is currently in federal prison serving a life sentence.[45]

OTHER PERSONS OF INTEREST

**Eyad Mohammed Mohammed Mustafa aka
Eyad M. Mustafa al Rababah**[46]
Place of birth: Jordan
Date of birth: July 21, 1972

3/21/99   Rababah entered the United States at New York City as a tourist and was admitted until September 20, 1999. He said he was going to Bridgeport, Connecticut.[47]

10/12/00   Rababah was arrested by the Virginia Department of Motor Vehicles for assisting persons to illegally obtain Virginia driver's licenses and Virginia identification cards. Rababah later pleaded guilty to a misdemeanor offense in connection with these charges.

5/01   Rababah told the FBI that he met two Saudi males, "Nawaf" and "Hani," at a 7-11 convenience store in Falls Church, Virginia. Rababah told the pair that he could assist them in obtaining driver's licenses.

6/01   Rababah received a phone call from his former roommate in
              Virginia that the two men he met—Nawaf and Hani—had
              tried to contact him. Rababah spoke to Nawaf who said that
              he had two other friends who would like to "travel around."
              Rababah, who had since moved to Connecticut, drove to
              Virginia to pick up the four men. The following day Rababah
              drove them to the Fairfield Motor Inn in Fairfield,
              Connecticut. They stayed for two nights.

9/28/01   Rababah voluntarily told the FBI in New Haven, Conn. that
              he may have known some of the 9/11 hijackers. The men were
              subsequently identified by Rababah as hijackers Ahmed al
              Ghamdi, Hani Hanjour, Majed Moqed and Nawaf al Hamzi.[48]

              The FBI contacted the INS Hartford office regarding
              Rababah's immigration status. At 11:30 P.M., two Hartford INS
              agents took Rababah into custody. The following day Rababah
              was charged with overstaying his tourist visa in violation of
              INA § 237(a)(1)(B), and detained.

9/30/01   A material witness warrant was issued against Rababah in
              connection with the 9/11 plot and he was transferred to the
              INS detention center in New York, and then to the
              Metropolitan Correctional Center (MCC). The INS filed a
              detainer with the MCC and closed the immigration
              proceeding against him since he was no longer in INS custody.
              The detainer directed the MCC to turn Rababah over to the
              INS when he was released.

11/16/01   A criminal complaint was filed against Rababah in the U.S.
              Court for the Eastern District of Virginia charging him with
              knowingly and without lawful authority producing an identity
              document, and aiding and abetting the same, in violation of 18
              USC § 2 and 8 USC § 1028(a)(1), § (b)(1)(A)(ii), and §
              (c)(3)(A). A federal arrest warrant was issued for Eyad M. Al
              Rababah for the document fraud charges.

12/8/01   The INS filed a detainer with the U.S. Marshal for the Eastern
              District of Virginia where Rababah had been transferred to
              stand trial.

5/20/02 Rababah was convicted and sentenced to six months imprisonment and ordered to pay a special assessment of $200. His sentence was conditioned on his cooperation with the INS and his agreement not to oppose any removal or deportation action.

The deportation hearing was postponed a number of times at the request of Rababah's attorney. Rababah sought to have his bail reduced so that he could be released in order to marry his American girlfriend. The INS legal counsel concluded that the special conditions included as part of the sentence were unenforceable because the federal court order involved matters of criminal law, but immigration hearings involved administrative law.

10/17/02 The INS received a letter from the FBI stating that Rababah was no longer of investigative interest to them.

10/22/02 A deportation hearing was held. Rababah requested political asylum, protection under the convention against torture, and relief from deportation. The Immigration Judge ruled that Rababah did not provide sufficient evidence to support his claims for relief and ordered him removed from the United States.

11/4/02 Rababah lost the appeal of his removal order.

7/10/03 Rababah was deported to Jordan via Paris.

Anwar Nasser Aulaqi aka al Awalaki[49]
Place of birth: Yemen
Date of birth: 1971

Aulaqi entered the United States at an unknown place as a J-1 Exchange Visitor. He enrolled in the civil engineering program at Colorado State University. He later obtained legal permanent residence status in the United States; we were unable to determine on what basis this status was granted.

Aulaqi was a cleric who preached at the Dar al-Hijrah Islamic Center in Falls Church, Virginia and at a mosque in San Diego. He became a "spiritual adviser" to hijackers Nawaf al Hazmi and Khalid al Midhar. Eyad al Rababah was also a member of the Falls Church mosque. Aulaqi's telephone number was found when police raided Ramzi Binalshibh's apartment in Hamburg, German.

Mohdar Mohamed Abdullah[50]
Place of birth: Yemen
Date of birth: May 8, 1978

4/14/99   Abdullah requested and received political asylum based on his claim of religious persecution in Somalia.

1/15/02   Nawaf al Hazmi and Khalid al Mihdhar arrived in Southern California. They eventually met Mohdar Abdullah who assisted them in their housing search and helped them with English translations.[51]

10/3/02   Abdullah received a "Notice of Intent to Terminate Asylum Status" before an immigration judge based on his fraudulent political asylum claim. The INS had determined that he was a citizen of Yemen, not Somalia, and had entered the United States as a temporary visitor on December 10, 1998, from Canada using a Yemeni passport. Abdullah had testified that he illegally entered the United States on December 7, 1998, in New York on an Italian passport.

     Abdullah was indicted in the Southern District of California for violations of 18 USC § 371 (Conspiracy), 18 USC § 1546 (False Statement in an Immigration Application), 18 USC §1001 (False Statements) and 18 USC § 2 (Aiding and Abetting).

7/19/02   Abdullah pleaded guilty to 18 USC § 1001 (False Statements) for submitting fraudulent documents in support of his political asylum claim. While in custody on these charges, Abdullah reportedly claimed that he knew about the 9/11 attack weeks before it happened.[52]

10/02/02   Abdullah was released from federal prison and transferred to the custody of the INS.[53]

5/21/04   Abdullah was deported to Yemen.[54]

LOS ANGELES AIRPORT MURDER ON JULY 4, 2002[55]

Hesham Mohamed Ali Hedayet aka Hadayet

Date of birth: July 4, 1961
Place of birth: Egypt

11/14/87   Hadayet was issued Egyptian passport 69662.

7/13/92   He received a multiple entry B-2 tourist visa from the U.S. Consulate in Cairo, Egypt.

7/31/92   He entered the United States at Los Angeles as a tourist and was admitted until January 25, 1993.

12/01/92   Hadayet filed an application for political asylum and permission to work. He claimed he would be persecuted for his religious beliefs if he returned to Egypt. Specifically, Hadayet claimed to be a member of "Assad Eben Furat Mosque Association," which called for a strict Islamist government. Hadayet also claimed to have been arrested many times over the previous 14 years by the Egyptian secret police for his strong religious beliefs. Based on his asylum application, he was approved for an Employment Authorization Document (EAD) by the Los Angeles INS office.

3/93   Hadayet's wife arrived in the United States with their son, an Egyptian citizen. There was no immigration record of their arrival.[56]

3/8/93   Hadayet's permission to work was approved for another year.

3/30/93   Hadayet was interviewed about his political asylum claim. He lied about the presence of his wife and son in the United States. Concealment of this material fact was grounds for denial of his petition.

3/18/94   Hadayet received another one-year renewal of his employment authorization. He worked as a chauffeur, mainly at the Los Angeles airport.

3/7/95   After reviewing all the facts in the case, the INS issued a
             "Notice of Intent to Deny the Political Asylum Claim."
             Hadayet was given thirty days to respond. He did not.

10/19/95   Deportation proceedings were initiated for his previous over-
             stay in 1992. Hadayet's permission to work was also terminated.
             His deportation hearing was scheduled for March 26, 1996. All
             case documents were sent to him via certified mail.
                  The certified mail was returned "undeliverable." Because he
             did not receive the official INS notification of his deportation
             hearing, under INS regulations he was not placed in the
             Deportable Alien Control System (DACS) system. Thus, no
             one at INS was tracking him or looking for him.

3/29/96   Deportation proceedings against Hadayet were terminated
             because he could not be located.

6/96   Hadayet applied to renew his employment authorization. The
             DACS was checked but because Hadayet's name was not
             entered, he received authorization to work another year.
                  Meanwhile, his wife won one of the 50,000 "diversity
             immigrant visas" issued in an annual lottery, and was granted
             legal permanent residence status in the United States.

1/97   Hadayet's wife filed an application for permanent residence for
             Hadayet based on her status as a legal resident.[57]

8/29/97   Hadayet was approved for permanent residence as an asylee.

5/3/00   Hadayet was issued a second California driver's license in the
             name Hesham Mohamed Hadayet. His previous driver's license
             was in the name of Hesham Mohamed Ali.

7/4/02   Hadayet drove to the Los Angeles Airport armed with a .45
             caliber pistol, a 9-millimeter automatic handgun and a hunting
             knife. He approached the El Al ticket counter and shot and
             killed an El Al employee and a man waiting in line. He was shot
             and killed by a security officer.

NOTES

Chapter 1

1. Intelligence report, interrogation of a detainee, Oct. 23, 2002. After Ramzi Binalshibh failed to obtain a U.S. visa in May 2001, Usama Bin Ladin (UBL) asked Binalshibh to act as a contact between himself and Mohamed Atta to relay operational details that were too sensitive to trust to telephone or email. His travel in this capacity illustrates the importance of "courier" travel to al Qaeda planning and operations. To facilitate his travel, KSM provided Binalshibh with a genuine Saudi passport in the name of Hasan Ali al Assiri and a round-trip ticket to Kuala Lumpur, Malaysia, where he was supposed to meet Atta. While in Kuala Lumpur, Binalshibh applied for a Yemeni passport. When Atta was delayed, Binalshibh went to Bangkok. Because Atta was still unable to meet him, Binalshibh traveled to Amsterdam on his Yemeni passport, took a train to Hamburg, and bought a ticket to Spain to meet Atta. Intelligence report, interrogation of a detainee, Oct. 1, 2002. Binalshibh finally met up with Atta in early July 2001 in Spain to discuss sensitive operational aspects of the 9/11 plot. Specifically, Binalshibh told Atta that UBL's instructions were to attack the U.S. Congress, the World Trade Center, and the Pentagon, the "symbols of America." Atta told Binalshibh, who passed the information to UBL through KSM, that planning had been completed with no problems and it could be operational in five to six weeks.

2. CIA analytic report, Analysis of Passports, Nov. 20, 2002, p. 1, 3. Atta, who reportedly learned these techniques in Afghanistan, cleaned Ramzi Binalshibh's passport of its Pakistani visa and travel cachets.

3. In addition to the 19 hijackers, the seven other conspirators who sought visas were Mohamed al Kahtani (a Saudi), Saeed al Ghamdi (a Saudi, not the hijacker), Mushabib al Hamlan (a Saudi), Zakariya Essabar (a Moroccan), Ali Abdul Aziz Ali (a Pakistani), Ramzi Binalshibh (a Yemeni), and Tawfiq bin Attash (a Yemeni, also known as Khallad). An eighth individual who was a possible pilot in the 9/11 operation, Zacarias Moussaoui, entered under the Visa Waiver Program.

4. CIA analytic report, "Name Variants and Aliases of 11 September Hijackers and Associates," Mar. 2004.

Chapter 2

1. Hani Hanjour was the first 9/11 hijacker to acquire a U.S. visa and come to the United States. He entered four times before September 11, three times to seek a U.S. education. Immigration records for Hanjour indicate that he acquired a B-2, or tourist, visa in Saudi Arabia before traveling to the United States in September 1991 and March 1996. Records of Hanjour's earlier visa applications were destroyed at the Jeddah post. DOS memo from Richard Baltimore, Consul General, Jeddah, Saudi Arabia, Nov. 28, 2001, describing a search that recovered "all applications and

documents available on file relating to issuance of their [the 9/11 hijackers'] visas," and stating that Hanjour's earliest application was his 1997 visa application. *See also* Consular Officer No. 5 interview (Mar. 2, 2004), describing how, generally, Jeddah post kept visa applications for two years. Hanjour entered the United States on these visas within a month of acquiring them on October 3, 1991, and Apr. 2, 1996. There is no record as to when Hanjour left the country after his first visit, although he was permitted a six-month stay. INS record, NIIS record of Hanjour, Oct. 3, 1991 and Apr. 2, 1996.

Hanjour's March 1996 tourist visa was issued with a notation on the application stating "prospective student, school not yet selected." INS record, NIIS record of Hanjour, Apr. 2, 1996 with visa issuance date of Mar. 19, 1996. Records indicate that when Hanjour returned on April 2, 1996, he received another six-month length of stay as a tourist. INS record, NIIS record of Hanjour, Apr. 2, 1996 with length of stay until Oct. 1, 1996. On June 7, 1996, Hanjour filed an INS I-539 application to change his immigration status from tourist to academic student to attend the ELS Language Center in Oakland, California. During this time, Hanjour also had contact with the Caldwell Flight Academy in New Jersey and the Sierra Academy in Oakland. Caldwell Flight Academy record of Hanjour, June 6, 2001, and Sierra Academy of Aeronautics record of Hanjour, Sept. 3, 1996. The application was quickly approved 20 days later, on June 27, 1996, and allowed Hanjour to stay in the United States until May 20, 1997. INS record, I-539 Application to Change Nonimmigrant Status of Hanjour, May 24, 1996. Hanjour attended the Sierra Academy from September 3 to September 9, 1996. Well before his length of stay expired, Hanjour departed the United States in November 1996. INS record, NIIS record of Hanjour April 2, 1996 with date of departure of Nov. 26, 1996.

On his November 1997 visa application, Hanjour answered "no" to the question "Have you ever applied for a U.S. visa before, whether immigrant or nonimmigrant?" He also answered "no" to the question "Have you ever been in the U.S.A.?" DOS record, visa application of Hanjour, Nov. 2, 1997. It is difficult to establish the intent behind these false statements. The application does bear a signature that appears identical to the signature on Hanjour's two 2000 visa applications. DOS record, visa applications of Hanjour, Sept. 10 and Sept. 25, 2000. However, the application form also indicated that it was prepared by "Siddiqi/Samara Travel." DOS record, visa application of Hanjour, Nov. 2, 1997. Thus, the false statements may have been made inadvertently by a travel agent who filled out the form on Hanjour's behalf. The consular officer who adjudicated Hanjour's 1997 visa application interviewed him on November 2, 1997. This officer said that they would interview 50–60 percent of the Saudi applicants. DOS Office of Inspector General Memorandum of Conversation (OIG MOC) with Consular Officer No. 5, Feb. 5, 2003. The officer who interviewed him about his application did not recall many details of the interview, but was able to reconstruct some aspects of it from notes on the visa application. DOS OIG MOC with Consular Officer No. 5, Feb. 5, 2003. The officer said he would not have known about Hanjour's prior travel to the United States unless it was reflected in his passport. The officer also said he could not understand why Hanjour would have sought to cover up prior travel to the United States, adding, "It's perplexing that they would hide that because it works in their favor." Consular Officer No. 5 interview (Mar. 2, 2004). He did say, though, that a Saudi who had been to the United States twice before, as Hanjour apparently had been, and who then applied to go to the United States for English studies would have "raise[d] an eyebrow" because a student visa applicant must demonstrate that he or she has made reasonable progress in their studies. Ibid. The officer said underperforming Saudi students were denied visas on some occasions. Ibid. In general, the officer told us, they felt they could make visa adjudications with only the basic biographical information Saudis typically provided. However, the officer made a point of telling us that "it bothered me; it disturbed me" to accept so many incomplete applications from Saudis. When they raised it at post, they were told by the local staff, "Well, we have always done it this way." Ibid. There is no evidence they sought to raise the question with their superiors.

Hanjour traveled to the United States on November 16, 1997 on that visa and was granted a two-year length of stay by an immigration inspector. The visa allowed Hanjour to attend the ELS Language Centers in Florida. But Hanjour instead began flight training at Cockpit Resource Management Airline Training Center in Scottsdale, Arizona. Seven months later, on June 16, 1998, Hanjour filed an I-539, seeking a change of status from academic student (F-1) to M1 vocational student (M-2) to attend the Cockpit Resource Management from July 30, 1998 to July 29, 1999. Eight months later, the INS asked Hanjour to supply supporting evidence for his request. INS record, I-539 Application to Change Nonimmigrant Status of Hanjour, June 9, 1998, and INS record, I-539 Notice of Action of Hanjour, June 16, 1998. The application was not approved until Jan. 16, 2001, for a retroactive length of stay from July 30, 1998, to July 29, 1999. Having attended the flight school and received a commercial pilot's license from the Federal Aviation Administration (FAA) in April 1999 without ever receiving INS approval to change his status, Hanjour left the country that month. For flight school attendance and FAA approval, *see* Penttbom Summary, Feb. 29, 2004. INS record, NIIS record of Hanjour, Nov. 16, 1997, with a departure date of April 28, 1999. His I-539 was not approved until January 16, 2001. By that point, Hanjour had already acquired a new academic visa and reentered the United States for his last time. DOS record, Visa Application of Hanjour, Sept. 25, 2000; INS record, NIIS record of Hanjour, Dec. 8, 2000.

2. INS memo, Ken Elwood, Deputy Executive Associate Commissioner, Office of Field Operations to the field, Nov. 11, 1998.

3. DOS record, NIV Applicant Detail of Nawaf al Hazmi, Nov. 19, 2001.

4. FBI record, copy of Nawaf al Hazmi's passport.

5. DOS record, visa application of Salah Saeed Mohammed Bin Yousaf, April 3, 1999.

6. Ibid.

7. Ibid. Yemenis has a 66 percent refusal rate for "B" visas in fiscal year 1999. DOS record, "Visa Issuance and Refusal Data for the Country of Yemen," June 18, 2004.

8. Khallad claims he applied for a visa before the 1999 application. DOS has searched for this application using his real name and known aliases, but has been unable to locate any records supporting this claim. However, the records could have been destroyed and no electronic record retained.

9. DOS record, NIV Applicant Detail of Khalid al Mihdhar, Nov. 8, 2001; Copy of Khalid al Mihdhar's passport number B721156..

10. FBI Penttbom Timeline, Dec. 5, 2003.

11. A consular officer serving in Jeddah at this time told Commission staff that Saudi citizens were considered security risks by Jeddah consular officers, that they interviewed "the majority" of Saudi males between the ages of 16 and 40, and that they were not shy about turning down Saudi male visa applicants on security grounds—including applicants whom the officers felt had no good reason to be going to the United States. This officer told us he would be "shocked" to learn that they had not interviewed Saudi males like Nawaf al Hazmi and Khalid al Mihdhar, who were between 16 and 40 years of age and traveling alone. However, he did not handle their visa applications. Consular Officer No. 12 interview (Feb. 24, 2004).

12. DOS OIG MOC with Consular Officer No. 6, Feb. 3, 2003.

13. Although today consular officers typically take notes electronically while interviewing an applicant—notes made part of the permanent CCD record—that was not the case in April 1999.

14. INS records, NIIS records of Nawaf al Hazmi and Khalid al Mihdhar, Jan. 15, 2000 and primary inspector interviews for both these entries (May 24, 2004).

15. CIA cable, "Activities of Bin Ladin Associate Khalid Revealed," Jan. 4, 2000.

16. DOS record, NIV Applicant Detail of Marwan al Shehhi, Nov. 8, 2001.

17. DOS OIG MOC with Consular Officer No. 7, Feb. 11, 2003.

18. Ibid.

19. Consular Officer No. 10 interview (Mar. 1, 2004).

20. DOS record, NIV Applicant Detail of Nawaf al Hazmi, Nov. 19, 2001, with visa expiration date April 2, 2001.

21. American Association of Motor Vehicle Administrators (AAMVA) memo, "9/11 hijacker driver license and identification paper trail," May 28, 2004.

22. DOS record, NIV Applicant Detail of Mohamed Atta, May 17, 2000. The hijackers received visas of different lengths dependent on reciprocal agreements in place between the United States and their countries of origin. A copy of Mohamed Atta's U.S. visa is attached in Appendix A.

23. Consular Officer No. 9 interview (Feb. 20, 2004).

24. DOS records, visa applications of Ramzi Binalshibh, May 16, June 5, Sept. 15 and Oct. 25, 2000. A copy of the first page of Binalshibh's first visa application is attached in Appendix A.

25. DOS record, NIV Applicant Detail of Ziad Jarrah, Nov. 8, 2001. Jarrah's original visa application was destroyed, but an electronic record, including his photograph, remains in the State Department's electronic records. A partly-burned copy of Jarrah's U.S. visa, recovered from the crash scene of Flight 93, is attached in Appendix A.

26. DOS OIG MOC with Consular Officer No. 8, Feb. 11, 2003.

27. INS record, NIIS record of Marwan al Shehhi, May 29, 2000, and Customs record, Customs Secondary Inspection Result of Marwan al Shehhi, May 29, 2000.

28. INS record, NIIS record of Mohamed Atta, June 3, 2000.

29. Ramzi Binalshibh's NIV Applicant Detail produced to the Commission by the State Department lists the adjudication dates of his Berlin visas as June 5, June 27, July 18, and Nov. 1, 2000.

30. That provision of law states: "No visa . . . shall be issued to an alien if (1) it appears to the consular officer, from statements in the application, or in the papers submitted therewith, that such alien is ineligible to receive a visa . . . under section 212, or any other provision of law, (2) the application fails to comply with the provisions of this Act, or the regulations issued thereunder, or (3) the consular officer knows or has reason to believe that such alien is ineligible to receive a visa . . . under section 212, or any other provision of law."

31. DOS regulations, Authority to Require Documents of Visa Applicants, 22 C.F.R. § 41.105(a)(1): "The consular officer is authorized to require documents considered necessary to establish the alien's eligibility to receive a nonimmigrant visa. All documents and other evidence presented by the alien, including briefs submitted by attorneys or other representatives, shall be considered by the consular officer."

32. 22 CFR § 41.103(b)(2) (additional information as part of application).

33. Consular Officer No. 9 interview (Feb. 20, 2004); 22 CFR § 41.121 (Refusal of individual visas) provides, "If the ground(s) of ineligibility may be overcome by the presentation of additional evidence, and the applicant has indicated the intention to submit such evidence, a review of the refusal may be deferred for not more then 120 days."

34. FBI report, "Summary of Penttbom Investigation," Feb. 29, 2004.

35. INS record, NIIS record of Ziad Jarrah, June 27, 2000.

36. FBI report, "Summary of Penttbom Investigation," Feb. 29, 2004.

37. Huffman Aviation enrollment records of Marwan al Shehhi and Mohamed Atta; DOJ OIG Memorandum of Investigation (MOI), interview of company president, Rudi Dekkers, April 10, 2002. Dekkers also stated that Atta and Shehhi had previously attended Jones Aviation in Sarasota, Florida, but were asked to leave that flight school because of their bad attitudes.

38. DOJ OIG MOI, interview of Rudi Dekkers, Apr. 10, 2002. FBI report of investigation, interview of Sue Costa, Sept. 15, 2001.

39. INS record, I-539 Application to Extend Nonimmigrant Status of Nawaf al Hazmi, July 12, 2000.

40. According to an official in the State Department's Visa Office within the Bureau of Consular Affairs, State records support a conclusion that Binalshibh's first two visa applications amounted to "one case" that was denied on July 18, 2000 under 214(b). The records themselves also support this conclusion. Copies of Binalshibh's visa application show no writing on his June 15, 2000, application. Rather, notes taken on the May 17, 2000, application described the reasons why both applications then pending were denied, and included the dates of June 5 and July 18—both dates of refusals, according to the State computer system. It appears that Binalshibh's two applications were first denied under 221(g) (on June 5 and June 27) without a face-to-face meeting with a consular officer—a common practice in Berlin during this time period; Binalshibh was denied under 214(b)—the more serious denial—only after a formal interview with a consular officer on July 18, 2000. This surmise is supported by a note

on Binalshibh's last application, denied November 1, 2000, on which a consular official wrote "two prior refusals"—i.e., one in Berlin and one in Sanaa, Yemen.

41. FBI report of investigation, interview of Sue Costa, Sept. 15, 2001.

42. DOS record, Visa Application of Ahmed al Ghamdi, Sept. 3, 2000.

43. The consular officer's testimony before Congress reflects his misimpression that Hanjour applied for this visa under the Visa Express program. Testimony of Consular Officer No. 3 before the U.S. House of Representatives, Committee on Government Reform, Aug. 1, 2002, p. 38. This error led the officer to state—incorrectly, we believe—that he had denied Hanjour a visa for administrative reasons under section 221(g) in order to call him in for an interview. Ibid, pp. 38–39. "I remember that I had refused him for interview, because he had applied for a tourist visa and he said that his reason for going to the United States was to study," the officer recalled.); Ibid, p. 39. In this case, it meant "No. Come in. I want to talk to you"). In fact, the date Hanjour applied (as shown on his written application) and the date he was denied (as shown both on the application and on State's electronic records) are the same: September 10, 2000. A copy of Hanjour's September 10, 2000, visa application is attached in Appendix A.

44. Ibid.

45. The student coordinator told the FBI that on "one occasion, Atta was very upset with the date of his visa and wanted it changed." Atta did not tell her what upset him about the date or why he wanted the visa date changed. (We assume this reference is to Atta's length of stay.) FBI report of investigation, interview of Nicole Antini, Sept. 13, 2001.

46. INS record, I-539 Applications to Change Status for Mohamed Atta, undated; and Marwan al Shehhi, Sept. 15, 2000. A copy of al Shehhi's I-539 is attached in Appendix A.

47. FBI report of investigation, interview of Ivan Chirivella, Sept. 16, 2001.

48. On his Oct. 25, 2000, visa application, Binalshibh lists the date of his Sanaa visa application as Aug. 12, 2000. However, the application itself is dated Sept. 15, 2000, and the date stamped on the application for the denial is Sept. 16, 2000.

49. Ibid.

50. Ibid.

51. DOS record, NIV Applicant Detail of Hanjour, Nov. 8, 2001. We were unable to interview the primary inspector who admitted Hanjour on Dec. 8, 2000, to determine how the tourist visa may have been changed upon Hanjour's entry at Cincinnati International to an academic student visa entry.

52. DOS record, visa application of Hamza al Ghamdi, Oct. 17, 2000.

53. FBI report, "Summary of Penttbom Investigation," Feb. 24, 2004.

54. DOS OIG MOC with Consular Officer No. 1, Jan. 22, 2003.

55. DOS record, visa application of Mohand al Shehri, Oct. 23, 2000. A copy of al Shehri's visa application is attached in Appendix A.

56. DOS OIG MOC with Consular Officer No. 4, Jan. 24, 2003.

57. Ibid.

58. DOS record, visa application of Ahmed al Nami, Oct. 28, 2000.

59. FBI report, "Summary of Penttbom Investigation," Feb. 24, 2004.

60. DOS record, visa application of Mushabib al Hamlan, Oct. 28, 2000.

61. INS record, NIIS record of Ziad Jarrah, Oct. 29, 2000.

62. FBI report of investigation, interview of Sue Costa, Sept. 15, 2001.

63. FBI report of investigation, interview of Karen Goduto, Sept. 14, 2001.

64. DOS record, visa application of Ahmad al Haznawi, Nov. 12, 2000. A copy of Haznawi's application is attached in Appendix A.

65. FBI report, "Summary of Penttbom Investigations," Feb. 24, 2004.

66. DOS record, visa application record of Saeed al Ghamdi, Nov. 12, 2000. A copy of al Ghamdi's visa application (in which he spelled his last name "al Gamdi") is attached in Appendix A.

67. DOS record, visa application record of Majed Moqed, Nov. 20, 2000.

68. DOS OIG MOC with Consular Officer No. 4, Jan. 24, 2003.

69. Ibid.

70. DOS record, visa application record of Satam al Suqami, Nov. 21, 2000.

71. Although Suqami had false travel stamps in his passport as of 9/11, we do not know if these stamps were placed in his passport before or after submission of his visa application, although the dates on some of the false stamps pre-date the date he applied for his visa.

72. Testimony of Consular Officer Number No. 2 before the House Committee on Government Reform, Aug. 1, 2002.

73. Ibid.

74. Customs record, TECS II Private Aircraft Enforcement System record of Ziad Jarrah, Nov. 25, 2000; and customs inspector of Ziad Jarrah on Nov. 25, 2000 interview (May 18, 2004).

75. INS record, NIIS record of Hani Hanjour, Dec. 8, 2000. On failure to attend school, *see* FBI report, "Summary of Penttbom Investigation," Feb. 29, 2004.

76. DOS record, visa application of Zakariya Essabar, Dec. 12, 2004.

77. FBI report of investigation, interview of Sue Costa, Sept. 15, 2001. At some point during their schooling, Atta and Shehhi were reportedly offered jobs as co-pilots for a new airline, "Flair" by Huffman's president, Rudi Dekkers. FBI draft report of investigation, interview of Nicole Antini, Sept. 13, 2004.

78. INS record, NIIS record of Mohamed Atta, June 3, 2000, with length of stay until Dec. 2, 2000, and a departure date of May 18, 2000. For the INS abandonment policy, *see* INS Memorandum of Tom Cook, Acting Assistant Commissioner for Adjudications addressed to all Service Center Directors, District Directors, and Officers in Charge, June 18, 200. It stated: "Service officers are reminded an alien on whose behalf a change of nonimmigrant status has been filed and who travels outside the United States before the request is adjudicated is considered to have abandoned the request for a change of nonimmigrant status. This has been, and remains, the Service's long-standing policy."

79. INS record, NIIS record of Ziad Jarrah, Jan. 5, 2001.

80. Primary immigration inspector of Mohamed Atta on Jan. 10, 2001 interview (Mar. 25, 2004); DOJ OIG primary immigration inspector interview, Nov. 27, 2001. INS record, Inspection Results Report record of Mohamed Atta, Jan. 10, 2001.

81. Primary immigration inspector of Mohamed Atta on Jan. 10, 2001 interview (Mar. 25, 2004). INS record, I-94 arrival record of Mohamed Atta, Jan. 10, 2001.

82. The "VOID" handwritten over top of this stamp is not the handwriting of the primary inspector, according to him. It is likely the handwriting of the secondary inspector, who told the Commission he could not recognize his own handwriting stating: "I've hurt my writing finger too many times and my handwriting keeps changing; couldn't recognize it."

83. This policy was in contradiction to the stricter language of the INS Field Guidelines, which had specifically delineated business categories for admission. Continued training as a pilot was not within the language of those guidelines.

84. Secondary immigration inspector of Mohamed Atta on Jan. 10, 2001 interview (Mar. 25, 2004); DOJ OIG interview of secondary immigration inspector of Atta on Jan. 10, 2001, Dec. 20, 2001. We asked these questions because under immigration law, "part-time schooling" is considered incidental to the primary purpose of a visit, and did not require a new student visa or a change of status from tourist to student.

85. Secondary immigration inspector of Mohamed Atta on Jan. 10, 2001 interview (Mar. 25, 2004). For the abandonment policy, see INS Tom Cook policy memo stating that pending benefits applications are considered abandoned if the alien leaves while the application is pending, therefore requiring the applicant to attain a visa abroad for that same benefit prior to re-entry. (There is no reference to this policy in the INS Field Inspectors' Manual.) In other words, if Atta wanted to study in the United States and filed an application to that effect but left the country while it was pending, he needed to get a student visa abroad in order to return to the United States. The initial application was considered no longer valid. For other inspectors aware of this policy, see Commission interview of inspector for Atta's deferred inspection on May 2, 2001.

86. Secondary immigration inspector of Mohamed Atta on Jan. 10, 2001 interview (Mar. 25, 2004). DOJ OIG interview of secondary immigration inspector of Atta on Jan. 10, 2001, Mar. 21, 2002.

87. Secondary immigration inspector of Mohamed Atta on Jan. 10, 2001 interview (Mar. 25, 2004). See also Justice Department Inspector General Report, The INS Contacts with Two September 11 Terrorists, (May 20, 2002), p. 56-58.

88. The eight-month time period is recalled by another inspector who reviewed Atta's I-94 arrival record in May 2001, as this inspector changed Atta's length of stay from eight months back to six months. The electronic admission record also noted an eight month stay. The admission stamp, (although hard to read), bares this secondary inspector's number. It appears that the secondary inspector wrote "VOID" on the primary inspector's one month B1 admission stamp in Atta's passport, and instead admitted Atta as a tourist for eight months, apparently to accommodate Atta's schooling. The same handwriting appears on Atta's I-94 arrival record as well, crossing out the primary inspector's one month stay and replacing it with a sloppy handwritten date which looks to be September 8, 2001, with the same length of stay that is listed on the original immigration arrival record.

89. If an alien files an application for a change of status while they are legally in the United States, they may stay in the country until the application is adjudicated. In addition, Atta could have qualified for a deferred inspection if the inspector was

convinced that "the case could possibly be resolved in the alien's favor," *see* INS Field Inspectors' Manual at 17.1.

90. Secondary immigration inspector of Mohamed Atta on Jan. 10, 2001 interview (Mar. 25, 2004).

91. Commission work product chart, *September 11 Hijacker border inspection interview results: Red Flags Resulting in Secondary Interviews*, May 20, 2004.

92. On deferred inspections, *see* INS Field Inspectors' Manual at 17.1.

93. INS record, NIIS record of Marwan al Shehhi, Jan. 18, 2001.

94. Primary immigration inspector of Marwan al Shehhi on Jan. 18, 2001 interview (Mar. 26, 2004).

95. INS record, INS Inspections Results Report record of Marwan al Shehhi, Jan. 18, 2001. In the interview of Marwan al Shehhi's primary immigration inspector, she said: "I referred him to secondary and he didn't want to leave the booth. 'What is your problem?' I said. He simply said, 'No.' I had to get out of the booth and take him into secondary because I thought he would bolt, and I sat him down. I told someone in secondary to watch him. He made me remember him; if he had been smart he wouldn't have done that," *see* Primary immigration inspector of Marwan al Shehhi on Jan. 18, 2001 interview (Mar. 26, 2004).

96. Secondary immigration inspector of Marwan al Shehhi on Jan. 18, 2001 interview (Mar. 22, 2004). For length of time Shehhi spent in secondary, *see* INS record, INS secondary inspection roster for JFK on January 18, 2001, during the time frame Shehhi was referred to secondary.

97. Secondary immigration inspector of Marwan al Shehhi on Jan. 18, 2001 interview (Mar. 22, 2004).

98. Ibid.

99. Ibid.

100. Ibid. For baseline time given for business visitors at JFK International Airport (the baseline differed amongst the air ports where the hijackers entered, *see* Commission work product chart, *September 11 Hijacker border inspection interview results: Primary Inspection Procedures Prior to September 11*, May 20, 2004). *See also* Commission interviews of three JFK inspectors who had contact with the 9/11 hijackers (March 22, March 25 and May 24, 2004).

101. INS record, NIIS record of Ziad Jarrah, Jan. 5, 2001with a departure date of Jan. 26, 2001.

102. INS record, NIIS record of Ziad Jarrah, Feb. 25, 2001. For baseline time given for business visitors at air ports of entry, *see* Commission work product chart, *September 11 Hijacker border inspection interview results: Primary Inspection Procedures Prior to September 11*, May 20, 2004.

103. INS record, NIIS record of Ziad Jarrah, Feb. 25, 2001 with a departure date of March 30, 2001.

104. AAMVA memo, "9/11 hijacker driver license and identification paper trail," May 28, 2004.

105. INS record, NIIS record of Ziad Jarrah, April 13, 2001 with a length of stay until July 30, 2001.

106. On Ahmed al Nami's passports, *see* DOS record, NIV Applicant Detail for Ahmed al Nami (Nov. 8, 2001).

107. DOS record, DOS visa application of Ahmed al Nami, April 23, 2001. A copy of al Nami's application is attached in Appendix A.

108. INS records, I-94 Arrival Records for Waleed al Shehri and Satam al Suqami, Apr. 23, 2001.

109. The passport was recovered by NYPD Detective Yuk H. Chin from a male passerby in a business suit, about 30 years old. The passerby left before being identified, while debris was falling from WTC 2. The tower collapsed shortly thereafter. The detective then gave the passport to the FBI on 9/11. *See* FBI report, interview of Detective Chin, Sept. 12, 2001.

110. Analytic reference report, Apr. 1, 2003. In addition, the Forensic Document Analysis of Satam al Suqami's passport indicates that on page 8, "An Arabic stamp impression located near the top of page 8 has been partially covered with correction fluid," *see* INS letter from John Ross, INS Supervisory Forensic Document Examiner, to Lorie Gottesman, FBI Document Examiner, Nov. 2, 2001.

111. Primary immigration inspector of Satam al Suqami interview (Apr. 23, 2001).

112. INS records, I-94 Arrival Records for Majed Moqed and Ahmed al Ghamdi, May 2, 2001 and Customs record, Customs Declaration for Majed Moqed, May 2, 2001. On the requirement to fill out electronic reports on amounts declared over $10,000, *see* Rick Colon interview, June 14, 2004.

113. INS record, NIIS record of Marwan al Shehhi, May 2, 2001 with a length of stay until Nov. 2, 2001.

114. In regard to the identification of Atta's companions, the inspector identified one of two. She said all three had olive skin tone and dark features. She told the Commission she would never forget Atta, whom she told a colleague was "an ugly man, he looked like a bulldog." The companion who first spoke to the inspector, she recalled "was a great looking kid," which she also mentioned to a colleague. When the FBI's Most Wanted photo of Adnan G. El Shukrijumah appeared on the inspectors' bulletin board after September 11, and after the FBI interviewed her, the inspector says she told her supervisor at the port that she was "75 percent sure" that she could identify the man who was with Atta as Shukrijumah. In checking Shukrijumah's immigration status, she learned that he was a legal resident and had worked in south Florida. Information about the September 11 plot has not to date associated Shukrijumah with the plot. However, Shukrijumah is considered a well-connected al Qaeda operative, otherwise known as "Jafar the Pilot" and he is still wanted by the FBI. Shukrijumah's father is a well known imam in South Florida, having testified on behalf of Sheik Rahman during his trial for the conspiracy to destroy New York landmarks in June 1993. The inspector cannot recall what the third companion looked like, and did not recognize any of the photos of other hijackers shown to her. The Commission, however, believes that Jarrah may have been one of Atta's companions. He was the only hijacker who matched the facts as told by the inspector, that Atta's "friend" had come back in January and received a six month stay. It is also known that Jarrah was with Atta later that day, driving north to get a Florida driver's license. *See* immigration inspector of Mohamed Atta on May 2 interview (Mar. 25, 2004).

115. *See* immigration inspector of Mohamed Atta on May 2 interview (Mar. 25, 2004).

116. Ibid.

117. Ibid.

118. Ibid.; a copy of Atta's May 2, 2001, INS record (I-94) is attached in Appendix A.

119. AAMVA memo, "9/11 hijacker driver license and identification paper trail," May 28, 2004. A copy of Atta's Florida Driver License is attached in Appendix A.

120. Ibid.

121. Ibid.

122. Intelligence report, interrogation of detainee, Apr. 2, 2004.

123. For departure date of May 16, 2001, INS record, Immigrant Admission Information of Satam al Suqami, Sept. 14, 2001and INS record, NIIS record of Waleed al Shehri, Apr. 23, 2001 with a departure date of May 16, 2001. There was a mistake on Shehri's port of departure on this record, however, stating that he left from Fall River, Massachusetts, as opposed to Fort Lauderdale. An FBI phone interview indicates that an immigration inspector in Freeport, Bahamas checked the local immigration records and noted that the two arrived together on Gulfstream Continental flight 9273 at 8:20 A.M. FBI report of investigation, interview of Freeport, Bahamas immigration inspector, Sept. 18, 2001.

124. Interrogation of Ramzi Binalshibh, Apr. 7, 2004.

125. FBI report of investigation, interview of Freeport, Bahamas immigration inspector, Sept. 18, 2001.

126. Preclearance stations existed prior to September 11 in Canada, Ireland, the Bahamas, and the Caribbean.

127. Customs record, Secondary Inspection record of Waleed al Shehri, May 16, 2001. The attempted three-day jaunt by Shehri and Suqami to the Bahamas would cause difficulty for the INS in assisting the FBI's investigation into 9/11 since the INS records indicated the two had left the United States and not returned. This is because when the two left Miami for the Bahamas, they handed in their I-94 departure records as required. They were turned around in the Bahamas for a lack of visas but under U.S. immigration law they never left the United States. However, they were not given new arrival records when they physically returned to the United States. Therefore, when the attacks occurred, investigators thought that Suqmai and Shehri had departed the United States, which is what the INS records indicated.

128. DOJ record, "Hijacker Identity Documents: Passports, Visas, Licenses/Identification Cards."

129. Nami obtained a Florida driver's license, but we do not know when. AAMVA memo, "9/11 hijacker driver license and identification paper trail," May 28, 2004.

130. INS records, I-94 Arrival Records of Hamza al Ghamdi, Mohand al Shehri, and Ahmed al Nami, May 28, 2001.

131. DOS record, DOS cable from the Embassy Riyadh to Secretary of State, Aug. 19, 2001.

132. INS records, NIIS records for Ahmad al Haznawi and Wail al Shehri, June 8, 2001.

133. DOS record, NIV Applicant Detail of Saeed al Ghamdi, Aug. 12, 2002.

134. DOS record, Visa Application of Saeed al Ghamdi, Nov. 19, 2001.

135. Ibid.

136. DOS record, visa application of Khalid al Mihdhar, June 13, 2001, and a digital image of Khalid al Mihdhar's C551754 passport.

137. DOS record, visa application of Abdul Aziz al Omari, June 18, 2001.

138. DOS record, DOS visa application of Fayez Banihammad, June 18, 2001.

139. Consular Officer No. 10 interview (Mar. 1, 2004).

140. FBI memo from Legat Riyadh, "Penttbom case," Oct. 25, 2001.

141. DOJ, "Hijacker Identity Documents: Passports, Visas, Licenses/Identification Cards," undated.

142. See CIA analytic reference report, "A Reference Guide for Terrorist Passports," Feb. 14, 2003.

143. Testimony of Consular Officer Number No. 2 before the House Committee on Government Reform, Aug. 1, 2002.

144. Ibid.

145. AAMVA memo, "9/11 hijacker driver license and identification paper trail," May 28, 2004.

146. Ibid.

147. INS records, NIIS records of Fayez Banihammad and Saeed al Ghamdi, June 27, 2001.

148. INS record, I-94 Arrival Record and Customs record, Customs Declaration of Fayez Banihammad, June 27, 2001. For admission of Banihammad, see primary immigration inspector for Fayez Banihammad interview (May 19, 2004).

149. Primary immigration inspector of Saeed al Ghamdi interview (Mar. 17, 2004). This inspector did not know that a September 11 hijacker came through his line until a colleague had told him a few months prior to the Commission's interview request. Most of the inspectors we interviewed were not aware they had adjudicated the entrance of a 9/11 hijacker.

150. INS record, INS Inspection Results record of Saeed al Ghamdi, June 27, 2001.

151. Customs record, Customs Declaration record of Saeed al Ghamdi, June 27, 2001 and primary immigration inspector of Saeed al Ghamdi interview (Mar. 17, 2004). Copies of Ghamdi's Customs Declaration and I-94 are attached in Appendix A.

152. INS record, INS Inspection Results record of Saeed al Ghamdi, June 27, 2001 and primary immigration inspector of Saeed al Ghamdi interview (Mar. 17, 2004). The Commission cannot verify whether Ghamdi's travel documents were clean since no copies survived the attacks or were recovered elsewhere.

153. INS records, I-94 Arrival Records of Abdul Aziz al Omari and Salem al Hazmi, June 29, 2001.

154. CIA analytic reference report, Apr. 1, 2003.

155. FBI record, Penttbom Major Case # 182, DOCEX document, undated.

156. DOJ document, "Hijacker Identity Documents: Passports, Visas, Licenses/Identification Cards," undated.

157. AAMVA memo, "9/11 hijacker driver license and identification paper trail," May 28, 2004. A copy of Salem al Hazmi's USA ID document is attached in Appendix A.

158. USSS report, "Physical examination of identifications of 'Salem Alhazmi' and 'Alhazmi' found at the Pentagon," Sept. 25 and 27, 2001.

159. AAMVA memo, "9/11 hijacker driver license and identification paper trail," May 28, 2004.

160. INS record, I-94 Arrival Record of Khalid al Mihdhar, July 4, 2001.

161. Commission work product chart, *September 11 Hijacker border inspection interview results: Primary Inspection Procedures Prior to September 11*, May 20, 2004.

162. A digital copy of Mihdhar's passport was recovered during a search of an al Qaeda safehouse.

163. Primary immigration inspector for Khalid al Mihdhar interview (May 24, 2001).

164. DOS record, visa application record of Mohammad al Kahtani, July 4, 2001 and DOS record, NIV Applicant Detail for Mohammad al Kahtani, Jan. 16, 2004.

165. Veronica Cates interview (May 25, 2004); Rocky Concepcion interview (June 15, 2004); and Rick Colon interview (June 14, 2004).

166. Veronica Cates interview (May 25, 2004); Rocky Concepcion interview (June 15, 2004); Rick Colon interview (June 14, 2004); Dan Cadman interview (June 14, 2004); and Kevin Rooney interview (Jan. 8, 2004).

167. Customs record, TECS II-Administrative Message record, July 6, 2001; and Rick Colon interview (June 14, 2004).

168. INS record, NIIS record of Mohamed Atta, Jan. 10, 2001, with departure date of July 7, 2001 and length of stay until July 9, 2001.

169. DOJ document, "Hijacker Identity Documents: Passports, Visas, Licenses/Identification Cards," undated.

170. AAMVA memo, "9/11 hijacker driver license and identification paper trail," May 28, 2004. A copy of Mihdhar's USA ID is attached in Appendix A.

171. INS record, INS I-539 Application to Change Status of Mohamed Atta, undated.

172. INS record, I-94 Arrival Record of Mohamed Atta, July 19, 2001.

173. Primary immigration inspector of Mohamed Atta on July 19, 2001 interview (May 17, 2004).

174. DOS record, NIV Applicant Detail record of Khalid Sheikh Mohammad under alias of Abdulrahman AA Al Ghamdi, Jan. 13, 2004. A copy of KSM's U.S. visa application is attached in Appendix A.

175. DOS record, visa application of Khalid Sheikh Mohammad under alias of Abdulrahman AA Al Ghamdi, July 23, 2001.

176. DOS record, NIV Applicant Detail of Saeed al Ghamdi, Nov. 19, 2001.

177. United States v. Kenys A. Galicia, U.S.D.C.E.D. Va., Oct. 2001 term, Indictment, Paragraphs 7, 8, Oct. 25, 2001.

178. United States v. Luis A. Martinez-Flores, Affidavit in Support of a Criminal Complaint and an Arrest Warrant, E.D.Va, Sept. 28, 2001.

179. *See* Martinez-Flores and Galicia cases.

180. For Moqed's use of the same address, *see* Virginia Department of Motor Vehicles Residency Form DL51 for Majed Moqed, Aug. 2, 2001.

181. Virginia Department of Motor Vehicles Residency Form DL51 for Ziad Jarrah, with residency certified by Hani Hanjour, Aug. 29, 2001. Hanjour used as his

address the same address he had fraudulently obtained on Aug. 1, 2001. Jarrah's listed address is fictitious.

182. United States v. Herbert Villalobos, Affidavit in Support of a Criminal Complaint and an Arrest Warrant, E.D.Va.

183. AAMVA memo, "9/11 hijacker driver license and identification paper trail," May 28, 2004. In addition, Hanjour had also acquired Arizona and Florida driver's licenses in 1991 and 1996, respectively. A copy of Ahmed al Ghamdi's Virginia identification document is attached in Appendix A.

184. INS record, I-94 Arrival Record of Mohammad al Kahtani, Aug. 4, 2001, with "Application Withdrawn to Depart Foreign Under Safeguard" stamped on the record. *See also* INS record, Withdrawal of Application for Admission/Consular Notification of Mohammad al Kahtani, Aug. 4, 2001.

185. A combination of evidence gathered by the FBI supports this conclusion: vehicle rental records for Atta during this time period; parking records for this vehicle at Orlando International Airport during the time frame in which Kahtani was attempting entry; and phone records from a public phone to a phone number associated with both Atta and Kahtani. FBI record, Documentation Sufficient to show Mohamed Atta's Presence at the Orlando International Airport on August 4, 2001, including rental vehicle, parking and calling card records, Aug. 11, 2003.

186. Primary immigration inspector of Mohammed Kahtani interview, April 18, 2004.

187. Jose Melendez-Perez testimony, Jan. 26, 2004. INS headquarters had previously interviewed the secondary inspector on a couple of occasions. However, no one from the FBI or intelligence community spoke to this inspector or to the primary inspector prior to Commission interviews.

188. Ibid.

189. Ibid.

190. We compared the copy of Kahtani's passport with the U.S. Government publication *Counterfeit Travel Stamp Directory* (Dec. 2003).

191. CIA cable to DOS, INS, FBI, and Customs, Aug. 23, 2001.

192. Customs records, TECS II records of Nawaf al Hazmi and Khalid al Mihdhar, Aug. 24, 2001.

193. DOS record, visa application of Ali Abdul Aziz Ali, Aug. 27, 2004 and DOS record, NIV Applicant Detail of Ali Abdul Aziz Ali, Jan. 13, 2004.

194. AAMVA memo, "9/11 hijacker driver license and identification paper trail," May 28, 2004.

195. Ibid.

196. FBI record, Customs Service information on TECS II database review of Khalid al Mihdhar, Sept. 12, 2001.

197. Reproductions of the USA ID cards of Salem al Hazmi and Khalid al Mihdhar, and the Virginia identification card digital image of Ahmed al Ghamdi, are in Appendix A.

198. INS record, Lookout Inquiry record for Khalid al Mihdhar, Sept. 4, 2001.

199. AAMVA memo, "9/11 hijacker driver license and identification paper trail," May 28, 2004.

200. FBI Report of investigation, Customs Service information on Khalid al Mihdhar, Sept. 12, 2001. The Commission was unable to locate the text of the lookout explaining what action the inspector should have taken.

201. AAMVA memo, "9/11 hijacker driver license and identification paper trail," May 28, 2004.

202. FBI records of airline personnel indicate that some recall specific hijackers presenting U.S. identification documents with their airline tickets. The American Airlines ticket agent at Logan Airport recalls the al Shehri brothers presenting drivers' licenses at check-in. FBI report of investigation, Elvia C., Sept. 13, 2001. When Hamza al Ghamdi and Ahmed al Ghamdi checked in at Logan Airport in Boston, Hamza al Ghamdi used his Florida driver's license and Ahmed al Ghamdi used his fraudulently obtained Virginia identification card. FBI report of investigation, interview of Gail J., Sept. 21, 2001. At Dulles, Khalid al Mihdhar and Majed Moqed provided their fraudulently obtained Virginia identification cards at the ticket counter. FBI report of investigation, interview of Susan S., American Airline ticketing agent, Sept. 13, 2001. A "Kingdom of Saudi Arabia Student Identity Card" was found in the rubble at the Pentagon with Moqed's name on it. Forensic examination indicated that it may have been fraudulent. United States Secret Service Forensic Services report for the FBI PENTTBOM investigation regarding the physical examination of forensic science research request, Oct. 10, 2001. Hijackers Omari, Wail al Shehri and Hanjour also had international driver licenses and Jarrah had an international student identification card.

203. FBI report of investigation, interview of Caprice C., Sept. 13, 2001. She was employed as a ticket agent by American Airlines at Logan Airport on September 11, 2001.

204. This sum does not include Hanjour's 1997 visa application in Jeddah because this pre-dates the plot.

205. Hanjour's second application in September 2000 was approved after he supplied additional paperwork.

Chapter 3

1. CIA document, Redbook, 1992 ed.

2. Ibid.

3. The CIA claimed that they did not receive new data to analyze. The FBI did not share what they gathered from their law enforcement investigations with the CIA. Commission interview, Feb. 25, 2004.

4. Gazi Ibrahim Abu Mezer, who planned to destroy the Atlantic Avenue subway in Brooklyn with explosives in 1997, was arrested on his third attempt to illegally enter the United States along the northwest border with Canada. He was arrested by the New York City police on July 31, 1997. Bombs were found in his apartment. Abdel Hakim Tizegha claimed to have entered the United States in Boston as a stowaway on the *Mustapha Ben Boulaid*, a tanker owned by an Algerian energy company used to transport liquefied natural gas.

5. CIA analytic report, "A Reference Guide for Terrorist Passports," Apr. 14, 2003.

6. *United States v. Mohammed A. Salameh, et al.*, No. 94-1312(L), U.S. Court of Appeals for the Second Circuit, p. 21.

7. His application was later denied. Abohalima was indicted as an accessory after the fact for assisting the WTC1 attackers.

8. Center for Immigration Studies, *The Open Door: How Militant Islamic Terrorists Entered and Remained in the United States, 1993 to 2001*, Stephen A. Camarota, p. 25.

9. Although there is no evidence that any of these marriages were fraudulent, Abu Zubaydah said that some al Qaeda operatives married American women to obtain U.S. visas. Usama Bin Ladin reportedly did not approve of this tactic, saying it violated the sanctity of marriage. KSM, however, allegedly believed it was a fantastic mechanism for operatives to acquire valid documents, Intelligence report, interrogation of Abu Zubaydah, Oct. 7, 2002.

10. *United States v. Mohammed A. Salameh, et al.*, No. 94-1312(L), U.S. Court of Appeals for the Second Circuit, p. 21.

11. Ibid., p. 22.

12. Ibid., p. 24.

13. Ibid., pp. 23, 26.

14. DOJ document, handwritten memo to file from Immigration Inspector at JFK, Sept. 2, 1992.

15. Trial testimony of Brian Parr re: interview with Yousef, Oct. 22, 1997, *United States of America v. Ramzi Ahmed Yousef and Eyad Ismoil* (S.D.N.Y).

16. *United States v. Mohammed A. Salameh, et al.*, No. 94-1312(L), U.S. Court of Appeals for the Second Circuit, p. 25.

17. An examination of Yousef's passport by the Forensic Document Lab at INS later reveals that the date of birth has been overwritten and the passport binding has been cut and un-stitched, but no other alterations were detected.

18. *United States v. Ahmad Mohammad Ajaj aka Khurram Khan*, Brief, p. 178.

19. Ibid.

20. Center for Immigration Studies, *The Open Door*, p. 27.

21. Alkaisi plead guilty in connection with the WTC1 plot.

22. Saleh was convicted of conspiracy for the bombing plot and subsequently deported to Egypt, his home country, on Nov. 19, 1996.

23. Testimony of Consular Officer No. 2 before the U.S. House of Representatives Committee on Government Reform, Aug. 1, 2002 (regarding an interview the officer conducted of the Sheikh before they began service as a State Department employee).

24. DOS OIG, Report of Audit, Review of the Visa-Issuance Process Phase I: Circumstances Surrounding the Issuance of Visas to Sheikh Omar Ali Ahmed Abdel Rahman, Mar. 1994, p. 1.

25. DHS document, immigration file A29 753 750.

26. Although it has long been suggested that the Sheikh was issued visas because of his assistance with Afghan Mujahadeen fighters who were then allies of the U.S., the Inspectors General of both the CIA and State Departments found "no evidence

. . . that any of these visas were granted to the Sheikh to serve CIA operational purposes." Talking Points prepared for the DCI by CIA OIG Frederick Hitz; Report of Audit, Review of the Visa-Issuance Process Phase I: Circumstances Surrounding the Issuance of Visas to Sheikh Omar Ali Ahmed Abdel Rahman, Mar. 1994, p. 19 ("What we did find, rather, was evidence of: sloppiness; poor performance by some American officers and Foreign Service Nationals (or local employees) involved; inadequate systems of control; and inadequate implementation of immigration laws, regulations, and guidelines.").

27. DOS OIG, Report of Audit, Review of the Visa-Issuance Process Phase I: Circumstances Surrounding the Issuance of Visas to Sheikh Omar Ali Ahmed Abdel Rahman, Mar. 1994, p. 20.

28. CIA document, Revised Chronology of Events Regarding Issuance of Visas to the "Blind Sheikh."

29. DOS OIG, Report of Audit, Review of the Visa-Issuance Process Phase I: Circumstances Surrounding the Issuance of Visas to Sheikh Omar Ali Ahmed Abdel Rahman, Mar. 1994, p. 22.

30. Ibid., p. 25.

31. Ibid., p. 22.

32. Ibid., p. 25.

33. Ibid., p. 27.

34. Ibid., p. 31.

35. Ibid., p. 29.

36. Ibid., p. 2, 17. According to documents produced by the Sheikh himself in connection with his asylum claim, he was arrested by Egyptian authorities for charges related to his preaching five times from October 1970 to April 1989. In April 1990, after his last incarceration and an extended period of house arrest, he was escorted to the airport where he made his way to the Sudan. Affidavit of Omar Ahmed Ali, A29-753-750, dated Aug. 11, 1992.

37. DOS OIG, Report of Audit, Review of the Visa-Issuance Process Phase I: Circumstances Surrounding the Issuance of Visas to Sheikh Omar Ali Ahmed Abdel Rahman, Mar. 1994, p. 35.

38. DHS document, In the Matter of Omar Ahmed Ali, File No. A29-753-750 (In Exclusion Proceedings), Mar. 16, 1993 (Meisner, J.), p. 3.

39. Ibid., p. 20.

40. He was arrested by the New York City police on July 31, 1997. Bombs were found in his apartment.

41. DHS document, immigration file A74 101 910.

42. Center for Immigration Studies, *The Open Door*, p. 31.

43. *Seattle Times*, "It Takes a Thief," June 23, July 7, 2002. Fateh Kamel would pay Ressam for stolen passports, credit cards and other identity documents. Kamel is now serving eight years in prison in France for his "activities related to association with terrorist enterprises." *Time*, Sept. 24, 2001. Ressam testified that he also sold stolen documents to Mohktar Haouari. U.S. v. Mokhtar Haouari, S4-00 Cr. 15, Testimony of Ahmed Ressam before United States District Court of the Southern District of New York, July 3, 2001.

44. Leo Nkounga was a document broker and an illegal alien in Canada from Cameron who failed to surrender himself for deportation in 1993. Canadian Deportation Order, Adjudication file no. AOT93-0077, Sept. 15, 1993. He said he obtained two genuine Canadian passports for Ressam, in both instances by submitting fake baptismal certificates to Canadian authorities CBC News, *Disclosure*, "Target Terrorism," Mar. 26, 2002. According to a senior al Qaeda detainee, an Algerian friend of Ressam "set up" the Canadian passport for him.

45. FBI letterhead memorandum, Ressam investigation, May 15, 2001, p. 7. Ressam told border officials that he did not have a visa for Pakistan because he was only transiting on his way to India.

46. PBS Frontline, "Trail of a Terrorist, The Ahmed Ressam Case and Passport Fraud," Oct. 25, 2001.

47. FBI case profile provided to Dale Watson, "Abdelghani Meskini," Feb. 8, 2000. Meskini, who spoke English, was to drive Ressam and to give him money, but Ressam never showed since he was arrested at the border. Meskini was arrested on Dec. 30, 1999, and charged with material support and interstate fraud. *See* Testimony of Dale Watson before the Senate Select Committee on Intelligence, Feb. 9, 2000, pp. 11- 12. On passports and visas provided by Haouari, *see United States v. Haouari*, 319 F. 3d 88, 91 (2d Cir. 2000).

48. There is no record of his entry into the United States; he claimed he entered in Miami in an unknown way.

49. Tizegha now claimed to have entered the United States in Boston as a stow-away on the *Mustapha Ben Boulaid*, a tanker owned by the Algerian energy company used to transport liquefied natural gas.

50. DHS document, immigration file A73603119.

51. FBI Communication Form, Re: Borderbom, July 26, 2001.

52. FBI letterhead memorandum, Ressam investigation, May 15, 2001.

53. FBI Communication Form, Re: Borderbom, July 26, 2001.

54. CIA analytic report, "Clandestine Travel Facilitators: Key Enablers of Terrorism," Dec. 31, 2002.

55. FBI documents, Jan. 17, 1999; FBI report of investigation, interview of Ali Abdelseoud Mohamed, March 8, 1999; FBI report of investigation, Re: Aman Gul, Mar. 21, 2000; FBI report of investigation, interview of Ahmed Ressam, May 16, 2001; Case file of Ramzi Yousef, convicted in WTC1 bombing in 1993.

56. FBI report of investigation, Re: UBL/al Qaeda, Jan. 16, 2001; FBI letterhead memorandum, Ressam investigation, May 15, 2001; Trial brief, *United States v. Ahmed Ressam*, CR99-666C, Mar. 2001.

57. FBI report of investigation, interview of protected source, Mar. 22, 2001.

58. FBI report of investigation, Re: UBL/al Qaeda, Jan. 16, 2001, pp. 30-31 FBI letterhead memorandum, Ressam investigation, May 15, 2001.

59. In 1995, Italian authorities in Milan cracked down on the ICI, an Islamic radical group that was facilitating Islamic militants going to fight in Bosnia. Its leaders were members of the Egyptian Islamic Jihad. When authorities raided the ICI office, two copies of the Redbook were found in Arabic, along with several seals, rubber stamps, blank and counterfeit documents and other tools used to forge documents; FBI

report of investigation, "Pakistani visa information pertaining to Kenbom/Tanbom subjects," May 13, 1999; Intelligence report, "Terrorism: Documents Associated with Apprehended Egyptian Islamic Jihad Member," Apr. 13, 1999. In addition. documents seized in the home of an Egyptian Islamic Jihad member included extensive evidence of passport fraud.

60. FBI report of investigation, UBL database, Jan. 19, 1999; FBI report of investigation, interview of Ali Abdelseoud Mohamed, Mar. 8, 1999; FBI communication, investigative summary re: the Islamic Army, Mar. 27, 2000; FBI report of investigation, Re: UBL/al Qaeda, Jan. 16, 2001, pp. 8, 14–15, 17, 18, 30–31.

61. FBI report of investigation, Re: UBL/al Qaeda, Jan. 16, 2001, p. 27; FBI letterhead memorandum, Ressam investigation, May 15, 2001.

62. FBI report of investigation, analysis of source reporting, June 16, 2000; FBI report of investigation, UBL database, Jan. 19, 1999, pp. 4, 11, 29

63. FBI report of investigation, interview of Ali Abdelseoud Mohamed, Mar. 12, 1999.

64. FBI report of investigation, interview of unidentified source, Oct. 2, 2000.

65. FBI report of investigation, Initial 90 day letterhead memorandum, July 24, 2000.

66. FBI report of investigation, request for evidence comparison, Jan. 26, 2000.

67. FBI document, Jan. 17, 1999; FBI report of investigation, interview of Ali Abdelseoud Mohamed, Mar. 8, 1999; FBI letterhead memorandum, Ressam investigation, May 15, 2001.

68. FBI report of investigation, interview of Abdul Rauf Chaudhry, Oct. 2, 1998; FBI report of investigation, interview of Ali Abouelsaud Mohamed, Oct. 3, 1999; FBI report of investigation "Pakistani visa information pertaining to Kenbom/Tanbom subjects," May 13, 1999; FBI report of investigation, "Possible visa fraud," April 20, 2001; FBI letterhead memorandum, Ressam investigation, May 15, 2001.

69. FBI report of investigation, UBL database, Jan. 19, 1999.

70. FBI Communication, investigation summary re: the Islamic Army, Mar. 27, 2000. Trial brief, *United States v. Ahmed Ressam*, CR99-666C, Mar. 2001.

71. Intelligence Report, interrogation of a detainee, Nov. 22, 2002.

72. Intelligence Report, interrogation of a detainee, Sept. 11, 2002.

73. CIA analytic report, Analysis of Passports, p. 1; Intelligence report, interrogation of a detainee, Nov. 20, 2002.

74. Intelligence Report, interrogation of Ramzi Binalshibh, Oct.11, 2002. Malaysia was also desirable because of its proximity to Afghanistan and Pakistan and its majority-Muslim population.

75. Intelligence report, interrogation of KSM, Sept. 9, 2003; CIA analytic report, "Al Qaeda Travel Issues," Jan. 2004, p.1. On the role of KSM, *see*, e.g., Intelligence report, interrogation of Binalshibh, Oct. 11, 2002. On the role of Abu Zubaydah, *see*, e.g., Intelligence report, biographical information on Abu Zubaydah, Feb. 25, 2002.

76. Intelligence report, interrogation of a detainee, Sept. 9, 2003; and Intelligence Report, interrogation of Abu Zubaydah, Apr. 12, 2003. The committee moved to Zormat, Paktia province in late 2001 and then to Karachi after the fall of Kandahar in late 2001.

77. On passport collection schemes, *see* Intelligence report, interrogation of KSM, Sept. 9, 2003. On recycled passports, *see* Intelligence report, Collection of Passports, June 7, 2002.

78. CIA analytic report, Analysis of Passports, p. 1, 3. Intelligence report, interrogation of detainee, Nov. 12, 2003; and Intelligence Report, Information on travel, training and indoctrination in training camps in Afghanistan, Nov. 19, 2001. A detainee said that he attended several security and specialized courses including counterfeiting and seal removal; Intelligence report, interrogation of detainees, Apr. 11, 2002.

79. CIA analytic report, Analysis of Passports, p. 19.

80. Intelligence report, information from Saudi detainees on mujahedin travel to Afghanistan via Iran, Mar. 13, 2002.

81. CIA analytic report, Analysis of Passports, p. 3. Mohamed Atta reportedly learned these techniques in Afghanistan, and used them to clean Ramzi Binalshibh's passport of its Pakistani visa and travel cachets.

82. Intelligence report, interrogation of Abu Zubaydah, June 20, 2002. Hassan Ghul was an important al Qaeda travel facilitator who worked with Abu Zubaydah assisting Arab fighters traveling to Afghanistan. In 1999, Ghul and Zubaydah opened a safe house under the cover of an import/export business in Islamabad. In addition, at Zubaydah's request, Ghul also successfully raised money in Saudi Arabia for the Khaldan camp; in exchange Zubaydah paid for Ghul's trips there so he could renew his residency.

83. Intelligence report, interrogation of a detainee, Mar. 31, 2003. For example, a detainee identified a person who made false documents. The detainee said he would supply this person with passport photos and the facilitator would turn them into false documents, including drivers' licenses, but not passports. The person could make false documents on computers, but he also had a contact who could get official documents from a government office, by either creating an actual file in a false name or by putting a supplied photo onto the biographical information from a legitimate file. Ibid.

84. Intelligence report, information on Abu Zubaydah, Aug. 24, 2000; Intelligence report, interrogation of a detainee, Feb. 25, 2002.

85. Intelligence report, interrogation of Abu Zubaydah, June 7, 2002. Abu Zubaydah claims he applied for a U.S. student visa in Riyadh, Saudi Arabia, sometime between 1987 and 1989, but claims he was denied. The State Department, however, was unable to locate a record of this. After one year in India, he claims he arranged to visit a computer programming school in Missouri with the help of a Palestinian friend in Saudi Arabia. As a Palestinian, he did not have a passport, but rather a refugee travel document so he said he borrowed the Kuwaiti passport of a friend to make the trip. Although he did not formally meet with anyone at the school and never enrolled, he said he walked around the campus and picked up some brochures.

86. Intelligence report, information on Abu Zubaydah, Aug. 24, 2000.

87. Intelligence report, interrogation of a detainee, Feb. 25, 2002.

88. Ibid.

89. Intelligence report, interrogation of Abu Zubaydah, July 10, 2002. In January 1999, Ahmed Ressam reportedly stayed at the Khaldan safehouse, where Abu Zubaydah bought his plane ticket to Canada and doctored the visa in Ressam's Canadian passport.

90. Intelligence report, profile of Abu Zubaydah, June 14, 2000.

91. Intelligence report, interrogation of Abu Zubaydah, May 23, 2002. Zubaydah claims that members of the Egyptian Islamic Jihad, various Algerian groups and others came to him to learn his techniques.

92. Intelligence report, interrogation of Abu Zubaydah, May 23, 2002. Zubaydah also strictly limited the movement of travelers, almost never allowing them to leave the safehouse for any reason. Instead, individuals who blended into the local community were used to get clothes, food and whatever else was needed.

93. Intelligence reports, interrogations of Abu Zubaydah, May 23, 2002, Oct. 29, 2002, and Nov. 7, 2002.

94. Intelligence reports, interrogation of Abu Zubaydah, Sept. 25 and Dec. 4, 2002.

95. Ibid.

96. Intelligence report, interrogation of a detainee, Apr. 24, 2003.

97. Intelligence report, interrogation of Abu Zubaydah, Dec. 4, 2002; Intelligence report, interrogation of a detainee, Apr. 24, 2003.

98. Intelligence report, interrogation of Abu Zubaydah, Dec. 4, 2002.

99. Intelligence report, interrogation of Abu Zubaydah, Sept. 25, 2002.

100. Intelligence reports, interrogation of Abu Zubaydah, Sept. 25, 2002, Dec. 4, 2002, Apr. 2, 2003, and Apr. 21, 2003. According to Abu Zubaydah, The African Facilitator procured construction and other necessary supplies in Pakistan and delivered them to Afghanistan, and although he operated openly in Afghanistan, he was more cautious in Pakistan.

101. Intelligence report, interrogation of Abu Zubaydah, June 9, 2003.

102. Intelligence reports, interrogation of Abu Zubaydah, Sept. 25, 2002, Dec. 4, 2002, and Apr. 2, 2003. "Ordinary" mujahid who needed help with their documents were required to report to The African Facilitator who would prioritize the work for the Kenyan forgers. Senior al Qaeda members could take a passport directly to the Kenyans.

103. Intelligence report, interrogation of Abu Zubaydah, Dec. 4, 2002.

104. Intelligence report, "Collection of 400 Passports of Dead Mujahidin," June 7, 2002.

105. Intelligence report, information on Riyadh, Jan. 26, 2002; Intelligence report, interrogation of Abu Zubaydah, Aug. 26, 2002.

106. Intelligence report, interrogation of Riyadh, Jan. 28, 2004; Intelligence report, interrogation of a detainee, Sept. 15, 2003.

107. Intelligence report, interrogation of a detainee, Sept. 15, 2003.

108. Intelligence report, information on Riyadh, Jan. 26, 2002.

109. Intelligence report, interrogation of Riyadh, Jan. 28, 2004; Intelligence report, interrogation of a detainee, Sept. 15, 2003.

110. Intelligence report, interrogation of Riyadh, Jan. 28, 2004; Intelligence report, Analysis of detainee interviews, Sept. 12, 2002. Many detainees mention Riyadh as a facilitator in Karachi, Pakistan. From Karachi, many were directed to another facilitator in Quetta, Pakistan, who arranged transportation over the border into Afghanistan. The large number of detainees who took the Karachi-Quetta-Kandahar route suggests that the facilitators were coordinating their activities.

111. Intelligence report, Interrogation of Riyadh, Jan. 28, 2004. For more on Riyadh's post 9/11 role as money facilitator *see* Intelligence report, interrogation of Riyadh, Apr. 6, 2004.

112. CIA analytic reports, "Clandestine Travel Facilitators: Key Enablers of Terrorism," Dec. 31, 2002 and Analysis of Passports, Jan. 2004.

113. CIA analytic report, "Clandestine Travel Facilitators," p. 3. According to Abu Zubaydah, in Turkey an Iraqi or a Kurd was a reliable forger. For $5,500 he would provide documents to travel to Europe. A Saudi-based forger from Chad bought real passports from foreign drug addicts and re-sold them. Zubaydah also claims that real Pakistani passports could be bought by anyone with money. *See also* Intelligence report, interrogation of Abu Zubaydah, Nov. 1, 2002, and Intelligence report, "Acquisition of Libyan passports by an Abu Zubaydah operative in the Netherlands," Dec. 6, 2000.

114. CIA analytic report, Analysis of Passports, pp. 11-12

115. Trial testimony of Brian Parr re: interview with Yousef, Oct. 22, 1997, *United States of America v. Ramzi Ahmed Yousef and Eyad Ismoil* (S.D.N.Y.).

116. CIA analytic report, Analysis of Passports, p. 12.

117. Intelligence report, interrogation of a detainee, Sept. 9, 2003.

118. FBI documents, Oct. 3, 1999; Intelligence reports, interrogation of Abu Zubaydah, Dec. 4, 2002 and Apr. 10, 2003.

119. Ibid. A travel agency arranged an Australian visa for Khalid Sheikh Mohamed (KSM), al Qaeda's chief operational planner and the mastermind of the Sept. 11 attacks. The agency submitted his visa application on Aug. 13, 2001, the same day they submitted an application for another al Qaeda operative. The same address and employer were listed on both applications. KSM received his visa, although there is no evidence he ever used it, FBI case file, June 21, 2002

120. Intelligence report, interrogation of Abu Zubaydah, Oct. 10, 2002. Abu Zubaydah discusses smuggling routes from Afghanistan into Pakistan and Iran, and assessed that Yemen was the easiest place to conduct smuggling operations. Intelligence report, "International organized crime: overview of Pakistani 'Mafia' activities in Azerbaijan," June 18, 2002.

121. CIA analytic report, "Clandestine Travel Facilitators," p. 3.

122. Intelligence report, "Information from Saudi detainees on Mujahedin travel to Afghanistan via Iran," Mar. 13, 2002.

123. CIA analytic report, "Clandestine Travel Facilitators," p. 1.

124. DHS email from Dan C. to Commission staff, "CODEL Brief," Apr. 16, 2004.

125. CIA analytic report, "Clandestine Travel Facilitators," p. 6.

126. Ibid.

127. Intelligence report, interrogation of a detainee, Sept. 9, 2003. KSM used an alias Saudi passport, adding entry and exit stamps to "age it." *See* Intelligence report, interrogation of a detainee, Nov. 20, 2002, in which a detainee maintains that the immigration stamps in his passport are false and were put in his passport by Abd al-Rahim al-Nashiri's support network in Karachi to cover up the detainee's time in Afghanistan. *See also*, FBI document, Feb. 9, 2003, reporting a detainee's claim that he went to Kandahar to pick up his passport after it had been modified with forged stamps showing him visiting Malaysia, Thailand, Egypt and Pakistan.

128. CIA analytic report, Analysis of Passports, p. 1.

129. Intelligence report, interrogation of a detainee, Sept. 9, 2003. KSM said that Usama Bin Ladin approved the use of all alias passports. In Intelligence report, Nov. 23, 2002 it is reported that a detainee said all Saudi jihadists in Pakistan used fake Saudi passports to prevent their true identity from being discovered by Pakistani authorities at the airports. *See also*, CIA analytic report, Analysis of Passports, p. 25, stating that terrorists also have used false supporting documents, including credit cards and video rental cards to support the alias under which they are traveling.

130. Intelligence reports, interrogation of Abu Zubaydah, May 27, 2002 and Nov. 1, 2002. According to Abu Zubaydah, it cost $400–$1,000 for a Saudi passport.

131. CIA analytic report, "Fraudulently Acquired Saudi Passports," p. 1.

132. Intelligence report, interrogation of Abu Zubaydah, May 27, 2002. According to Abu Zubaydah, KSM preferred to use Saudi Arabia as a transit point because it was easy for Saudi passport holders to acquire tourist and student visas to the United States.

133. Intelligence report, interrogation of a detainee, Sept. 9, 2003.

134. Intelligence reports, interrogation of Abu Zubaydah, Aug. 26, 2002 and Nov. 1, 2002. According to Abu Zubaydah, he had access to a number of forgers who, for a relatively small amount of money, would alter the passports of many countries.

135. CIA analytic report, "Fraudulently Acquired Saudi Passports," p. 1.

136. CIA analytic report, "Fraudulently Acquired Saudi Passports," p. 2.

137. CIA analytic report, Analysis of Passports, p. 13; Intelligence report, interrogation of a detainee, Sept. 9, 2003. KSM photo-substituted an alias Saudi passport with his own picture in proper Saudi attire.

138. CIA analytic report, Analysis of Passports, p. 15.

139. CIA analytic report, Analysis of Passports, p. 19.

140. CIA analytic report, "Expanding Links Between Human Smugglers and Extremists: Threats to the United States," July 6, 2001, p. ii.

141. CIA analytic report, "Expanding Links," p. 1.

142. One smuggler, Salim Boughader-Mucharrafille, smuggled Lebanese nationals sympathetic to Hamas and Hizbollah into the United States and relied on corrupt Mexican officials in Beirut, Mexico City and Tijuana to facilitate their travel. Specifically, Boughader obtained Mexican tourist visas from an official at the Mexican embassy in Beirut to facilitate the travel of humans to Mexico. DOJ, INS Background or briefing paper on Operation Tabouli, Nov. 14, 2002; CIA analytic report, "Expanding Links," p. ii.

143. CIA analytic report, "Expanding Links," p. ii.

144. Human smugglers are also logistical experts, arranging for lodging and travel. CIA analytic report, "Expanding Links," p. ii.

145. CIA analytic report, "Clandestine Travel Facilitators: Key Enablers of Terrorism," Dec. 2002, p. 3.

146. Ibid.

147. Boughader was charged with human smuggling and sentenced to 11 months in prison. After serving his sentence he was deported to Mexico where he was arrested along with several other members of his smuggling ring. They face criminal charges and if convicted could serve lengthy jail times.

Chapter 4

1. Annual Strategic Intelligence Review for Counterterrorism, Oct. 1995, p. 8. Terrorist surveillance capabilities were directly linked to their ability to travel unimpeded around the world, which is why training in document forgery was a part of al Qaeda's terrorist instruction.

2. Annual Strategic Intelligence Review for Counterterrorism, Apr. 1998, p. 13.

3. For example, in June 1998 a joint USG–Albanian operation acted on information that a forgery operation was producing passports, visas and other documents to support the travel of al Qaeda operatives. A raid turned up visa stamps, blank Egyptian birth certificates, and a forged passport; CIA took exemplars of all stamps. FBI CART Report, Aug. 14, 1998. In another case, the arrest of a suspected operative turned up a photo-substituted Italian passport and a British passport previously reported stolen and various other passports, photographs and identity cards, FBI CART Report, July 16, 2002.

4. The Terrorist Mobility Unit was created in October 2001.

5. Memorandum for the Record, Keith M.

6. Ibid.

7. DOS report, 1990 Report of the Visa Office, released Oct. 1991. The INS shared with State the authority for administering immigrant visa and refugee applications, inspecting all travelers arriving at ports of entry, adjudicating applications for change of status, and (through its Border Patrol component) interdicting aliens attempting to enter without inspection. INS Special Agents were responsible for enforcement of immigration laws in the interior of the United States. On an average day, INS inspectors at ports of entry collectively handled the admission to the United States of over one million individuals, 85 percent of whom entered through the land borders with Canada and Mexico. Agencies playing a lesser role in the immigration system were the Federal Bureau of Investigation (FBI), which participated in the screening of visa applicants for certain domestic national security-related concerns; the CIA and other intelligence agencies, which participated in screening visa applicants for counter-intelligence and counter-terrorism concerns and which participated in overseas anti-smuggling efforts, and the Coast Guard, which addressed significant episodes of migration by sea.

8. U.S. House of Representatives Committee on Government Reform transcript, "Telephone Interview of Consular Officer 1," Aug. 1, 2002 (Consular officer in Saudi Arabia discussing visa policy as supportive of other U.S. policy goals in the country).

9. DOS report, Bureau of Consular Affairs, "1990 Report of the Visa Office," Oct. 1991.

10. Ibid.

11. Ibid.

12. INA § 221(h), "Nothing in this Act shall be construed to entitle any alien, to whom a visa or other documentation has been issued, to be admitted [to] the United States, if, upon arrival at a port of entry in the United States, he is found to be inadmissible under this Act, or any other provision of law."

13. Immigration officers today work within the Department of Homeland Security.

14. In fiscal year 2001, approximately 175 million U.S. citizens were inspected at U.S. ports of entry.

15. 22 C.F.R. § 53.2(b). According to the Department of Homeland Security, Bureau of Customs and Border Protection, a U.S. citizen entering from Canada "may use" a certified copy of their birth certificate to reenter the United States under this regulation. However, the regulation itself contains no such requirement.

16. 22 C.F.R. § 41.2(a).

17. The Immigration Reform and Control Act of 1986 (P.L. 99-603) created the Visa Waiver Program as a pilot. It became a permanent program in 2000 under the Visa Waiver Permanent Program Act (P.L. 106-396, Oct. 30. 2000). The countries in the program at the time of the September 11 attacks were: Andorra, Austria, Australia, Belgium, Brunei, Denmark, Finland, France, Germany, Iceland, Ireland, Italy, Japan, Liechtenstein, Luxembourg, Monaco, The Netherlands, New Zealand, Norway, Portugal, San Marino, Singapore, Slovenia, Spain, Sweden, Switzerland, United Kingdom, and Uruguay.

18. GAO report, "Implications of Eliminating the Visa Waiver Program," GAO-03-38, Nov. 2002.

19. DOS report, Bureau of Consular Affairs, "2000 Report of the Visa Office," June 2002.

20. Ibid.

21. Ibid.

22. Ibid.

23. In addition, Zacarias Moussaoui, an al Qaeda operative suspected of being primed as a possible pilot in the 9/11 plot, entered the United States February 23, 2001, from London, England using a French, "visa waiver" passport. He overstayed his term of admission under that program, and was arrested by the INS for this immigration violation on August 16, 2001.

24. DOS report, Bureau of Consular Affairs, "2000 Report of the Visa Office," June 2002.

25. Mary Ryan interview (Sept. 29, 2003).

26. The 1952 Immigration and Nationality Act (P.L. 82-414; 8 U.S.C. Sec. 1101 et seq.) has been amended several times since 1952, more recently by the Immigration Act of 1990, the Illegal Immigration Reform and Immigrant Responsibility Act of 1996 (P.L. 104-208), the USA PATRIOT Act of 2001 (P.L. 107-56), the Enhanced Border Security and Visa Entry Reform Act of 2002 (P.L. 107-173), and the Homeland Security Act of 2002 (P.L. 107-296).

27. Before 9/11, neither the Office of the Secretary of Homeland Security nor the Department of Homeland Security existed. Under the Homeland Security Act, the INS was transferred to the Department of Homeland Security (Section 402), and control over the policy governing the issuance and denial of visas to enter the United States was also transferred to DHS (Section 403).

28. INA section 101(a)(3).

29. *See* Immigration and Nationality Act of 1952, as Amended; Title 8 Code of Federal Regulations—Aliens and Nationality; Title 22 Code of Federal Regulations—State Department (Parts 40-53). 22 CFR Sections 41.103 (Filing an Application and

Form OF-156), 41.104 (Passport requirements), 41.105 (Supporting documents and fingerprinting).

30. The assistant secretary for consular affairs reports to the under secretary of state for management, who, in turn, reports to the deputy secretary of state. Richard Moose interview (Jan. 14, 2004).

31. *See*, e.g., *Centeno v. Schultz*, 817 F.2d 1212 (5th Cir. 1987), *cert. denied*, 484 U.S. 1005 (1988).

32. Before this time, a name check was mandatory but it was performed with a number of systems, including scanning microfiche for the names of potential terrorists. This weakness in the name-check system was laid bare in the Blind Sheik episode, referred to in chapter 3, and was corrected by the mid-1990s.

33. 22 C.F.R. §41.121(a)–(c).

34. 22 CFR § 41.121(d).

35. INA § 222e, 22 CFR § 41.102.

36. This aspect of State Department policy is described in the next chapter.

37. DOS report, Bureau of Consular Affairs, "2000 Report of the Visa Office," June 2002.

38. 8 U.S.C. § 1184 (2002).

39. DOS Office of Inspector General report, "Review of Nonimmigrant Visa Issuance Policy and Procedures," Dec. 2002.

40. DOS report, Bureau of Consular Affairs, "2000 Report of the Visa Office," June 2002.

41. The statutory language reads: "No visa or other documentation shall be issued to an alien if (1) it appears to the consular officer, from statements in the application, or in the papers submitted therewith, that such alien is ineligible to receive a visa or such other documentation under section 212, or any other provision of law, (2) the application fails to comply with the provisions of this Act, or the regulations issued thereunder, or (3) the consular officer knows or has reason to believe that such alien is ineligible to receive a visa or such other documentation under section 212, or any other provision of law."

42. A denial under 221(g) was considered a "soft" refusal because the applicant could overcome the denial and obtain a visa fairly easily by reapplying with the necessary documentation. Hanjour did this and acquired his student visa on September 25, 2000. By contrast, a 214(b) refusal was considered a "hard" refusal: it was much more difficult to overcome and had far more lasting consequences. In the pre-9/11 era, many posts used section 221(g) as a workload-processing tool. They would deny a visa application using 221(g) by sending a letter to the applicant and without interviewing the applicant. If the applicant persisted and was unable to overcome this initial denial—after a personal interview—then they would deny the applicant under 214(b).

43. *Terrorist activity* means any of the following acts if illegal where committed or unlawful in the United States: (1) the hijacking or sabotage of any conveyance (regardless of type); (2) the seizing or detaining, and the threat to kill, injure, or continue to detain, any person in order to compel an action by a third party as a condition for releasing the detained individual; (3) a violent attack on an internationally

protected person or on his or her liberty; (4) an assassination; (5) the use of any biological or chemical agent, nuclear weapon or device, or explosive or firearm (other than for mere personal monetary gain) to endanger the safety of another individual or to cause substantial property damage; or (6) a threat, attempt, or conspiracy to commit any of the above actions. INA § 212(a)(3)(B); 9 FAM 40.32 (note N2.1).

44. Under the INA, such acts include (1) preparing or planning a terrorist activity, (2) gathering information on potential targets for terrorist activity, (3) providing any type of material support to any individual or entity that the alien knows or has reason to believe has committed or plans to commit a terrorist act, (4) soliciting funds or other things of value for terrorist activity or for any terrorist organization, and (5) recruiting any individual to engage in terrorist activity for membership in any terrorist organization or government. INA § 212(a)(3)(B); 9 FAM § 40.32 (Note N2.2).

45. Section 601 of the Immigration Act of 1990 (P.L. 101-649). This Section amended and renumbered the grounds for immigrant and non-immigrant visa refusal under section 212(a) of the INA, effective June 1, 1991.

46. INA § 212(a)(27).

47. Below are the number of aliens found ineligible for a non-immigrant visa on grounds of terrorism for the fiscal years 1992, when the grounds for denial explicitly included terrorism, through 2001.

Year	# Ineligible on Terrorism Grounds	Year	# Ineligible on Terrorism Grounds
1992	28	1997	35
1993	73	1998	63
1994	38	1999	101
1995	79	2000	99
1996	41	2001	83

48. DOS memo, "Machine Readable Visa Program," Mar. 9, 1990. Although the machine-readable visa (MRV) took State officials an additional one minute and 48 seconds to process, the MRV program helped State to resolve problems stemming from internal control weaknesses in the visa issuance process and the physical weakness of the then-current U.S. visa. Ibid. These weaknesses included inaccurate counting of visas issued by the old Burroughs visa-issuing machines, relative ease of counterfeiting the old visa, and a lack of biographical data included in the old visa. Ibid.

49. Other bureaus who work closely with CA in fulfilling its mission are the Bureau of Diplomatic Security, the Bureau of Intelligence and Research (INR), and the various regional bureaus within whose regions consular officers work.

50. Mary Ryan interview (Oct. 9, 2003).

51. DOS record, "History of the Department of State During the Clinton Presidency (1993-2001)," Chapter 9, The Consular Function, www.state.gov/r/pa/ho/pubs.

52. DOS Congressional Presentation Document, Fiscal Year 2003, Bureau of Consular Affairs "Strategic Goals," Oct. 31, 2000, p. 369.

53. INA § 222 (h) states, "**Nonadmission upon arrival**. Nothing in this Act shall be construed to entitle any alien, to whom a visa or other documentation

has been issued, to be admitted [to] the United States, if, upon arrival at a port of entry in the United States, he is found to be inadmissible under this Act, or any other provision of law. The substance of this subsection shall appear upon every visa application."

54. By July 2001, INS officials were posted at approximately 40 of the 230 visa-issuing posts.

55. As discussed later, State and INS did cooperate on the creation and operation of the terrorist watch list. Beginning in 1991, State provided the INS with a subset of the information in its TIPOFF watch list which the INS used to scan visitors at ports of entry. This was a subset because TIPOFF included information on potential terrorists that was not specific enough to use when screening passengers quickly at a port of entry. For example, TIPOFF might include a data file on an Egyptian terrorist named "Ahmad" reported to have participated in a meeting of other terrorists at a certain date and time. This information, while important to keep and build upon, almost certainly would not be sufficient to justify an INS decision to stop all Egyptians using the name "Ahmad" attempting to enter the United States upon suspicion of involvement in terrorism unless extraordinary circumstances warranted.

56. DOS record, "History of the Department of State During the Clinton Presidency (1993-2001)," Chapter 17, Personnel and Professional Development, www.state.gov/r/pa/ho/pubs.

57. Richard Moose interview (Jan. 14, 2004).

58. Ibid.

59. Ibid.

60. DOS record, "Program Performance Report FY 2001," at www.state.gov/m/rm/rls/perfpt/2001/pdf.

61. Richard Moose interview (Jan. 14, 2004).

62. The Inman Commission's recommendations in June 1985 continue to be the standards for the State Department's overseas security measures to this date. Congressional Research Service Report for Congress, "Embassy Security: Background, Funding and the Budget," updated Oct. 4, 2001.

63. Ibid.

64. Ibid.

65. It recommended spending in three basic categories: (1) enhancement of work place security, (2) improvement of crisis management systems and procedure, and (3) improvement of intelligence and information sharing and assessment. "Embassy Security: Background, Funding and the Budget," Congressional Research Service Report for Congress, updated October 4, 2001. State's Bureau of Diplomatic Security proposed a Global Security Enhancement Strategy to improve security at all U.S. embassies, especially those formerly considered "low risk." DOS record, "History of the Department of State During the Clinton Presidency (1993-2001)," Chapter 3, Security Policies, www.state.gov/r/pa/ho/pubs.

66. During this same time period, State also increased funding from machine-readable visa (MRV) fees to the Diplomatic Security (DS) section for increased personnel, antiterrorism and crime programs, and visa fraud investigations. "Embassy Security: Background, Funding and the Budget," Congressional Research Service

Report for Congress, updated October 4, 2001. MRV funding of DS increased from $13.3 million in FY 1997 to $18.5 million in FY 2001.

67. DOS record, "History of the Department of State During the Clinton Presidency (1993-2001)," Chapter 17, Personnel and Professional Development, www.state.gov/r/pa/ho/pubs.

68. Ibid.

69. Ibid.

70. Ibid.

71. It was not until fiscal year 2001, that State began to hire above the attrition rate. *See* DOS record, "Program Performance Report FY 2001," at www.state. gov/m/rm/rls/perfpt/2001/pdf ("After years of downsizing, we began to hire above attrition in FY [Fiscal Year] '01").

72. Mary Ryan interview (Sept. 29, 2003).

73. Because of the Visa Waiver Program, nonimmigrant visa demand shrank from a high of 8,769,709 visas issued in 1988 to a low of 5,359,620 visas issued in 1993. After 1993, nonimmigrant visa demand rose again through the 9/11 terrorist attacks. In FY 2001, State issued 10,569,194 nonimmigrant visas.

74 . The Immigration Reform and Control Act of 1986 (P.L. 99-603) created the Visa Waiver Program as a pilot in 1986. It became a permanent program in 2000 under the Visa Waiver Permanent Program Act (P.L. 106-396, October 30, 2000). Persons traveling to the United States for other purposes, for example to study or work, are required to have a visa.

75. The Departments of State and Justice also evaluate the country's political and economic stability. DOS memo, "Creating a Permanent Visa Waiver Program," Mar. 15, 1990, listing the four criteria for inclusion as (1) average visa refusal rate of 2% or less in the previous two fiscal years, (2) visa refusal rate of no more than 2.5% in each of those years, (3) reciprocal waiver of visa requirements for U.S. citizens, (4) no detriment to U.S. national security, and (5) a program to develop a machine-readable passport. Based on the first two of these criteria, Saudi Arabia, Kuwait, the United Arab Emirates, Bahrain, and Qatar all qualified for inclusion in the visa waiver program. DOS letter, Eagleburger to Thornburgh, Jan. 28, 1991, with attachment stating "Countries meeting the statistical criterion whose inclusion in the VWPP is not recommended: Saudi Arabia," and stating as the reason: "The government does not extend reciprocal visa waiver privileges to American nationals. We do not believe it would be useful to again approach them on this matter."

76. 8 U.S.C. § 217(c)(1) (1986).

77. DOS memo, "Continuation of a Nonimmigrant Visa Waiver Program," Jan. 11, 1990; DOS memo, "Creating a Permanent Visa Waiver Program," Mar. 15, 1990.

78. DOS memo, "NIV Waiver Pilot Program," Jan. 20, 1988. However, State believed there would be very few permanent position savings. Rather, the savings would come from not having to hire employees in the future to handle projected increases in demand for nonimmigrant visas from the affected countries. Initially, the Justice Department, at the urging of the INS—and based on security concerns— sought to require any potential participating country to "consent to the presence of an INS pre-inspection operation at that country's principal international airport,"

DOS memo, "Implementation of the NIV Waiver Pilot Program," Dec. 11, 1987. However, this desire was quelled by the substantial objections of the State Department, which feared such an expansion of U.S. personnel abroad would result in demand for increased resources, raise host country sovereignty concerns, and prove infeasible because of "airport facility constraints." Ibid.

79. Ibid.

80. Ibid.

81. DOJ memo for William Bradford Reynolds, Aug. 8, 1987.

82. DOS memo, "The nonimmigrant Visa Waiver Pilot Program," July 28, 1988.

83. DOS memo, "Continuation of a Nonimmigrant Visa Waiver Program," Jan. 11, 1990.

84. Ibid.

85. Ibid.

86. Because of the Visa Waiver Program, nonimmigrant visa demand shrank from a high of 8,769,709 visas issued in 1988 to a low of 5,359,620 visas issued in 1993. After 1993, nonimmigrant visa demand rose again through the 9/11 terrorist attacks. In FY 2001, State issued 10,569,194 nonimmigrant visas. DOS congressional presentation document, Bureau of Consular Affairs "Strategic Goals," Oct. 31, 2000 ("Most visas now issued at high visa risk posts.")

87. Ibid.

88. DOS memo, "Creating a Permanent Visa Waiver Program," Mar. 15, 1990; DOS memo, "Draft Report to Congress on the Visa Waiver Pilot Program," Apr. 6, 1990.

89. Mary Ryan interview (Oct. 9, 2003).

90. Not all U.S. diplomatic posts issue visas.

91. DOS record, Presentation to the Consular Systems Information Resources Management Program Board, Apr. 25, 1995. The MRV was mandated by the Anti-Drug Abuse Act of September 1988, and installation began in September 1989 in Santo Domingo, Dominican Republic. State also developed a Machine Readable Passport at the same time, pursuant to the same Act. DOS memo, "Machine Readable Visa Program," Mar. 9, 1990.

92. GAO report, "Passports and Visa: Status of Efforts to Reduce Fraud," GAO/NSIAD-96-99, May 1996.

93. DOS record, Presentation to the Consular Systems Information Resources Management Program Board, Apr. 25, 1995. By February 1993—when the World Trade Center was bombed—104 posts were on the real-time network, 17 used the distributed name check system, and 111 posts were still relying on microfiche to perform name checks. In general, posts in the so-called "first world" were more automated, while posts in remote and undeveloped locations tended to be the ones using the more archaic technology.

94. Chaired by State and funded by the Defense Department.

95. The TIPOFF database was searchable using a sophisticated language algorithm that allowed a searcher to identify multiple variations on a name, for example, transliterated from Arabic to English. For example, the Blind Sheik, Sheik Omar Ali Abdal Rahman would produce 486 "hits" in State's name check system. DOS record,

Presentation to the Consular Systems Information Resources Management Program Board, Apr. 25, 1995.

96. The agreement with Canada, while signed by the State Department, required a separate memorandum of agreement among the intelligence community members in which they agreed to supply their TIPOFF data with Canada.

97. DOS record, TIPOFF power point presentation, "History of the Visas Viper Program," Nov. 1, 2003.

98. The criteria for inclusion were that there was reasonable suspicion that the subject has or might engage in terrorism, and that there was sufficient biographic data for positive identification of the individual. Ibid.

99. GAO report, "Passports and Visa: Status of Efforts to Reduce Fraud," GAO/NSIAD-96-99, May 1996.

100. Following the 9/11 attacks, CA Assistant Secretary Mary Ryan met with CIA Director George Tenet, and expressed her frustration with the CIA's failure to provide State with the names of two 9/11 hijackers: Khalid al Mihdhar and Nawaf al Hazmi, whose names were in the possession of the CIA as early as January 2000. In the wake of the 9/11 attacks and this meeting between Ryan and Tenet, Visas Viper experienced a "dramatic" increase in submissions. Mary Ryan interview (Sept. 29, 2003).

101. On April 30, 1994, President Clinton signed the Foreign Relations Authorization Act, which authorized the Secretary of State to charge and retain a fee for processing MRVs. P.L. 103-236 (1994).

102. History of the Department of State during the Clinton Presidency (1993–2001), Chapter 9, The Consular Function.

103. DOS record, Supplementary Information provided in connection with interview of Travis Farris, Nov. 26, 2003. A Hispanic algorithm was implemented beginning in September 2002. Ibid.

104. Travis Farris interview (Sept. 29, 2003).

105. DOS record, Supplementary Information provided in connection with interview of Travis Farris, Nov. 26, 2003.

106. Ibid.

107. GAO report, "Border Security: Visa Process Should be Strengthened as an Antiterrorism Tool," GAO-03-132NI, Oct. 2002.

108. Mary Ryan interview (Sept. 29, 2003). According to the State Department, each post received a single hard copy of the *Best Practices Handbook* (an edition dated February 1998), which included a series of 14 cables. Over time, additional cables were added to the *Handbook* by posting them to the Consular Affairs Web site. The last cable (No. 49) was dated April 1999. DOS record, Consular Best Practices Handbook, 2000 edition.

109. General Accounting Office, "Border Security: Visa Process Should be Strengthened as an Antiterrorism Tool," GAO-03-132NI, Oct. 2002.

110. Ibid.

111. DOS record, "History of the Department of State During the Clinton Presidency (1993-2001)," Chapter 9, The Consular Function.

112. Ibid.

113. GAO report, "Border Security: Visa Process Should be Strengthened as an Antiterrorism Tool," GAO-03-132NI, Oct. 2002; Mary Ryan interview (Sept. 29, 2003) ("They were telling us they were burned out.")

114. *See* DOS record, Consular Best Practices Handbook, 2000 edition, Section 1.1 Overview which states "One reason best practices have been developed in consular work is to help those sections with growing workloads and static resources to 'get the job done.'"

115. Ibid.

116. Ibid.

117. DOS record, Consular Best Practices Handbook, 2000 edition, Cable No. 6: The Context for Best Practices, Oct. 1997.

118. Ibid.

119. Cable No. 6: The Context for Best Practices, State 185823, October 1997; RDOS03004151.

120. Id. at p. 2, Letter of Assistant Secretary Mary Ryan introducing the *Handbook* addressed "Dear Consular Colleagues."

121. As of March 1, 2003, the Immigration and Naturalization Service (INS) was reorganized, renamed and removed from the Justice Department and housed in the Department of Homeland Security.

122. The Naturalization Act of 1790 was the first immigration law passed that set federal standards for naturalization, permitting citizenship within two years of residency. Article 1, section 8, clause 3 of the Constitution gives Congress the power to "regulate commerce with foreign nations, and among the several states and with the Indian tribes."

123. By Acts passed Aug. 3, 1882, 47 Cong. Chap. 376, §§ 2, 3; 22 Stat. 214, and Feb. 23, 1887, 49 Cong. Chap. 220, 24 Stat. 415, charging the Secretary of the Treasury with "supervision over the business of immigration to the United States." States were required to process, deny entry, and care for passengers arriving within their state from abroad.

124. By Acts passed March 3, 1891, 51 Cong. chap. 551, § 7 and March 2, 1895, 53 Cong. Chap. 177.

125. By Act passed March 3, 1891. This act set out some of the basic parameters of federal immigration authority, including the list of persons to be excluded from entry, *see* § 1; the discretion of border inspectors to determine admissibility; the requirement that incoming vessels provide lists of incoming passengers including the "name, nationality, last residence, and destination of every such alien, before any of them have landed" and for pre-landing inspections by U.S. border officials; the authority to remove "unlawful" aliens and create rules to facilitate travel over the land borders, *see* § 8.

126. In 1895, the Bureau of Immigration was created and placed under the Secretary of the Treasury. In 1903, the bureau moved to the newly created Department of Commerce and Labor, taking the name the Bureau of Immigration and Naturalization in 1906. When the Department of Labor was created in 1913, the bureau moved with it. In 1933, these functions were consolidated to form the Immigration and Naturalization Service under a commissioner. In 1940, the Service was transferred to the Department of Justice where it remained until March 2003. *See*

"History of Immigration and Naturalization Agencies," 8 U.S.C. § 1551. In addition, there are at least 150 statutes providing the legislative history of immigration.

127. An example of the interdependence of the enforcement and services sectors of INS is a 1984 memo addressing the priorities of INS interior enforcement: "More broadly, interior enforcement capabilities were to have a significant effect on the deterrence of illegal immigration through the prosecution of fraud facilitators, removal of criminal aliens, reduction of employment opportunities for illegal aliens and prevention of alien access to entitlement benefits." INS memo, "Control of Nonimmigrant Students" Dec. 13, 1984.

128. George Regan interview (Oct. 21, 2003), former Assistant Commissioner for Intelligence (1989-Nov. 1996) and subsequently Acting Associate Commissioner for Enforcement through Aug. 1997.

129. INS records, INS organizational charts signed by Attorney General Reno, 1998 and 2000.

130. Mary Ann Wyrsch interview (Oct. 10, 2003), Deputy Commissioner, March 1998–October 2000 and Acting Commissioner, November 2000–March 2001.

131. Jamie Gorelick interview (Jan. 13, 2004); Eric Holder interview (Jan. 28, 2004). Budget and national security issues pertaining to the INS were handled out of separate offices at main Justice, including the Terrorism and Violent Crime Section, the Office of Immigration Litigation, and the Justice Management Division.

132. When James Ziglar became INS Commissioner on Aug. 4, 2001, he found an agency he described as severely lacking enforcement agents—he estimated that to address the illegal population in the United States, INS would need 46,000 agents as opposed to the 2,000 of the previous decade. *See* Ziglar power point to Attorney General Ashcroft, Nov. 2001. In addition, Ziglar also noted that technology development had been ad hoc, and there were no systems interconnecting INS. Development of a technology platform became a priority. James Ziglar interview, Nov. 14, 2003.

133. Doris Meissner interview (Nov. 25, 2003); DOJ records, INS Weekly agendas 1997–1998; Janet Reno interview (Dec. 16, 2003); Jamie Gorelick interview (Jan. 13, 2004); Eric Holder interview (Jan. 28, 2004). For example, when the White House Counterterrorism Security Group sought INS information on special interest cases and student tracking, or when FBI director Louis Freeh sought help from Deputy Attorney General Gorelick on the same subject.

134. She had previously served as an Acting INS Commissioner.

135. Gustavo de la Vina interview (Nov. 19, 2003).

136. Doris Meissner interview (Nov. 25, 2003).

137. House Appropriations Committee Report 105-636 (1999) and Congressional Appropriations Conference Reports (1996-1998).

138. *See* Dan Cadman interview (Oct. 7, 2003), of the INS National Security Unit; Bill West interview (Oct. 3, 2003), INS supervisory special agent in South Florida; Harvey Adler interview (Apr.16, 2004), INS detailee to the CIA; George Regan interview (Oct. 21, 2004), of the INS Intelligence Unit; Laura Baxter interview (Feb. 26, 2004), of the INS National Security Law Unit; Sarah Kendall (Mar. 15, 2004), of the INS National Security Law Unit; Tim Goyer interview (Oct. 1, 2003), of the INS

Lookout Unit, which also discusses the TIPOFF liaison, Bob Neighbors of the INS Lookout Unit; Greg Bednarz interview (Oct. 9, 2003), an Acting Assistant Commissioner for INS investigations policy and budget); Morrie Berez interview (Oct. 2, 2003), of the INS Student Tracking Task Force and its first coordinator.

139. The 9/11 hijackers only used international airports to gain entry to the United States.

140. Customs and Border Protection (CBP) power point record, Sept. 12, 2003, stating the legacy INS mission.

141. Zacarias Moussaoui, an al Qaeda operative suspected of being primed as a possible pilot in the 9/11 operation, used a French, "visa waiver" passport to come into the United States and attend flight school.

142. Although visitors from a Visa Waiver country could only stay in the United States for 90 days, they were not required to show a return airplane ticket out of the United States valid within those 90 days. Rather, the ticket could be valid for up to one year.

143. At the international airports the immigration inspectors worked the immigration lines, determining aliens' admissibility, prior to a selective review of the luggage and currency accompanying those same aliens by the Customs Service. At many land border ports of entry INS and Customs officials worked in tandem processing U.S. citizens and aliens. On the northern border, this included 86 land ports of entry and 124 crossings, which were smaller stations with limited working hours. On the southern border it included 24 land border ports of entry and 43 crossings.

144. INA § 286. INS News, October, 1997, *Service Reaching 45-Minute Flight Inspection Goal,* "The Service is close to reaching the 45-minute flight-inspection time mandated by Congress in Section 286 of the INA on most flights…" *See also* 8 USCS § 1752, which altered the law after 9/11, requiring adequate staffing so as not "compromise the safety and security of the United States." To put the atmosphere in which the inspectors worked in context, in 2001, 90 percent of aliens entering the United States were visitors for pleasure (tourists). Total nonimmigrant visitors in 2000 were over 30 million, nearly a doubling in entries from the 17 million in 1995, *see Annual INS Statistical Report,* 2001.

145. Many of the inspectors interviewed by the Commission complained these lights were often broken. Inspectors had the option of conducting an "Accelerated Citizen Examination" of U.S. citizens, called "ACE," consisting only of a document check but not a watchlist name check. The watchlist also contained information on lost or stolen passports. The INS was wholly dependent for this information on the State Department and the intelligence community. Prior to 2004, the real-time Interpol database of lost and stolen passport numbers was not available to immigration inspectors. On details of how travelers are processed at airports of entry, *see* JFK International briefing (July 28, 2003); Dulles International site visit (Feb. 27, 2004). *See also* Commission work product chart, *September 11 Hijacker border inspection results: Primary Inspection Procedures Prior to September 11,* May 20, 2004.

146. If the traveler was a hit on any of the watchlists, specific instructions appeared on the computer monitor visible only to the inspector. Instructions varied depending

on the type of record. An outstanding arrest warrant could result in an immediate arrest. On the other hand, the inspector could be told to admit the individual for operational reasons, such as to gather intelligence on the individual's contacts and activities while in the United States.

147. "Pocket litter" consists of paper, documents, receipts, photos, etc. carried on the person or in the baggage of the traveler.

148. A translator and IDENT were used to screen Kahtani. The photographing and fingerprinting of Kahtani on August 4, 2001, at Orlando International Airport would later help federal authorities identify him as the same individual captured in Afghanistan subsequent to September 11.

149. The State Department was consistently responsive to TIPOFF hits at ports of entry, according to the INS Lookout Unit manager.

150. Prior to September 11, the FBI-led Joint Terrorism Task Forces, which usually had INS detailees, would be called in occasionally on watchlist hits. On these occasions, sometimes the JTTFs would show up at the port for more information or to interview the individual.

151. Danny Chu interview (May 28, 2003).

152. INS Commissioner Meissner responded to the 1993 World Trade Center bombing by providing funds to the State Department's Consular Affairs bureau to automate its paper terrorist watchlist, known as TIPOFF, for use by consular and border inspectors. (Meissner MFR)

153. Commission work product chart, *September 11 Hijacker border inspection results: Primary Inspection Procedures Prior to September 11*, May 20, 2004.

154. Only one inspector out of 26 interviewed had heard of TIPOFF prior to September 11.

155. This agreement gave only the INS, not Customs, the authority to deny entry to visitors reasonably suspected of terrorist activity.

156. The standard of "reasonable suspicion" was taken from a confidential task force report written in the early 1980s. The report suggested a border watchlist be created to improve national security. The task force suggested that the watchlist database hold names of those who may seek admission for criminal purposes. The reasoning was that since the database only compiled names of those who may seek admission, the higher standard of excludability need not be met.

157. According to the INS Lookout Unit manager, beginning in 1997, the INS would receive new TIPOFF referrals for entry into the INS database in weekly batches on a compact disc, along with supporting intelligence. The six person staff of the INS Lookout Unit would then review the materials for entry into the lookout database, NAILS, which was available to primary inspectors at ports of entry.

158. Tim Goyer interview (Oct. 2, 2003).

159. Ibid.

160. The initial hits totaled 327 at all U.S. ports of entry out of a total 40,000 records, but many of these were mismatches or lacking sufficient information to deny entry. These numbers do not contain terrorist exclusions that were based on reasons

other than terrorism, such as Kahtani, who, as we shall see, was excluded for suspicious behavior. DOS report, DOS power point presentation, 1998.

161. Ibid. Total TIPOFF exclusions included 36 Saudis, 53 Egyptians, 125 Lebanese, and 1 Emirati. The largest number of exclusions came from the United Kingdom, a visa waiver country, with 328.

162. The program operated out of Rome, Italy; Jakarta, Indonesia; Thailand, and countries in Europe. The INS Forensic Document Lab provided expert advice in training carriers on the most common types of fraudulent travel documents. Taxes applied to airline tickets helped pay for the program. Airlines selected for the program were those who tended to bring a higher quantity of improperly documented, and thus inadmissible, aliens to the United States. Tim Goyer interview (Oct. 2, 2003).

163. In 2000 Saudia, the Saudi airline, requested training due to its concern about improperly documented non-Saudis traveling on their airline. Saudi Arabia was a popular transit point for travel in the Middle East. Neither the State Department, nor INS, nor Saudia expressed concerned about Saudi nationals themselves or the possibility that they might carry fraudulent documents. Only one 9/11 hijacker used Saudia airlines on a return flight into JFK International Airport on July 4, 2001. Tim Goyer interview (Oct. 2, 2003).

164. Passenger Analytic Units (PAUs) used inspector expertise at large airports of entry to replicate the work of the Lookout Unit, which also conducted checks on selected flights prior to their arrival at ports of entry. The purpose of the PAUs was to prepare for travelers identified through lookouts that were arriving on an incoming flight. This included information gathering, paperwork, and escorting the traveler directly from the plane to the secondary inspection area.

165. What started out as a handful of experts grew to approximately 20 experts by September 11, including five fingerprint specialists, twelve document examiners, and a half dozen intelligence analysts producing fraud alerts for the field. Forensic Document Lab briefing (July 18, 2003).

166. Forensic Document Laboratory briefing (July 18, 2003). DHS document, "Tripwire," Dec. 2003.

167. Forensic Document Laboratory briefing (July 18, 2003).

168. When the Forensic Document Laboratory was asked to analyze the surviving hijacker travel documents, they did not note the fraudulent stamps now associated with al Qaeda. See INS reports, Forensic Document Lab analyses of passports of Satam al Suqami and Abdul Aziz al Omari, Nov. 2, 2001 and Sept. 19, 2001.

169. Testimony of Phyllis Coven, INS Director, Office of International Affairs, before the House Appropriations Subcommittee on the Departments of Commerce, Justice, and State, the Judiciary, and Related Agencies, May 1, 1996.

170. Dan Cadman interview (Nov. 21, 2003).

171. Testimony of Phyllis Coven, INS Director, Office of International Affairs, before the House Appropriations Subcommittee on the Departments of Commerce, Justice, and State, the Judiciary, and Related Agencies, May 1, 1996.

172. INS memo, Investigations Assistant Commissioner to Deputy Commissioner, "Discontinuance of Arab Nonimmigrant Overstay Program," May 21, 1974.

173. INS memo, Enforcement Associate Commissioner to Regional Commissioners, Sept. 26, 1994; INS memo, Deputy Commissioner Chris Sales to Special Assistant to the Deputy Attorney General Amy Jeffress, "Policy Instructions regarding Locating and Processing Certain Libyan Students in the United States," July 11, 1983.

174. On the quality of this student/school compliance database, *see* Morrie Berez interview (Oct. 2, 2003).

175. Memorandum from FBI Director Louis Freeh to Deputy Attorney General Jamie Gorelick, "Improving DOJ's law enforcement capabilities re: aliens entry and departures from the U.S." and "Status Report on Foreign Student Controls Task Force," (September 26, 1995). *See also* DOJ memo, Meissner to Gorelick, "Immigration Controls on Foreign Students," May 11 1995, stating that a "top-down review of the current process of scrutinizing, admitting, and monitoring foreign students in the Untied States, and assessing risks and vulnerabilities relative to issues of security." The memo notes that the FBI, U.S. Information Agency, and the State Department will be part of the review team.

176. INS report, *INS Final report by the Task Force on Foreign Student Controls: Controls Governing Foreign Students and Schools that Admit Them*, Dec. 22, 1995.

177. Ibid.

178. Ibid. *INS Final report by the Task Force on Foreign Student Controls: Controls Governing Foreign Students and Schools that Admit Them*, Dec. 22, 1995. The Introduction states: "Americans have a fundamental, basic expectation that their Government is effectively monitoring and controlling foreign students. While the extent of any individual student being involved in a terrorist or major criminal activity is unknown, history tells us it does occur. Because there have been high profile instances where terrorists and criminal aliens have been linked to student visas, there is a growing degree of public concern about this issue. The American people need to have some basic level of comfort in the knowledge that its government is guarding against this danger. Americans deserve and expect it. Although there is no quantitative way to measure the intangible benefits gained through Americans having confidence and trust in their Government, it is fundamental to the mission and role of government. Without it, our nation's stability can be adversely impacted. This guiding principle was fundamental to the Task Force's effort." The reference to terrorist use of student visas here is a reference to Eyad Ismoil, the Jordanian who had driven the truckload of explosives into the parking garage at the World Trade Center on February 26, 1993. Ismoil had entered the United States in 1989 on a student visa, attending Wichita state University in Kansas for three semesters. He then dropped out of school and continued living in the United States illegally. *See also*, DOS letter, Frank Moss to Nancy Sambaiew, "Systems Priorities-Coordinated Interagency Partnership Regulating International Students," Feb. 5, 1999, stating at p. 3, "Development of a fully deployed CIPRIS is considered to be an important and valuable tool for countering both fraud and terrorism."

179. P.L. 104-208 § 641 (1996). The legislation states that the first foreign students to come into the new tracking system should be those from state sponsors of terror.

180. Congressional appropriation conference reports for the INS (1996-2000).

181. Morrie Berez interview (Oct. 2, 2003). The INS received $800 million in technology monies between 1995 and 1997, but examiners were generally critical of its technology efforts, *see* GAO Report 01-046, Information Technology: INS Needs to Strengthen its Investment Management Capability, Dec.2000. DOJ OIG Audit Report 99-19, Follow Up Review Immigration and Naturalization Service Management of Automation Program, July 1999.

182. *See* INS report, CIPRIS Information Packet, 1998. The success of the biometric student card was acknowledged by senior management at an INS Policy Council meeting in August 1998. The minutes read: "The CIPRIS pilot is in operation and appears to be working well. Current plans for the pilot call for the introduction of a new card that would replace the [paper forms now required of schools and students]. Advantages of proceeding to introduce the card as planned include the desire of the stakeholders, especially the participating schools. The card would replace some of the workload on schools with respect to entries and exits. It would also be more durable and more counterfeit-resistant than the current paper documents carried by students. Concerns about the card include the fact that it is . . . not a travel document. The Policy Council decided that issuance of the student cards should be deferred to allow time to explore other options." INS record, INS Policy Council Meeting minutes, Aug. 28, 1998. The Commission also spoke to John Smith, a former IBM vice president who helped develop the project. He stated the "biometrics were feasible at the time," *see* electronic communication to Commission staff, Oct. 21, 2003. The biometric scanners were linked between the Atlanta airport, the Texas Service Center and the United States Information Agency.

183. Doris Meissner interview (Nov. 25, 2003); Mary Ann Wyrsch interview (Oct. 20, 2003), Dan Cadman interview (Oct. 7, 2003); Tom Cook interview (Jan. 14, 2004); Morrie Berez interview (Oct. 2, 2003). *See also* Daniel Benjamin and Steven Simon, "A Problem of Distance" in *The Age of Sacred Terror* (Random House, 2002), p. 307-311.

184. *See* Presidential Decision Directive 62, 1998.

185. INS letter, Rep. Chuck Schumer to Attorney General Reno, "Student Visas and the implementation of CIPRIS," Feb. 19, 1998; INS letter, Senators Jon Kyl and Rick Santorum to Commissioner Meissner, "Implementation of CIPRIS," Mar. 31, 1998.

186. Testimony of Tom Fischer before the House Judiciary Subcommittee on Immigration, Border Security, and Claims re: *Immigration Student Tracking: Implementation and Proposed Modifications*, (Sept. 18, 2002).

187. INS record, INS Senior Leadership Policy Council meeting, Aug. 26, 1998.

188. INS electronic communications, "CIPRIS Stop Work, Task 402," Feb. 4-9, 1998.

189. The National Association of International Educators supported an amendment that would have repealed the 1996 legislation mandating the program. Web site of NAFSA: Association of International Educators, "NAFSA Endorses CIPRIS Repeal Legislation, Issues Action Alert," 2000.

190. Mary Ann Wyrsch interview (Oct. 20, 2003) and Tom Cook interview (Jan. 14, 2003).

191. Tom Cook interview (Jan. 14, 2003). *See also* Doug Pasternak, "American Colleges are Weapons U. for Iraq," *U.S. News and World Report,* Mar. 9, 1998; American Council of Education (ACE) letter to its members, "CIPRIS Foreign Student Fee Collection System Issue Summary," Jan. 10, 2000; ACE letter, Terry Hartle, Senior Vice

President to Kevin Rooney, Acting INS Commissioner, April 4, 2001, "Implementation of the Student and Exchange Visa Program/Coordinated Interagency Partnership Regulating International Students (SEVP/CIPRIS);" and Bob Bach interview (May 14, 2004), Executive Associate Commissioner for Policy and Planning, 1994–2000.

192. INS record, INS Senior Leadership Policy Council meeting, Aug. 26, 1998.

193. Tom Cook interview (Jan. 14, 2003). *See also* Bob Bach interview (May 14, 2004). Mary Ann Wyrsch, however, states she removed the project manager because he did not have a "good technology plan." Mary Ann Wyrsch interview (Oct. 20, 2003). John Smith, the technology consultant on the program, states he never did brief Wyrsch, but did brief the research group that reported to her. *See* electronic communication from Smith to Commission staff, Oct. 21, 2003.

194. INS letter, Senator Spencer Abraham and 20 other senators to Meissner, "INS Student Tracking," Feb. 22, 2000.

195. American Camping Association website, "CIPRIS," Nov. 1, 2000, states: "Appropriation language introduced by Senator Judd Gregg, Chairman of the Commerce, Justice, State Appropriations Subcommittee, would essentially eliminate CIPRIS altogether."

196. Mary Ann Wyrsch interview (Oct. 20, 2003)

197. Tom Cook interview (Jan. 14, 2003).

198. Illegal Immigration Reform and Immigrant Responsibility Act (IIRIRA) § 110, 1996.

199. Congressional appropriations conference reports, 1996–2000.

200. Ibid.

201. Doris Meissner interview (Jan. 12, 2004). *See also* INS record, contemporaneous notes on conversations between Meissner, Bach, and the Canadian government regarding the implementation of (IIRIRA) § 110, June 1999. *See* Canadian/American Border Trade Alliance record, notes on a presentation from Commissioner Meissner: "[Commissioner Meissner] thanked CAN/AM BTA for its pivotal role in educating Congress on the realities and needs of the northern Border and especially in its involvement in convincing Congress to delay the implementation of Section 110;" INS electronic communication, Jackie Bednarz to senior management, stating that Governor Howard Dean of Vermont said that entry-exit would be a "disaster" for Vermont, 1998.

202. *See* Congressional bill, S. 1217 § 102: "Departments of Commerce, Justice, and State, the Judiciary, and Related Agencies Appropriations Act, 2000 (Placed on Calendar in Senate)," where it reads, "Section 110 of Public Law 104-208 is repealed." *See also* Doris Meissner interview (Jan. 12, 2004).

203. Ibid.

204. The INS Web site at the time stated that the intelligence unit "collects, evaluates, analyzes, and disseminates information relating to all INS mission, both enforcement and examination. Intelligence also directs the Headquarters Command Center, which maintains communications with other offices and agencies 24 hours a day."

205. Doris Meissner interview (Nov. 25, 2003).

206. This 1995 CIA briefing had as its goal the detailing of INS agents to the CIA. INS email, Bednarz to Meissner, "CIA Briefing of INS Top Management—current

Threat Assessment of Islamic Fundamentalist groups and Impact upon INS" (Oct. 16, 1995).

207. Doris Meissner interview (Nov. 25, 2003) and Gregory Bednarz statement (Oct. 9, 2003).

208. Doris Meissner interview (Nov. 25, 2003).

209. Cliff Landsman interview (Oct. 27, 2003). Landsman ran the intelligence unit from 1998-2003, when the INS was abolished. *See also* George Regan interview (Oct. 21, 2003).

210. Janet Reno interview (Dec. 16, 2003).

211. Cliff Landsman interview (Oct. 27, 2003).

212. *See* Majority Staff Report, Hearing on "Foreign Terrorists in America: Five Years after the World Trade Center," Feb. 24, 1998, p. 138-139. On the 2,000 special agents, *see* Gregory Bednarz statement, (Oct. 9, 2003). On the 4,500 inspectors, *see* Immigration and Naturalization News Release, "INS to Hire More Than 800 Immigration Inspectors Nationwide," Jan. 12, 2001: "The new inspectors will join the ranks of a current staff of more than 4,500 who perform more than 500 million inspections of people entering the United States each year." *See also*, INS Communique, Vol. 23. No. 1, "INS Commissioner Doris Meissner Announces Departure," Jan. 2001: "The Service is significantly bigger, with a workforce of 18,000 to now 32,000 employees. The Border Patrol alone has doubled in size, from 4,036 to 9,100 in the past seven years."

213. Majority Staff Report, Hearing on "Foreign Terrorists in America: Five Years after the World Trade Center," Feb. 24, 1998, p. 152.

214. Cliff Landsman interview (Oct. 27, 2003).

215. Harvey Adler interview (Apr. 16, 2004) and Cliff Landsman interview (Oct. 27, 2003).

216. INS records, INS enforcement personnel statistics, 1990-2000.

217. On the 1986 plan, *see* INS report, Investigations Division, "Alien Terrorists and Undesirables: A Contingency Plan," May 1986; Daniel Cadman interview (Oct. 17, 2003). On the 1995 plan, *see* INS memo, Bramhall to Bednarz and Hurst, "Draft Counter-Terrorism Strategy Outline," Aug. 11, 1995. On the 1997 plan, *see* INS email from Cadman, "EAC briefing document," Dec. 5, 1997, with attachment entitled "Counterterrorism/National Security Strategy and Casework Oversight".

218. Doris Meissner interview (Nov. 25, 2003) and Dan Cadman (Oct.17, 2003). The manager of the unit put together a report for the INS investigations division in 1986 titled, "Alien Terrorists and Undesirables: A Contingency Plan," which recognized the INS as "the agency charged with manning those borders and screening potential entrants to ensure that they are not entering with the intent to commit acts of terror either against our own government and people, or those of any other nation."

219. INS report, "National Security Unit Strategy proposal," 1997.

220. Dan Cadman interview (Oct. 17, 2003).

221. Ibid.

222. INS memo, Ken Elwood to the field, "Advisement to all offices and employees of the indictment of Usama bin Laden, international terrorist, and direct heightened security measures," (Nov. 4, 1998).

223. Dan Cadman interview (Oct. 17, 2003) and Laura Baxter interview (Feb. 26, 2004).

224. Rocky Concepcion interview (June 15, 2001).

225. Veronica Cates interview (May 25, 2004), Rocky Concepcion interview (June 15, 2004), DHS electronic communication, Cadman to Commission staff and subsequent phone conversation (June 14 and 16, 2004), and Kevin Rooney interview (Jan. 8, 2004). *See also*, INS report, Cates to Cadman, "White House briefing," July 5, 2001.

226. Doris Meissner interview (Nov. 25, 2003).

227. A supervisory special agent in Florida wrote memos to headquarters beginning before the first World Trade Center bombing in 1993 urging the INS and the Department of Justice to take on counterterrorism investigations under its broad immigration authority. He also suggested using classified evidence to help remove terrorist aliens. The memos never received a response. *See* INS memos, Bill West to Bill Yates and headquarters, 1993-1995.

228. INS Memo, William Slattery, INS Field Operations Executive Associate Commissioner, to Alexander Alienikoff, Program Executive Associate Commissioner, "INS Task Force Report," Oct. 29, 1996.

229. INS Memo, Meissner to John Keeney, DOJ Acting Assistant Attorney General, Feb. 7, 1997.

230. Ibid. It took until 1999 for the Justice Department, White House and Congress to establish a baseline for INS commitment to supporting JTTFs and until 1999, after the African embassy bombings, for Congress to specifically fund INS "participation in joint task forces on terrorism, to assist in the identification and apprehension of alien terrorists." By 2000, Congress allotted more than 900 new positions to interior enforcement, for a total of 3,024 available positions, and INS detailees were considered integral to the Joint Terrorism Task Forces. *See* Congressional Conference Committee Report 105-825, 1999.

231. Individuals still could claim political asylum and receive a hearing to determine if the fear of persecution was credible. Resolution of such a claim cold delay the expedited removal charge. *See* Antiterrorism and Effective Death Penalty Act §§ 422, 403; IIRIRA § 302.

232. Ibid.

233. INS Fact Sheet, "Update on Expedited Removals," July 9, 1997.

234. INS record, INS Policy Council Meeting Minutes, June 4, 1997 and Laura Baxter interview (Feb. 26, 2004).

235. INS record, Immigration "A" (Alien) file of Abu Mezer.

236. INS record, INS Policy Council Meeting Minutes, June 4, 1997 and Laura Baxter interview (Feb. 26, 2004).

237. Testimony of Seth Waxman before the Senate Judiciary Committee during consideration of the proposed Omnibus Counterterrorism Act of 1995, quoted in Senate Judiciary Committee Hearing record 105-703, p. 149.

238. *See* Rules for the Alien Terrorist Removal Court of the United States, May 28, 1997.

239. Majority Staff Report, Hearing on "Foreign Terrorists in America: Five Years after the World Trade Center," Feb. 24, 1998, p. 152.

240. James Reynolds interview (Mar. 31, 2004).

241. 8 U.S.C. section 1534 (e)(1)(A), INA § 504.

242. Doris Meissner interview (Nov. 25, 2003); Dan Cadman interview (Oct. 7, 2003); Laura Baxter interview (Feb. 26, 2003); and James Castello (Nov. 7, 2003). *See also*, DOJ memo, Laura Baxter memo, "The Use of Classified Evidence in Immigration Proceedings: Background Information and Legislation," Feb. 16, 2001. One example of the difficulties in pursuing a suspected terrorist through immigration violations is the case of Sami al Arian, which was initiated in 1994 and was repeatedly reviewed by the Justice Department for possible prosecution or initiation of removal proceedings prior to September 11. *See* Bill West interview (Oct. 3, 2003) and testimony of Steven Emerson before the Senate Judiciary Subcommittee on Technology, Terrorism and Government Information, Feb. 24, 1998, p. 101. The Justice Department brought charges after 9/11.

243. Doris Meissner interview (Nov. 25, 2003).

244. James Castello interview (Nov. 7, 2003) and Laura Baxter interview (Feb. 26, 2003).

245. Dan Cadman interview (Oct. 17, 2003) and Rocky Concepcion interview (June 15, 2004).

246. Those in the latter two groups sought U.S. residency on the basis of fear of persecution in their home country: asylees made their claim after entering the United States or at the border, and refugees made it from abroad.

247. INS record, "A" file of Aimal Kansi.

248. INS record, "A" files of Mohamed and Mahmud Abouhalima.

249. The SAW applicants had to provide evidence that they had worked on perishable crops for at least "90 days" between May 1, 1985, and May 1, 1986; their residence did not have to be "continuous" or "unlawful." Nearly 1 million illegal aliens had received legal permanent residence under SAW, twice the number of foreigners normally employed in agriculture.

250. Testimony of Paul Virtue before the House Judiciary Subcommittee on Immigration, 1999.

251. The Patrol's official mission statement read as follows: "To detect and prevent the illegal entry of aliens into the United States. The Border Patrol helps maintain borders that work—facilitating the flow of legal immigration and goods—while preventing the illegal trafficking of people and contraband." *See* CBP power point record, Sept. 12, 2003.

252. Gus de la Vina interview (Nov. 19, 2003), a 31-year Border Patrol veteran and its Chief, 1999–2003.

253. The primary entry points were San Diego, California followed by El Paso, Texas.

254. Gus de la Vina interview (Nov. 19, 2003)

255. Where the Patrol did receive outside federal help and support was from the Defense Department in three areas: (1) military personnel who, until the mid 1990s, worked at listening posts as "eyes and ears" on land and water; (2) National Guard units constructed such things as fences, gates, and towers; and (3) technological "leftovers" such as binoculars, infrared glasses, and sensors. The Defense Department no longer

supplied military personnel at listening posts after a mistaken shooting of a civilian by military personnel. Known as the Redford incident, its ramifications were to be felt in the aftermath of September 11, as the Patrol's request to DOD for military personnel help at listening posts was denied, and the Patrol received instead technology and intelligence analysts.

256. INS newsletter, "INS Commissioner Meissner Announces Departure," Jan. 2001.

257. Numbers derived from statistics set forth in DOJ OIG report, *Border Patrol Efforts Along the Northern Border,* Apr. 2000.

258. For numbers of agents on the Canadian border, the Canadian situation generally, and the Inspector General's recommendations, *see* DOJ OIG *Follow-up Review of the Border Patrol Efforts Along the Northern Border,* Apr. 2000. On terrorists entering the U.S. via Canada, *see* e.g. INS report, *Record of Deportable Alien Abu Mezer,* June 24, 1996. Mezer was able to stay in the United States despite three apprehensions for illegal entries along the northern border. In regard to the detailing of northern border patrol agents to the southern border, Doris Meissner stated in a memo to Mary Demory, Assistant Inspector General for Inspections at DOJ, that the INS would stop detailing border patrol agents to the southern border, p. 5 of above-mentioned DOJ OIG report.

259. Gus de la Vina interview (Nov. 19, 2003).

260. Gus de la Vina interview (Nov. 19, 2003).

261. DOJ, Executive Office for Immigration Review, Statistical Year Book 2000, p. D-1, 214; 982 immigration hearings were held for deportation, exclusion and removal.

262. BJA, Compendium of Federal Justice Statistics, 2000, p. 1. Immigration offenses for FY 2000 totaled 16,495.

263. INS has assigned special agents to the Organized Crime Drug Enforcement Task Forces since 1987.

264. There was also the problem that the paper "Alien" files that were located throughout the U.S. were not available for review after hours.

265. The term "aggravated felon" refers to aliens who have been convicted of serious felony crimes such as illicit trafficking in drugs or firearms, money laundering, and alien smuggling. 8 USC § 1101(a)(43).

266. Access to the center was available through an existing dedicated law enforcement telecommunication system, the National Law Enforcement Telecommunications System (NLETS). The first state to have access to the LESC was Arizona. To obtain immigration information on a possible criminal alien suspect, a simple query screen on the NLETS system was completed. Basic biographical information was required with optional fields available to better define the search. The query screen was available to all law enforcement agencies in the state. The INS attempted to answer all queries and returned any information within 20 minutes. The LESC conducted extensive training to officers in the state on immigration law and the new system.

267. The LESC was also used to locate criminal aliens who were detained in county jails for criminal activity. The Maricopa County Jail in Phoenix was the first detention facility to program an automated interface with the LESC so that all foreign-born inmates who were booked into the jail on criminal charges were checked for immigration status.

268. 8 U.S.C. § 1357 (1996).

269. This "sanctuary" policy was first published by Mayor Edward Koch on August 7, 1989, and directed city "line workers" who had contact with the public to not transmit information respecting any alien to federal immigration authorities. However, it exempted the police and the Department of Corrections and directed them to continue to work with federal authorities "in investigating and apprehending aliens suspected of criminal activity." Koch, executive order, Aug. 7, 1989.

Chapter 5

1. Atta is believed to have piloted Flight 11 and Jarrah Flight 93.

2. DOS OIG MOC, Consular Officer No. 9, Feb. 5, 2003. The names of consular officers, immigration inspectors, and intelligence officials have been changed or omitted, in accordance with Commission policy and agreements.

3. Consular Officer No. 9 interview (Feb. 20, 2004).

4. Ibid.

5. Consular Officer No. 9 interview (Feb. 20, 2004).

6. Ibid.

7. Ibid.

8. Ibid.

9. Ibid.

10. DOS OIG MOC, Consular Section Chief Levy and ACS Officer Wolfson, Jan. 27, 2003.

11. Ibid.

12. Consular Officer No. 10 interview (Mar. 1, 2004); DOS OIG MOC, Consular Officer No. 7, Feb. 11, 2003; DOS OIG MOC, Consular Officer No. 10, Jan. 19, 2003.

13. DOS OIG MOC, Consular Officer No. 10, Jan. 19, 2003; Consular Officer No. 10 interview (Mar. 1, 2004).

14 . Consular Officer No. 10 interview (Mar. 1, 2004).

15. Ibid., stating "From a security standpoint, we viewed them as safe bets."

16. DOS OIG MOC, Consular Officer No. 10, Jan. 19, 2003.

17. Ibid.

18. Consular Officer No. 10 interview (Mar. 1, 2004).

19. DOS OIG MOC, Consular Officer No. 7, Feb. 11, 2003.

20. Ibid.

21. Consular Officer No. 10 interview (Mar. 1, 2004); DOS OIG MOC, Consular Officer No. 10, Jan. 19, 2003.

22. DOS OIG MOC, Consular Officer No. 7, Feb. 11, 2003.

23. DOS OIG MOC, Consular Officer No. 10, Jan. 19, 2003.

24. DOS OIG MOC, Consular Officer No. 7, Feb. 11, 2003.

25. DOS OIG MOC, Consular Officer No. 10, Jan. 19, 2003.

26. Consular Officer No. 10 interview (Mar. 1, 2004).

27. Ibid., estimating that 70% used the drop box and 30% the travel agency.

28. DOS OIG MOC, Consular Officer No. 7, Feb. 11, 2003; DOS OIG MOC, Consular Officer No. 10, Jan. 19, 2003.

29. Albert A. Thibault, Jr. interview (Nov. 5, 2003).

30. Arthur M. interview (Oct. 14, 2003).

31. Testimony of Consular Officer No. 1 before the U.S. House of Representatives, Aug. 1, 2002.

32. Carl C. interview (Oct. 29, 2003). Consular officials in Saudi Arabia and in Washington uniformly told the Commission that they could not recall receiving any letters from Congress urging them *to deny* visas before 9/11. Rather, consular officials told the Commission that members of Congress were their most faithful correspondents and were constantly urging them *to issue* visas to individuals in Saudi Arabia who were constituents' family members or other individuals with connections to their legislative districts.

33. Consular Officer No. 6 interview (Oct. 14, 2003); Consular Officer No. 11 interview (Dec. 30, 2003).

34. Ibid.

35. This statistic is an estimate prepared by consular officials in Saudi Arabia at the request of the General Accounting Office and memorialized in GAO workpapers. The difficulty in measuring this more precisely is that the State Department electronic record-keeping system did not record whether a visa applicant was interviewed prior to September 11, 2001. Travis Farris interview (Sept. 29, 2003).

36. Carl C. interview (Oct. 29, 2003).

37. Consular Officer No. 11 interview (Dec. 30, 2003).

38. Ibid.

39. Ibid.

40. Ibid.

41. Carl C. interview (Oct. 29, 2003).

42. DOS memo to Riyadh Consul General Allen K., May 7, 2000.

43. GAO record, telephone interview of Allen K., July 10, 2002.

44. Ibid.

45. DOS cable, Jeddah 001185, Dec. 10, 2001.

46. DOS cable, "Riyadh Fraud Issues," Aug. 4, 2000.

47. Ibid. (emphasis added).

48. Carl C. interview (Oct. 29, 2003).

49. DOS cable, Jeddah 001225, Nov. 9, 1999.

50. DOS email, from Allen K. to Judith McCloskey, Aug. 5, 2002.

51. INA sec. 214(b), 8 U.S.C. sec. 1184(b); testimony of Consular Officer No. 1 before U.S. House of Representatives Committee on Government Reform, Aug. 1, 2002.

52. Testimony of Consular Officer No. 3 before U.S. House of Representatives Committee on Government Reform, Aug. 1, 2002.

53. Tom Furey interview (Dec. 5, 2003); testimony of Consular Officer No. 2 before U.S. House of Representatives Committee on Government Reform, Aug. 1, 2002.

54. *See* DOS cable, Riyadh Fraud Issues, Aug. 2000, stating "Saudis are generally good visa risks, and most Saudi applicants are processed without interview."

55. DOS OIG MOC, Consular Officer No. 11, Jan. 20, 2003; testimony of Consular Officer No. 3 before U.S. House of Representatives Committee on Government Reform, Aug. 1, 2002.

56. Consular Officer No. 11 interview (Dec. 30, 2003); DOS OIG MOC, Tom Furey, Jan. 28, 2003.

57. Consular Officer No. 11 interview (Dec. 30, 2003); DOS OIG MOC, Consular Section Chief Miguel O., Jan. 23, 2003; testimony of Consular Officer No. 3 before U.S. House of Representatives Committee on Government Reform, Aug. 1, 2002, stating "It was the same way that that's the presumption for many Europeans;" Tom Furey interview (Dec. 5, 2003), stating Saudis were treated like citizens of countries in the Visa Waiver Program and for the same reasons.

58. DOS OIG MOC, Consular Officer No. 11, Jan. 28, 2003.

59. DOS OIG MOC, Tom Furey, Jan. 28, 2003; DOS OIG MOC, Catherine Barry, Dec. 13, 2002, quoting Ms. Barry as saying that both Saudi Arabia and the UAE were "de facto visa waiver countries."

60. CIA research paper, "Saudi Arabia's Islamic Awakening," Feb. 1993.

61. INS record, 2001 Statistical Yearbook, Table 58 (Deportable Aliens Located by Status at Entry and Region and Country of Nationality Fiscal Year 2001). This was fewer than from Liechtenstein (42) and Norway (49), and contrasts with the 1,315,678 from Mexico.

62. DOS cable, Riyadh 10070, Nov. 25, 1991.

63. GAO analysis of economic data on Saudi Arabia, prepared by Bruce Kutnick, July 16, 2002.

64. CIA research paper, "Saudi Arabia's Islamic Awakening," Feb. 1993.

65. Testimony of Consular Officer No. 2 before U.S. House of Representatives Committee on Government Reform, Aug. 1, 2002.

66. Testimony of Consular Officer No. 3, before U.S. House of Representatives Committee on Government Reform, August 1, 2002.

67. Testimony of Consular Officer No. 2, before U.S. House of Representatives Committee on Government Reform, Aug. 1, 2002; testimony of Consular Officer No. 3 before U.S. House of Representatives Committee on Government Reform, Aug. 1, 2002, stating "they weren't looking for jobs even though they were unemployed."

68. Testimony of Consular Officer No. 4 before U.S. House of Representatives Committee on Government Reform, Aug. 1, 2002.

69. DOS OIG MOC, Consular Officer No. 13, Jan. 23, 2003.

70. DOS memo, Tasker #252, prepared in the summer of 2000, "Best Practices already in effect at post include . . . interview by exception for applicants from Saudi Arabia, Bahrain, Oman, Qatar, Kuwait, and the United Arab Emirates;" Consular Officer No. 11 interview (Dec. 30, 2003).

71. DOS cable, "Interviews by Exception," 98 State 160236.

72. Consular Officer No. 11 interview (Dec. 30, 2003).

73. This view is supported by findings of the General Accounting Office which compiled statistics on the refusal rates for Riyadh and Jeddah during the year before September 11, 2001. According to the GAO, consular officers in Riyadh refused .15 percent of Saudi citizen visa applicants during the period from September 11, 2000 to April 30, 2001, while consular officers in Jeddah refused approximately 1.07 percent of Saudi citizen applicants in the same time period. For reasons discussed, infra, the interview rate for Saudi citizens applying in Jeddah probably dropped beginning in September 2000, so the difference may have been greater before that date.

74. Consular Officer No. 5 interview (Mar. 2, 2004); DOS Office of Inspector General Memorandum of Conversation, Consular Officer No. 5, Feb. 5, 2003.

75. Consular Officer No. 12 interview (Feb. 24, 2004).

76. Ibid.

77. Ibid.

78. Ibid.

79. Ibid.

80. Consular Officer No. 6 interview (Oct. 14, 2003).

81. Testimony of Consular Officer No. 1 before U.S. House of Representatives Committee on Government Reform, Aug. 1, 2002.

82. Ibid.

83. Testimony of Consular Officer No. 2 before U.S. House of Representatives Committee on Government Reform, Aug. 1, 2002.

84. Consular Officer No. 13 interview (Feb. 24, 2004).

85. Ibid.

86. DOS OIG MOC, Consular Officer No. 13, Oct. 9, 2002.

87. DOS OIG MOC, Consular Officer No. 11, Jan. 20, 2003.

88. Consular Officer No. 11 interview (Dec. 30, 2003).

89. DOS OIG MOC, Consular Officer No. 11, Jan. 20, 2003.

90. DOS OIG MOC, Consular Officer No. 11, Jan. 20, 2003.

91. Consular Officer No. 14 interview (Feb. 2, 2004).

92. DOS OIG MOC, Consular Officer No. 13, Jan. 23, 2003; Consular Officer No. 14 interview (Feb. 2, 2004). Consular Officer No. 13's supervisor said that he had taken "a lot of flack" about Consular Officer No. 13's high refusal rate. He said there had been "overt hostility" to Consular Officer No. 13's high refusal rate before 9/11.

93. Consular Officer No. 14 interview (Feb. 2, 2004); Consular Officer No. 13 interview (Feb. 24, 2004).

94. GAO report, "Visa Process Should be Strengthened as an Antiterrorism Tool," GAO-03-132NI, Oct. 2002, stating "For example, consular officers held different opinions about whether they should use INA section 214(b) to refuse visas to questionable applicants, that is, those who either did not appear credible or who could not convince them of the purpose of their visit, regardless of the applicant's income or ties to a residence abroad. Many consular officers told us they were using the provision for this purpose. Consular managers and individual consular officers whom we interviewed differed on whether consular officers should be using INA section 214(b) to screen applicants in this manner."

95. DOS OIG MOC, Tom Furey, Jan. 28, 2003.

96. Tom Furey interview (Dec. 5, 2003); DOS OIG MOC, Tom Furey, Jan. 28, 2003.

97. Tom Furey interview (Dec. 5, 2003).

98. Testimony of Consular Officer No. 2 before the U.S. House of Representatives, Committee on Government Reform, Aug. 1, 2002.

99. Ibid.

100. DOS OIG MOC Consular Officer No. 11, Jan. 20, 2003.

101. The Gulf Cooperation Council countries are: Saudi Arabia, Bahrain, Kuwait, Oman, Qatar and the United Arab Emirates.

102. Tom Furey interview (Dec. 5, 2003).

103. Ibid.

104. Ibid.

105. Ibid.

106. DOS cable no. 6, The Context for Best Practices, Oct. 1997.

107. DOS cable no. 10, Non-Immigrant Visa Appointment Systems, State 227586, Nov. 1997.

108. Tom Furey interview (Dec. 5, 2003).

109. DOS cable no. 7, Drop Box and Personal Appearance Waiver (PAW) Programs, Nov. 1997.

110. Ibid.

111. Testimony of Consular Officer 2 before the U.S. House of Representatives Government Reform Committee, Aug. 1, 2002.

112. DOS cable no. 19, Interviews By Exception, 98 State 160236, Aug. 1998; DOS cable no. 9, Remote Data Entry, State 223398, Nov. 1998; DOS cable no. 4, Off-Site Fee Collection, State 059404, Apr. 1997.

113. DOS cable, "U.S. Visa Express Program Transforms NIV Scene in Saudi Arabia," Riyadh 02326 (Aug. 19, 2001).

114. Ibid.

115. Tom Furey interview (Dec. 5, 2003); testimony of Consular Officer No. 2 before the U.S. House of Representatives Government Reform Committee, Aug. 1, 2002.

116. See, e.g., Memorandum of Understanding Between Kanoo Holidays Travel Company in Saudi Arabia and the United States Embassy in Riyadh and U.S. Consulate General in Jeddah, Saudi Arabia Concerning U.S. Visa Express (Nonimmigrant Visa Service).

117. DOS cable, "U.S. Visa Express Program Transforms NIV Scene in Saudi Arabia," Riyadh 02326 (Aug. 19, 2001); testimony of Consular Officer No. 2 before the U.S. House of Representatives Government Reform Committee, Aug. 1, 2002.

118. DOS report, "U.S. Visa Express Program Transforms NIV Scene in Saudi Arabia," Riyadh 02326, Aug. 19, 2001.

119. Testimony of Consular Officer No. 2 before the U.S. House of Representatives Government Reform Committee, Aug. 1, 2002.

120. DOS Report of the Accountability Review Boards on the Embassy Bombings in Nairobi and Dar Es Salaam, Jan. 1999. In his introduction to the Report, Review Boards Chairman Admiral William J. Crowe said the following: "In our investigation of the bombings, The Boards were struck by how similar the lessons were to those drawn by the Inman Commission over 14 years ago. What is most troubling is the failure of the U.S. Government to take the necessary steps to prevent such tragedies through an unwillingness to give sustained priority and funding to security improvements."

121. Ibid., Recommendations 7 and 8.

122. Kevin O. interview (Feb. 12, 2004).

123. DOS email from Tom Furey to Mary Ryan, dated "Tuesday, June 26, 2001, 8:06 A.M."

124. Testimony of Consular Officer No. 2 before the U.S. House of Representatives Government Reform Committee, Aug. 1, 2002.

125. Testimony of Consular Officer No. 3 before the U.S. House of Representatives Government Reform Committee, Aug. 1, 2002. In a cable this officer drafted but did not send during this time period, the officer stated, "requiring all applicants to apply through travel agents has gummed-up the process in Jeddah. The NIV officer must now review the applications of those who were previously ineligible for Visa Express twice, once on paper and then again several days later at the window." The officer recommended returning Visa Express to the "original guidelines (Saudi nationals and TCNs with prior visas)." Visa Express in Jeddah—Suggested Modifications (undated).

126. Consular Officer No. 11 interview (Dec. 30, 2003); State OIG MOC with Consular Officer No. 11, Jan. 20, 2003, "The program also eliminated the need for interviews of first time student visa applicants."

127. Testimony of Consular Officer No. 3 before the U.S. House of Representatives Government Reform Committee, Aug. 1, 2002.

128. Consular Officer No. 11 interview (Dec. 30, 2003).

129. Testimony of Consular Officer No. 3 before the U.S. House of Representatives Government Reform Committee, Aug. 1, 2002; Visa Express in Jeddah—Suggested Modifications (undated), "It also created incentives to issue 'borderline' cases in order to decrease interview workload."

130. Tom Furey interview (Dec. 5, 2003).

131. Consular Officer No. 11 interview (Dec. 30, 2003).

132. Ibid.

133. Testimony of Consular Officer No. 4 before the U.S. House of Representatives Government Reform Committee, Aug. 1, 2002, p. 10, "Nothing changed. Only the way the applications were coming to me," Tom Furey interview (Dec. 5, 2003), Visa Express did not change Saudi interview policy since "[t]hey were already not being interviewed."

134. Testimony of Consular Officer No. 4 before the U.S. House of Representatives Government Reform Committee, Aug. 1, 2002.

135. GAO report, "Border Security: Visa Process Should be Strengthened as an Antiterrorism Tool," GAO- 03-132NI (Oct. 2002), p. 19, fn. 29. Although the State Department's Inspector General concluded that "the consular officers who issued visas to the terrorist hijackers . . . acted in accordance with policies that prevailed at their missions at the time the visas were issued," the State OIG did not specifically address whether the Visa Express Program affected the quality or quantity of interviews in Saudi Arabia. DOS OIG report, "Review of the Issuance of Visas to the September 11, 2001, Terrorists," ISP-CA-03-27 Mar. 2003.

136. All the Memoranda of Understanding between the U.S. Government and the Visa Express travel agencies contained language mandating that "the American embassy and consulate agree to return the processed visas (barring any need for personal interview of applicant) the following day."

137. The Commission produced charts in the different subject areas discussed during the interviews to aid in a better empirical understanding of the border inspections of the hijackers. Charts used to support the discussion in this section include: Commission work product chart, *September 11 Hijacker border inspection interview results: Primary Inspection*

Procedures Prior to September 11, May 20, 2004; Commission work product chart, *September 11 Hijacker border inspection interview results: Red Flags Resulting in Secondary Inspection Prior to September 11*, May 20, 2004. The remaining 12 inspectors who were not interviewed were no longer employed by the INS (now in DHS) and were unavailable to the Commission. Our interviews were conducted between March and June 2004.

138. The inspector told us she is "75 percent sure" one of Atta's companions was Adnan Shukrijumah, listed by the FBI as one of their ten most wanted. Immigration inspector of Mohamed Atta on May 2, 2001 interview (Mar. 25, 2004). The Commission has reason to believe that the other companion was Ziad Jarrah, *see* Chapter 2, note 114.

139. Because none of the hijackers were from a visa waiver country, they all had to obtain visas.

140. Despite the well-known information about the use of fraudulent travel documents in the prosecutions of the Blind Sheikh and the World Trade Center conspirators, the Department of Justice failed to make systematic use of this information as a counterterrorism tool.

141. Commission work product chart, *September 11 Hijacker border inspection interview results: Primary Inspection Procedures Prior to September 11*, May 20, 2004.

142. The inspector subsequently changed his mind and sent Atta to secondary where he—incorrectly—received an eight-month tourist stay.

143. Commission interview of immigration inspector for Suqami and al Shehri's April 23 inspection (May 19, 2004). Other inspectors verified that the I-94 arrival record and customs declaration had little to no bearing on the length of stay determination. Sometimes a return ticket would be requested as well, but this was not a consistent request by inspectors since return tickets are not required by law as they are, for example, in the United Kingdom.

144. Commission interview of immigration inspector for Atta's July 19 inspection (May 17, 2004). Atta came to the United States first in June 2000 and was admitted for six months. He overstayed his six month length of stay by five weeks, and left again in early January 2001, returning January 10, 2001. Atta left again after six months in early July 2001, and returned July 19, 2001, staying until the execution of the plot.

145. Of 34 attempted hijacker entries, only 13 of these declarations were available for Commission review. This is because Customs' declarations are all paper and destroyed every six months. None of the information is made a permanent electronic record, which is what the INS does with I-94 arrival records, manually downloading them into an entry database called NIIS, the Non-Immigrant Information System.

146. The answers to questions about how much currency the hijackers were carrying did not result in secondary inspections. Seven hijackers declared less than $10,000. The currency amounts on the declarations of Majid Moqed and Ahmed Al Ghamdi, was initially left blank and then later apparently completed by an inspector, who circled that both Moqed and al Ghamdi possessed more than $10,000 in cash.

147. This information was provided by a DHS intelligence office to the Commission.

148. In general, the information contained in this section is derived from Commission work product, *September 11 Hijacker border inspection interview results: Work Environment Prior to September 11*, May 20, 2004.

149. Indeed, no inspector interviewed by the Commission could read Arabic, or ever checked the authenticity of travel stamps in passports. Arabic speakers were rare at ports of entry in general and if an inspector could not communicate with a visitor, the inspector would either reluctantly rely on an airline representative for translation, if someone was even available, or refer the traveler to a secondary immigration inspection where an interpreter was available by phone. A lack of communication skills was the basis of the referral of Kahtani.

150. Immigration and Nationality Act § 286.

151. In general, the information contained in this section is derived from Commission work product, *September 11 Hijacker border inspection interview results: Training Prior to September 11*, May 20, 2004.

152. Primary inspector of Saeed al Ghamdi interview (Mar. 25, 2004).

153. Inspectors also received extensive firearms training. However, no inspector interviewed was ever permitted to carry a firearm while conducting airport line inspections. Firearms were carried in secondary inspection areas, general aviation and sea cargo inspections.

154. This was the only version ever produced.

155. Two immigration inspectors were familiar with the later version of the book, the *Passport Examination Manual*, which focused on generic document fraud, not documents used by terrorists.

156. Secondary inspector of Marwan al Shehhi on Jan. 18, 2001 interview (Mar. 22, 2004). The Commission obtained a copy of this bluebook from JFK airport immigration officials.

157. In general, the information contained in this section is derived from Commission work product, *September 11 Hijacker border inspection interview results: Work Environment Prior to September 11*, May 20, 2004.

Chapter 6

1. Timothy S., Chief of the Terrorist Mobility Branch, interview (Oct. 30, 2003).

2. Examples of finished intelligence produced by the Terrorist Mobility Branch include: *A Reference Guide for Terrorist Passports,* CIA, Directorate of Intelligence, Oct. 21, 2002; *Clandestine Travel Facilitators: Key Enablers of Terrorism,* CIA Directorate of Intelligence, Dec. 31, 2002; and Analysis of Passports, CIA, Directorate of Intelligence, Jan. 2004.

3. Timothy S. interview (Oct. 30, 2003).

4. Ibid.

5. Ibid.

6. For example, CIA Director George Tenet wrote to Dale Watson, the Assistant Director of the FBI's Counterterrorism Division, on Nov. 15, 2001 requesting FBI assistance in obtaining the passports and supporting documents of the 9/11 hijackers that were under FBI control for the purpose of developing actionable intelligence. There was no response to this request.

7. DOS designated Regional Security Officers employed by State's Bureau of Diplomatic Security to be the liaison at foreign posts with the FBI in the collection of evidence. Through this process, the FBI collected from State the visa applications of the September 11 hijackers once their identities were established.

8. Mary Ryan interview (Sept. 29, Oct. 3, Oct. 9, 2003).

9. Ibid.

10. DOS cable, "Muslims Need Not Apply: Fear and Rumors Lead Hejazis to Cancel U.S. Travel," Oct. 3, 2001.

11. Investigators from the State Office of Inspector General who visited Saudi Arabia in 2002 described "a feeling of lack of support, almost betrayal by CA and the Department" among consular personnel in Jeddah. DOS OIG record, "Findings in Jeddah," undated.

12. Included in the border security equipment provided to each host nation are passport readers, cameras, a flatbed scanner and fingerprint reader. The United States government pays for installment and maintenance.

13. DOS document, "Follow-up to A/S Harty's Meeting on 11/21, 9/11 Commission," Dec. 31, 2003.

14. Ibid.

15. Ibid.

16. DOJ document, Memorandum for the Attorney General, Final Report on Interview Project, Feb. 26, 2002.

17. We addressed the matter of the "special interest" detainees in the Final Commission Report, and so do not do so here.

18. DOJ document, Memorandum for the Attorney General, Final Report on Interview Project, Feb. 26, 2002.

19. John Ashcroft interview (Dec. 17, 2003).

20. DOJ document, Memorandum for the Attorney General, Final Report on Interview Project, Feb. 26, 2002, fn 2. 681 had left the United States; 1,097 of the individuals in the country could not be located; 785 were determined to have moved, complicating the effort to locate and interview them. Fewer than 20 were arrested in connection with the interviews, most charged with immigration violations. Three individuals were arrested on criminal charges, none related to terrorism. At least 10 individuals refused to be interviewed.

21. GAO report, Justice Department's Project to Interview Aliens after September 11, 2001, GAO-03-459, April 2003. In March 2003, when the Interview Project was the subject of a GAO investigation and report, law enforcement officers had interviewed 3,216 aliens, or about 42 percent of the 7,602 non-duplicate names on the original interview list. Because of uncertainty with the identity, address, and entry-exit information regarding the 7,602 potential interview subjects, it was not possible to state with certainty how many of the names represented unique individuals, and how many of those individuals were in the United States and, therefore, eligible to be interviewed.

22. Commission document, Department of Justice Document Request Number 9, Question 12 (Oct. 20, 2003).

23. In addition, DOJ asserts that it strengthened the bonds between federal, state and local law enforcement and improved relations between the law enforcement officers and the Muslim communities involved.

24. Ken Wainstain interview (May 5, 2004).

25. DOS document, "Follow-up to A/S Harty's Meeting on 11/21, 9/11 Commission," Dec. 31, 2003.

26. 8 USC § 1253 (failure to depart, imprisonment up to four years, 10 years if a criminal); 8 USC § 1324d (failure to depart, civil fine of $500 a day); 8 USC § 1326 (reentry after deportation, imprisonment from two to 20 years).

27. James Ziglar interview (Nov. 24, 2003).

28. FBI document, National Crime Information Center (NCIC) 2000 Operating Manual Section 5.6, "Operator's Lesson Plan," Jan. 2004.

29. James Ziglar interview (Nov. 13, 2003). The directive from the Attorney General did not define what was meant by "from countries . . ." Under the immigration law, this could apply to citizens of a country or persons who were born in one of these countries.

30. Ibid.

31. Ibid.

32. DAG Thompson said that the first group to be investigated would be "a group of fewer than a thousand, many of whom appear to be convicted felons." These "special interest countries" were Afghanistan, Algeria, Bahrain, Bangladesh, Djibouti, Egypt, Eritrea, Indonesia, Iran, Iraq, Jordan, Kazakhstan, Kuwait, Lebanon, Libya, Malaysia, Morocco, Oman, Pakistan, Philippines, Qatar, Saudi Arabia, Somalia, Sudan, Syria, Tajikistan, Thailand, Tunisia, Turkey, Turkmenistan, United Arab Emirates, Uzbekistan, Yemen, Territories of Gaza and the West bank. DHS document, Closing Report for AAI Project when it was transferred from Investigations, National Security Unit to Detention and Removal Office prepared by Immigration and Customs Enforcement, July 10, 2003.

33. DOJ document, Memorandum from the Deputy Attorney General to Commissioner, Immigration and Naturalization Service, Director Federal Bureau of Investigation, Director, U.S. Marshals Service, U.S. Attorneys, Subject: Guidance for Absconder Apprehension Initiative, Jan. 25, 2002.

34. The Commission believes that the FTTTF did remove some subjects from the list; we have not yet learned how many and whether these subjects remained of interest to the FBI on terrorism grounds. Lou Nardi interview (Oct. 20, 2003).

35. Ibid. *See also*, Testimony of Joe Greene, INS Assistant Commissioner for Investigations before the House Judiciary Subcommittee on Immigration, June 19, 2002.

36. To meet the terrorist-related reporting requirements imposed by the Department of Justice, the NSU developed special reporting requirements to ensure that all encounters with designated absconders were treated as a "significant incident" and therefore reported within 24 hours. In the usual course of immigration enforcement activity, significant incidents are those that involve death or injury of an officer, significant public and media interest, or an unusual event, such as the apprehension of large numbers of smuggled aliens.

37. James Ziglar interview (Nov. 13, 2003). These additional officers organized leads, made copies of the documents in the file, created working files, and kept track of the case assignment.

38. Lou Nardi interview (Oct. 20, 2003).

39. DHS document, Closing Report for AAI Project when it was transferred from Investigations, National Security Unit to Detention and Removal Office prepared by Immigration and Customs Enforcement, July 10, 2003.

40. Not all records were entered into the NCIC because immigration files do not always provide the documents required by NCIC to support entry into the system. For

example, INS files frequently do not have fingerprints, photographs or final deportation orders.

41. A continuing problem is the failure to have a compatible fingerprint system between the FBI and immigration. The FBI standard uses 10 fingerprints, as does the criminal database used by state and local law enforcement, NCIC. Immigration, however, continues to use the two index finger prints that can be matched in their watchlist database. In other words, if a terrorist enters the country and is fingerprinted on entry, as the U.S. VISIT system now requires of some travelers, these fingerprints cannot be checked against the databases used by the FBI or state and local law enforcement. The joining of the two systems has been under development for many years but is behind schedule. DOJ OIG, "IDENT/IAFIS: The Batres Case and the Status of the Integration Project," Mar. 2004.

42. The Law Enforcement Support Center (LESC) confirmed all NCIC hits on immigration absconders in the NCIC Immigration Violators File. Not all law enforcement agencies arrest immigration absconders even after they have received a "hit" from NCIC. Some agencies believe that they cannot legally arrest or detain an alien unless a criminal arrest warrant has been issued.

43. Craig E. Ferrell, International Association of Chiefs of Police, "The War on Terror's 'Absconder Initiative,'" found at www.theiacp.org/documents, stating, "The NCIC database has always been used to aid law enforcement officers in identifying persons wanted criminally. The FBI and the Department of Justice should take steps to immediately remove those individuals from the database who only have civil absconder warrants."

44. Some multiple immigration files were created when the alien applied for immigration benefits and the original immigration file was not located or known, resulting in the alien having more than one file. One permanent file may be on the *enforcement side* of INS and another "A" file on the *service side* of INS. With over a million aliens arrested each year and over a million aliens applying for benefits in most years, the INS was overwhelmed. As discussed earlier, Sheikh Omar Ali Abdel Rahman who was convicted of terrorism, had two immigration files at the same time. He did this by changing his name slightly and filing for immigration benefits at New York City and Newark, New Jersey. *See also*, GAO Report I-2003-004, "The Immigration and Naturalization Service's Removal of Aliens Issued Final Orders," Feb. 2003.

45. BREAKDOWN OF 4,074 AAI CLOSED CASES

Administrative closing	55
Asylee/Refugee	14
Board of Immigration Appeals	42
Convention Against Torture	3
Deceased	24
Duplicate	12
Identified as Females[45]	55
In State or Federal Custody	45
In Legal Non-Immigrant Status	11
LIFE Act Applicant	8
Legal Permanent Resident	191
Motion to Reopen Deportation Hearing	64

No Final Deportation Order	99
Under Order of Supervision	72
Other[45]	56
Pending Application for Immigration Benefits	47
Prior Removal	99
Refused Entry	7
Released on Bond	122
Removed from the U.S.	704
Released on Order of Recognizance	25
Self-deported[45]	390
Stay of Deportation or Removal[45]	10
Temporary Protected Status (TPS)[45]	18
Unable to Locate or Leads Exhausted	1807
United States Citizen	80
Waiver Approved	5
Withholding	9
Total	4,074

46. Testimony of Mike Dougherty, Director of Operations, Bureau of Immigration and Customs Enforcement (ICE), Department of Homeland Security, before the House Judiciary Subcommittee on Immigration, May 8, 2003. A total of 41 were charged with criminal immigration violations.

47. DOS document, "Follow-up to A/S Harty's Meeting on 11/21, 9/11 Commission," Dec. 31, 2003.

48. DOS document, Letter from Karl Hoffman to Daniel Marcus, Apr. 5, 2004.

49. DHS document, "National Security Entry-Exit Registration System: Program Overview and Analysis of Effectiveness as a Law Enforcement Tool," Prepared by Bureau of Immigration and Customs Enforcement, NSEERS Project Coordinator, May 22, 2003. The Attorney General's authority to mandate this program is spelled out in 8 CFR 2§ 64.1.

50. Ibid.

51. Ibid.

52. A total of 750 NSEERS terminals were deployed to 270 legacy INS offices nationwide and 4,633 INS personnel were trained in NSEERS. DHS document, "National Security Entry-Exit Registration System: Program Overview and Analysis of Effectiveness as a Law Enforcement Tool," Prepared by Bureau of Immigration and Customs Enforcement, NSEERS Project Coordinator, May 22, 2003.

53. DOJ document, Memo from Johnny Williams, Executive Associate Commissioner of Field Operations to the field, "Summary of NSEERS," Sept. 9, 2002.

54. DHS document, "National Security Entry-Exit Registration System: Program Overview and Analysis of Effectiveness as a Law Enforcement Tool," Prepared by Bureau of Immigration and Customs Enforcement, NSEERS Project Coordinator, May 22, 2003. For example, if the nonimmigrant made unexplained trips to Afghanistan or the nonimmigrant met characteristics established by current intelligence updates and advisories. Ibid.

55. Ibid.

56. Ibid.

57. After the initial registration, usually within two weeks of the registration, NSEERS registration information also was checked against databases of derogatory information—the TIPOFF terrorist watch list and the FBI's Violent Gang Terrorist Organization Files (VGTOF)—by the FBI's Foreign Terrorist Tracking Task Force (FTTTF). Any potential matches to records were sent to the INS National Security Unit (NSU) for investigation. DHS document, "National Security Entry-Exit Registration System: Program Overview and Analysis of Effectiveness as a Law Enforcement Tool," Prepared by Bureau of Immigration and Customs Enforcement, NSEERS Project Coordinator, May 22, 2003.

58. Ibid.

59. A person is subject to NSEERS registration each time they enter.

60. DHS document, "Compliance Enforcement Summary," May 4, 2004, NSEERS Statistics.

61. DOJ document, "NSEERS Statistics September 11, 2002 through January 29, 2003," undated.

62. DHS document, "Compliance Enforcement Summary," May 4, 2004.

63. DHS document, "National Security Entry-Exit Registration System: Program Overview and Analysis of Effectiveness as a Law Enforcement Tool," Prepared by Bureau of Immigration and Customs Enforcement, NSEERS Project Coordinator, May 22, 2003.

64. Ibid. INS officers were permitted to grant NSEERS waivers for aliens who crossed the border frequently and for aliens who sought to depart from an undesignated port. Memo from Johnny Williams, Executive Associate Commissioner for Field Operations to the field, "Guidance for Special Registration, or NSEERS Waivers," Sept. 30, 2002.

65. Ibid. We did not receive data for departure interviews conducted as of May 4, 2004.

66. Ibid.

67. Ibid.

68. Ibid.

69. DHS document, "Compliance Enforcement Summary," May 4, 2004.

70. DHS document, "National Security Entry-Exit Registration System: Program Overview and Analysis of Effectiveness as a Law Enforcement Tool," Prepared by Bureau of Immigration and Customs Enforcement, NSEERS Project Coordinator, May 22, 2003.

71. The precise number of NSEERS domestic registrants who were arrested and processed for removal is unclear. One document, the "National Security Entry-Exit Registration System: Program Overview and Analysis of Effectiveness as a Law Enforcement Tool," Prepared by Bureau of Immigration and Customs Enforcement, NSEERS Project Coordinator, May 22, 2003, states variously that "over 13,000" call-in registrants were arrested and that "10,000 to 12,000 individuals who appeared for call-in registration and were found to be illegally in the U.S. were arrested." In other words, the document appears to not take a consistent position, let alone attempt to precisely quantify the number arrested. A May 2, 2004 summary of NSEERS statistics lists the number of Notices to Appear issued as 10,037. DHS document, "Compliance Enforcement

Summary," May 4, 2004. It is not clear to us how this number could be lower than the 13,000 figure contained in the May 22, 2003, summary since the Notice to Appear is the standard form used to begin an immigration removal proceeding.

72. DHS document, "National Security Entry-Exit Registration System: Program Overview and Analysis of Effectiveness as a Law Enforcement Tool," Prepared by Bureau of Immigration and Customs Enforcement, NSEERS Project Coordinator, May 22, 2003.

73. Ibid. "The discrepancy between the high number of NSEERS violators and the relatively low number of target folders is due to data integrity issues. . . . Since the release of version 5.4, FIELD OPS has seen a dramatic decrease in the numbers of possible NSEERS violators being reported in error."

74. Ibid.

75. DHS document, "Compliance Enforcement Summary," May 4, 2004.

76. James Ziglar interview (Nov. 13, 2003).

77. Robert Mueller interview (Jan. 13, 2004).

78. For example, on September 27, 2002, the Canadians wrote Secretary of State Powell expressing "considerable disappointment" that NSEERS applies to Canadians born outside Canada. Letter to Secretary of State Colin Powell from Canadian Foreign Affairs Minister Bill Graham, Sept. 27, 2002; in 2003, representatives of the affected countries began having meetings with the Attorney General and Homeland Security Secretary Ridge. Ambassadors from Pakistan and Indonesia expressed concern to the White House and the Secretaries of State and Defense about the detentions and removals of their nationals from the United States. The ambassador of Pakistan said that inclusion in NSEERS had the "potential to weaken the government and President Musharraf." DOJ record, "Aide Memoire," Jan. 29, 2002; Pakistan's foreign minister met with the Attorney General, the Secretaries of State and Defense, and the National Security Advisor. DOJ record, "Meeting Between the Attorney General and Milan Khurshid Mahmoud Kasuri, Foreign Minister of Pakistan," Jan. 28, 2003; In a Department of State cable of January 3, 2004, the American Ambassador in Islamabad concluded a seething description of NSEERS, stating, "To a large extent, the U.S. cannot win here on NSEERS, regardless of the facts (35 percent of Pakistanis in the US are out of status.) There are few things that Benazir Bhutto and President Musharraf agree on, but NSEERS is one of them." DOS cable, "Sharp Pakistani Criticism of NSEERS," Jan. 3, 2003.

79. White House memo, "National Security Entry Exit Registration System (NSEERS) Global Message," Mar. 31, 2003.

80. DHS document, "Compliance Enforcement Summary," May 4, 2004, NSEERS Statistics, Country or Citizenship and Birth Records.

81. Ibid.

82. DHS document, "National Security Entry-Exit Registration System: Program Overview and Analysis of Effectiveness as a Law Enforcement Tool," Prepared by Bureau of Immigration and Customs Enforcement, NSEERS Project Coordinator, May 22, 2003.

83. DOJ document, NSEERS Violator List, Analysis Target Folder List given to HQINV, Dec. 17, 2002.

84. DHS document, "National Security Entry-Exit Registration System: Program Overview and Analysis of Effectiveness as a Law Enforcement Tool," Prepared by Bureau of Immigration and Customs Enforcement, NSEERS Project Coordinator, May 22, 2003.

85. Ibid.

86. Ibid.

87. Prepared testimony of David Martin before the National Commission on Terrorist Attacks Upon the United States hearing, Dec. 8, 2003.

88. Intelligence report, interrogation of KSM, May 10, 2003.

89. Ibid.

90. Ziglar was sworn into office on Aug. 6, 2001. He would remain Commissioner until Dec. 2002, until the abolition of the INS was announced and the recreation of immigration functions in the Department of Homeland Security. James Ziglar interview (Nov. 14, 2003). Chuck Winwood was stranded in Canada on September 11. The person acting in his place that day was John Varrone, the head of investigations, who also told the Commission he spoke to Ziglar that morning regarding the tightened security measures. John Varrone interview (April 29, 2004).

91. Both Ziglar and Robert Bonner, who was sworn in as Customs Commissioner within days of 9/11, used this phrase to describe the highest level of inspection guidelines provided at the borders, *see* James Ziglar interview (Nov. 14, 2003), and Robert Bonner interview (Dec. 18, 2003).

92. James Ziglar interview (Nov. 14, 2003) and John Varrone interview (April 29, 2004).

93. The initial identity of the hijackers was completed within about 24 hours of the attack by both Customs and INS. Determining the immigration histories of the hijackers, without biometric identifiers accompanying their files or the ability to share data between INS facilities or databases, would take months. *See* drafts of INS record, Texas Service Center Enforcement Operations Division 9/11 Terrorist Review, Sept. 2001-June 2002.

94. James Ziglar testimony, Jan. 26, 2004; and James Ziglar interview (Nov. 14, 2003).

95. INS Memo, Michael Pearson, Executive Associate Commissioner for Field Operations, to Regional Directors, "Authority to Carry a Firearm Performing Inspections at Air Ports of Entry," Sept. 12, 2001.

96. INS power point record, "INS Request for Military Support," autumn 2001. The Border Patrol soon thereafter requested 480 military personnel to help shore up the porous northern border.

97. James Ziglar testimony, Jan. 26, 2004.

98. INS Statistics, PAS G-22.1, 2000.

99. U.S. Bureau of Transportation Statistics (online at www.bts.gov).

100. Customs memo, Director of Field Operations to Executive Director of Trade Programs, re: "Blocking Property and Prohibiting Transactions with Persons who Commit, or Support, Terrorism," Sept. 28, 2001.

101. Robert C. Bonner testimony, Jan. 26, 2004.

102. James W. Ziglar interview (Nov. 14, 2003); and Robert Bonner interview (Dec. 18, 2003).

103. Robert C. Bonner testimony, Jan. 26, 2004.

104. Customs memo, Director of Field Operations to Executive Director of Trade Programs, re: "Blocking Property and Prohibiting Transactions with Persons who Commit, or Support, Terrorism," Sept. 28, 2001.

105. Robert C. Bonner testimony, Jan. 26, 2004.

106. Ibid.

107. INS Memo, Michael Pearson to Regional Directors, "Progressive and In-transit Clearance," Sept. 18, 2001 with addendum "Emergency Guidance re: TWOV and unable to depart due to FAA grounding," Sept. 11, 2001.

108. Customs memo, Executive Director of Passenger Programs, Field Operations, to all Directors of Field Operations, "Suspension of Progressive and In-transit Processing," Sept. 12, 2001.

109. Customs memo, Director of Field Operations to Executive Director of Trade Programs, re: "Blocking Property and Prohibiting Transactions with Persons who Commit, or Support, Terrorism," Sept. 28, 2001.

110. Customs memo, Executive Director of Passenger Programs, Field Operations to all Directors of Field Operations, "Clarification of Suspension of Progressive and In-transit Processing," Sept. 17, 2001.

111. Robert C. Bonner testimony, Jan. 26, 2004.

112. Peter F. Verga testimony, Jan. 26, 2004.

113. INS Memo, Michael Pearson to Regional Directors, "Guidance on Department of Defense title 10 (Anti-Terrorism) Support," Mar. 8, 2002.

114. *Message to the Congress of the United States re: the Department of Homeland Security*, George W. Bush, June 18, 2002.

115. This change was mandated by the Homeland Security Act § 428.

116. Ibid.

Appendix B

1. FAA record, Response to Questions for the Record (QFR) No. 1, June 8, 2004.

2. Ibid.

3. Ibid.

4. Ibid.

5. *See*, e.g., Port Authority of New York and New Jersey, Response to QFR, July 9, 2004, stating, "There were restrictions for GA flights that lasted until early October."

6. The following airports met FAA's new security requirements and reopened on September 13, 2001 at the times listed: Tampa International (11 A.M.), Tampa International Airport record, Response to QFR, June 7, 2004; Lexington-Blue Grass (12:50 P.M.), Lexington Blue Grass Airport record, Response to QFR, June 8, 2004; Lambert-St. Louis International (11 A.M.), Lambert-St. Louis International Airport record, Response to QFR, May 27, 2004; Los Angeles International (12 P.M.), Los Angeles International Airport record, Response to QFR, June 2, 2004; Orlando International (11 A.M.), Orlando International Airport record, Response to QFR, June 8, 2004; Washington-Dulles (11 A.M.), Washington-Dulles Airport record, Response to QFR, June 8, 2004; New York-JFK (11:04 A.M.), Port Authority of New York and New Jersey record, "Review of JFK Operations Chrono for 9/11 Incident," attachment to Response to QFR, June 4, 2004. Boston-Logan International Airport reopened to commercial activity at 5 A.M. on September 15, 2001. Massachusetts Port Authority, Responses to the Logan International Airport Questions for the Record, June 17, 2004. The Transportation Security Administration has confirmed that the following airports were open when the Saudi flights arrived or departed from them:

Tampa, Lexington, Providence, St. Louis, Los Angeles, Orlando, Washington-Dulles, Boston-Logan, Las Vegas, New York-JFK, and Hanscom. Christine Beyer interview (July 14, 2004).

7. Rihab Massoud, Deputy Chief of Mission, Kingdom of Saudi Arabia, interview (May 11, 2004); Dale Watson interview (June 3, 2004). Watson recalls that Massoud called late at night and told him that they were having a problem getting a plane released that carried "just family members." Ibid. Massoud recalls making clear that the plan was to gather all members of the Bin Ladin family on one flight, making several stops, before departing the United States. Rihab Massoud, Deputy Chief of Mission, Kingdom of Saudi Arabia, interview (May 11, 2004). Minister Massoud told the Commission that he worked to secure the departure of three flights with Saudi nationals sponsored in some fashion by the Saudi government; one flight with the Saudi Deputy Defense Minister on Saudi Airlines departing from Newark, New Jersey on September 14, 2001; one flight from California by the Governor of Mecca on a plane registered to the Republic of Gabon that departed from Las Vegas on September 19, 2001; and the flight of Bin Ladin family members that departed Boston-Logan Airport on September 20, 2001. All three flights took place after the national airspace had reopened. It appears from these records that State coordinated with the FBI and FAA to allow screening by the FBI of flights with Saudi nationals on board.

8. Michael Rolince interview (June 9, 2004).

9. Michael Rolince interview (June 9, 2004); Massoud corroborates this account. He said the FBI required the names and personal information of all departing passengers sponsored for departure by the Saudi Embassy. Rihab Massoud, Deputy Chief of Mission, Kingdom of Saudi Arabia interview (May 11, 2004).

10. Michael Rolince interview (June 9, 2004). Mueller responded by telling Rollince that this was the first he had heard of the Saudi flights issue. Ibid.

11. Michael Rolince interview (June 9, 2004); Massoud corroborates this account. He said the FBI required the names and personal information of all departing passengers sponsored for departure by the Saudi Embassy. Rihab Massoud, Deputy Chief of Mission, Kingdom of Saudi Arabia, interview (May 11, 2004).

12. Michael Rolince interview (June 9, 2004).

13. Jack Salata interview (June 14, 2004). The FAA representative put the FBI in direct communication with FAA air traffic control, which would not clear any flights to depart until the FBI gave their clearance. Ibid.

14. See DOS record, "State Terrorist Attack Task Force Log," June 3, 2004, stating in a log entry dated September 19, 2001, 8:34 P.M., "FAA requested DOS clearance for Saudi Registered aircraft to depart Las Vegas bound for Geneva, I checked with the FBI Las Vegas office. They confirmed that they had completed their interviews and had no objections to their departure. I then cleared their departure." Records of State's Terrorist Attack Task Force established after 9/11 contain 13 references to U.S. government coordination regarding flights of Saudi nationals, the earliest of which—involving the Saudi Deputy Defense Minister—occurred after the reopening of national airspace on September 13, 2001. Ibid. One entry on September 15, 2001 regarding a proposed flight of Saudi royalty states "there is no issue of whether the Saudis may or may not depart the country, the only issue is whether they qualify for diplomatic clearance which would expedite their departure

vs. waiting in backlogged airport for routine clearances." Ibid. In other words, diplomatic clearance expedited departure once the decision whether a person was allowed to depart had already been made. There is no evidence from these records or elsewhere that State worked to limit the FBI's ability to screen passengers on the departing Saudi flights. *See* Jack Salata interview (June 14, 2004), stating that the State Department did not press the FBI to take any shortcuts in checking out passengers on the Saudi flights.

15. Richard Clarke Testimony before the Senate Judiciary Committee, Subcommittee on Terrorism, Technology and Homeland Security, Sept. 3, 2003, stating that the week of September 11, the State Department asked if the Saudis could evacuate some of their citizens; that he (Clarke) directed that the flight manifests for all the flights be vetted by the FBI and that the FBI "sign off" on the concept of Saudis being allowed to leave. "And as I recall, all of that was done."

16. Richard Clarke interview (Jan. 12, 2004).

17. President Bush and Vice President Cheney meeting (Apr. 29, 2004); Condolezza Rice meeting (Feb. 7, 2004); Prince Bandar interview (May 5, 2004); Richard Clarke interview (Jan. 12, 2004); Richard Clarke testimony, Mar. 24, 2004 ("I would love to be able to tell you who did it, who brought this proposal to me, but I don't know"). Andrew Card, the White House Chief of Staff has told us that neither he, nor anyone else in the Chief of Staff's Office, to his knowledge, got any call from the Saudis or told Clarke to do anything. Andrew Card interview (Mar. 31, 2004). However, he recalls "being aware" of the request or the issue as early as September 11 or September 12. Ibid. This appears to be the highest level within the U.S. government to which the matter rose.

18. *See*, e.g., FBI record, Information on "Bin Ladin" Family Flights that Departed the United States in September 2001, May 28, 2004, stating "Contacts with an SSA at FBIHQ (whose name was not recalled) coordinated this departure to occur as soon as the FAA had authorized air traffic. SSA Foster further noted that during the hectic days following 9/11/2001, he spoke with several supervisors at FBIHQ concerning these issues, but did not keep specific records." FBI Assistant Director Tom Pickard recalled being in the SIOC on September 13 or 14, and being told by one of three people—Dale Watson, Mike Rolince, and Steve Jennings, who has told us he had no involvement in the Saudi flights issue (Steve Jennings interview (June 9, 2004)—that the issue of a UBL family flight had come up on a secure video teleconference. Both Pickard and Watson told us that they did not participate in SVTC communications with Dick Clarke, and that the person frequently involved in those conferences in the SIOC was Mike Rolince. Tom Pickard interview (June 3, 2004); Dale Watson interview (June 3, 2004). Pickard was not able to recall who—he was told—had raised the issue on the SVTC, and said to us that he thought it had come from Richard Clarke or the State Department. He understood that the issue was that they wanted to leave the country. But, he told us, there was no information suggesting that they were "here illegally or clandestinely." Tom Pickard interview (June 3, 2004). Pickard said that he knew prior to 9/11—when Usama Bin Ladin had been placed onto the FBI's Most Wanted List—that UBL had family members inside the U.S., that the FBI had "looked at them," and that the FBI had found "no connections" between these family members and UBL himself. "Now we had this extended family who wanted permission to leave," Pickard said. At the time, he said that he viewed the issue as a "low priority," given what he had been told and what he already knew about

the Bin Ladin family members. Pickard said that his approach was to tell his subordinate to handle the matter. He told us that he did not believe he conveyed the need to come back to him about it. In the scheme of things, Pickard said, he did not see anything to raise an alarm. Pickard did not recall discussing any other flights beyond this one Saudi flight. Ibid. Similarly, Dale Watson recalls that at about the same time he received the call from Rihab Massoud, the Deputy Chief of Mission of the Saudi Embassy in Washington, the issue "came up to him" from within the FBI, possibly raised by Mike Rolince. Watson recalled being told in this discussion that all the individuals on the flight had been identified and there was no one of interest on the flight. Watson said he recalled telling whoever it was who raised it with him words to the effect of "that's fine." Dale Watson interview (June 3, 2004).

19. *See* 8 CFR § 231.2 (Requiring that air carriers submit "a departure manifest" to an immigration officer "at the port of departure . . . within 48 hours of the departure.")

20. For example, as the Commission has previously reported, the 768 so-called "Special Interest" Aliens detained after 9/11 by the INS in conjunction with the FBI were detained lawfully on immigration violations.

21. United States law provides that no alien may depart the United States "if his departure would be prejudicial to the interests of the United States," 8 C.F.R § 15.2(a)(implementing INA § 215 —Travel control of citizens and aliens), and includes within that category any alien "who is needed in the United States as a witness in, or as a party to, any criminal case under investigation." 8 CFR § 215.3(g). However, the power to prevent departure under this law is vested in "departure control officers" that, prior to the creation of the Department of Homeland Security, were employees of the Immigration and Naturalization Service, not the FBI. 8 CFR § 215.1(i) ("The term *departure-control officer* means any immigration officer as defined in the regulations of the Immigration and Naturalization Service"). In addition, persons prevented from departing under this provision of law are provided with a hearing before a "special inquiry" officer and the law sets out the procedures and evidentiary requirements for such a hearing. 8 CFR § 215.4 (Procedure in case of alien prevented from departing from the United States), § 215.5 (Hearing procedure before special inquiry officer). Thus, before an individual on one of these flights could have been prevented from departing, the FBI would have needed some evidence that they had information about either the 9/11 attacks or some other terrorist activity. By insisting that they be able to identify all persons on these flights, and by checking the biographical information of these persons against databases with derogatory information, such as terrorist watchlists, the FBI took the logical steps necessary to develop such evidence.

22. According to FBI Special Agent Tim D., the Terrorist Screening Center (TSC) found one name match, but the TIPOFF record was for an individual born in 1980, and the "Bin Ladin flight" passenger was listed on the manifest as born in 1962. Tim D. interview (March 30, 2004).

23. In order to be as comprehensive as possible, the TSC checked the names on the manifests listed on the House of Bush/House of Saud Web site using the biographical information contained on those manifests. With minor exceptions, the Web site contained data previously checked by the TSC prior to our April hearing.

24. This information was reported on the House of Bush/House of Saud Web site as having been obtained by the Judicial Watch organization from DHS pursuant to a

FOIA request. However, the materials produced to Judicial Watch did not have complete biographical information such as the name and passport number of the individuals on these flights. The FBI obtained the complete records from DHS, and, at our request, ran the complete list of names and other biographical data against the TIPOFF Terrorist watchlist. There were no matches. Tim D. interview (June 30, 2004).

25. Although the FBI states that "a total of 18 Saudi passengers [were] aboard this flight," that does not seem possible since at least two of the names of the passengers— Gualberto Simpao Glore and Gilles Gerard—do not have Arabic names, and their passport numbers are not consistent with Saudi issuance.

26. We do not know the destination of this flight.

27. Kathy Steele, "Phantom Flight From Florida," *Tampa Tribune*, Oct. 5, 2001. It was featured prominently in an article in *Vanity Fair* magazine and in articles and op-ed pieces in major newspapers and magazines. It has been discussed on television news shows. A U.S. Senator requested that the Justice Department Inspector General investigate it. Letter from United States Senator Charles Schumer to DOJ Inspector General Glenn Fine, June 16, 2004, stating "I am troubled that such a flight could have been allowed to take place just two days after the terrorist attacks of 9/11."

28. This security detail began when one of the Saudis contacted a Tampa police officer and requested security fearing they would be attacked. Tampa police officers were then hired off-duty and were paid to provide security. John Solomon interview (June 4, 2004); Mike Fendle interview (June 4, 2004). We have reviewed documents provided by the Tampa Police Department regarding "extra-duty pay" provided for six hours by Detective Mike Fendle to "Sultan Bin Fahad" on September 13, 2001.

29. John Solomon interview (June 4, 2004).

30. Ibid.

31. Ibid.

32. Ibid.

33. Ibid.

34. Dan Grossi interview (May 24, 2004); Manuel Perez interview (May 27, 2004).

35. John Solomon interview (June 4, 2004); Mike Fendle interview (June 4, 2004).

36. Mike Fendle interview (June 4, 2004); Dan Grossi interview (May 24, 2004).

37. Mike Fendle interview (June 4, 2004).

38. The Tampa officers were paid through the Tampa Police Department according to routine procedures. Mike Fendle interview (June 4, 2004); John Solomon interview (June 4, 2004). Dan Grossi reimbursed the Tampa Police Department with money he obtained in Lexington, Kentucky later on September 13. John Solomon interview (June 4, 2004); Dan Grossi interview (May 24, 2004).

39. Dan Grossi interview (May 24, 2004); Manuel Perez interview (May 27, 2004); Christopher Steele interview (June 14, 2004).

40. Christopher Steele interview (June 14, 2004); Barry Ellis interview (June 14, 2004).

41. Christopher Steele interview (June 14, 2004); FAA record, Supplemental Response to QFR No. 1, June 16, 2004.

42. Christopher Steele interview (June 14, 2004); Barry Ellis interview (June 14, 2004).

43. Barry Ellis interview (June 14, 2004).

44. Christopher Steele interview (June 14, 2004).

45. FAA record, Supplemental Response to QFR No. 1, June 16, 2004.

46. FAA record, Response to QFR No. 1, June 8, 2004.

47. Dan Grossi interview (May 24, 2004); Manuel Perez interview (May 27, 2004).

48. Tampa's system captures the noise made by planes taking off and landing at the airport and attaches that information to the aircraft type and flight identification number. Gigi Skipper interview (June 4, 2004). Tampa's system recorded HPJ32, model LJ35 arriving at 3:34 P.M., departing at 4:37 P.M., arriving back in Tampa at 8:23 P.M. and departing for the last time at 8:48 P.M. Tampa International Airport record, Responses to QFRs, June 7, 2004.

49. FAA records show 30 flights departing Tampa Airport on September 13, including commercial flights departing as early as 12:43 P.M. FAA record, Response to Questions for the Record (QFR) No. 1, June 8, 2004.

50. The aircraft which arrived before this flight took off included: two general aviation flights, four "passenger" flights that included commercial airlines and four flights categorized as "other." The aircraft that departed before this flight included one general aviation, eight passenger flights that included commercial airlines, and three flights categorized as "other." Tampa International Airport record, responses to QFRs, June 7, 2004.

51. FAA record, Supplemental Response to QFRs, June 18, 2004.

52. Daniel Walsh interview (June 14, 2004); Dan Grossi interview (May 24, 2004); Manuel Perez interview (May 27, 2004); Christopher Steele interview (June 14, 2004); FAA record, Supplemental Response to QFR No. 1, June 16, 2004, indicating that this flight took off heading back to Tampa at 6:43 P.M.

53. Lexington-Blue Grass Airport record, Response to QFRs, June 8, 2004.

54. Mark Barnard interview (June 7, 2004), in which Barnard commented, "It happened. They flew from Tampa to Lexington," and "Trust me. It landed. I was there." *See also*, TAC Air record, Response to QFR, June 9, 2004, Statement of Daniel Walsh, General Counsel that "I am aware of a trip that did arrive with persons of Arab descent. If my memory served me correctly, this aircraft was a Learjet." Dan Grossi interview (May 24, 2004); Manuel Perez interview (May 27, 2004).

55. Dan Grossi interview (May 24, 2004); Manuel Perez interview (May 27, 2004).

56. Mark Barnard interview (June 7, 2004). These three individuals departed the United States days on a separate flight on September 16, 2001. Their departure is discussed below.

57. TAC Air record, Response to QFRs, June 9, 2004, with attachment TAC Air Daily Fuel Disbursement Report for "9/13/01" indicating a "Lear" with Tail "32HJ" received fuel at approximately 6:45 P.M.—the time on the log is unclear; FAA record, Supplemental Response to QFR No. 1, June 16, 2004.

58. Dan Grossi interview (May 24, 2004); Manuel Perez interview (May 27, 2004); Christopher Steele interview (June 14, 2004).

59. The FBI agrees that this flight occurred. James M. interview (June 18, 2004). Special Agent M. told the Commission that approximately one week after the 9/13/01 flight, he spoke with a Lexington Police officer who had provided security to the

16

Saudi nationals on this flight. M. asked how the three young Saudis on the Tampa-Lexington flight arrived in Lexington and, when informed that they had flown, he questioned whether this was possible. M. says the officer "hemmed and hawed," and then suggested that the three young Saudis actually drove to Lexington and said they had flown to avoid the displeasure of their elder male relative in Lexington. Special Agent M. told the Commission he now believes based on his own independent investigation that this flight in fact took place. Ibid.

60. FBI record, "All Passports Obtained by the FBI of Individuals on Northstar Aviation Flight from Providence, Rhode Island (Departing on or about September 14, 2001)," June 15, 2004. We have reviewed the copies of these passports collected by the FBI, and have not found anything unusual.

61. FBI record, "Final Draft of Response to October 2003 Vanity Fair Article (re: Bin Laden Family Departures after 9/11/2001)," Sept. 24, 2003.

62. Christine Beyer interview (July 14, 2004).

63. According to the FBI, airport accounting records and log sheets prepared by airport personnel indicate the plane departed the airport at this time. Tim D. interview (July 14, 2004).

64. FBI record, "Documents related to Saudi Arabian Airlines Flight from Newark Airport," June 2004.

65. Ibid.

66. Port Authority of New York and New Jersey record, Responses to QFRs, July 9, 2004.

67. The FBI has provided us with a copy of the manifest for this flight. FBI record, "All Passports Obtained by the FBI of Individuals on a Chartered Boeing 727 flight from Lexington, Kentucky (Departing on or about September 16, 2001)," June 15, 2004.

68. We have reviewed copies of those passports and found nothing unusual.

69. FBI record, "Final Draft of Response to October 2003 Vanity Fair Article (re: Bin Laden Family Departures after 9/11/2001)," Sept. 24, 2003; FBI record, Summary of "Information Regarding Flights Taken by Saudi Citizens, Including Members of the Binladen Family, Out of the United States Shortly After September 11, 2001," Oct. 29, 2003.

70. Lexington-Blue Grass Airport record, Response to QFR, June 8, 2004.

71. FBI record, "All Passports Obtained by the FBI of Individuals on a Chartered Boeing 727 flight from Lexington, Kentucky (Departing on or about September 16, 2001)," June 15, 2004.

72. Craig Unger, "Questions," *Boston Globe*, April 11, 2004, citing Gerald Posner, "While America Slept."

73. CIA record, Response to QFR, June 23, 2004. We found no evidence for this assertion in the interrogation reports of Abu Zubaydah we reviewed.

74. Boston-Logan Airport reopened to commercial air traffic at 5 A.M. on September 15, 2001. Massachusetts Port Authority record, Response to the Logan International Airport QFRs, June 17, 2004.

75. FBI record, Report of Leads Covered from FBI Las Vegas Office, Sept. 25, 2001.

76. Ibid.

77. Ibid.

78. FBI record, "Final Draft of Response to October 2003 Vanity Fair Article (re: Bin Laden Family Departures after 9/11/2001)," Sept. 24, 2003; FBI record, Flight manifest for Republic of Gabon Flight, Feb. 26, 2004.

79. FBI record, "Final Draft of Response to October 2003 Vanity Fair Article (re: Bin Laden Family Departures after 9/11/2001)," Sept. 24, 2003.

80. Ibid.

81. FBI record, Report of Leads Covered from FBI Las Vegas Office, Sept. 25, 2001.

82. FBI record, "Final Draft of Response to October 2003 Vanity Fair Article (re: Bin Laden Family Departures after 9/11/2001)," Sept. 24, 2003.

83. Las Vegas-McCarran International Airport reopened at 5 A.M., PST, on September 14, 2001. McCarran International Airport record, Responses to QFRs, June 17, 2004.

84. FBI record, Report of Leads Covered from FBI Las Vegas Office, Sept. 25, 2001; FBI record, Flight Manifest, Sept. 24, 2001. Although the FBI states that "a total of 18 Saudi passengers [were] aboard this flight," that does not seem possible since at least two of the names of the passengers—Gualberto Simpao Glore and Gilles Gerard—do not have Arabic names, and their passport numbers are not consistent with Saudi issuance.

85. FBI record, "Final Draft of Response to October 2003 Vanity Fair Article (re: Bin Laden Family Departures after 9/11/2001)," Sept. 24, 2003; FBI record, Flight manifest for Republic of Gabon Flight, Feb. 26, 2004.

86. Ibid.

87. Ibid.

88. Las Vegas-McCarran International Airport reopened at 5 A.M., PST, on September 14, 2001. McCarran International Airport record, Responses to QFRs, June 17, 2004.

89. James C. interview (June 3, 2004).

90. Ibid.

91. FBI record, Report of Leads Covered from FBI Las Vegas Office, Sept. 25, 2001.

92. James C. interview (June 3, 2004).

93. There is conflicting evidence on which one of two individuals were actually on the flight. In its summary of these flights, the FBI lists "Maria Bayma" as a passenger on the flight manifest. However, another FBI record of this flight indicates that Khalil Bin Laden "and his wife and son" boarded in Orlando, Florida. FBI record, Report of Leads Covered from FBI Los Angeles Office, Sept. 25, 2001. An analyst comment then states: "Khalil Bin Laden's wife's name is Isabel Bayma." Ibid. Thus, it is unclear whether Isabel or Maria Bayma were on Flight 441. The FBI's records indicate that Maria Bayma "appears to be a relative of Khalil Bin Laden's wife, Isabel Bayma." Ibid.

94. FBI record, "Final Draft of Response to October 2003 Vanity Fair Article (re: Bin Laden Family Departures after 9/11/2001)," Sept. 24, 2003. Although the *Vanity Fair* article states Abdullah Bin Laden was on this flight, there is no evidence that Abdullah Bin Laden was on Ryan Air Flight 441.

95. In total, the FBI conducted 22 interviews of the 23 passengers on Ryan Air Flight 441. FBI record, "Final Draft of Response to October 2003 Vanity Fair Article (re: Bin Laden Family Departures after 9/11/2001)," Sept. 24, 2003.

96. FBI record, "All Interview Reports for Any Passengers on the Flights," containing reports dated Sept. 13 through Sept. 26, 2001.

97. FBI record, Summary of "Information Regarding Flights Taken by Saudi Citizens, Including Members of the Binladen Family, Out of the United States Shortly After September 11, 2001," Oct. 29, 2003.

98. According to FBI records, in Boston, 17 people got onto this flight in Boston, and one person—a security guard—got off the plane. FBI record, "Final Draft of Response to October 2003 Vanity Fair Article (re: Bin Laden Family Departures after 9/11/2001)," Sept. 24, 2003.

99. Ibid.

100. Ibid.

101. FBI record, Report of Leads Covered from FBI Los Angeles Office, Sept. 25, 2001.

102. FBI record, "All Interview Reports for Any Passengers on the Flights," containing reports dated Sept. 13 through Sept. 26, 2001; FBI record, "Final Draft of Response to October 2003 Vanity Fair Article (re: Bin Laden Family Departures after 9/11/2001)," Sept. 24, 2003.

103. FBI record, "All Interview Reports for Any Passengers on the Flights," containing reports dated Sept. 13 through Sept. 26, 2001.

104. FBI record, "Final Draft of Response to October 2003 Vanity Fair Article (re: Bin Laden Family Departures after 9/11/2001)," Sept. 24, 2003. The FBI agent reported that this flight was delayed two hours because flight crew members refused to fly upon learning "the identities of the passengers." According to the agent, "The matter was resolved after the charter company agreed to pay each flight crew member an additional five thousand dollars." FBI record, "All Interview Reports for Any Passengers on the Flights," containing reports dated Sept. 13 through Sept. 26, 2001.

105. FBI record, "All Interview Reports for Any Passengers on the Flights," containing reports dated Sept. 13 through Sept. 26, 2001.

106. FBI record, "Final Draft of Response to October 2003 Vanity Fair Article (re: Bin Laden Family Departures after 9/11/2001)," Sept. 24, 2003.

107. Ibid.

108. Ibid.

109. FBI record, Report of Leads Covered from FBI Los Angeles Office, Sept. 25, 2001.

110. We say apparently because New York-JFK Airport informed us that they have no information on this "VIP" flight. James Begley email, June 10, 2004.

111. The Web site is www.houseofbush.com.

112. State Department logs contain a number of references to "VIPs" and "Saudi royals" in connection with proposed flights out of the country prior to this flight. In each case it is clear that the FAA and/or the FBI was involved in clearance for the flight. DOS record, "Terrorist Attack Task Force log," September 16 and 17, 2001.

113. New York-JFK Airport reopened on September 14, 2001, at 10:58 A.M. Port Authority of New York and New Jersey record, facsimile from the Law Department, June 4, 2004.

114. Hanscom Airfield reopened to commercial air traffic at 5 A.M. on September 15, 2001. Massachusetts Port Authority record, Response to the Hanscom Airfield QFRs, June 17, 2004.

115. FBI record, "Final Draft of Response to October 2003 Vanity Fair Article (re: Bin Laden Family Departures after 9/11/2001)," Sept. 24, 2003.

116. Ibid.

117. FBI record, Flight Manifest, Sept. 19, 2001.

118. FBI record, "Final Draft of Response to October 2003 Vanity Fair Article (re: Bin Laden Family Departures after 9/11/2001)," Sept. 24, 2003.

119. Las Vegas-McCarran International Airport reopened at 5 A.M., PST, on September 14, 2001. McCarran International Airport, Responses to Questions for the Record, June 17, 2004.

120. Letter from Christopher Farrell of Judicial Watch to 9/11 Commission Executive Director Philip Zelikow, June 1, 2004.

121. Kelly B. interview (April 27, 2004).

122. Tim D. interview (June 30, 2004).

Appendix C

1. *See* DHS document, immigration file A72 415 284 and immigration file A93 249 086.

2. The new passport contained a curious notation that the correct name on the passport should be "Kansi."

3. Immigration Reform and Control Act of 1986, *Eligibility for Temporary Resident Status Under the Main Legalization Program.*

4. He also provided a completed form requesting status in a class action lawsuit against the INS by the League of United Latin American Citizens (LULAC).

5. DHS/CIS Press Release, *Federal Courts Approve Settlements in CSS and LULAC Legalization Cases,* Mar. 23, 2004.

6. *See* DHS document, immigration file A93 249 086.

7. Kansi's roommate, Zahed Ahmad Mir, was visited by law enforcement authorities after the CIA attack and permitted the police to seize two handguns and magazines for the AK-47 believed to be used by Kansi in the shooting. Mir was later arrested and convicted of fraud for his application for amnesty under the Seasonal Agricultural Worker (SAW) provisions of the Immigration Reform and Control Act of 1986. This provision permitted illegal aliens who had engaged in seasonal agricultural work for at least 90 days to apply for amnesty and receive legal residence in the United States. Mir falsely asserted on his SAW application that he entered the United States in 1985 and picked "watermelons, cantaloupe and assorted other crops" for a farm in Georgia. *See* DHS document, immigration file A93 001 385.

8. Mir Aimal Kasi v. Commonwealth of Virginia (Virginia Supreme Court), Circuit Court of Fairfax County, Record Numbers 980797 and 980798, Nov. 6, 1998.

9. *See* DHS document, immigration file A73 140 727.

10. Department of Justice, U.S. Attorney's Office for the Southern District of New York, Press Release, Aug. 3, 1995.

11. *See* DHS document, immigration file A 91 184 226.

12. The petitioner on his behalf, Lee Artis Breedlove, a Florida farm owner, claimed to have employed Abouhalima and others. Breedlove pled guilty in federal court to issuing 260 fraudulent employment records used by aliens in their SAW applications.

13. Department of Justice, Federal Bureau of Prisons.

14. *See* DHS documents, immigration files A71 495 857, A93 003 841 and A94 010 816. Only parts of these files were available for our review.

15. *The Cell,* John Miller and Michael Stone, Hyperion, 2002, p.49.

16. Section 244 of the Immigration and Nationality Act grants temporary protected status (TPS) to eligible nationals of designated countries (or parts thereof) as determined by the Attorney General. TPS can be given to aliens in the United States who are temporarily unable to safely return to their home country because of ongoing armed conflict, the temporary effects of an environmental disaster, or other extraordinary and temporary conditions.

17. Alkaisi could not get TPS as a citizen of Jordan. Lebanon was a designated Temporary Protected Status country.

18. 18 USC § 1001 (False Statements).

19. Memorandum of Record, "Request for Recommendation re: Revocation of Naturalization," from Warren Louis, INS District Director, Newark, NJ to Carol D. Chasse, Regional Director, INS Eastern Region, May 28, 1996.

20. His INS immigration file (A 90 678 144) was not available for review. Although the Department of Homeland Security (Bureau of Immigration and Customs Enforcement) stated that the file had been located in New York City, it was not provided to the Commission. They did state that the individual was not a legal permanent resident or naturalized citizen.

21. Trial exhibit, WTC 1, U.S. District Court, Southern District of New York.

22. His INS immigration file (A 90 568 993) was not available for review. DHS informed us that the Privacy Act barred the Commission from obtaining immigration files on legal permanent residents and naturalized citizens, even those convicted of terrorism or related crimes.

23. *See* DHS documents, immigration files A41 066 738 and A27 520 221.

24 . This was Cortez's second marriage; her first husband, Jonathan Rivera Rosario, was also an alien. *See* DHS document, immigration file A27 520 221.

25. The petition was for Wahid Mohamed Ahmed (alias for Saleh) with a date of birth of June 13, 1950.

26. INA Section 213, Conditional Residence, states "this status, based on marriage, lasts for two years after entry if the marriage was less then two years prior to day you have received your permanent residence."

27. This was a violation of 21 USC § 841(a)(1) and 18 USC § 2.

28. 18 USC § 371, 18 USC § 844 (i) and 18 USC§ 842(a)(3)(A).

29. Under immigration law, because the INS had placed a detainer on him, Saleh ordinarily would have been turned over to them for deportation following his release.

30. Relief from deportation is available to someone convicted of terrorism under immigration law if they can show "hardship," which Saleh could not do based on his terrorism and drug convictions.

31. His Immigration file (A 23 406 577) was not available for review. The Privacy Act barred the Commission from obtaining this file.

32. Many birth records were destroyed in an earthquake in Nicaragua on December 23, 1972. Applications for Nicaraguan passports do not require a personal visit.

33. INS Memo to File from District Counsel, INS, Newark, New Jersey, undated.

34. He also might have held an Iraqi passport M0887925 in the name of Abdul Rahman S. Taher. *See* FBI fugitive web site www.fbi.gov/mostwant/topten/fugitives/fugitives.

35. United States v. Omar Ahmad Ali Abdel Rahman, El Sayyid Nosair, Ibrahim A. El-Gabrowny, Siddig Ibrahim Siddiq Ali, Clement Hampton-El, Amir Abdelgani, Fares Khallafalla, Tarig Elhassan, Fadil Abdelgani, Mohammed Saleh, Victor Alvarez, Matarawy Mohammmed Said Saleh, US District Court, Southern District of New York.

36. DOJ, Federal Bureau of Prisons.

37. Ibid.

38. Ibid.

39. Ibid.

40. *See* DHS document, immigration file A73 442 758.

41. A warrant of arrest was issued by Aaron Miller, Assistant Chief Patrol Agent, Bellingham, Washington for Khalil's immigration violations.

42. On August 11, 1997, the INS requested that Khalil be tried in New York, rather than in Arlington, Virginia since he was being held in New York City as a material witness in the attempted bombing. The judge agreed to move the case.

43. DOJ, Federal Bureau of Prisons.

44. 9/11 Commission Report, page 489, endnote 13.

45. Department of Justice, Federal Bureau of Prisons.

46. *See* DHS document, immigration file A78 392 527. The A file contains poor quality copies of two passports belonging to Rababah. Jordanian passport E041890 was issued on March 3, 1994 and was valid until March 8, 1999. Jordanian passport G263860 was issued on March 1, 1999 and was valid until March 12, 2004.

47. He had entered the United States two times before on a B-2 multiple entry tourist visa.

48. Testimony of Michael E. Rolince, Section Chief, International Terrorist Operations Section, Counterterrorism Division, Federal Bureau of Investigation in Bond Proceedings before the Executive Office for Immigration Review, Oct. 23, 2001.

49. His INS immigration file was not available for review. The Privacy Act barred the Commission from obtaining immigration files on legal permanent residents and naturalized citizens.

50. *See* DHS document, immigration file A75 628 802.

51. 9/11 Commission Report, pp. 215–220.

52. 9/11 Commission Report, p. 220.

53. Department of Justice, Bureau of Prisons.

54. *Man held as a material witness in 9/11 probe deported to Yemen*, The San Diego Union-Tribune, May 26, 2004.

55. *See* DHS document, immigration file A70 640 955.

56. Testimony by William Yates, Deputy Executive Associate Commissioner, Immigration Services Division before the House Subcommittee on Immigration, Border Security, and Claims, House Committee on the Judiciary, Oct. 9, 2002.

57. Since Hadayet's wife was a legal permanent resident alien, her immigration file is covered by the Privacy Act and the Commission was barred from reviewing it.